Praise for Ensouling the Effigy

"Every now and then you approach a book with high expectations, based on foreknowledge of the author. Sometimes those expectations are superseded and you realise that what you are reading is an essential contribution to the field of magical practice, a modern classic that fills a hole that most people had not even realised was there! *Ensouling the Effigy* is such a modern classic, providing not just a breath of fresh air but a veritable gust of wind into the ever-increasingly more popular area of working with spirits as an essential part of magical practice.

Matthew Venus combines historical scholarship with decades of practice to provide a work that manifests his views and experience of the world. It is rich with lucidity and insight and will both reinforce and challenge the reader's own insights. Decades of experience literally sing off the pages in this comprehensive, accessible and extremely practical work. *Ensouling the Effigy* is not a book to just be read; it is itself a spirit vessel that guides the reader through a wealth of practices. The practices are provided with a concise clarity that everybody will learn from, irrespective of their level of experience. There is a lifetime of invaluable material within this book, please do not ignore it, but treat it as the treasure that it is."

—David Rankine, author of the *Grimoire Encyclopaedia*

"*Ensouling the Effigy* by Matthew Venus is a book that lives and breathes and is itself an example of the art that it teaches. As you turn the pages you are transported through times and places to follow the development of ideas and methods to call and create objects of power and spirit. This book is a trip to the witches' sabbath that waits outside of time. While it is the best book I've read on poppets, effigies, spirit vessels, and the like, it is so much more. It is a true guide for any that wish to embrace the spirit work at the core of witchery. The author's passion and vast experience are undeniable and compelling. I will be reading this book several times because I am sure it will answer questions I am yet to formulate."

—Ivo Domínguez Jr., author of *Spirit Speak: A Comprehensive Guide to Connect Beyond the Veil*

"*Ensouling the Effigy* is a work that goes straight to the heart of one of the most venerable of all magical arts, the ecstatic process of creation, whereby material objects assume spiritual power.

Going beyond the familiar use of poppets in 'sympathetic magic', Matthew's work provides an engaging and erudite discussion of the making and en-spiriting of vessels, which may serve the cunning as points of mediation between spirit and flesh.

Filled with practical formulae, and a comprehensive discussion of the history and philosophies underpinning this noble art, *Ensouling the Effigy* is a welcome addition to the library of any who seek to understand the role of magician as maker, and who desire to learn of the means by which body is given unto spirit."

—Martin Duffy, author of *Effigy: Of Graven Image and Holy Idol*

Ensouling the Effigy

The Witch's Arte of Enspirited Objects

About the Author

Matthew Venus is an artist, folk magician, and witch in Salem, Massachusetts. His craft centers around animism and ancestral, land-based traditions. His practice is enriched as Tata Ndenge in a lineage of Quimbanda de Angola and his experiences as an Aborisha in the Lucumí Orisha tradition. Over two decades, Matthew has shared his teachings worldwide through courses on witchcraft and folk magical traditions.

Matthew owns the apothecary of Spiritus Arcanum (@spiritus_arcanum), a shop that specializes in handcrafted incense, oils, and talismanic art. He co-founded the Salem Witchcraft and Folklore Festival (@SalemWitchFest), which hosts events around magical education, community building, and activism.

Ensouling the Effigy

The Witch's Arte of Enspirited Objects

Matthew Venus

Foreword by Mat Auryn

Illustrations by Adrienne Rozzi

Chicago, IL

Paperback ISBN: 978-1-964537-03-0
Hardcover ISBN: 978-1-964537-38-2
E-Book ISBN: 978-1-964537-93-1

Library of Congress Control Number on file.

Published by:
Crossed Crow Books, LLC
518 Davis St, Suite 205
Evanston, IL 60201
www.crossedcrowbooks.com

Printed in the United States of America.
IBI

For my Mother

Acknowledgements

Eternal honor to the ancestors and to the spirits who guide my feet, my heart, my hands, and my head in this life.

My endless love and appreciation to Alex for his unfailing encouragement and support.

Deepest gratitude to Elizabeth Autumnalis, Devin McElderry, Jesse Hathaway-Diaz, Grant Hanna, Jacqui Allouise, Dr. Alexander Cummins, Mat Auryn, K Siner, Kelden, Sasha Ravitch, Sarah Jezebel Wood, Gary Noriyuki, Austin Fuller, Professor Charles Porterfield, Phoebe Hildegard Finch, Ben Stimpson, Summer Grimes, Dame Wilburn, Christopher Penczak, and to Cabula Maville Kitula Kia Njilla for all of your inspiration, your wisdom, your friendship, and for the unparalleled magic that each of you brings into this world.

Special thanks to Adrienne Rozzi for crafting the truly exceptional imagery that accompanies this work. My appreciation to Blake Malliway, Gianluca Pelagatti, Lee Anderson, and the entire team at Crossed Crow for your support in making this work possible.

And finally, my sincerest gratitude to Martin Duffy and Kamden Cornell, both of whose written works in the realm of effigies and whose kindness and correspondence have affirmed and enriched my own efforts in this often underexplored corner of the craft.

May the following work be a testament to all whom I've encountered as teachers, students, friends, lovers, acquaintances, and enemies whose presence in my life has served to inspire and motivate me towards greater fulfillment, achievement, magic, and revelation.

Lux in Tenebris.

Tenebrae in Luce.

M

Table of Contents

Foreword

The best books on witchcraft and magic tend to share a few key traits. They contribute meaningfully to the ongoing conversation rather than just parroting what's already been said. They offer systems that are both rooted and usable, grounded in practice while remaining adaptable to the reader's path. Some stand out by illuminating devotional relationships. Others excel through clear, accessible guidance for spellwork or folk practice. A few deepen the reader's understanding of history, spiritwork, or magical theory with precision and care. The books that endure are the ones that manage to do this while remaining alive in the hands of the practitioner. The book you are reading is all of those things.

We live in an interesting era where occultism no longer hides in the shadows as it did with our ancestors. There are countless books on witchcraft, from broad overviews and accessible entry points to those focused on specific and highly specialized topics. Yet among this expanding body of literature, very few focus on one of the witch's oldest and most intimate artes: the creation and care of spirit vessels. The subject might appear in passing, a footnote, a brief mention, or a single chapter, but it rarely stands at the core. *Ensouling the Effigy* is remarkable for reviving and recentering this work as a complete system of magical relationship, grounded in lived experience rather than treated as a side practice or folkloric curiosity. With this book, Matthew Venus accomplishes a long-overdue restoration of the creation, care, and conjuration of spirit vessels back to the heart of magical practice for the witch.

As someone who works clay into figures and fetiches in private, and who has walked the crooked path of the witch for decades, I can say with certainty that few approach the nexus of material craft and magical arte with the depth and integrity of Matthew Venus and that I fully believe that there isn't a single person more qualified to write this book. His devotion to both is seamless. The breath that moves through his body moves through his creations. He has a kind of Midas touch where everything he commits himself to is nothing short of excellence, and that excellence is imbued in all that he does. This book is no exception. We're fortunate to have it, and through it, to share in the power of that touch.

I first met Matthew over a decade ago at Templefest, where he was teaching a class on crossroad spirits. I remember reading the description and knowing instantly that I needed to be there. The session didn't disappoint me. I found his discussion engaging, well-structured, and deeply rooted in lived experience as well as historical insight. I left struck by both his clarity and presence. Since then, I've held Matthew in the highest regard and have remained in awe of both his depth of knowledge and his magical ability. It was the beginning of a friendship that would grow over the years, deepening during our shared time in Salem.

I'm far from alone in my admiration for Matthew and his work. Over the years, I've watched his influence quietly shape entire corners of contemporary witchcraft. I've also seen others attempt to adopt his visual language, spiritual approach, and perspectives; sometimes without crediting the source, with some even going so far as to rewrite the story and claim his insights as their own. Much of what's now recognized as the "traditional craft" aesthetic has been greatly influenced by his work. Still, there's something in Matthew's work that resists replication. It isn't just that the spirits within it are real. It's that each piece bears the mark of his hand, his will, and his offerings. Though his aesthetic is refined, it never stops at appearances. His work doesn't aim to look "witchy;" it emerges as a natural extension of his witchcraft itself.

With this book, we're now lucky enough to bring that current into our own magickal practices. The teachings, techniques, and formulas he shares give us the tools to recreate the kind of spirit-led arte he's become known for. Still, what emerges won't be a carbon copy of Matthew's magic, nor should it be. The magic he offers is rooted in relationship: with the spirits we call, the vessels we craft, and the spirit that lives within us. That relationship will take a different shape in every pair of hands and every unique breath of the practitioner. It will speak in different voices, wear different faces, and move in ways unique to each witch who decides to do this work.

As I mentioned, his spirit effigies hold a magical current. I keep one of his crow fetiches on my wall, a piece I bought from his shop all those years ago when we first met. The spirit within it is palpable and undeniably alive. Its presence registers across the room with an unmistakable weight. That kind of charge doesn't come from aesthetics alone; it's the result of a cultivated relationship, shaped through knowing, listening, and genuine magical craft.

A few years ago, I interviewed Matthew for my blog and asked him about the name of his business and magical practice, *Spiritus Arcanum*. His response stayed with me:

> *Spiritus speaks in some ways to spirit, but also to the breath. Breathwork and breathing are a way in which I imbue a lot of my work with life. It is the songs we sing, the words we speak or whisper, which enspirit much of our work in magic. The witches' breath... Arcanum can mean a secret, something occult, a mystery. The hidden lore which fuels our magic.*

This is exactly the spirit of his approach that runs through every page of this book. Matthew writes without compromise. Spirits move through these pages as immediate presences. Animism and panpsychism are treated as conditions for the practice, not abstract philosophy. Spirit contact is direct, embodied, and experiential. This approach extends to even the *materia* engaged in the process of this craft, where wood, wax, clay, feather, stone, and bone are respected as animate, responsive, and integral. Nothing is inert. Everything is a participant, approached through relationship. And while his work is rooted in decades of lived experience, it remains grounded and pragmatic, balancing historical understanding with hard-earned personal insight.

Matthew shares a scholarly level of historical insights drawn from a wide range of cultures and time periods, offering rich context for the practices he presents. Even with this breadth, he maintains clear and respectful boundaries. He's careful never to cross into the territories of closed or initiatory traditions and speaks firmly against doing so. Nothing in this book is taken from where it doesn't belong. Every technique, formula, and rite offered here is something any practitioner can engage with fully, respectfully, and without causing harm or disrespect to living traditions and those within them, whether human or spirit.

The rites and formulas within this book stand apart from those found in the broader corpus of witchcraft literature. Each ritual arises from the demands of direct spirit engagement and was shaped to meet specific needs within that lived context. What Mathew has given us is neither solely a historical survey with a few practices appended, nor a collection of workings presented without context. Instead, it is a rare balance of both. The reader is shown not only how these rites function, but why they matter. This is a field-forged manual for engaging spirit through object. Within these pages are methods for meeting and working with spirits on their own ground through the Otherworld, alongside techniques for anchoring them in the physical through effigies and vessels. You'll learn how to communicate with spirits through psychic and divinatory means and how to craft alliances and pacts with them.

Ensouling the Effigy is the kind of book you'd expect to see commanding a high price from one of the fine-edition occult publishers known for limited-run esoteric texts aimed at deeply experienced practitioners willing to dive deep into their pockets to pay for it. However, it was important to him that it be both accessible to acquire and accessible in content, serving as a guide that carries the reader from foundational principles to intermediate and advanced work. For those just beginning, it offers structure and direction. For those well along their path, it sharpens discernment, deepens skill, and levels up your relationship with spirits. Wherever you begin, the work will change you. It will shift your perception of spirit and the relationship that is possible with them. It will expand what you believe your hands and breath can do.

The appendices alone make this book worth the cost. Within the formulary are workings and recipes found nowhere else: the Smoke of the Hallowed Tongue, a wash for the mouth when calling spirits, the Suffumigation of Ensouling, Transvection Oil, and many more. These are not the run-of-the-mill formulas you often run into. They are original, field-tested contributions from Matthew himself. His recipes have long been closely held, sought after by witches who know their quality and value. As if that weren't generous enough, he even shares magical doughs specifically crafted for building your own spirit effigies.

I found myself deeply inspired by the information and praxis in this book. This book moves like breath through the reader, animating thought, stirring the spirit, and calling the hands to act to craft and ensoul. In the pages that follow, you'll see for yourself why so many of us are deeply in love with Matthew's work and are sure to find yourself inspired in your own magical work, just as I have been.

—Mat Auryn
Author of *Psychic Witch, Mastering Magick,* and *The Psychic Art of Tarot*

Introduction

There is a crimson thread sewn through the diverse and rich spiritual and magical traditions humanity has crafted throughout our history. A thread drawn through conjuring lips and hallowed by the breath of life that stitches together the embodied realm and the Otherworld and binds both spirit and body by acts of devotion, desire, and demand. This vivifying thread is, of course, the arte of crafting and working with enspirited objects, or what many refer to as *spirit vessels.* Within contemporary witchcraft, though many written works will touch upon or allude to this work, there are very few written works that have dedicated themselves solely to an exploration of this arte. It is this gap in the greater dialog of contemporary magic and witchcraft that this book seeks to contribute to.

Outside of witchcraft, this type of work is often more explicitly expressed within many living traditions of the world, such as Shintoism, Buddhism, Hinduism, African Traditional/Diasporic Religions, and many indigenous practices. However, I believe that the lack of focused attention to the work of creating enspirited objects within witchcraft leaves us with a major blind spot, impoverished of important praxis, and at a disadvantage when crafting an enduring vision of contemporary witchcraft. Further, I believe that mindfully integrating animistic approaches and embracing our work with spirits, ones which are centered on reciprocity and relationship as it dances between the embodied world and the Otherworld, stands as an atavistic reclamation of forms of witchery many of us lost long ago through religious imperialism and colonization.

Who is this Book is For

This book is intended for anyone with an interest in working with spirits and who is curious about the arte of creating spirit vessels. Though this book will be helpful to beginners in some ways, and I have made efforts to speak to newer magical practitioners throughout, it is predominantly designed for more intermediate to advanced practitioners. Ideally, the reader will have a pretty solid idea of what magic is and also be fairly familiar and experienced with ritual processes such as creating ritual space and both banishing and cleansing. That said, I have included numerous exercises for newer readers throughout this book in hopes that this may help get them started. There are also a great deal of resources listed throughout in the form of recommended additional reading which may prove helpful. Though this book approaches this subject of enspirited objects primarily from an animist view of traditional witchcraft, reflective of how I practice it, the work here can be easily adapted to almost any spiritual or magical tradition.

Who I Am

I began upon a path of witchcraft over thirty years ago as a young boy. Throughout the past twenty years, it has been my privilege to serve the craft as a teacher as well. I came to this specific work of crafting enspirited objects many years ago as my magical and spiritual practices began to increasingly intersect and inform my works of artistry and artifice. I feel I have always had an animist heart and looked upon the world as actively and dynamically enspirited. In hindsight, it seems quite inevitable to me that the arte of witchcraft and the art of crafting objects would quite naturally merge and eventually stand as a central part of my practice.

My witchcraft falls into what is most often categorized as traditional or folkloric craft and draws upon a deep connection to the land, spirit work, and both historical and folkloric understandings of the witch. My personal study and practice of magic is more diverse and is further informed by the reclamation of ancestral folk traditions as well as training within certain traditions of Southern Conjure. Additionally, I am an aborisha in the Afro Cuban tradition of Lucumí and a Tata Ndenge in a lineage of Quimbanda de Angola. I mention these treasured influences because, though this book explores this work from an animistic witchcraft approach, to pretend that these other aspects of my spirit work have not contributed to a greater understanding would be to do them a disservice and disrespect both my teachers and spirits in those traditions. Additionally, as I will occasionally make mention of these traditions for points of comparison, I want to be clear that when doing so, I am speaking with some level of firsthand experience.

On Appropriation and Closed Practices

At various points throughout this book I will highlight practices found within other magical and spiritual traditions, this should not be taken as a suggestion that the reader co-opt the specifics of these practices as an outsider to the traditions mentioned. When pointing out such examples, my intention is to show how many aspects of this work are expressed and can be found in traditions around the world. There is always a line between what serves as information/inspiration and what becomes appropriation, and the reader is encouraged to be mindful here. Many of the examples given in these cases exist within closed traditions. This means that to effectively and respectfully perform them as they are described would require that you have been initiated and welcomed into these traditions or otherwise born into them culturally.

How This Book is Organized

This book is arranged into four sections. The first, *On an Enspirited World,* establishes a vision of the witch as well as approaches towards spirit work. The second part, *On Enspirited Objects,* will delve into the history and various forms of spirit vessels as well as approaches towards their construction. The third section, *Ensouling the Effigy,* will explore the magical process involved in creating and working with enspirited objects. And the final section, *A Book of Secrets,* provides a formulary for the creation of various incenses, oils, and other formulas to aid in this work as well as a selection of magical workings. You will also find a collection of appendices at the end of the book relevant to points discussed throughout the text.

Most chapters of this book will include a recommended reading section at the end. These are meant to give the reader further resources which may give greater context and guidance for topics discussed throughout this work. These recommendations come from a variety of sources, and though

I believe each of them can provide greater elucidation to the reader, my inclusion of them here should not be seen as a complete endorsement of all the ideas espoused in each source or of their authors. In some cases, the authors I recommend directly contradict some of my own ideas. This is valuable as I believe a well-rounded witch should be exposed to a variety of ideas in order to better develop their unique approaches towards the craft.

When I find I am truly interested in a subject, I like to read as much as I can from all manner of sources. After all, some good ideas may be found in otherwise bad books, and a few bad ideas may be found in good books. I will nod to Timothy Leary here and encourage the reader to think for yourself and question authority when forming your own conclusions.

General Advice and Precautions

As with most things worth doing, witchcraft is not free from risk. Whenever engaging in magical work, particularly when working with spirits, there exists a possibility for delusion, obsession, or any number of other adverse situations to arise. Though I have included many warnings and instructions throughout this work regarding establishing protections and exercising discernment, the reader is encouraged, as much as possible, to approach this work from a place of preexisting stability in their life situations and mental health. If you find that engaging in this work, or magical work in general, begins to cause imbalance in your life, you should seek the aid and counsel of spiritual elders, trusted and objective peers, and medical professionals as needed.

The work presented within this book should be considered neither inherently safe nor unnecessarily dangerous. However, each individual's experiences will vary, and there are seldom any guarantees in the realm of spirits. Whenever we are exploring new corridors of magical work, it is paramount that we regularly check in with ourselves and take stock of our physical, mental, and spiritual health in relation to the work we are doing. In approaching any of the more rewarding and challenging corners of the magical arte, what will always serve the witch best is a regularly applied effort to actively and truly *Know Thyself.*

The Purpose of this Book

My goal in writing this work is to contribute my own voice, insights, and experiences in this realm based upon my own practice over the years, and also to encourage what I hope will become a greater conversation and exploration around the role of spirit vessels both within contemporary witchcraft as well as in magical practice more broadly. Throughout this book, I will present many of my own ideas around spirit work as well as my own approaches towards the crafting and birthing of enspirited objects. Though I hope that the reader might discover much here that contributes to their understanding of spirits and this particular arte, what exists here is only one perspective among many. As such, the reader is encouraged to take from this book what is both meaningful and effective for them and to leave what does not serve them behind. If this book leaves the reader with inspiration and motivation towards embracing this work for the first time or in new ways, then there is little more I can ask for as a mark of success.

Part One:
On an Enspirited World

Chapter One

The Birthing of Spirits: On Animism, Consciousness, and Spirits

In the depths of a primordial cave, roughly forty thousand years ago, a conjuration began that would alter the course of humanity. Within the cave's darkness, illuminated only by the light of a crude oil lamp burning bison tallow as its fuel, one of our earliest ancestors began a ritual. A rite designed to call something forth from the Otherworld and into our own. Equipped with the simplest of tools, in a process estimated to have taken some four hundred hours, a spirit was given form.

The axis around which this ancient ritual revolved, a piece of mammoth ivory, served as the medium by which she would conjure him. With each measured stroke of her stone blade, she sang to him, carving and etching new forms and calling him forth. The transfigural work of her hands, a bewitching of our reality, as she pierced the visceral membrane between the intangible and the embodied. By her inspired desire, artistry, and agency, she would alter the material realm, reach into the Otherworld, and embrace the other-than-human so that she might midwife this spirit into our realm.

At the conclusion of her tireless primeval conjuration, in the lamplight of the cave, what stood before her was a new being, the likes of which our world had never seen. Its body was that of a man. Its head was that of a lion. And by its birthing, we would forever be changed.

This figure, known to us now as the *Löwenmensch* (Lion Man), was rediscovered by archeologists in 1939 in a cave called Hohlenstein-Stadel in what is now Southern Germany. As millennia had eaten away at this effigy, upon being unearthed, it initially seemed only to be a collection of ivory shards. These were summarily cataloged, gathered, stored away, and forgotten.

It was not until 1969 that an archeologist by the name of Joachim Hahn reexamined the over two hundred pieces of broken ivory and, in an act nothing short of necromantic, began piecing them back together in their originally crafted form. Once again, revealing the Lion Man and bringing his form into our world.

The *Löwenmensch,* now resurrected, stands at thirty-one centimeters and, at the time of this writing, represents the earliest undisputed sculpture in the world. Though not to be ignored in the history of artistry and icons, it is also from around this period in the Upper Paleolithic that early humans began creating painted and drawn images from red ochre upon the walls of caves. The Lion Man, however, is our first example of a sculptural figure with human characteristics.

Yet with the addition of its feline head, it is more accurately a therianthrope (combining both human and animal elements) and represents a being that, until it was sculpted, did not exist in this world. When we consider that such therianthropic figures have been present in the mythologies and religions of various cultures throughout history, it is perhaps not a great leap to imagine that this lion-man might have been a devotional object or an effigy meant to serve as the physical embodiment of a spirit.

This figure becomes our first effigy, our first known idol, our first tangible, portable, and sculptural representation of a spirit born into our realm. It is also, therefore, the earliest example of the magic this book seeks to explore. Here we stand at the eternal crossroads of artistry and evocation to vivify for the reader a sorcerous endeavor begun by our earliest ancestors and continued throughout human history. One that is the birthright of every witch. Herein lies an arte of conjuration, of craft, and of spirits embodied.

On the World of Spirits

We exist in an enspirited world.[1] This was known by our Paleolithic ancestors who crafted images from ochre, bone, and clay, and it is the foundation of all animistic traditions. Each of the plants and fungi that populate the forests and fields, each creature of the land, sea, and sky, exists within a vast, diverse, and interconnected ecosystem of spirits. It is the work of understanding this relationality and establishing relationships with nonhuman people that fuels the fires that illuminate the dark caverns of the witch's arte.

Such an understanding of personhood extends beyond biological lifeforms and towards a recognition of *all* naturally occurring material forms and phenomena as being enspirited. The stones and the soil, rivers and mountains, canyons, and caves all have their spirits. Within the falling snow, the storm clouds, the lightning, the winds, and the wildfires, so too the spirits dwell. Each planet and star represent a great spirit, one which plays host to its own litany of indwelling, attendant, and emissary spirits.

My craft and artistry delve deeper into the cave of spirits and ideas around consciousness. Ending not with recognition of the spirits inhabiting the natural world, but extending towards recognizing the spirits present within the forms crafted by human hands and machines alike. Further, it recognizes that immaterial creations such as music, words, and philosophical concepts may also have their own associated spirits.

An animistic craft of this kind might manifest as understanding and engaging with our homes as an ecosystem where a diversity of spirits can be found, and approaching the home itself as a spirit. Or in recognizing that the street you live on, or the town you live in, might also be engaged with as spirits. The everyday objects you encounter: a piece of jewelry, your

1 Instead of the more common *inspirited,* which is primarily used to mean encouraged or strengthened, I have made the stylistic choice to favor the more archaic spelling of *enspirited* in order to set its usage throughout this work apart when referring to that which is imbued with spirit.

electronic devices, and the very book you are holding might all be approached, and indeed respond to us, as individual spirits. For the particularly skilled witch, this might even take the form of conjuring forth and engaging the spirits that are associated with specific words, colors, concepts, or memories.

Within my craft, each of these things not only contains some essence of spirit but also a form of what we might understand as consciousness. A personhood that can be conjured, communicated with, and consciously engaged with as such. These beliefs often blur the object/subject dichotomy and create a foundation for spirit work, which I refer to as a form of *Panpsychic Animism.*[2]

Panpsychic Animism, as I approach it, is a fusion of two similar yet distinct philosophical/spiritual thoughts and holds these two beliefs at its core:[3]

- Firstly, that consciousness permeates the entirety of existence. So much so that reality as we experience it might be said to be composed primarily of consciousness.
- Secondly, that spirits, embodied or otherwise, are understood as unique patterns of consciousness which we are able to directly engage with when equipped with the necessary cognitive and sensory tools. This stands as the working definition for spirits throughout this text.

It helps us to clarify here that all embodied beings, meaning anything with a material form that we can physically interact with, may indeed be viewed as spirits by the above definition. However, when speaking of *spirits* within the context of this book, I am most commonly referring to patterns of consciousness that are not entirely dependent upon physical

---

2 Within philosophy, *subject* refers to beings who possess agency, have conscious experiences, and are therefore able to interact with and observe their surroundings. Conversely, *object* refers to the things experienced or observed by a subject and believed to lack agency.

3 When using the term *belief* throughout much of this work, it should not be mistaken for a declaration of unassailable objective truth, but instead an approach towards understanding which serves as an operative view and valuable tool. I encourage the skeptical reader to embrace the approach of 'belief as tool' often employed within chaos magick circles here.

forms (bodies) and who often, or primarily, exist independently from them. In essence, when speaking of spirits throughout this work, I am usually referring to disembodied forms of consciousness.

In order to more fully explore the implications of a Panpsychic Animism, I believe it serves us to take a very brief journey into these terms, their history, and their prospective meanings. This is meant to serve for establishing a greater understanding of the perspectives that my approach towards this kind of spirit work, artistry, and witchery is born from. And to possibly inspire others towards experimenting with and embracing similar perspectives. Though the techniques of this book can certainly be adapted to the practices of the hard polytheist pagan, the ceremonial ritualist, and the chaos magician alike. I believe it is helpful to have a grounding in some of the concepts which underlie my approach towards spirits so that it might establish a foundation for the particular arte explored later in this text, namely conjuring spirits both from and into the material.

On Animism

In its simplest form, animism is the belief that some or all things have a spirit or soul. The term was coined in 1871 by British anthropologist Sir Edward Burnett Tylor[4] and draws upon the Latin *anima,* a term simultaneously referring to breath, spirit, and life.[5] Tylor defined animism as the "theory of the universal animation of nature."[6]

Though ascribing this particular label to the beliefs of people is a more recent development, the great tree of animism is both incredibly ancient and still very much alive. Its branches stretch across cultures, and whether they outwardly recognize it or not, the seeds of its fruit are present within most spiritual traditions. It is a tree with primeval roots that extend through the fertile chthonic soils of time and reach out to, cradle, and preserve the bones of our earliest ancestors. This animate and enspirited view of existence is believed to be humanity's earliest form of what might

---

4 Borrowing from earlier writings by Georg Stahl.

5 Take note of this association with life, breath, and spirit as it will be a recurrent theme throughout this work.

6 "Origin & History of Animism," *Etymonline,* https://www.etymonline.com/word/animism

be called "religion". And in the minds of many of its adherents, animism offers us a path towards our greatest potential as a species for existing in harmonious engagement with the world around us.

Animism is not a structured monolithic religion, and it may function quite differently from one animistic culture to the next. Instead, animism is simply a way of describing an awareness of our world as being enspirited. In general, animistic belief structures are not anthropocentric, meaning they do not center humanity to the exclusion of nonhuman persons. Nor is humanity generally viewed as being of greater value or virtue than other forms of spirit. Contrasting with beliefs often promoted within a Christianized culture, humanity is not viewed as separate from the natural world and given dominion over it. Instead, humanity exists as a part of and within nature and in correlational community with the land and its spirits.

With this in mind, it is worth pausing here to note that, though I will primarily use the terms *spirit* or *Others* when referencing disembodied other-than-human persons, we should not mistake this as imposing unnecessary distance between ourselves and the Others, as our existence is intertwined. We share in the quality of being spirits, we share in the quality of personhood, and we exist concurrently within an interrelated spiritual ecosystem.

The earliest usage of the term *animism* presented a variety of problems worth addressing. It is generally believed that our Neolithic and Paleolithic ancestors understood and engaged their world through an animistic world-view. During the time period when animism emerged as a descriptor, historians and anthropologists knew very little about the complexities of Paleolithic and Neolithic peoples. As a result, our early ancestors were often depicted simply as ignorant brutes lacking any semblance of culture or civility. Because of this, animism was regarded by many early anthropologists, including Tylor, as a mistaken, primitive, and regressive way of understanding the world.

In Tylor's work, *Primitive Culture,* he presents a Darwinian view of cultural and spiritual evolution that established animism as an archaic expression of religion. Such a framing of animistic beliefs presents them as an inferior stage in the natural progression of human religion and intellect. The evolution of religion as framed by Tylor advances from animism towards polytheism and eventually develops into a monotheist belief viewed as the greatest expression of culture. Within this view, European

Protestant Christianity was commonly centered as the most evolved and idealized form of monotheist belief.[7] Theories such as those put forth by Tylor framed indigenous animistic cultures as being less functional or desirable and painted them as societies of savages who hadn't yet seen the error of their ways. Animism was treated not as a destination unto itself, but instead, as humanity's underdeveloped juvenile first steps towards a destination of greater understanding and civility.

These perspectives were further promoted and developed by Western anthropologists, psychologists, and philosophers of the late nineteenth and early twentieth centuries. Individuals who, whilst possibly enjoying a somewhat romantic view of the polytheist cultures of antiquity, primarily identified as monotheists or as atheists. For instance, in the third chapter of Sigmund Freud's *Totem and Taboo,* he psychologizes animism and reinforces an evolutionary idea of religious thought. In his case, highlighting scientific rationalism as the pinnacle of that evolutionary arch. Freud's view of animism was also that it was a regressive and mistaken attribution of personhood. A result of projection that imagines the world as we wish to see it, as a reflection of ourselves. Humans had a personhood/psyche/soul, yes, but to Freud, it was an error to believe anything else might. Freud's framing of animism linked it to delusional disorders and obsessive thinking and relegated it to the beliefs of "primitive" peoples and neurotics.[8]

These early ideas about animism were formed from within an imperialist culture during a time when many of the world's polytheist and animistic peoples were being (as many still are today) exploited or exterminated. These are ideas created by the same colonizing forces who often benefited from self-serving narratives around the backward nature and beliefs of the people they were subjugating as a rationale for treating them as less than human. Whenever an external force imposes its own created labels and worldviews upon cultures they are not a part of, whether intentionally or not, there is ample opportunity to misrepresent and erase what makes those cultures unique. Early usage of animism tended towards it being applied by anthropologists and scholars as a catchall label to reference the beliefs of almost all non-Western cultures who exhibited recognition

7 Justine Quijada. "Do Mountains Have Souls?" *SAPIENS,* 15 Nov. 2022, www.sapiens.org/culture/new-animism/.

8 S Freud. *Totem and Taboo.* (Hogarth Press, 1958)

and reverence for an enspirited world. In short, animism became a lens through which European and American colonialist powers often devalued the spiritual framework and cultural traditions of indigenous communities.

Shackled to this evolutionary theory of religious progression, animism quickly became a term entangled in the strangling vines of imperialism, colonization, and white supremacy. Thankfully, by the mid-twentieth century, many anthropologists came to recognize the inherent problems and cultural biases accompanying animism's early applications as an identifier. As a result, animism as a way of referring to cultures that believed in an enspirited world largely fell out of favor amongst academics for several decades.

In the latter part of the twentieth century, however, this began to change. Many realized that when it came to understanding animistic cultures and beliefs, though the bathwater was rather filthy, the baby might have been just fine. A revisiting of animism began, and the construction of a "new animism" was proposed by voices within anthropology, psychology, and religious studies.

More powerfully, perhaps, animism started becoming adopted by a variety of indigenous communities, as well as many pagan and earth-based religions, as a self-designated term for defining their beliefs.[9] A purging of old animism's belief in evolutionary religion and its racist foundations became paramount, and in its stead, animism became embraced as a term by people who felt it was representative of their beliefs. In this new approach, aided by academic works such as those of Nurit Bird-David[10] and Graham Harvey,[11] animism became further divorced from the more problematic application and implications given to it by those outside of animistic cultures. A caution against ethnocentrism and superimposing a Western ontology upon indigenous cultures remains central to new animism. In its current form, the study of animism is an ongoing conversation between those living within animistic cultures and the academics and scholars outside of them. With a further respect towards understanding

9 Graham Harvey. *Animism: Respecting the Living World.* (Columbia University Press, 2006). 3.

10 Nurit Bird-David. "'Animism' Revisited." *Current Anthropology,* vol. 40, no. S1, Feb. 1999, S67–91. https://doi.org/10.1086/200061

11 Graham Harvey. *Animism: Respecting the Living World.* (Columbia University Press, 2006).

that animistic beliefs are not a monolith and that they can and do vary quite a bit from one culture to the next.

As exhibited by indigenous groups such as the Ojibwe, most animist cultures recognize that there are many nonhuman people we live in community with. That a personhood/spirit/consciousness may be viewed as present within animals, plants, and stones. Such beliefs are not simply a projection of humanity upon other beings in order to grant them personhood. They are instead an understanding that human beings represent only one kind of *people* in a world populated with many nonhuman people.[12]

This understanding of different kinds of persons and our relationships to, and with, them is deeply critical in the work of the witch as I know it, and one which will be explored in greater depth throughout this work. As one who, by their nature, consorts with spirits, the witch is tasked with the development and maintenance of relationships with other-than-human persons as a central pillar of their arte. As such, the spirits with who we work with, care for, learn from, and align ourselves with are an integral aspect of the witch's craft.

Such an understanding of spirits is also still very much alive throughout the world. Though its presence is more clearly identifiable among traditions such as Shintoism, African traditional religions, and many Indigenous spiritualities. Animism plays a greater or lesser role in all religions that believe in any form of enspirited being.

As animism encourages a relationality and responsibility towards our environment and its inhabitants, it has also played an increasing role in ecological conservation efforts and activism. Efforts that have largely been led by Indigenous peoples. For example, animist-backed ecological efforts have pushed for Environmental Personhood and often succeeded in securing recognition of land and locales as sacred and sovereign entities, as people. Some incredible successes in this realm have included the recognition of the Te Urewera National Park, the Whanganui River in New Zealand, as well as the Magpie River in Canada, as legally recognized people with their own rights and protections.

It is also heartening to find that in more recent decades, animism as a label, worldview, and point of discussion has become increasingly adopted, applied, and emphasized by many operating within contemporary witchcraft,

---

12 Harvey, *Ibid.* 17-19.

paganism, and folk magic frameworks. At this critical point in the Earth's history, human beings need now, perhaps more than ever, to embrace our role and responsibilities in the great ecosystem of nonhuman people that we exist within. And I believe that embracing an animistic perspective has the potential to be both a transformative and powerful medicine for the future of our world.

On Panpsychism

Whereas a materialist understanding of conscious experience believes that consciousness is emergent, meaning that it arises out of the neurological mechanisms (brains) of biological lifeforms, Panpsychism argues instead that consciousness is not unique to humans and animals, but fundamental and ubiquitous in the natural world.[13] In short, a panpsychic view does not believe consciousness is reliant upon biological life. Instead, it recognizes the universe as being filled with consciousness.

Further, panpsychism suggests that all material forms, down to the smallest particles, can be said to possess at least a rudimentary form of consciousness. In some forms of panpsychism, all things within the universe are believed to be a part of and exist within one great mind or consciousness. This allows for an experience of consciousness as existing in both microcosmic and macrocosmic forms. And might be understood to mean that, though each bacterium and microbe on your body could be recognized as possessing a form of consciousness, the collective contributes to the entirety of the consciousness that creates you. Furthermore, each creature that exists upon the Earth contributes to the great conscious entity that is Earth. Additionally, many schools of panpsychism argue that what we experience as matter is itself a form of consciousness.

Though similar beliefs are found in spiritual theologies such as pantheism and panentheism, both of which view the universe as, or a part of, God. Panpsychism is a concept most commonly discussed within the realms of philosophy and psychology when grappling with "the hard problem of consciousness". Essentially, referring to the challenge that science, being

---

13 Phillip Goff, William Seagar, and Sean Allen-Hermanson. S. Panpsychism. *Stanford Encyclopedia of Philosophy*, 5 May 2022. https://plato.stanford.edu/entries/panpsychism/#PanpHistWestPhil

objective, cannot agree upon an explanation for why a person has conscious subjective experiences. And though the term panpsychism wasn't coined until much later, we do find written accounts of similar concepts being explored among ancient Greek presocratic philosophers such as Thales of Miletus.

Among the adherents of panpsychism, there are varying beliefs about the ways in which consciousness exists and functions. Though all things possess a degree of consciousness, it is generally recognized that human beings represent a unique and complex form of it.[14] A uniqueness that leads us towards engaging with spirits in the diversity of ways we have throughout history. This has gifted us the magic of embodying the intangible through ritual, artistry, and artifact since our ochre-reddened hands first traced images upon the walls of ancient caves and carved imaginal creatures from ivory.

Recommended Additional Reading

Practitioner Resources:

Path of the Moonlit Hedge: Discovering the Magick of Animistic Witchcraft by Nathan Hall. Llewellyn Publications, 2023.

Academic Resources:

Animism: Respecting the Living World by Hurst & Company, 2017.

The Handbook of Contemporary Animism edited by Graham Harvey. Routledge, 2015.

Braiding Sweetgrass: Indigenous Wisdom, Scientific Knowledge and the Teachings of Plants by Robin Wall Kimmerer. Milkweed Editions, 2020.

The Spell of the Sensuous: Perception and Language in a More-Than-Human World by David Abram. Pantheon Books, 1996.

The Mind in the Cave: Consciousness and the Origins of Art by David Lewis-Williams. Thames & Hudson, 2016.

Panpsychism in the West, revised edition by David Skrbina. The MIT Press, 2017.

The Routledge Handbook of Panpsychism edited by William Seager. Routledge, 2021.

14 Note the intentional choice of the words unique and complex here as opposed to anthropocentric terms such as greater, or more advanced.

Chapter Two

Conjuring the Witch: On Origins, Identifiers, and the Witch Embodied

The witch belongs to no one. In this lies her eternal power.[15] She is a figure both adaptable and mutable. A shapeshifter who slips through the fingers of those who, in their hubris, imagine they might strictly define her or keep her in a cage.

It is neither my desire nor is it within the power of any one of us to control or contain the witch. Nor to tell her she is unrecognized in the faces of those she empowers in the breaking of chains, to police the realms the witch might inhabit, or the myriad masks she might choose to wear. With such in mind, it should be understood that the vision of the witch provided here is not one I wish to impose upon the reader unwillingly. In short, I am not here to tell you who or what the witch is *to you*.

That said, I recognize that my understanding of the witch and her craft may at times be incongruous with many contemporary understandings of witchcraft. This is a part of why I felt this chapter was a necessary

---

15 Throughout much of this section, I speak of the witch using feminine pronouns. Though I do often experience the spirit of the witch as female presenting it should be understood that the witch is ageless, eternal, transcendent of gender, and intrinsically queer. In short, the witch will inhabit the bodies she chooses regardless of any specific gender or sexual expression.

addition to our work. For instance, I am of the opinion that the witch may be viewed as a spirit in her own right. One which may breathe into, inhabit, and enspirit us. Bewitching us that we might, in turn, go forth as an embodiment of the witch within the world. Becoming 'witched' in such a manner is an alteration of self which may be sought out or occasionally be thrust upon an individual as a result of a spirit encounter or the circumstances of their birth.[16] There are any number of ways one might become witched, and each sincere seeker will find their initiations where they will.

No matter the road that has led to her, though, each individual so touched exists as a uniquely embodied avatar of the witch. This in mind, in order to best lay a foundation for the work ahead, I believe it serves us to chart certain points on the map of the witch's history and highlight elements that have commonly identified her whilst we form a vision of the witch as she might live amongst these pages.

Here we come to the edge of the dark forest, to the midnight crossroads, the Bald Mountain, the Brocken cave, and the Heath of the He-goat to meet the witch as we shall understand her throughout this work. In hopes that we might take flight with her upon the night's tempest and together embrace the mythic truths the witch shall embody here.

On the Wings of Night

When excavating our earliest origins, it serves us to examine some of the creatures that inform our first understandings of, and are often synonymous with, the witch. Monstrous ancient ancestors, which are often more closely aligned with vampires, werewolves, and haints than with the human sorcerer, necromancer, or enchantress. While following this prominent branch of the witch's family tree, we are inevitably met by the looming yellow eyes and sharp black talons of the vampiric *strix* of Roman and Greek mythology.

As opposed to being classed as a revenant of the dead, as many vampiric creatures are, the *strix* is said to be the result of metamorphism. An early

16 Within some traditions, indicators such as be born with a caul, or being born as the seventh son of a seventh son suggested an individual may be inclined towards witchery.

Greek account of the *strix*, written by Boios in his *Ornithologia* and preserved by Antoninus Liberalis in *Metamorphoses*, relates the story of Polyphonte and her sons Agrios and Oreios, who, as punishment for engaging in cannibalism, were transformed into *striges* (plural of *strix*).

According to tales of antiquity, *striges* were most commonly understood as large nocturnal birds of prey with sharp talons, large eyes, and gray or dark plumage. *Striges* were bloodthirsty creatures that feasted upon human flesh and drank human blood, particularly that of infants. Their screeches and screams were said to pierce through the night as a harbinger of misfortune.

The *strix* was viewed as a supernatural creature of ill omen and believed to be either part woman and part bird, or a creature with the ability to transform from its avian form into that of a woman. Parts of the *strix's* body were also believed to possess powerful magics. For those brave enough to collect them, her feathers were reputed to be effective in works of both love and malediction.[17]

Though *striges* have sometimes been compared to bats, they are most commonly associated with owls, particularly the screech owl. This contributes to a very long history allying witches with owls, and also to the modern-day nomenclature of nocturnal birds. The ornithological terms *Strigiformes*, *Strigidae*, and *Strix* all derive from the *strix* of myth and refer respectively to the order, family, and genus designations for owls.

The *strix*, and its cognates such as the Albanian *shtriga*, Polish *strzyga*, and the Italian *strega*, all become terms that tend to blur definitions and might equally be applied to supernatural vampiric creatures, literal owls, night flying hag spirits, or the witch in the form of a human. Here we find the witch emerging as an embodied supernatural spirit. A creature that might appear human if she desires, but is equally seen as malefic, monstrous, and inhuman.

A notable parallel of the *strix* worth highlighting here is found in the figure of Lilith from Mesopotamian and Jewish folklore. Though her stories vary and her history is ancient within some Abrahamic traditions, Lilith is often said to have been the first woman. She was created at the

---

17 Samuel Grant Oliphant. "The Story of the Strix: Ancient." *Transactions and Proceedings of the American Philological Association*. 1913. 133. https://doi.org/10.2307/282549

same time as Adam and was his wife before Eve. Lilith refused to behave as a subservient to Adam and was banished from Eden as a result. After this banishment, she becomes transformed into a vampiric progenitrix of both demons and witches. An anti-mother who is antagonistic towards life, who seduces men and robs them of their seed, and who abducts and feeds off of newborns. Much like the strix, Lilith is envisioned as both a woman and a nocturnal flying monster, and her name is most often translated as "night hag" or "screech owl."

In this vision of Lilith, we see a reflection of cultural anxieties around women who dare to seek autonomy and independence of body and mind as well as the resultant demonization of such inclinations. A deep-rooted misogyny that has accompanied the witch throughout her history and continues to plague women and witches of all genders into the present. As such, it is unsurprising that many contemporary witches embrace the figure of Lilith as a powerful emanation of the Witch Mother.

On Nightmares and Boo Hags

This understanding of the witch as a supernatural being, neither fully human nor spirit, is also found in the Germanic and Slavic lore of the mare. A creature often viewed as both an embodied witch in human form and a malevolent spirit. The mare sits and presses, or rides upon people's chests while they slumber to steal their breath or drain them of vitality. The mare also brings about sleep paralysis, restless sleep, and frightening dreams or "nightmares". The lore of the mare usually includes elements of vampirism, nocturnal flight, and shapeshifting as well. By the light of day, the mare might appear in human likeness, but by night, they would send their spirit out in the form of an animal to torment others.

This same sort of creature finds many variations in cultures throughout the world, such as the night hags of Great Britain and Ireland, and the boo hag of the Southern United States. They are almost always presented as beings who appear human by some illusion or who were born human but who have the ability to slip out of their skin at night in spirit form. Usually, with the intention of sneaking into the homes of others through a window, a crack in the wall, or a keyhole to steal their vitality while they sleep. Such creatures were commonly believed to steal horses and ride them throughout the night, often leaving the horses exhausted and sickly in the morning. Both the boo hag and the mare were said to creep into the homes of unsuspecting humans, braid their hair into a brindle, and ride them through the night, depleting their energy and ultimately draining their health and vitality.

The associated phenomena became known as *hagriding* or being *hagridden* and spoke to the experience of people and animals being ridden and drained of their life force. It is also from this folkloric inhuman hag that the hagstone (a stone with a naturally occurring hole in it) derives its name. And such stones were often hung above beds and in animal stables or worn on the person as an apotropaic charm to keep these malevolent creatures at bay.

As displayed above, depending upon the source, the mare, hag, or witch may be viewed as an entirely supernatural creature that takes on a human form when convenient. Or instead, as a human being who sends out their spirit at night. Regardless, such beings have always been framed as malevolent in nature, a threat to the community, and cause for very real concern, which often resulted in very real consequences.

On the Woman Turned Witch

Elements associated with the monstrous *strix*, the mare, and the hag, particularly those of nocturnal flight and sowing misfortune, inform our later understandings of the witch. It is this nebulous separation between humanity and the monstrous, coupled with a weaponized fear, that eventually results in countless innocent people finding themselves labeled as witches and accused of engaging in nocturnal attacks and malefic magic. Throughout early modern Europe and into the Colonial Americas, such accusations often resulted in people, predominantly women, being targeted and murdered by their own communities.

As opposed to being classified as a monstrous creature, within Early Modern Christendom, a more common image of the witch becomes that of a human being who derives their power through consorting and making pacts with diabolical spirits. Primarily, (as the church and its officers would tell it), with the intent of causing harm to the community. In many cases, those accused of being witches were said to participate in libidinous and blasphemous behaviors, theft, causing misfortune to others, and engaging in infanticide and cannibalism. Such charges often allowed communities to dehumanize their neighbors, cast them as monsters, and, in turn, engage in monstrous behaviors towards them.

A variety of things might lead to a person being branded a witch. Being said to possess supernatural gifts and abilities, being an outspoken or free-willed woman, or angering a neighbor might all lead to an accusation. But one of the more consistent elements of such accusations, and one which transformed an otherwise ordinary citizen into a witch in the eyes of their persecutors, was the act of consorting with spirits.

In such an environment, engaging with the spirit world on any level becomes a potentially deadly practice, as in the eyes of the church, most, if not all, spirits become increasingly viewed as deceptive agents of evil. As a result, wherever the colonizing forces of Christendom plant their flags, indigenous practices become labeled as witchcraft and idolatry, and the spirits of the land become maligned as demons and devils. Decade after decade, generation after generation, century after century, the people of that land become increasingly subjugated, indoctrinated, and either converted or eradicated within a religious overculture designed to impose its own narrative upon the land and rewrite the history of its people.

The old gods, the ancestors, and the spirits that once sustained communities and tied them to their land become, quite literally, demonized forces said to lead the souls of humanity astray. Animistic and pagan practices become increasingly stamped out, suppressed, erased, and occasionally stripped for parts and absorbed by the church. As a result, those who maintain earlier spiritual practices become potential targets for persecution and prosecution. Due to this, many animistic magical traditions are only preserved by being hidden away from the church, or through being woven into and throughout a Christianized tapestry of folklore and folk magic.

On the Spirit Made Witch

Many who were labeled as witches were completely innocent of trafficking with spirits and were instead the unfortunate victims of community insecurity turned mass hysteria. A prominent example of this being the 1692-1693 witch trials of Salem, Massachusetts, where individuals were charged with witchcraft and accused of consorting with the devil, keeping familiar spirits, and sending these spirits, as well as their own, out to afflict others. As a result of these accusations, nineteen people were executed, one died while being tortured, and several more died while incarcerated. In the Salem cases, and many more throughout history, the accused were almost certainly not involved in any real form of spirit conjuration. Instead, the accused were targeted by members of their community who were fearful that their own misfortunes were the result of their neighbor's misdeeds. Or, in some cases, the accused were targeted by people who had a vendetta against them.

In other cases, those accused of witchcraft appear to have had genuine relationships with spirits. One such example is Bessie Dunlop, a Scottish woman who, during her sixteenth-century confession, described meeting a familiar spirit named Thomas Ried while she was facing personal hardship. Thomas, once a human who was killed in battle, now claimed to serve the Queen of Elphame and offered Bessie magical knowledge in healing and divination. With his help, she became a respected midwife and cunning woman in her community until she was accused of witchcraft, likely by a displeased client, and ultimately executed.[18]

A similar example from around the same time in Scotland is found in the 1597 confession of cunning man Andrew Mann. Andrew confessed that the Queen of Elphame had granted him magical gifts in exchange for his kindness. Mann also claimed he became one of her lovers and fathered children with her. He further described attending otherworldly gatherings of faerie spirits and spirits of the dead, including the ghosts of King James IV and Thomas the Rhymer. These gatherings resembled many folkloric accounts of witches' meetings and included feasts, dancing, spirit flight, and magical instruction. At one such assembly, Mann encountered a spirit named Christonday, said to be the Queen's consort, who could appear as an angel, a devil, or a stag, and who marked Mann with a witch's sign and revealed apocalyptic visions. Mann, too, was executed for witchcraft after confessing to these encounters.[19]

The confessions of Dunlop and Man are only two examples among many confessions found throughout Europe and the Americas. However, they illustrate some elements of what was commonly believed to make a person a witch and the role of spirits in relation to the witch.

---

18 L. Henderson. "Witch, Fairy and Folktale Narratives in the Trial of Bessie Dunlop." Essay. *Fantastical Imaginations: The Supernaturalin Scottish History and Culture,* (Birlinn Ltd, 2009) 141–66.

19 Charles Sinclair. *Scotland's Wicked Witches.* (Goblinshead, 2011) 38

Firstly, they reinforce a common belief that witches were thought to gain power through their relationship with spirits. This might take the form of a spiritual gift such as prophecy or healing bestowed upon them by a spirit, as instruction and information being offered by spirits, or as the witch employing spirits to do their bidding.

Secondly, they illustrate the kinds of spirits a witch might traffic with. Dunlop and Mann engaged with spirits described as fairies, angels, and devils, as well as spirits of the dead.[20] When it came to defining a witch, in some cases, it wasn't the act of consorting with spirits alone that caused a person to be accused so much as the *classification* of spirit they were said to be working with. There were plenty of healers and cunning folk throughout this period who uttered charms calling upon the intercession of Jesus and Mary, and worked with angels, the sainted dead, or with fairies. In some cases, these individuals were largely permitted to do their work free from accusations of witchery. In fact, the work of many cunning folk, pellars, and faerie doctors revolved around freeing their clients from bewitchment, performing exorcisms, creating protective charms, and identifying the sources of malefic magic.

In such a dichotomy, these folk practitioners were the protective opposing forces that stood against malevolent witches believed to be actively antagonistic towards the well-being of their community. Cunning folk were often believed to source their abilities from God or the faerie folk. In contrast, witches were thought to be agents of evil who sourced their power from the Devil and demonic beings. In most cases, when individuals were conjuring spirits of the dead, this was largely treated as a form of necromancy and generally considered equivalent to, or synonymous with, witchcraft.

However, the line between being viewed as a benevolent cunning person or a malefic witch was a tenuous one at best. One which became much thinner depending upon one's relationship with their community and the opinions adopted by the church. In time, such liberal distinctions between classes of spirits and the people who conjured them largely disappeared, particularly once Protestant sensibilities began to spread. As a result, the definition of witchery expanded, and the type of people who

20 It is interesting to note here how their stories demonstrate the often blurred lines between fairies and spirits of the dead.

might be considered witches along with it. Throughout the Early Modern period, depending upon the location, those believed to be working with *any* kind of spirit, or practicing any kind of folk magic and healing, might find themselves accused of witchcraft. In many cases, all it took was for a dissatisfied neighbor or client to blame a cunning person for causing them illness or harm, and they might quickly become dragged before the magistrate and branded a witch.

On Nocturnal Flight

While transforming into a more human form, the witch maintained certain characteristics of the *strix* and mare. The most persistent of these being transvection, or the ability to fly. In nearly all the lands and languages the witch has found herself represented, she has been a figure believed to go forth in flight during the night. It's clear in many cases that this magical flight allowed witches to travel at great speed and the ability to move unseen. Witches were often accused of using this ability to steal milk, butter, or much like their monstrous precursors, the vitality of their neighbors and their livestock.

In other cases, these nocturnal journeys took the witch to otherworldly gatherings. Witches might fly to forest clearings, or sacred trees, to congregate and meet with goddess figures such as Herodias, Diana, Holda, and Abundia. As in the case of Andrew Mann, they might go forth to Elphame to engage in revelry with the faerie folk and their queen. Or they might fly to forbidden caves or mountains and attend the witches' sabbath to pay homage to their Devil. Though it was certain in the minds of those seeking to define and prosecute witches that they did in fact fly, there was some debate on how exactly this was achieved.

In the eleventh-century *Canon Episcopi,* we find accounts of "certain wicked women" taking flight upon beasts in the night to engage in revelry with the goddess Diana or Herodias. These accounts are discounted as real experiences and instead relegated to the realm of dreams and phantasms. From this view, the witches' night flight, and much of witchcraft, is not treated as a reality, but a delusion created by Satan and placed into the minds of people to test their faith. For a person to experience such dreams was seen as an error to be corrected, however for someone to believe in and promote the reality of these dreams would be seen as heresy.

In 1484, Pope Innocent VIII issued the papal bull *Summis desiderantes affectibus,* which altered this position and declared witchcraft a reality. This laid the path for the *Malleus Maleficarum,* various legal acts throughout Europe labeling witchcraft a capital crime, and the waves of witch trials and death that would follow in their wake. In this new interpretation, the flight of witches was no dream or delusion but a very real phenomenon.

Within contemporary traditional witchcraft, the flight of witches is approached as a form of spirit flight and is often referred to as transvection or hedge crossing. This practice shares some common elements with those present in other magical traditions such as shamanic journeying, astral travel, dreamwalking, or pathworking. In later chapters, we will take a more practical approach to this type of work and explore its relevance to the contemporary practitioner, as well as how it might assist the witch in the creation of enspirited objects.

On the Witching Artes

The types of magic attributed to the literate and learned classes throughout history often involved complex astrology, alchemical processes, or elaborate tools and rituals of evocation. In contrast, the witch's arte is largely practical in its approaches, using what is readily available. Outside of the magics performed through transvection, shapeshifting, and spirit companions, there are two additional forms of magic common to the witch worth mentioning here: the magic of objects and the magic of breath.

The arte of bewitching or conjuring everyday objects is one inseparable from the witch. This is reflected in many of the tools commonly associated with witches, such as the cauldron, the broom, and other domestic implements transformed by witchery. Historically, through the work of a witch, butter churns might become bewitched, causing them to fail; a towel tied around an axe handle could be milked like an udder in order to steal from the neighbor's cow, and lengths of cord could bestow healing or capture the wind within their knots. In the hands of the witch, everyday objects become awakened, empowered, and enspirited. Under the broader heading of such *Object Magic,* we find the concepts of both contagion magic and sympathetic magic.

In many cases, those accused of witchcraft were said to have taken a personal item from their victim, such as a hair comb or shoe, in order to influence or harm them. These are examples of what is often called *contagion magic.* A magic steeped in the belief that objects or beings that have once been in contact with each other retain a connection even after being separated. Contagion magic relies upon contact and relationship. Within this sphere of magic, possession of a part of something allows the witch to hold a measure of control over the whole. This branch of magic largely relies upon remnants and residue; locks of hair, fingernail clippings, bodily fluids, clothing, a handwritten signature, or personal items are all imbued with a person's essence. Such items provide a link to their original owner and a potent key for magical influence, either for blessing or bane.

Sympathetic magic, on the other hand, relies upon sympathy (similarity) and mimicry. This magic operates under the belief that when manipulated by the witch, objects that share sympathy may exert an influence upon each other. This belief is commonly reduced to the simple idea that 'like effects like.' Red-colored thread might be used for a charm to stop bleeding, a root shaped like a hand might empower our artistry, and a golden yellow marigold might draw upon the power of the Sun. This corner of sympathetic magic falls into the realm of symbols and shared qualities that often inform magical correspondences.

More relevant to both the history of the witch and our work here, sympathetic magic also includes *imitative magic.* Imitative magic implies the ritual use of objects which function as sympathetic links to those things we wish to influence. A good illustration of this is found within poppetry, a practice wherein the witch sculpts, draws, or otherwise constructs a physical likeness to represent a target. The poppet becomes a primary example of imitative magic throughout the ages, and witches have been known to craft such effigies from wax, cloth, clay, and other materials for the purpose of both hexing and healing.

By creating a simulacrum, be it a figurine, a drawing, or any crafted image, the witch casts a net over the spirit of the target, be they distant or nearby. This magic asserts that, as if the two were twinned by invisible forces at the moment of the image's creation, to affect the effigy is to affect the subject. Each brush stroke, shaping of clay, or carved sigil acts as a whispered pact with the universe, asserting an alliance between material bodies and enacting influence over the spirit tethered to such an effigy.

This form of magic dances upon the threads of connectivity, suggesting that bonds formed by similarity in appearance, quickened by the witch's conjurations, hold a power deep enough to be harnessed and manipulated by those who are wise to their subtleties. It is through these invisible threads that the witch weaves their intent, binding their will to the resonance between objects, symbols, and the powers they wish to influence.

The second of the two primary forms of magic is *breath magic.* As mentioned earlier, one of the charges often made against the witch was that through stealing the breath of others while they slept, they could steal their power and lifeforce. The witch's magic extends to the spoken word, which, when empowered by the witch's breath, may effectively transform simple utterances into charms, incantations, evocations, blessings, and curses. Certainly, spoken conjurations and the like appear within learned traditions of magic, such as those found in the grimoires as well. However, the utterance of the witch's word can heal the sick, remove or administer the evil eye, blight fields, call up storms, steal a man's fertility, or otherwise cause calamity.

Whether it be the healing charms uttered by a cunning person, or maledictions spewed forth from the diabolical witch, the word and the breath become a primary vehicle for the sorts of magic popularly attributed to witchery. In some cases, an otherwise innocent person could find themself accused of witchcraft simply because, in a moment of frustration, they insulted or spoke ill wishes to their neighbor, only for their neighbor to then encounter some misfortune and blame it upon them. Of course, people cursed at each other and argued in the past, just as many do today. However, when spoken by the witch, a curse, or even a compliment, might bring misfortune in its wake.

This fear of the witch's word is reflected in a Scottish practice enacted upon Bessie Dunlop and many other accused witches, known as "*scoring abune the breath.*"[21] In such cases, the accused would be cut somewhere above their nostrils, often in the form of a cross carved into the forehead.[22] This practice hinged upon the belief that a witch's power could be neutralized and they would be rendered unable to effectively speak or employ breath in their magic if they were subjected to such cuts.

---

21 Cutting above the breath.

22 Joseph McKenzie McPherson. *Primitive Beliefs in the North-east of Scotland* (Longmans Green, 1929) 221

On Confronting Historical Accounts

Before moving on, it is worth pausing a moment to mention that, when excavating the somber boneyards and ash heaps of history for glittering jewels with which to adorn our contemporary witchcraft, we should always apply a discerning eye to the ways our earliest witch lore was transmitted. Though I have made reference to witchcraft confessions throughout this chapter, it would be ill-advised for any of us to believe without question that what individuals confessed to is a faithful reflection of their actual lived experience.

We must remember that in the majority of these cases, the confessions extracted from those believed to be witches were only secured after the accused was subjected to imprisonment in abhorrent conditions. Sleep deprivation, malnourishment, and extreme forms of torture were often employed to extract such confessions. This makes it difficult to point to any one case and confidently state that what is claimed or confessed by the accused is an accurate or true account, as, understandably, many people under such duress are known to provide false confessions.

Further, during such confessions, the accused were often led by their interrogators into saying whatever it was they wished to hear. This results in a macabre form of collaborative storytelling and mythmaking which illustrates and reinforces ideas about what a witch is. And, though a good deal of what is recorded is quite likely fabricated, much of the testimony provided in these confessions offers the historian, folklorist, and practitioner alike a patchworked snapshot of how both the accused and their accusers understood spirits and witchcraft at the time.

Witch trial transcripts, and the narratives spun by works such as the *Malleus Maleficarum* (1486), King James's *Daemonologie* (1597), and Matthew Hopkins's *The Discovery of Witches* (1647) all contributed to, and are reflections of, how the witch was defined by the church, the state, and the common people long before more contemporary expressions or reimaginings of witchcraft came into consideration. We must never forget that the earliest codified understanding of the term *witch* existed, not as a self-designation, but as an accusation.[23] One that marked the witch as the other. A person

23 Here I am specifically speaking to the English word "witch" as opposed to any earlier terms for magical practitioners or those which originate in other cultures and often become treated as synonyms.

who stood in opposition to the norms imposed by the overculture and cast them as a scapegoat for the community's woes, an embodiment of societal fears, and a means by which those fears might be exorcised.

The witch was viewed as someone who turned away from the church and, by extension, their community. As a person who engaged in unsanctioned magic and belonged outside of godliness. As someone who, through pacts with spirits, exchanged a part of their humanity for power.

On a Contemporary Traditional Craft

As cultural fears and beliefs around witches began to shift and laws against witchcraft began to be taken off the books in Europe and the Americas, people had room once again to more publicly practice magic, divination, and spirit work. Additionally, due to the work of folklorists and anthropologists like Margaret Murray, Charles Godfrey Leland, and James Frazer, an updated, if not romanticized and often ahistorical, template for witchcraft and paganism was provided, and a modern movement towards witchcraft as a self-designation followed. In the early to mid-twentieth century, a reclaiming, or perhaps more appropriately, a rebranding, of witchcraft occurred. Influenced by individuals like Gerald Gardner, Doreen Valiente, Alex Sanders, Robert Cochrane, and many others who publicly claimed the title of witch. This vision of witchcraft was quite often presented as an earth-centered religion equivalent or adjacent to paganism.

As there are many wonderful books devoted solely to the exploration of contemporary witchcraft history, and it is far beyond the scope of this work, I'd rather not bog us down here by attempting to trace all of the developments in modern witchcraft from Gardner's Wicca through the current landscape of witchcraft in an age of social media. Or with exploring all of the reasons a person might identify as or become a witch. Instead, I'll encourage the reader to explore some of the titles on the recommended reading list at the end of this chapter for deeper insights into these realms.

What I wish to illustrate instead are some of the ways in which a historical and folkloric image of the witch has influenced certain pockets of contemporary witchcraft. As well as, perhaps by contrast, highlight some of the ways that contemporary witches often leave behind important elements previously mentioned in this chapter.

My craft, as it exists today, falls more closely into the realm of what is often referred to as traditional or folkloric witchcraft. Under the broader heading of Traditional Witchcraft, you will find lineaged and initiatory traditions such as the Clan of Tubal Cain and the Cultus Sabbati, as well as less publicly known craft lineages and cultural traditions with origins that claim to predate the modern witchcraft movement. In other cases, traditional witches may be unaffiliated with any particular lineage or they may be solitary practitioners who, by the nature and necessity of traditional craft, have practices that may differ quite significantly from one witch to another. With this all in mind, I will attempt an explanation of traditional witchcraft as I have come to understand and approach it.[24]

In contrast to many contemporary expressions of witchcraft, traditional witchcraft is primarily informed by historical understandings of the witch as well as preserved folk magical traditions and folklore. Though this will vary from one practitioner to another, the bulk of this is often drawn from Early Modern sources. Much of traditional witchcraft is heavily animist in its ideology and is very much tied to the spirits of the land. As a result, traditional witchcraft tends to favor a *spirit model* of magic wherein most traditional witches perform their magic by partnering with spirits through various methods of conjuration and the making of pacts. Meaning that much of the traditional witch's practice will be influenced by, and reflective of, a relationship to their localized spiritual ecosphere. Further, traditional craft commonly employs methods of spirit flight and shapeshifting as additional means for interacting with spirits and performing magic.

In an extension of this spirit-centered approach, traditional witchcraft often emphasizes working with ancestral spirits and the preservation or resurrection of ancestral traditions. Additionally, many traditional witches do not approach their craft from a heavily polytheist perspective or one that centers devotion to a deity. Though the line between gods and spirits is often quite a narrow one, and plenty of traditional witches do have meaningful partnerships with deities.

In many cases, the primary spirit a traditional witch will ally with and be instructed by is their familiar spirit. In addition to this, any number

24 Traditional/folkloric witchcraft is not a monolith, and the explanation and framing provided here is not a definitive exploration of how it may be understood and approached by all who fall under its broader umbrella.

of land spirits, spirits of the dead, plant spirits, animal spirits, faeries, daemons, or any other spirit beings the witch develops a relationship with may be partnered with. When approaching herbs, stones, and other magical *materia*,[25] instead of working from an *energy-centered* model, or simply with symbolic correspondences, we will often elect to conjure and ally with the spirit (personhood) of the given *materia.*

Traditional witches might also recognize any number of greater patron spirits within their craft. With such beings often treading that line betwixt what might be understood as spirit or deity. Some may approach them as the Witch Mother or Witch Father. While others might know them as the Queen of Elphame or the Devil himself.

On Sympathy for the Devil

Though the Devil has been expelled from most expressions of contemporary witchcraft, he is often embraced within corners of traditional craft. Of course, I should stipulate that plenty of traditional witches do not work with any spirit whom they would label the Devil, and those who do work with the Witches' Devil seldom consider themselves Satanists.

To me, the Witches' Devil exists as the spirit of challenge, catalyst, change, chaos, and choice, which is encountered at the crossroads center. He is the untamed horned and hirsute spirit of the wild and wooded places. He is lord of the dead and of resurrection. The first tiller of the field and Lord of the Greenwood. The Magister of the Sabbath and bestower of benedictions and maledictions. He is an infernal star, the celestial shadow, the first magician, the first blacksmith, and the rebellious light-bearer who steals fire from the heavens and alights the brow with gnosis that we might be tempered by witchfire. He wears manifold masks, only one of which is called "Devil". Many witches will have their own names for him. Some known through the ages, with others only whispered under the cover of darkness.

Within traditional craft, we resurrect shadows of the old gods and conjure forth the spirits often relegated to the realm of devils by a puri-

25 The term *materia* (Latin for material) is used throughout this text in reference to botanical, mineralogical, and animal materials employed by the witch for magical purposes.

tanical overculture. We center a deep connection to the spirit world, the plants, animals, and unseen forces, and a recognition of their agency. An animistic traditional craft aligns us with our earliest ways of seeing the world and sharply contrasts the hierarchical, human-centered worldview often central to Christianity and other dominant religions.

Existing in such an opposition to many of the values espoused by popular culture places witchcraft in the inherently subversive role of challenging established norms, reclaiming marginalized knowledge, and embracing practices that value immanence over transcendence. It is a perspective that simultaneously values personal sovereignty and community, as well as a relationship with, and responsibility towards, the natural world.

The spirits we honor have been maligned as demons and devils by the overculture, and our values, philosophies, and practices branded as witchcraft. In the face of this, we stand in defiance and declare: "If what I do is witchery, then I shall be the Witch, and if serving the spirits is devilry, then it is the Devil I shall serve."

On a Working Definition of Witch

Before diving in here, I wish to reiterate some earlier sentiments and affirm that my personal beliefs are that the witch is a title, role, responsibility, and very real spirit that one may embody through various means, or occasionally have thrust upon them. The Craft is what one does with it. And there are as many expressions of witchcraft as there are witches.

This in mind, as informed by what we have explored throughout this chapter and as reflected within my practice, for the purposes of this book, it should be understood that the primary characteristics by which we might define the witch are as follows:

- The witch conjures, contracts, and consorts with spirits.
- The witch is a liminal creature who works both within this realm and the Otherworld and often employs transvection and shapeshifting whilst doing so.
- The witch practices magic. Most often through the aid of spirits, the use of breath, and by transforming otherwise ordinary objects into magically active and enspirited objects.

- Finally, the witch seeks alignment with and develops relationships within the spiritual ecosystem they inhabit.

What much of humanity has discarded or forgotten, often to its own detriment, the witch tends to and preserves, often at great personal cost. Though she may move through a world shaped by dogmatists and materialists, who would mock her, scorn her, or seek her eradication, she does not truly belong to it. Nor is she entirely claimed by the Otherworld. Instead, the witch exists as a paradox. Neither wholly here nor there, neither fully human nor fully Other. She dwells at the threshold of otherness, a bridge, a nexus, and emissary between the embodied realm and the realm of spirits. She speaks with the dead, recognizes and is recognized by the spirits of her land, and at night she slips from her skin to travel in spirit, passing betwixt the world of the living and those hidden landscapes that lie beyond sleeping eyes. To embody the witch is to ride upon the winds to the beat of an animist heart. It is through this pulse, through conjuring, through relationship, and through spirit pacting that new bodies may be shaped and new spirits brought forth.

In the crafting of effigies and fetiches, the witch stirs and calls upon the virtues and spirits of each material element. Each bone, herb, feather, or stone lending itself to the whole. Through the witch's work, such objects transcend the material and symbolic and are understood as enspirited and alive. Indwelt by a chorus of voices drawn together in unison by the witch's will and breath. As to the witch, it is known that the body, whether of flesh or a crafted form, is seldom the dwelling place of a single spirit. Instead, it is understood as a constellation, an assembly of spirits working in concert, moving and singing forth as one.

On the Ethics of Witchery

Whenever the topic of witchcraft arises, so too do the inevitable questions and debates that surround the ethical application of it. In essence, witchcraft and magic are amoral, and the ethics are solely determined by the operator.

An analogy I've shared with students for years is that witchcraft is like a knife. A knife can dig a trench for planting seeds. It may be used to harvest fruits and vegetables. It can assist us in building a shelter for ourselves. A knife can artistically carve images and ornaments. Knives are required in many life-saving surgeries, and with a knife, we could hunt food for ourselves and skin animals or extract botanical fibers for making clothing. We may cut ourselves free from bondage or defend ourselves against an animal or human attack with a knife as well.

So too is the nature of magic. Magic can assist us in creating prosperity, securing protection, establishing stability, and it can aid us in healing. Magic can also be used to exact justice or inflict harm. This amorality of magic should not be taken as a carte blanche license to behave however we please. Each witch is a sovereign being, but not one immune to the effects of their own choices. And though there are no universally agreed-upon ethics inherent in witchery, it is generally agreed that for each action, there is a cost. As I have observed many times, the cost of regularly indulging our petty and vengeful impulses serves only to amplify them in a manner that turns their poisons inward and against ourselves. It is up to each witch to determine what is justified, what is ethical, what is necessary, and what serves us best in the course of our work and in our lives.

Recommended Additional Reading

Practitioner Resources:

People of the Outside: Witchcraft, Cannibalism, and the Elder Folk by Lee Morgan. Moon Books, 2024.

A Deed Without a Name: Unearthing the Legacy of Traditional Witchcraft by Lee Morgan. Moon Books, 2013.

Treading the Mill: Workings in Traditional Witchcraft by Nigel Pearson. Troy Books, 2017.

Traditional Witchcraft: A Cornish Book of Ways by Gemma Gary. Troy Books, 2008.

The Crooked Path: An Introduction to Traditional Witchcraft by Kelden. Llewellyn Publications, 2020.

The Witches' Sabbath: An Exploration of History, Folklore & Modern Practice by Kelden. Llewellyn Publications, 2022.

The Witches' Devil: Myth and Lore for Modern Cunning by Roger J. Horne. 2022

Academic Resources:

The Witch: A History of Fear, from Ancient Times to the Present by Ronald Hutton. Yale University Press, 2018.

Cunning-folk and Familiar Spirits: Shamanistic Visionary Traditions in Early Modern British Witchcraft and Magic by Emma Wilby. Sussex Academic Press, 2013

The Visions of Isobel Gowdie: Magic, Witchcraft and Dark Shamanism in Seventeenth-Century Scotland by Emma Wilby. Sussex Academic Press, 2013.

Ecstasies: Deciphering the Witches' Sabbath by Carlo Ginzburg. University of Chicago Press, 1991.

The Oxford Handbook of Witchcraft in Early Modern Europe and Colonial America. Edited by Brian Levack. Oxford University Press, 2015.

Chapter Three

Throughout and About: On the Witch's Spirits and Going Forth in Flight

This chapter and the following are primarily intended for those readers who may not be terribly familiar or experienced in engaging with spirits and the Otherworld, particularly from some of the approaches present within much of traditional witchcraft. My goal is to provide some foundational concepts and precursory techniques to serve as a starting point for those newer to these aspects of the craft. Though some of the material presented here may appear somewhat rudimentary to more seasoned practitioners, it is my hope that it might still prove of some interest and value to experienced witches as well. As always, I encourage the reader to consider what is provided here and determine how the material may best inform your own practice.

In approaching spirit work, I believe it is best to begin by examining some of the cultural assumptions we may have unconsciously adopted regarding this arte, specifically, those which may stand in the way of our success.

On Fear and Loathing in the Otherworld

The Otherworld is neither more nor less dangerous than our own. It is simply other. Why is it then that so many people, including a surprising number of magical practitioners I've encountered, often approach spirits with such a disproportionate level of trepidation?

There are a variety of factors that I believe contribute towards this tendency. Firstly, when dealing with spirits, we are engaging with a host of beings that have unique concerns, values, and preferences, and existences which are quite different from our own. Add to this that they are often imperceptible to the average person, yet quite capable of positively or negatively influencing aspects of our world, and we might begin to see why some people feel intimidated about approaching spirit work.

Additionally, I believe we are heavily enculturated towards a misunderstanding of spirits, which both disempowers us in our access to them and maligns most spirits as unworthy of our trust. This often frames the Otherworld and its inhabitants as more dangerous than our own. All of this encourages a certain social anxiety towards the Other Folk and their ways, which is often a detriment to our work with them and deserves a more thorough examination.

On How We Learned to Fear Spirits

The Otherworld exists intertwined with our own. Though we use the terms *Otherworld* and *Others* when referring to immaterial spirits and their realm, it should not be taken to imply distance between us so much as a difference in qualities and culture between us. We may craft and chart cosmological maps as imaginal landscapes of the spirits, however they are only tools. Though they are valuable tools in helping us approach unseen realms, they do not define a universal truth nor impose a hard cosmic geography upon the spirits themselves. This is because the Otherworld is present alongside of, and atop of, our own, and just as we find ourselves existing within biomes and ecosystems in the embodied world, the same is true of the spirit realm.

If we imagine our earliest hunter-gatherer ancestors viewed their world through an animistic lens, recognizing themselves as existing within the realm of spirits, it would make little sense that they would conceive of the Otherworld as somehow *more* volatile than our own. On any given day, they would have been more likely to encounter benign plants and animals than they would poisons and predators. Of course, life-threatening encounters did occur; danger and death are a part of life. However, the likelihood one might stumble into the cave of a bear or ingest a deadly plant was greatly reduced for those who were familiar with their environment and its inhabitants. This understanding may also be applied to the Otherworld.

Of course, there *are* harmful and violent spirits/deities who are potentially dangerous for humans to interact with. Beings who are detrimental to incarnate life inhabit all realms of existence. However in cultures that live in a more reciprocal relationship with the land, we tend to find that the Otherworld, its spirits, and their potential dangers appear as a fairly balanced reflection of the very real dangers present in the physical world. So unsurprisingly, for each Apophis or Ahriman in the realm of the gods, a cataclysmic earthquake or deadly plague might be found as a threat in our world.

Over time, early human cultures became less nomadic, moving into cities, and becoming both more protected from the unpredictability of the natural world and further removed from the wild spaces where feral beasts roamed. A further separation from untamed and chaotic spirits occurred as well, and we created a more domesticated and 'civilized' understanding of the spirits in turn. This leads towards a greater cultural shift which increasingly demonizes chthonic, chaotic, and bestial spirits as they are distanced from humanity. There are those spirits who are welcome within the city walls and those who are not. Here, we find greater delineation between spirits and epic myths relaying the interplay between good and evil.

In contrast to such a dichotomy, the witch does not shy away from a panoramic understanding of the enspirited world. Instead, we are charged with recognizing the interplay of all things and understanding the value of creation and destruction, life and death. Though we might understandably choose to distance ourselves from spirits that are detrimental to a healthy and happy life. The witch recognizes the limitations of framing spirits in terms of good and evil and instead embraces the utility in discerning what is helpful or harmful to us. Of course, this is not generally the case on a broader cultural level. So, how did we arrive at such a dichotomy in regards to spirits? Further, how did we arrive at the belief that spirits in general are something to be feared?

As human societies became increasingly urbanized and empires expanded, the dominant religions often reflected the aims of the empire. Though it is far from the first religious tradition to engage in such, as Christianity spread throughout the world, it weaponized the outlawing and demonization of most indigenous spirits and traditions it encountered. As a result, a hard line became increasingly drawn between which types of disincarnate beings were acceptable to venerate and which ones should be avoided at all costs, at least in the eyes of the church.

As the distance between cultures and their old gods grew and the relationships, rituals, and recollections of those spirits were stamped out or faded away, the view of those spirits became even more monstrous. Instead of simply being untamed, unpredictable, or undesirable beings, they become increasingly framed as evil, demonic forces, anathema to all goodness. Beings desirous of our ruin, both in this realm and the next. An alteration that pushes the needle much further toward a disenchanted world wherein any form of engaging certain spirits becomes understood as an ungodly and dangerous endeavor for ordinary humans.

Within the confines of Catholicism, a sliver of space still existed for spiritual intercession from the souls in purgatory, the sainted dead, angelic beings, and the Holy Mother. This shifted for much of Christendom during the Protestant Reformation; however, when Martin Luther and John Calvin denounced many Catholic doctrines, including the intercession of saints and the Virgin Mary. Instead, one's faith and spiritual attentions were intended to be reserved for Christ alone. As a result, within Protestant lands, engaging with spirits is increasingly viewed as either inaccessible (the sainted dead), heretical (the souls in purgatory), or evil (any other sort of spirit). This narrowing of the enspirited world offered little interpretive structure for those who witnessed ghostly apparitions or divine visitations, a void filled in part by Ludwig Lavater's pivotal 1569 work *De Spectris (Of Ghostes and Spirites).*

Originally published in German, *De Spectris* was incredibly popular amongst clergy and the laity alike. Within the first hundred years of its initial publication, nearly twenty additional editions were made, and it was translated into Latin, English, French, Italian, and Dutch. As a result, it became one of the most influential books on the subject of spirits in the history of Europe, and its influence upon popular conceptions of spirits still persists.[26] In crafting an explanation of spirit phenomena, *De Spectris* recognizes delusional fantasy and other possibilities for such experiences while still firmly arguing for the reality of spirits. It further asserts that spirits of the dead are unable, or at least very unlikely, to appear to the living. Instead, it establishes that spirits exhibit an aversion and antagonism towards

---

26 Justin Sledge. "Are Ghosts Really Demons? The Most Important Textbook on Ghosts -Ludwig Lavater 1569 de Spectris." Esoterica, YouTube, 16 June 2023, www.youtube.com/watch?v=5JiSlez9kZo

the Christian faith and that such apparitions are the work of demonic beings meant to mislead the living. *De Spectris* goes on to argue that true divine visitations are incredibly rare outliers. As such, the appearance of any spirit at all should not be trusted and instead assumed to be the illusory work of devils.[27]

Lavater's work, and those that echoed its beliefs, such as the *Demonologie of King James* (1597), and Pierre Le Loyer's *Discours et histoires des spectres* (1605), created a perception of spirits that was embraced across much of Europe and its colonized lands. It was echoed by the Puritans, and it still permeates the theology of spirits espoused by most contemporary Christians, whether they be Baptists, Evangelicals, or otherwise.

Such theological shifts imposed upon a good portion of the world have left many cultures amnesic of our animist origins, largely divorced from ancient paganism, and with a Christendom completely exorcised of its mysticism. As a result, many in the world are left disenchanted, and with a model of the Otherworld almost entirely inhabited by the demonic. Regardless of whether or not we have direct experience within religious institutions that espouse such beliefs, such an understanding of spirits still thoroughly permeates the overculture. It is a belief echoed and reinforced in Faustian tales, pulp novellas, and countless supernatural horror films and television programs. More pertinent to the work of this book, it is a view of spirits often left unexamined, unconsciously accepted, and subconsciously perpetuated by many who wish to practice magic. One which betrays our earliest instinctual understanding of the enspirited world and instead maintains and perpetuates a simple belief: that spirits are not to be trusted.

With such a cultural inheritance, it is unsurprising that some people might approach working with spirits with some degree of fear. However, when we are fearful, our emotions, expectations, and unconscious symbol systems often color our experiences in a way that is contrary to effective spirit work. I am not arguing for an absence of caution here. Unfamiliar territory in our world or the Otherworld should always inspire us to maintain a level of awareness, discernment, and caution. That said, a cautious approach

27 Lewes Lauterus. *Of Ghostes and Spirites, Walking by night and of Straunge Noyses, Crackes, and Sundrie Forewarnings, Which Commonly Happen before the Death of Men: Great Slaughters, and Alterations of Kingdoms.* (Thomas Creede, 1596). www.gutenberg.org/cache/epub/51038/pg51038-images.html

and a fearful one are quite different things, and we should endeavor to measure our fears in proportion to the level of actual threat we are facing.

Based upon observations I've had with students, if a person enters into spirit work expecting something frightening to occur, there is a greater likelihood their results will match that expectation. Our experience of spirits is a co-creative process, and when we are working from a place of fear, we are not maintaining control or sitting within our power. An important aspect in developing and maintaining our sense of centeredness and power lies in establishing a framework for understanding the Otherworld and our place within it. For me, the first step in this begins with establishing an understanding of our baseline experience of being and developing tools for relaxing the body and mind.

PRAXIS: Establishing a Touchstone

This is a simple practice designed to perform a basic assessment of ourselves and our environment. It is meant to provide us with a baseline or 'touchstone' awareness of our state of being before engaging in any form of spirit work or magic.

1. You should begin by arranging your body in a relaxed position.
2. Breathing from the diaphragm, take a few deep cleansing breaths being sure to thoroughly exhale. Then softly close your eyes and return to your regular breathing.
3. Mentally scan your body from the top of your head down to the tips of your toes. As you do so, take note of what you are currently sensing.
   - Does your body feel warm or cold?
   - What does the surface of your skin feel like?
   - How does the clothing you are wearing feel?
   - Are there any areas of discomfort or tension in your body?
   - Do you feel tired, alert, happy, melancholic, or hungry?
   - Are you feeling focused or distracted?
   - Are there any particular images that are cropping up in the mind?
   - Are there any daily concerns or anxieties that keep surfacing in your thoughts?
   - What does your current environment sound like?

- What does it smell like?
- What, if anything, do you taste?

These questions allow us to focus our awareness on the present and our current state. Though spirits will at times make their presence overtly known, in many cases, particularly for those who are still developing psychic senses and mediumship abilities, the ways they present may be experienced more subtly. The introduction of new sensory stimuli often accompanies spirit contact. By consciously taking a moment to examine our starting point, we are better able to assess the more subtle mental, emotional, physical, and environmental changes that may occur during or after spirit conjuration and magical workings.

Whether it be a slight breeze, flickering candles, or pictures rattling in their frames, when we encounter shifts in sensory input, it is best to simply note these changes as they occur rather than overly fixating on them or distracting from the experience by overreacting to each slight breeze or twitching toe. The time for a more critical assessment of your experience is after your ritual work has concluded. At the end of any magical working or spirit conjuration, be sure to note any changes that seem significant so that you can compare them to your earlier touchstone and future experiences. For instance, a slight ringing of the ears when calling upon a spirit may not mean anything if it happens once. However, if it happens whenever you call upon that spirit, it may very well be an indicator that they have arrived.

PRAXIS: Stilling the Body and Mind

Building off the previous exercise, this technique should be employed before most magical workings and attempts at transvection. It is a simple method for preparing us physically and mentally and adjusting our baseline state of being to one more conducive to such practices.

1. Establish your touchstone as in the previous exercise.
2. Mentally scan your body again from the top of your head down to the tips of your toes, paying attention to any areas of tension.
3. Then, starting again at the top of your head, begin intentionally relaxing your body. It can help to imagine a wave of relaxation

traveling down your body. Unfurrow your brow, unclench your jaw, relax your shoulders, and continue down your body, relaxing any areas of tension. Continue this down to the tips of your toes. Do this two to three times, or as many are needed to help get your body in a calm and relaxed state.

4. If you find that your mind will not quiet, it may help to envision any distractions or fleeting thoughts as images or words projected upon a screen in your mind. Then envision this screen being crumpled up as though it were on a sheet of paper and placed into an imaginal cauldron. Next, visualize a heavy lid being placed on top to keep such distractions from intruding upon your work. Let the image of the cauldron fade away, taking those distractions with it and transforming them into focused attention in the process.
5. Take mental note again of your body and the environment before moving on to any magical work or spirit flight. This becomes your new touchstone.

Establishing your touchstone and relaxing your body and mind become much easier with regular practice over time. I have found with many students that once you practice and become adept at this, it should become something that can be accomplished quite easily in just a few minutes.

On the Three Realms of the Witches' Tree

In beginning our approach to the Otherworld, it is important that we have an understanding of how we might access its various realms and inhabitants. Within my own practice and many other expressions of witchcraft, particularly when engaging in transvection, the Otherworld is approached through a cosmological perspective commonly framed as a *three-worlds* model, which envisions the universe as being vertically arranged into three separate realms:

The Supernal Realm

This is the Upper World. Often understood as the abode of many of the types of beings often classified as deities, celestials, and planetary spirits, as well as the realm of the mighty dead. And though not all witches work with them, this is also the abode of angelic beings. In my practice, this realm is overseen by a great bird of flame called *Athalez.*[28]

The Terrestrial Realm

This is the Middle World. Most aligned to the incarnate world of humans, animals, plants, minerals, and their associated spirits. It is also home to land spirits, elementals, and many faerie spirits.

The Infernal Realm[29]

This is the Underworld. Understood as the abode of chthonic deities and spirits, ancestors and spirits of the dead, and many daemonic/demonic beings. Within my practice, this realm is overseen by *Pa'arosh,* a great serpent of the watery depths.

This cosmological map is seldom understood in a rigid or overly literal way, and it often belies a strict categorization of the spirits or experiences that may be encountered in each of its realms. For instance, you may encounter a faerie being in the supernal realm or a deity within the infernal realm. When employing any model of the Otherworld, it is always best to understand again that cosmological maps are simply a tool; they are not the terrain.

Within this cosmology, the Witches' Tree or World Tree acts as our *Axis Mundi,* the central axis around which the universe revolves and an access point between all worlds. Such concepts of a sacred tree are found within numerous spiritual traditions throughout the world. The roots of this great tree dive deep into the underworld, its branches extend high into the upper world, and its trunk stands firm in the middle world, bridging the supernal and infernal.

In various cultures, the world tree has been associated with the ash, the oak, the ceiba, the olive, the iroko, and many other species of tree. The

---

28 I mention this for context because the imagery of the bird and serpent will appear later in some of the workings in this book.

29 It is important to note here that though most will associate the term *infernal* with meaning something diabolical, the term originates from the Latin *infernalis,* which is used in reference to the underworld and the realm of the dead. It is not until later that the term is adopted by Christianity in reference to Hell.

Witches'Tree will present itself differently to each witch. For me personally, it is often a great oak, other times it appears as a magnificent walnut tree. It might be any sort of tree that appears to the witch in visions or even a hybrid of differing species.

During transvection, the world tree often functions as a point by which we might travel throughout the Otherworld and access various spirit abodes. Within such travels, we might find ourselves in the temples of ancient celestial gods, enraptured by rhythmic drumming deep within ancestral caves, or receiving wisdom and healing from plant spirits within verdant gardens. We may also find ourselves swept up within the greater ecstasy and revelation of the witches' sabbath.

On The Witches' Sabbath

In the process of transvection or while dreaming, many witches will have an experience of the Witches' Sabbath. Referred to sometimes as the oneiric sabbath or the eternal sabbath, this is not an event or location within the material realm. Instead, it might be understood as a state of being and nonbeing experienced as a great conclave of spirits occurring within the Otherworld. The witches' sabbath is an ecstatic dreamscape existing outside of space and time where we are returned towards an understanding of all that we are and participate in a communal exchange betwixt the embodied and the disincarnate.

Here we may dance, feast, and engage in ritual and revelry with the patron spirits of our craft. Here we might commune with the Devil and his dame, the Queen of Elphame, alongside a diverse array of imps, daemons, faerie spirits, and any number of ancient and nameless gods. Here too, we may consort with and ally ourselves to various spirits of the living, the dead, animal and plant spirits, and with spirits of the land.

Though it has no static location or expression in the Otherworld, the sabbath is sometimes envisioned as taking place in a large cave, upon the top of a mountain, at a large crossroad, or at the base of the Witches' Tree. In my experience, the sabbath may at times present as supernal and luminous, and others infernal and viscerally primal. Still other experiences of it have been ineffable, serving as a transmutation and augmentation of spirit. The sabbath presents in many guises. However, its essence might be crudely summarized as one of communion, transformation, and revelation.

The witches' sabbath is the hallowed ground upon which we seek wisdom, forge alliances, encounter our witchkin, and emerge renewed. It is at once an experience of devotion and communion between witch and Other and a deep empowerment presented through transgressive, amorphous, and prismatic displays which are a bellows upon the witching fire.

On The Spirits of the Witch

Though many people tend towards envisioning themselves as a singular identity defined by and tethered to their bodies, this is not the only framework by which we might understand who and what we are. In many spiritual traditions, it is understood that what we recognize as *self* is not an individual entity but instead any number of spirits. Such a belief is sometimes referred to as *dualistic pluralism* or soul dualism.

In its most basic expression, soul dualism suggests that we have at least two parts of the soul/spirit. The first, sometimes referred to as the bodily spirit or 'body soul', is most associated with our physical body and its functioning. The second, sometimes referred to as the spirit body or *wandering soul,* is the aspect of self that is not entirely tethered to our physical form and is often viewed as eternal.

Beyond a simpler two-soul model, various cultures have embraced a diversity of multi-soul models of greater complexity. The ancient Egyptians divided the soul into anywhere from seven to nine parts. The Platonic model suggests we are made up of three souls, the *Logos* or *Logistikon* (located in the head and associated with logic and intellect), the *Thymos* or *Thumetikon* (located in the heart and associated with anger, passion, and will), and the *Eros* or *Epithumetikon* (located in the stomach and associated with desires).

In parallel to a three-worlds model of the cosmos, many contemporary witches embrace a tripartite perspective of our spirits as well. Understanding the witch not as a singular entity, but as a grouping of spirits that function so seamlessly that they often feel as though they are one. It is only by shifting our perspectives and focusing upon engaging with them as individual parts of self, that we better understand each as their own unique expressions of consciousness, and by extension, gain a greater understanding and mastery of all that we are.

Within my craft, the first of these spirits, referred to as the *Grand Genius,* is aligned to the supernal realm/upper world. It is this spirit that acts as a guide upon the path of our life's work. It functions in the realm of ideas and ideals and is the primary conduit for the transmission of inspiration, revelation, and spiritual gnosis. The *Grand Genius,* as I have experienced it, is somewhat comparable to the personal daimon of Greek antiquity and the Holy Guardian Angel as understood by many occultists. It represents the highest, most enduring expression of ourselves, and it is this aspect that reincarnates.

The second of our spirits, the *Fetch,* is aligned to the infernal realm/underworld and is associated with primal instincts, physical survival, and our baser needs and desires. It is where our fight/flight responses arise, as well as our passions, hunger, and sexual drive. It is also where a good deal of our instinctive and intuitive abilities are rooted. In the Otherworld, and sometimes in our own, the Fetch sometimes appears as a double of ourselves and has been compared to ideas surrounding both the doppelganger and *fylgja.*[30] It is believed that this double can, on occasion, appear to us or others during waking states as a warning of danger or an omen of death. The fetch may appear in a variety of forms, and within some traditions, it may also act as a companion akin to a familiar spirit or a spirit lover.

When engaging in transvection, this is the part of ourselves that we let loose from the body to send forth during our spirit flight. In such cases, it is not uncommon for the Fetch to appear as, or transform into, the form of an animal. All humans have a Fetch; however, as alluded to in the previous chapter, it is generally believed that one of the things that sets the witch apart is their ability to intentionally send this spirit forth and transform its appearance at will. Historical accounts of witches going forth in spirit and flying to the sabbath, of shapeshifting and appearing in the likeness of animals or other people, and entering the dreams of others are all considered examples of the Fetch at work.

Finally, within my practice, our third spirit is referred to as the *Crafter.* This aspect of ourselves is aligned with the middle world and tends to act as a bridge between the more immediate drives of the Fetch and the greater designs of the Grand Genius. The Crafter mediates between the guidance of the Grand Genius and the instincts of the Fetch and is con-

30 A spirit companion within Norse traditions.

cerned with the actual *doing* of things in the material realm. It is equally concerned with ensuring that we are physically safe and provided for, as it is that we are being led by a sense of greater purpose. The Crafter enacts the manifestation of our highest potentialities as met and balanced by our practical needs and desires. The Crafter is concerned with how all parts of ourselves impact and are impacted by the world around us. While we are in this incarnation, it is the most identifiably "self" part of ourselves. As such, it is often equated with the ego.

These three spirits become a foundational understanding of how we might begin to understand the constellation of spirits that inhabit the witch. Within and around this, the witch may develop ties to any number of additional spirits with whom they become so deeply allied with that they might be said to both inhabit and be inhabited by each other. This is experienced by some witches in relation to their familiar spirits. Though such relationships are not recommended for those inexperienced with spirit work and witchcraft. Without a developed level of discernment and the proper tools to navigate and negotiate spirit work, this sort of 'spirit grafting' can lead to adverse effects for the witch. Not the least of which include physical and mental illness. For this reason, I highly caution the reader in actively pursuing such experiences and arrangements without a deep understanding of all that they require and imply.

PRAXIS: A Basic Ritual Alignment

The following is an exercise designed to help center the witch and align oneself with the three realms and the three parts of the self. It may be performed as a daily practice, as a preparation before doing ritual or spirit work, or whenever you are feeling magically/spiritually imbalanced.

1. Center yourself by standing straight with your feet firmly on the ground.
2. Place your hands with the palms together at heart level in a praying position and say:

    "I stand as Axis Mundi and am centered between all realms."

3. Point your right hand to the heavens and your left hand to the Earth.

4. Envision or try to sense the power of the upperworld high above you. Some may envision this as a sphere of golden energy. Consciously connect to the part of yourself that is the Grand Genius spirit. Imagine as though you are speaking as the Grand Genius and then say:

   "I reach up to the Supernal realm, to the world above, and draw its power towards center."

5. Envision drawing this power down and then bring your right hand down to heart level, making one half of a praying hands gesture.
6. Envision or try to sense the power of the underworld deep below you. Some may envision this as a sphere of silver, murky gray, or black energy. Consciously connect to the part of yourself that is the Fetch spirit. Imagine as though you are speaking as the Fetch and then say:

   "I reach down to the Infernal realm, to the world below, and draw its power towards center."

7. Envision drawing this power up and then bring your right hand up to heart level, completing a praying hands gesture.
8. At your heart, feel the centering of Upperworld and Underworld on the terrestrial plane. Consciously connect to the part of yourself that is the Crafter spirit. Imagine as though you are speaking as the Crafter and then state:

   "Reside in the heart terrestrial, the crossways betwixt all realms."

9. Keeping your hands in the prayer position at heart level, imagine that all three parts of self, the Grand Genius, the Fetch, and the Crafter, are speaking together, and then state:

   "Between the realms I stand as center and the point of limitless potentiality.
   By my words, my work, and my will, it is so!
   By the setting and rising of the sun, it is done!"

10. Let your arms fall gently at your sides to conclude the exercise.

On Transvection

As mentioned in Chapter Two, one of the persistent identifiers of the witch cross-culturally has been the ability to go forth in spirit flight. Throughout history, explanations for how witches achieved this flight varied widely. They might enchant everyday objects like brooms, distaffs, or pitchforks to ride upon, or shrink themselves and fly within eggshells or sieves. Some accounts describe witches employing magical unguents or oils said to be gifted by the Devil or made from baneful and noxious ingredients, such as poisonous botanicals and the fat of unbaptized children, to enable their flight. Much like the mare and boo hag, witches were also said to ride upon bewitched animals, spectral beasts, or even human victims, leaving their mounts drained of vitality and sickly by morning. In other cases, their flight might be accomplished by riding upon familiar spirits or faerie steeds.

During the medieval and Early Modern period, debate persisted over whether witches flew in body or in spirit. Works such as the seventeenth-century *Compendium Maleficarum* suggested that the witch placed an effigy of twigs, straw, or other items into their bed to serve as a false body.[31] Then, through employing glamour and illusion, these were made into a realistic double with the ability to fool any observer into believing she was in a deep sleep when in truth she was away, physically flying through the night. However, the overwhelming majority of historical opinions, recorded confessions, and the experiences of most living practitioners will attest that it is the witch's spirit that goes forth in flight while their physical body remains. For many contemporary witches, spirit flight becomes one of our primary methods for engaging with the Otherworld and its inhabitants. Much like our forebears, this is accomplished by sending out the fetch either as a spirit double or in animal form.

When going forth, I most commonly adopt a bestial form as I find it allows me to more swiftly navigate through the Otherworld. This form provides an altered and heightened perception, whilst often attracting less unnecessary attention from spirits. Given practice and experience, we are

31 For the purposes of this book an effigy should be understood as an object which is humanoid in appearance and employed for magical purposes.

able to shift the fetch form into a diversity of guises. Though outside of the purview of this work, the development of such spirit-shifting techniques can also be brought into our waking world to assist us in magic and glamour.

Within the dreamscape of the Otherworld, we gain access to the vast realm of the spirits. It is here that we are able to engage with all manner of spirits outside of the constraints presented by the embodied realm. In our spirit flight, we might more easily engage with ancestral spirits, the spirits of the land, and those spirits who have never existed in material forms. Here, the spirit of a particular plant might appear to us in an anthropomorphized form with whom we might forge a deeper relationship. A river might speak with us, teach us, and reveal its diverse magics to us. We might even meet with the personified spirits of a work of art, piece of music, or philosophical concept so that we might better engage with and understand them.

Praxis: Transvection Exercise - The White Room and Going Forth

This presents one approach to beginning spirit flight, which many find an approachable and fairly easy way to begin. That said, it may not be a perfect fit for everyone, and there are many ways to engage in transvection. I will touch upon other approaches to spirit flight later in this work, and there are additional resources at the end of this chapter for the reader to explore in order to develop their own practice of spirit flight. I highly recommend reading through this exercise several times and the notes that follow it before attempting to perform it.

1. In a place where you will not be interrupted, begin by preparing your ritual space however best suits your comfort level and personal practice. This might involve laying a compass, casting a circle, calling upon guardian spirits or guides, wearing oils and talismans, or holding tools that bolster protection or aid in spirit flight.
2. Arrange your body in a relaxed position. I prefer to sit in a comfortable chair with my back straight, my feet flat on the floor, and my hands lightly resting upon my thighs with my palms upwards. Alternatively, laying down is also a good option so long as you

are certain that you will not completely drift off to sleep. For this reason, if possible, it's best to avoid doing this in your bed.

3. Breathing from the diaphragm, take a few deep cleansing breaths, being sure to thoroughly exhale. Then close your eyes and return to your regular breathing.
4. Using the previously given exercises, establish your touchstone and relax the body and mind.
5. Next, going from ten to one, you will begin mentally counting down into a deeper state of relaxation. You may do this aloud or silently in your head. I find it helps to imagine that I am descending a set of stairs. Each number, being a step down towards a greater state of physical and mental relaxation. While doing this, it should also be understood that with each step, your fetch spirit is stepping a bit further apart from your waking consciousness.
6. Repeat step five one more time, counting down again, and becoming even more relaxed this time.
7. You should be in a state of considerable relaxation at this point. If needed, you can repeat steps five through six.
8. Now, with your inner eye, envision yourself as though you are standing in a completely featureless white room.[32] In this space, you are protected, and it is entirely your own domain. Think of it as a form of spiritual cleanroom free from any external influence and entities. I tend to experience this as though I am in a space that is like a bright white void.
9. Think upon what it is you wish to accomplish through your transvection. As this relates to the work here, this could be as simple an intention as wishing to develop greater aptitude at spirit flight. This technique can be employed as a means of connecting to the three parts of ourselves as well. In these cases, you needn't leave the white room, and you can call forth the Fetch, Grand Genius, and even the Crafter to further understand their roles and nature. In time, your transvection might include things like exploring various

32 Not all witches experience these things in a strictly or vividly visual manner. This is okay. Please see the *On Our Otherworldly Senses* section of the following chapter for more on this.

spirit realms and meeting new spirits to form relationships with, learn from, or eventually pact with. The purpose of transvection may often include attending the Witches' Sabbath as well.

10. Once you have your purpose firmly in mind, conjure a door by willing it to appear before you. Take note of what this door looks like. Does it look ancient or modern? What material is it made from? Is there a symbol/sigil etched or painted on it? Try to commit this symbol to memory if so. If no symbol is on the door, not to worry. It is not required. I have found in my practice that doors to the different realms will often appear with sigils on them. These sigils have become keys for me to more easily access the power of these realms and the influence of their spirits within magical workings.
11. When you feel prepared, open the door and step into the realm you wish to explore. As a starting point, I usually recommend that you envision stepping out into a verdant and calm meadow where the Witches' Tree stands at its center. From here, you might travel up or down the tree to explore the supernal and infernal realms. In many cases, we will be seeking out and traveling to the location of the Witches' Sabbath, though there are limitless options for where you might go.
12. Take your time to explore. In some cases, an experience of transvection may feel as though it lasted hours, when in truth it was only a few moments. The obverse of this may be equally experienced as well.
13. When you are ready to conclude your journey, give thanks to any of the spirits you have had positive experiences with. Then either return to the door or summon it to appear where you are in the Otherworld. If at any time you feel uncomfortable or in danger during transvection, you may conjure your door and return to the white room. This room represents a sovereign place to you where nothing may enter unless you explicitly invite it.
14. Step back through the door into the white room. Close the door and envision it disappearing.
15. Next, allow the image of the white room to fade away.
16. Begin counting up from one to ten, envisioning that you are ascending a staircase with each number, and returning to waking consciousness. Do this twice, or as many times as you counted down initially. While

counting up, it may help to begin wiggling your fingers and toes a bit to draw your consciousness back to the physical body.

17. Once you have counted back up, open your eyes and stretch your body in whatever way feels best. You may also wish to shake out your hands, arms, and legs a bit to awaken the body and boost circulation. I find this helps to more fully return the consciousness of the fetch spirit to the physical body.
18. Stretch your arms above your head. Interlock your fingers. Then sweep your interwoven hands down your body towards the Earth, unlocking them near the knees and directing your fingers towards the Earth whilst releasing a powerful exhalation towards the ground at the same time. This step is intended to sweep away any residual power and return it to the earth, whilst giving us a final clearance.
19. Lastly, immediately record notes from your experience in a journal. This is an important step as, just as with dreams, our memory of Otherworld experiences is freshest just after returning to our awakened state.
20. Close your ritual space as you normally would.

Some notes on this practice:

Whenever engaging in spirit flight, or really any spirit conjuration/communion work, avoid overanalyzing or searching for deeper meaning in the moment. Instead, *be* in the moment and let the experience unfold without being overly critical or questioning it as it is occurring. Instead, after it has occurred, record what has happened in a journal, and then, over the next few days or weeks, you can revisit it and analyze it more thoroughly.

It may be beneficial to envision carrying a skeleton key into the Otherworld, which can be used to conjure any door to yourself as needed. The industrious witch might also create a twin to this key in material form that they might wear or hold while engaging in spirit flight.

If you intend on going into more challenging or potentially dangerous corners of the Otherworld, it is recommended you properly prepare yourself. This might take the form of carrying or wearing protective fetiches or anointing yourself with a protection oil like that found in the *Formulary* section. If you are skilled with conjuring in the imaginal, you might envision yourself wearing a form of spiritual armor or carrying weaponry. Once you have established relationships with spirits you trust, you might also request that they accompany you on Otherworld journeys to lend their aid and counsel. In the following chapter, we will explore the nature of spirits as well as ways we might establish relationships with spirits invested in our protection.

Recommended Additional Reading

A Broom at Midnight by Roger J. Horne. Moon Over The Mountain Press, 2021.

The Witches' Sabbath: An Exploration of History, Folklore & Modern Practice by Kelden. Llewellyn Publications, 2022.

By Moonlight and Spirit Flight: The Praxis of the Otherworldly Journey to the Witches' Sabbath by Michael Howard. Three Hands Press, 2019.

A Witch's Guide to Fetch Work by Blake Malliway. Crossed Crow Books, 2025

Chapter Four

Approaching the Otherworld: On the Nature and Language of Spirits

Over the centuries, we have compiled vast libraries of lore about spirits, as well as countless magical grimoires, spiritual traditions, and religious frameworks to better understand and approach them. With this in mind, it would be impossible to present a unified understanding of diverse spirits that reflects every possible tradition here. Instead, I wish to explore some of the ways that we as human beings interface and interact with spirits more generally, as well as explore the nature of spirits and spirit relationships with a broader lens.

Spirits have their own likes, dislikes, motivations, agendas, and methods of communication, which are varied and diverse. They also have their own cultural values, and the things we might consider good manners or the moral codes we live by may not be shared by them. As previously discussed, this doesn't mean that a spirit whose morality doesn't match our own is "evil" or that we are incapable of finding common ground with them. Only that we need to have appropriately measured caution and exercise discernment when determining if we wish to engage with them.

In meeting any spirit, allow yourself time to better understand them and their motivations before choosing to become too involved with them, and particularly prior to making any agreements with them. As is true of the humans we encounter throughout our day, simply because a spirit wants your attention or desires a relationship with you does not mean you are obligated to engage with them. Relationships of *all* kinds should be weighed against our desires and the standard of what we personally find advantageous or detrimental to our greater aspirations.

On Unsavory Spirits

The spirits of Rot and Decay are derided by many, yet they serve an incredibly important role in the cycle of all things. In the witch's work, they might be of help when trying to get rid of, transform, or break down an undesirable situation. In some cases, they might even serve in works of healing. However, you may not want them around when doing magic to increase growth, vitality, and fertility.

The spirits of Anger and Violence are essential entities as well. They exist as a corollary to the diversity of forms of anger and violence within our own world. Anger might manifest itself in ways that are productive or destructive. Depending upon the way it materializes, violence might be experienced as senseless, cruel, or sadistic. Or it might instead be understood as a swift, effective, and unavoidable companion to Justice.

From the animist's perspective, violence simply exists. Almost all of the food that sustains us is harvested through some form of violence. The cutting and uprooting of plants is violence. The tilling of soil is violence to the creatures that inhabit it. The killing and butchering of animals is violence. Our judgment of it is not universal but simply an assessment based upon whether it is more or less necessary, and more or less desirable, in relation to our personal values and its proximity to us. It benefits the witch to interrogate our own judgements and place them in relation to greater truths whilst still maintaining the values which serve us.

I will reiterate, though, that just as encountering a scorpion in the desert needn't imply that you bring it home with you as a pet, you are not obligated to form relationships with potentially detrimental spirits simply because they appear before you. The work of the witch is to develop our abilities and our discernment in order to conjure forth and strengthen those alliances that best suit our aims. Not to dive headfirst into abusive relationships or splay ourselves out as chum before a sea of hungry ghosts out of eagerness to make friends in the Otherworld.

On Knowing the Terrain

If you were suddenly transported to a remote village in the Amazon, you would likely find the experience incredibly alien to you. You might have difficulty communicating, and what is considered morally acceptable behavior in your culture might be seen as offensive or taboo in theirs. The same would be true if you were to be whisked away to an unfamiliar location in the Otherworld.

Just as when embarking upon a trip somewhere in this world, having a sense of where you are going and what to expect from your destination is incredibly helpful before engaging in spirit flight. This allows us to determine who we might encounter there, what we might experience, and what challenges we might face. Most importantly, it allows us to know when we've reached our intended destination.

For this reason, it is suggested that you establish some form of cosmological map, such as the Witches' Tree, that you might work with to orient yourself. A cosmological map is a human-made model of a particular culture, religion, or spiritual tradition's understanding of the Otherworld that the spirit realm will often conform to in order to meet the expectations of those working with it. Just like any other map it provides a layout and terrain for the Otherworld. The Buddhist Bhavachakra, the Norse Yggdrasil, and the Qabalistic Tree of Life are all examples of this. Again, it is important that we recognize that a cosmological map is not a static and concrete reality but rather a tool that helps us navigate it.

In approaching the Otherworld, it is important to study up on the lore and mythology surrounding the places you wish to go and the type of spirits you hope to encounter, as well as any associated cautions or cultural taboos. Additionally, talking directly with other magical practitioners about their experiences of the Otherworld and its inhabitants can be beneficial. This helps give some insights into what you *might* experience there. Keep in mind, however, that just as no two people's experiences of a trip to Europe will be the same, no two people's experiences of a journey into the Otherworld and its inhabitants will be the same. Additionally, keep in mind that some people are unreliable narrators.

Just as plenty of folks have opinions about countries they have only visited once or twice or share gossip about people they have little to no experience with, the same is not unheard of when magical practitioners begin discussing the Otherworld and spirits. Highly sensationalist stories and mischaracterizations often abound in occult forums amongst people who have often done very little research and had even less direct experience with the realms and spirits they are speaking on behalf of. So when preparing yourself and learning about various spirits and their place in the Otherworld, it's best to get a diverse set of information to pull from. After all, we each bring our own unique desires, expectations, biases, fears, and symbol systems to the Otherworld, and how we experience it is often a reflection of the things we project upon it, either consciously or unconsciously.

On What is Real

Let's consider the ways in which we perceive all things, including spirits, embodied or otherwise. Human beings receive the raw data about our experience of existence through our sensory experience (sight, hearing, smell, etc.), which gathers the data required for crafting our understanding of reality. The next step is the analysis of that data, which usually involves filtering out less immediately important information, such as not bothering to note the room's temperature when you've just stubbed your toe. This is then followed by the complex internal processes that draw upon our personal and cultural symbols and our memories to ascribe meaning and understanding to our sensory experiences. This usually includes the attachment of emotional weight and values to those experiences. All of this then informs how we respond physically and psychologically.

Not to belabor earlier points, but what deserves highlighting here is how tremendously individual our experiences of what we perceive to be "reality" are. There are a multitude of sensory factors that might lead to two people having very different perceptions of the world. Vision alone is highly variable. We have no way of determining that what each of us sees is the same experience for another, or that the experience I have of what we agree upon as the color red is the same as yours. Add to this that some people are colorblind, some have vision impairments, and some have no experience of sight at all, and it becomes very clear that we cannot rely upon sight as a universal experience. This extends to all of the senses as well; our experiences of sound, scent, and touch can vary quite a bit from person to person, and we do not all have the same taste receptors.

When we take into consideration that we are each further informed by a lifetime of unique experiences, social programming, individual or culturally created symbol systems, and any number of other factors related to neurodiversity, we are left with a vast ocean between each of us in determining a collective experience of what reality *is*. We often take for granted that other people are inherently 'like us' when, in truth, we are each a universe unto ourselves. Within all of this diversity of experience, it is a beautiful wonder that humans have developed such successful methods for creating communication, culture, and community amongst ourselves.

On Spirits and Symbolism

Given all of the above, I've never been much of a fan of lists that pretend to create a universal catalog of magical correspondences or dream interpretations. Certainly, these might be excellent tools for exploring a more broadly agreed-upon symbolic language of magic. In studying them, you might even choose to mindfully adopt their attributions as your own. That said, the most powerful symbols are usually those that we have a deep understanding of, and a personal meaning attached to.

A book may tell you that roses stand for romance, love, honor, and purity. However, if, as a small child, you fell into a bramble of roses that badly scratched and cut you, you might have a deeper understanding of roses, which suggests pain and danger. So, what meaning might you discern if a spirit were to appear to you carrying a bouquet of roses or accompanied by the smell of roses? Will you gauge your level of caution based upon a book of correspondences, or approach the encounter based upon your own emotional/memory symbolism of the rose?

There is no single book that will offer us the kind of insights and magical keys that are gifted to us when we put effort into truly *knowing ourselves*. This means that, as an integral part of our witchcraft and spirit work, we must spend time on introspection and meditation. That we challenge our own beliefs, we are aware of our strengths and weaknesses, and we question our conclusions and biases. Particularly that we examine things that we have simply accepted as true with little experimentation. Within the realm of spirit work, it is imperative that we establish a clear and ongoing understanding of ourselves. Primarily because our symbols, memories, assumptions, biases, desires, values, virtues, and vices are all means by which the spirits will engage and influence us towards either our benefit or detriment.

On Anthropomorphism

Humans have an inclination towards attributing human-like characteristics and qualities to the non-human beings we encounter. This tendency towards anthropomorphism is made quite evident by endless examples of artistry and effigy, which almost always depict spirits and deities as humanoid to some degree. While personifying spiritual entities can help serve as an effective bridge when engaging them, it is not without its risks. Within magical and animistic practices, anthropomorphism left unexamined can potentially obscure the true nature of a being, weakening the integrity of our relationships with them. When taken to an extreme, rather than meeting spirits on their own terms, we risk imposing familiar narratives and expectations that may hinder genuine communion or even provoke unintended consequences. So while anthropomorphism is a natural, and I would argue a necessary tool for communicating with spirits, it should be tempered with humility, curiosity, and an awareness of its limits.

That established, when working with disincarnate spirits, it is my belief that this tendency towards anthropomorphism is not a bug, but an important feature. A necessary part of engaging with spirits is establishing a shared mode of communication. As spirits work with our senses and memories to communicate, it naturally follows that spirits will adopt elements of humanity in an effort to better engage with and relate to us. A meeting in the middle, as it were.

We might see an artist's rendering of the goddess Hekate, read up on her, and study her history, and as a result of our expectations, she might appear to us in a form influenced by what we've read and the artist's depiction of her. There is nothing inherently wrong with this, so long as we are aware of our influences and biases. If it serves the purposes of building a genuine relationship with a spirit, then it has served you well.

I've generally found those initial experiences to be a starting point, however, and many spirits I've worked with have revealed themselves in new guises and unexpected forms throughout the course of our relationships. A spirit might at once appear both youthful and ancient, as a human one moment, then a coyote, then a therianthrope combining the two. In essence, it should be understood that when the fetters of a material form are cast off, all spirits, including you and me, are shapeshifters. As such, many spirits will often choose the path of least resistance and, at least initially, draw upon our preconceived notions of them when making their presence known. However, we should try to avoid boxing them in by our own designs.

On the Wardrobe of Memory

When we have no prior expectation of how a spirit might appear, our subconscious often fills the gap by clothing them in symbols drawn from the wardrobe of our memory. This is less a fabrication than it is a translation. The result of a conscious entity shuffling through our gray matter and attempting to communicate using the most immediately accessible toolset available, the database of symbols and sensory experiences found within our subconscious.

If you had never seen a fedora or durian fruit, it would be unlikely for a spirit to show up wearing a fedora and requesting durian as an offering. Because they are primarily drawing from our own set of symbols. Similarly, when we "hear" spirits, they are often drawing upon our own understanding of language. Of course, some exceptions to this exist, such as with spirits of the dead, as they often have their own memories of previous incarnations to draw upon. This is also true of group encounters where multiple people experience the same spirit in the same way. It's not that all those present must know what a fedora is, so long as one person does.

Shaped by their own intentions and our inner landscape, spirits may present themselves in guises that are alluring, abstract, or frightening. It is the work of the witch to decipher what is being communicated by the ways a spirit presents itself and communicates. A spirit who appears fearsome and threatening may be signaling power, danger, or simply testing how easily you scare. Understanding which is which requires experience and stepping back to examine our assumptions, emotions, and the context of the encounter. This same discernment should be applied to all spirits, including those who appear beautiful; much as with humans, the nature of a spirit cannot be determined by its appearance alone.

This interplay that occurs between spirit and psyche feeds the long-standing debate within magical circles between the psychological and spirit models. In short, the former suggests spirits are projections of the mind, while the latter asserts they are autonomous beings. But these need not be mutually exclusive. Spirits are conscious entities who often connect with humans by directly interfacing with our cognitive processes. In this way, every spirit encounter becomes a co-created event, part revelation, part reflection; bridging the liminal space between self and Other.

On the Sensing of Spirits

When engaging with a spirit, any number of phenomena may occur. You might feel a cold spot in a room, smell your grandmother's perfume, or see an apparition appear before you. Spirits may also influence the material realm and create strange encounters with animals, uncanny natural phenomena, or other synchronistic occurrences. In rarer occurrences, we might experience furniture moving or objects being knocked over. However, interactions with spirits will often be much more outwardly subtle, though they may have no less of an impact on us. You might dream of a spirit, "hear" them with an inner voice, "see" them with our inner eye, feel them move through you, or sense their presence through other subtle shifts of sensation.

As witches, it generally behooves us not to ignore the more subtle movements and messages of spirits in a search of the fantastical. It may be thrilling and affirming to see a spirit fully manifest, or to witness all of the candles in a room suddenly extinguish themselves; however, *this type of experience is the exception, not the rule.* Such acts tend to exert a lot of energy for spirits and often amount to little more than the parlor trick of proving themselves. It is not generally the type of interaction we should encourage in a spirit relationship. I personally prefer for my spirits to reserve the jump scares and showmanship and instead expend their energy actively working towards mutually agreed upon goals. Unless your goal is to be the cajoling host of an exploitative paranormal investigation series, such displays accomplish little in regard to forming meaningful relationships with spirits.

More importantly, if we are constantly waiting for fantastical outliers to provide validation of spirit experiences, then we are more likely to ignore the much more common, subtle forms of communication that spirits employ when seeking our attention. This is why the practice of establishing a touchstone laid out in the previous chapter is such an important one. It allows us to take note of the more subtle mental, emotional, and sensory changes in ourselves and in our environment that often accompany the presence of spirits.

On Our Otherworldly Senses

When we are engaging in spirit flight and encountering the Otherworld, there is often much emphasis placed upon what is commonly referred to as *visualization*. This phrasing can be a bit of a misnomer for framing what we might expect and the diversity of ways we might experience the Otherworld. For instance, if I were to tell a group of people to bring forth the image of an orange in the mind's eye, some might be able to vividly see an orange, whilst others may see nothing at all.

In contrast, I tend to prefer to use the term *sensualization* here instead. Though it may be difficult for you to "see" an orange, you may be able to conjure the memory of its smell and its taste. You might also be able to recall the feeling of holding an orange and the texture of its skin. We are able to effectively employ diverse aspects of our sensory memory when engaging in this work.

Instead of exclusively focusing on seeing yourself in spirit flight, try to bring forth the idea of flight. What does this feel like in your body? What does the night wind feel like upon your skin or sound like whistling in your ear? For some, the process of going to the Otherworld may be experienced through a form of internal storytelling akin to telling yourself you are walking in an otherworldly meadow and then conjuring forth the feel of the sun on your skin and the scent of that meadow. Or telling yourself, "I am descending down the Witches' Tree into the underworld" and then feeling and smelling the cool, rich earth as you descend.

The point being that we shouldn't focus upon only one of our senses when encountering the Otherworld to the exclusion of others. Such a singular approach does not allow room for the diversity of sensation and experience. Nor should you feel defeated or incomplete if some of your sensory experiences of the Otherworld are less pronounced than others. There are many paths towards successful engagement with spirits, and the witch is nothing if not resourceful and adaptable.

PRAXIS: Exploring the Fetch Sight

This is an exercise designed to practice shifting our awareness, developing skill sets for sensing spirits and points of power, as well as to aid us in sending our fetch forth in spirit flight. As stated above, in the case of this exercise, "sight" should not be taken literally. This kind of work may involve any of the senses, and the visions provided are inward and imaginal revelations received by the witching eye, which perceives in manners greater than sight alone.

The fetch spirit and the physical body are intrinsically linked, so though we are able to send this double out from ourselves, it is never fully disconnected from our bodies while we are alive. Some witches, particularly those just beginning this practice, may prefer to envision a spectral cord similar to an umbilical cord attached at the waist of the physical body and similarly linked to the fetch. This cord is subtle and can extend indefinitely. Should you ever feel in need of returning swiftly, "pulling" upon this cord may act as a means to quickly reunite the physical body and the fetch.

1. Begin in a place where you will not be interrupted. Prepare your ritual space however best suits your comfort level and personal practice. This might involve laying a compass, casting a circle, or calling upon guardian spirits or guides.
2. Light a single candle in the room and turn out the other lights. You may wish to dress the candle and anoint yourself with some of the *Oil of the Sight* found in the formulary towards the end of this book.
3. Arrange your body in a relaxed position.
4. Breathing from the diaphragm, take a few deep cleansing breaths, being sure to thoroughly exhale. Then close your eyes and return to your regular breathing.
5. Establish your touchstone and relax your body and mind.
6. Begin to establish a communion and direct awareness with the fetch self, your spirit double. I sometimes find that focusing my attention on the areas where my consciousness extends beyond my body is a good start.
7. Envision the fetch self as a double of yourself, resting within your body, but just a bit larger than your physical form. If you are not feeling this yet, take a deep, slow breath in, and upon exhaling, expand the body of the fetch a bit until it exists just beyond your skin.
8. Remember that in spirit form, the witch is a shapeshifter. Meaning that the fetch and its awareness can often be expanded or contracted, grown or shrunk, at will.

9. Once you have established a feeling of connection with the double, begin to more fully inhabit this spirit form of yourself with your consciousness. Shift your awareness to the feeling and experience of the spirit body of the fetch and less upon a conscious awareness of the physical body.
10. When you feel ready, allow the fetch to slowly slip from the skin. Meaning that the fetch spirit will more fully step out of and away from the body.
11. Aligning our awareness more fully to the fetch self and stepping away from our physical bodies and waking consciousness in this way can often feel like a splitting of our consciousness. This assists in creating a state between waking and sleep where all of our imaginal and mediumistic senses become more present and heightened.
12. Allow your fetch spirit to move around the room you are in. You may see this space as clearly as if you were walking around it embodied. You might instead only gain a sense of your consciousness traversing the space and receive flashes of images, scents, or other sensations relevant to the space. Both of these experiences are valid.
13. What we are attempting to do here is establish how the fetch expresses itself for you and how you receive information from it. Understanding that this part of yourself exists in-between the material realm we tend to take for granted as 'reality' and the Otherworld.
14. Draw your attention to the candle in the room. How does your fetch-self perceive this? Are you able to "see" it with the inner witching eye? Does it appear differently than it did in the material realm? Or does it appear in flashes of imagery or symbols? Perhaps you do not see it at all, but instead, you sense its warmth, its light, or the power emanating from it. Perhaps its scent is altered or heightened, or it emits a spectral sound. These are all ways in which you might perceive things whilst engaged in spirit flight.
15. You may wish to explore the room around you further to get a sense of how the fetch experiences the world when awakened in this way.
16. When you are ready, draw yourself back to your physical body and allow the fetch to slowly sink back into it. Some find it helps to shift their conscious awareness back to the physical body by

drawing in deep breaths, and while doing so, integrating the fetch self more and more back into the physical body.

17. Once you feel more fully integrated begin moving your fingers and toes, shake out your extremities a bit, and stretch your body as feels best. You want to really feel your physical body and allow the fetch to consciously inhabit it.
18. Next stretch your arms above your head. Interlock your fingers and sweep your interwoven hands down your body towards the Earth, unlocking them near the knees and directing your fingers towards the Earth whilst releasing a powerful exhalation towards the ground at the same time. This step is intended to sweep away any unnecessary residual power we may have picked up and return it to the earth whilst giving us final clearance.
19. Close your ritual space as needed.
20. Lastly, immediately record notes from your experience in a journal. This is an important step as, just as with dreams, our memory of Otherworld experiences is freshest just after returning to our awakened state.

This is a small beginning step into this kind of work and establishing a better understanding of our spirit senses. It is highly recommended that the newer practitioner look over the exercises throughout this book, explore the recommended reading at the end of this chapter, and invest time in practice and experimentation until they have developed a good level of comfort and adeptness with understanding and inhabiting the fetch self. This practice can be greatly expanded upon in time, allowing the witch to go forth in flight to other realms, encounter spirits in this realm, or engage in acts such as distance healing or reconnaissance and remote viewing.

The process of *skin slipping* may only happen a bit at a time, and you may not find success on your first few attempts. This is okay. Not all methods are effective for all witches. That said, I recommend practicing this several times before exploring alternate methods.

Some witches find it more effective to envision a spectral double of themselves standing in front of, or hovering above, their physical form. This exists as an empty vessel, which they may then breathe themselves into in order to animate it and go forth. I also encourage the reader to experiment with the *quickening breath* technique provided later in this book and explore it as a method for projecting the fetch outward.

On Categorizing Spirits

The manner in which spirits may be classified and categorized is far from universal and will vary quite a bit based upon culture and tradition. With this in mind, I encourage the reader to delve deeply into the lore and literature of the types of spirits they wish to work with, whether they be plant spirits, angels, fairies, or daemons. To this end, I have created a list of resources in the recommended reading at the end of this chapter for you to begin a deeper exploration of various classes of spirits. For the purposes of this work, instead of getting bogged down by delving into every possible classification of spirit, I will share some questions for determining the nature of the spirits you may encounter, touch upon a few broader categories of spirits for beginners, and conclude by discussing the *maumet* a very specific category of spirit relevant to the work of this book.

To begin, I should share that in my experience, the types of spirits best suited for ensouling into objects generally fall into the categories of sublunar and chthonic spirits. This essentially refers to spirits that are not higher celestial beings or deities and instead fall into the realm of plant spirits, animal spirits, land spirits, elementals, and spirits of the dead. This also extends to spirits under the broader categories of daemons/demons, faerie spirits, and domestic or household spirits. This isn't to say that an effigy cannot be made for and dedicated to a deity or celestial power as a devotional locus; it certainly can. However, I have generally found that the degree to which such spirits truly "inhabit" a spirit vessel tends to feel a bit more fluid and less anchored than in the case of sublunar spirits.

On the Nature and Roles of Spirits

When encountering a new and unknown spirit, I prefer to approach it with curiosity and let it reveal information about its nature. This is further informed by a series of questions that I will ask of spirits, which usually include the following:

- Do you enjoy the company of, or have an interest in, engaging with humans?
- Do you enjoy or have an interest in working in partnership with humans?
- What areas of the embodied realm do you have knowledge of?
- What areas of the spiritual and magical realm do you have knowledge of?
- What areas of the embodied realm do you have influence over?
- What areas of the spiritual and magical realm do you have influence over?
- Are there any areas of life or magic that you are particularly adept at influencing?
- Is there a particular place in the embodied realm or the Otherworld that you originate from?
- Is there a particular place in the embodied realm or the Otherworld that you live or call home?
- Are there any particular cultural groups in the embodied world you are aligned with?
- Are there any particular cultural groups in the Otherworld you are aligned with?
- Have you ever lived as a human?
- Have you ever lived as a plant or animal?
- Are there any particular symbols, colors, sensations, scents, or sounds that are representative of you or that you enjoy?
- Is there a preferred appearance you wish to take on? (Again, spirits are shapeshifters, and I sometimes find it helpful to invite them to show me a preferred form or image of themselves if they desire it.)
- Is there a particular title, name, or symbol you wish to be called by? (Some spirits will find it rude of you outright ask, "What is your name?".)
- What, if any, kind of partnership are you interested in with humans?
- Are there particular types of work you are willing to do with and for humans?
- What sort of exchange do you seek for such work?
- Would you like to meet again in the future?
- What is the best method for me to use in order to meet with or call upon you in the future?

Through working through this series of questions, I am able to get more of a sense of the type of spirit I'm engaging with upon first meeting. These types of questions may be reworked, added to, or rephrased to better suit your practice and the spirits you are encountering. They may also be reworded a bit for use with the simple divination methods mentioned in the next chapter. Keep in mind that you may at times receive answers from spirits that seem inconsistent or unreliable. Before immediately deciding a spirit is dishonest, bear in mind it may be because the spirit doesn't understand the question, and it needs rephrasing. There may also be a "language barrier" or general misunderstanding. Just as there are plenty of humans who are not very experienced in communicating with spirits, there are also spirits who are not terribly experienced in interacting with humans. Be patient, seek understanding, and always exercise discernment because some spirits are indeed dishonest.

Keep in mind that simply because you may recognize certain identifying characteristics of a spirit doesn't mean that everything you think you know about that type of spirit applies to the specific spirit you are talking to. That's a bit like imagining that all hairdressers or all Germans are the same. Simply because a spirit fulfills a particular role or comes from a particular cultural group of spirits doesn't mean that they may not display unique characteristics, skill sets, interests, knowledge, and personality.

In general, I tend not to become so hung up on seeking to define spirits by preexisting categorizations beyond what they show me of themselves. For me, it is often more about determining *who* they are as opposed to enforcing ideas around *what* they are. As a result of this approach, I have met and worked with spirits which, in another context, folks may consider land spirits or fairies or daemons. However, I've personally taken to affectionately referring to many of the spirits I encounter more broadly as imps. Not as a terribly rigid categorization of them but instead drawing upon witchlore wherein the imp broadly refers to the sorts of 'little devils' who work with witches.

On Plants, Animals, and Spirits of the Land

I will cover plant and animal spirits a bit more in Chapter Seven, but for now, I wish to encourage the reader who is just starting to work with spirits to begin developing relationships here. Start by being curious about the flora and fauna that are native to your area. Do research into their biology and folklore. Connect with them by observing them in their natural habitat, if possible, or engage in transvection to meet with their spirit forms in the Otherworld. As they are much more tied to the Middle World, they are usually more approachable for the beginner than some of the more celestial or demonic forces might be. Though some may underestimate the power of plant or animal spirits, I generally find these folks have never seen how Coyote engages in cunning or how a properly conjured Saint John's Wort can cause demons to flee. These spirits can stand as powerful protectors, allies, and guides in our work, and, if we take the time to build relationships with them, they may aid us in creating very effective magic. In connecting with the flora and fauna of our locale, we are also learning more about the spiritual ecosphere we live in, and this can further help us connect with spirits of the land.

Land spirit is a *very* broad term and generally is applied to any manner of spirit beings who inhabit and are tied to the land around us. This can include any number of faerie beings, but also includes the spirit of our local park, the land our house is built upon, the guardian spirit of the local cemetery, or the spirits who live in a nearby mountain or stream. They, too, are spirits tied to the embodied Middle World. Land spirits, particularly those who exist near where we live, can often provide gateways to understanding all of the spirits around us and how many of them interact with each other. They usually have a vested interest in the local community, and if we do as well, they may make excellent partners, protectors, and providers for us in our magic.[33]

On Protector Spirits

For those new to working with spirits, one of my first recommendations is to establish relationships with protector spirits. Considering everything we've explored so far, this shouldn't imply that you absolutely need a bodyguard everywhere you go in the Otherworld; you don't. However, if things ever do get odd or uncomfortable, you'll be happy you have one. Essentially, what you'll be looking to do is to determine which spirits

---

33 For an example of crafting a spirit vessel for a land spirit see the *Nest of the Genius Loci* in the Selection of Workings section towards the back of the book.

that you have fairly easy access to are most likely to effectively provide protection for the type of work you wish to do. A person who desires to conjure demons may need more powerful backup than someone who is primarily working with plant spirits, for instance.

One of the easiest ways to establish such relationships is to do a bit of research and choose a plant that is known for spiritual protection. Particularly one that either grows near you, or that you can at least get some dried material from. Plants like St. John's Wort, Rue, Rowan, and Angelica each have a very long history of providing protection against potentially harmful spirits. Go into the Otherworld or use one of the methods discussed in the next chapter for connecting with spirits. It is helpful to have some fresh or dried material from the plant with you when doing so. Seek an audience with the plant spirit and ask it if it is willing to help protect you and if the plant spirit would like anything in exchange. If all goes well, then afterwards the plant material may be added to a pouch or made into a fetich for protection.

If you have an established practice with a patron Deity, then you likely already have a protector willing to assist on some level. In fact, whether we have identified them or not yet, almost everyone has at least a few protective spirits who walk with them. However, to get started, you may wish to do a bit of research on any protective spirits and saints that are relevant to your spiritual tradition, ancestry, or locale. Or if you have a diviner or medium that you trust, you may be able to get a reading to determine which spirits walk with you. This is often a good place to begin seeking connection and establishing allyship with the Others. For instance, many witches I know turn to Archangel Michael as a protector. This angelic being has a very long history that stretches into the ancient world, and his influence and protections extend across many cultures and traditions.

Establishing a good relationship with proctors allows us to have allies to turn to, who can essentially act as spiritual bouncers, give us warning and insight about other spirits, and aid us in banishing and exorcising any spirits we may not want around us. In time, as your practice develops further, you will likely develop a variety of protectors who each contribute a unique quality and fulfill slightly different roles. For now, however, it's best to begin with what feels in alignment with your needs and provides quick and effective results.

PRAXIS: Establishing a Protector Spirit

This exercise will be using the format of the transvection exercise in Chapter Three, but with some additional wording and preparation. It is designed to ideally connect you with a spirit that will serve as an ally in protecting you from physical and spiritual harm. This general outline can also be adapted to other works when you seek to meet with spirits willing to serve as partners in other areas of your craft.

Items Needed:

- A red candle—a taper, household, or chime candle will do.
- A candle holder.
- Spirit Summoning Oil from the formulary or, in a pinch, olive oil will do.

1. In a place where you will not be interrupted, begin by preparing your ritual space however best suits your comfort level and personal practice. It is recommended that you lay a compass, cast a circle, and wear a protective oil such as the *Oil of Protection* listed in the Formulary section.
2. Put a bit of oil on your hands. Pick up the candle and begin to dress it (coating it with oil) from the bottom to the top in a way where your hands are moving away from your body. State:

   "By my ancestors and the spirits who walk with and watch over me, both known and unknown, named and unnamed, do I cast away any and all creatures of spirit or fantasy that do not serve the work of my protection and greatest exaltation."

3. Next, begin dressing the candle in the opposite manner. This time you will draw the oil from the top to the bottom and towards your body as you say:

   "I call now to those spirits who will serve as protectors and allies in my work. Let my call to you echo through the Otherworld, and may you be guided on a path laid forth and enforced by my ancestors

and all of the spirits who walk with and watch over me, both known and unknown, named and unnamed. I ask one of you now to make yourself known and to step forth and meet me in the Otherworld."[34]

4. Place the candle in its holder, light it, and state:

   "Let the light of this flame be a beacon which calls forth those spirits which act as guardians, sentries, and sentinels, and let it, in turn, burn the eyes of any and all who would seek to interfere with, or act with falsity in my work. By my ancestors and the spirits who walk with and watch over me, both known and unknown, named and unnamed, and by the setting and rising of the sun, it is done. As it is spoken, so it is."

5. Next, arrange your body in a relaxed position.
6. Breathing from the diaphragm, take a few deep cleansing breaths, being sure to thoroughly exhale. Then close your eyes and return to your regular breathing.
7. Using the previously given exercises, establish your touchstone and relax the body and mind.
8. Next, going from ten to one, you will begin mentally counting down into a deeper state of relaxation.
9. Repeat step eight one more time, counting down again and becoming even more relaxed this time. You should be in a state of considerable relaxation at this point. If needed, you can repeat steps seven and eight again.
10. Now, with your inner eye, envision yourself as though you are standing in the white room. In this space, you are protected, and it is entirely your own domain. Think of it as a form of spiritual cleanroom, free from any external influence and entities.
11. Think upon your desire to establish a relationship with a protector spirit and set this as your goal for going forth.
12. Once you have this purpose firmly in mind, conjure a door by willing it to appear before you. Take note of what this door looks like. Does it look ancient or modern? What material is it made

34 This can be adapted from this point to be performed with other forms of spirit communication such as scrying and divination if desired.

from? Is there a symbol/sigil etched or painted on it? Try to commit this symbol to memory if so as it may potentially serve as a sign of protection for you in the future.

13. When you feel prepared, open the door and step into the realm of this spirit. Take note of anything you encounter. Does this place appear as a city, a garden, a cave?
14. What is the spirit that appears to you? Do they appear as a plant spirit or an animal? Are they an ancestral or angelic being? It may seem immediately clear what the spirit you have encountered is. This is helpful, but don't rush to assumptions.
15. When/if the spirit appears, begin a dialog with it as you are able. Employ the questions given earlier in this section and establish how this spirit will work with you and begin to form the foundations of this relationship. You may need to visit this spirit on more than one occasion to firmly create a bond/pact with it.
16. If the spirit has not appeared or made itself known, using your inner voice, restate your call (or a personal variation of it) to them again:

    "I call now to those spirits who will serve as protectors and allies in my work. Let my call to you echo through the Otherworld, and may you be guided on a path laid forth and enforced by my ancestors and all of the spirits who walk with and watch over me, both known and unknown, named and unnamed. I ask one of you now to make yourself known."

17. If you still find that nothing is appearing, take your time to explore the environment you find yourself in and see what may be revealed. You may then return and try this exercise another day.
18. When you are ready to conclude your journey, give thanks to the spirit you have encountered for its attention. Then either return to the door or summon it to appear where you are in the Otherworld.
19. Step back through the door into the white room. Close the door and envision it disappearing.
20. Next, allow the image of the white room to fade away.

21. Begin counting up from one to ten, envisioning that you are ascending a staircase with each number and returning to waking consciousness. Do this twice, or as many times as you counted down initially. While counting up it may help to begin wiggling your fingers and toes a bit to draw your consciousness back to the physical body.
22. Once you have counted back up, open your eyes and stretch your body in whatever way feels best. You may also wish to shake out your hands, arms, and legs a bit to awaken the body and boost circulation. I find this helps to more fully return the consciousness of the fetch spirit to the physical body.
23. Stretch your arms above your head. Interlock your fingers. Then sweep your interwoven hands down your body towards the Earth, unlocking them near the knees and directing your fingers towards the Earth whilst releasing a powerful exhalation towards the ground at the same time. This step is intended to sweep away any residual power and return it to the earth whilst giving us a final clearance.
24. Lastly, immediately record notes from your experience in a journal.
25. Close your ritual space as you normally would and allow the candle to fully burn as an offering to the spirit you have met.

On Ancestral Spirits and Spirits of the Dead

Establishing a connection with ancestral spirits is also a good place to begin with spirit work. Primarily because these are generally going to be spirits that have a vested interest in your progression, protection, and prosperity in this world. Perhaps not all of your ancestors will be a fit for you; this is okay. You needn't invite people to eat at your dinner table who are not there to support you. Even if every deceased family member you've known in life is not a spirit you'd want to work with, if you go far enough back, there will always be folks in your line who are willing to stand with and look after you, whether you know their names or not. For this purpose, when I call to my dead, I do so with the following phrase included:

> *"I call upon my ancestors. I call to those who stand behind me, walk beside me, and lay the path before me. I call to those who will support*

and strengthen me in achieving the truest, most fulfilling, and most joyful expression of myself. Guide me and protect me that I be both a worthy descendant to those who have gone before me, and a worthy ancestor to those who will follow me."

In addition to familial dead, we will also have ancestral spirits associated with any spiritual traditions we are a part of, and many witches will attest that there are numerous ancestral witch spirits willing to make contact and assist us. You may even have ancestral connections to spirits allied to certain vocations and trades you are involved with. Lineage and ancestry are not strictly about blood; they are equally relevant to the spiritual or trade lineages, traditions, and families we are adopted into. With this in mind, I highly encourage the reader who is just getting started to begin by establishing a connection with their ancestors as an initial line of guardians and guides. For more in-depth guidance on this, please see the recommended reading at the end of this chapter.

We might also form relationships with other spirits of the dead. These kinds of spirit relationships are often more approachable for the beginner because you will be dealing with spirits who have lived as humans and therefore have the most in common with us amongst any of the spirits. In this category, we may seek to develop relationships with those we feel lived exemplary lives or who possessed qualities we admire and wish to cultivate. This might include forging relationships with historical figures, artists, performers, leaders, and magical figures in order to secure their patronage and guidance.

There is, of course, also the option of calling upon, honoring, and working with the spirits of people we have known and loved in this life who have passed on. We might also develop relationships with our local dead and enlist their aid in our work. I usually encourage my students to get to know their local cemetery and begin to establish an understanding of who is there, who the guardian spirits of the place are, and determine how this might inform them more about the place they live and aid them in developing relationships with the dead. There are often historical spirits of the dead associated with the towns we live in or even the houses we inhabit, and forging relationships with our local dead can prove a valuable and illuminating part of our spirit work.

On Household Spirits

Another broad category of spirits, the term *household spirit* is generally applied to any spirit beings that are tied to our home and the land it is on, and/or those spirits that live in our homes and are usually helpful for keeping the home and its inhabitants safe and prosperous. Though household spirits may come in many forms, a few examples include the Slavic *Domovoi,* the Swedish *Tomte,* and the *Brownies* and *Hobgoblins* of English and Scottish tradition. These spirits often require fairly consistent attention and offerings to keep them happy and keep us in their good graces, as some household spirits may act out if they become upset. However, when we give proper care and consideration to domestic spirits, they often reward us greatly with blessings for the home and family. In some cases, these household spirits may choose to move with us from home to home, and some become allied to particular families for generations.

Household spirits may also include any that we have intentionally enshrined in the home to act as protectors and allies. Examples of this can be found in the *Sentry Maumet* working and the *Nest of the Genius Locii* found in the Selection of Workings section at the back of this book. Additionally, and alluded to earlier, we may also consider the spirits of the dead who are tied to our homes as household spirits when and if they make themselves known and are willing to aid us in domestic magics.

On Familiar Spirits

The term *familiar* is derived from the Latin word *familiaris,* which suggests both domesticity and servitude, and by extension might also imply domestic or household spirits. More commonly, a familiar spirit is understood to refer to a spirit with which we share a certain bond, pact, or familiarity. Familiar spirits might alternately be referred to as the aforementioned Imp (often implying an infernal association), *Puckril* (often implying a faerie association), or as a *Magistellus,* a term meaning "little master". Though in some craft traditions that latter term is reserved more specifically for the type of spirits which have been granted to a witch by a deity or the Witches' Devil, and become interwoven with the witch's own spirit. Though often mentioned in relation to witchcraft, there are historical and contemporary magical practitioners of all kinds who have had established relationships with familiar spirits, regardless of whether they used that specific term to describe them.

In popular culture, living animal companions to the witch (pets) are commonly referred to as familiars. However, this concept is a largely ahistorical one, as in the vast majority of cases throughout history, familiars are not presented as incarnate animals but instead as disincarnate spirits who merely shapeshift into an animal form. This in mind, though I have great affection for my animal companions, it should be understood here that I am speaking of spirit companions, not living animals.

The familiar spirit is not defined so much by the kind of spirit it is as by its relationship to the witch. Familiar spirits can be a spirit of the dead, a faerie spirit, a plant spirit, a land spirit, a demon, or any other sort of spirit that the magician or witch has developed a close bond with. This is usually a tutelary relationship where the familiar acts as a protector, guide, ally, and often as a teacher who assists the witch in their magic. The relationship is often accompanied by a pact that binds both spirit and witch to certain agreements. This relationship is usually a reciprocal one in which the spirit receives payment and/or sustenance of some kind from the witch to strengthen their bond and in exchange for their continued aid.

In many cases, the familiar spirit is the primary spirit a witch will work with in their craft. It may go forth and perform tasks on their behalf, provide instruction for performing a spell, give counsel, aid in divination or healing, or warn us of potential danger. Familiar spirits will often assist witches during spirit flight, and in some cases may appear as an animal steed which we might ride upon whilst traversing through the Otherworld.

The familiar is a partner in our craft. In many cases, this partnership is one which lasts throughout the witch's life. In others, a familiar spirit might accompany a witch for several years and move on once their work together has come to an end. As such, a witch might have more than one familiar spirit relationship during their life, or even at the same time. Just as a person might have several romantic partners or trusted human confidants at the same time, you might find yourself in a similar situation with familiar spirits.

Historically, familiar spirits were acquired by a magician or witch in a variety of ways. They might be encountered in the wild or conjured by ritual means. They may be given to a witch by another spirit, such as the Queen of Elphame, the Devil, or a demon. They might also be given to, or inherited from, another witch. In some cases, familiar spirits lived in or around the witch's home or garden. Relevant to our work here, they were also housed in bottles, boxes, or baskets lined with wool. In rarer cases, familiar spirits might even inhabit the witch's own body as a form of spirit grafting and augmentation.

The arte of creating spirit vessels is one incredibly well-suited to working with familiar spirits, as it offers a way of strengthening our bond with our familiar spirits as well as creating a greater point of power and stability for them. Additionally, the creation of a spirit vessel may be incorporated into the ceremony of formally establishing our relationship and pacting with a familiar spirit. In such a case, we are more fully inviting the spirit into our lives and homes, whilst actively taking on the responsibility of caring for the spirit vessel and the familiar that inhabits it.

On Supernal and Infernal Spirits

Supernal or celestial spirits are those allied to the Upperworld. This generally includes certain classes of faerie beings, planetary spirits, many deities, and those beings we might think of as angels. Conversely, Infernal or chthonic spirits are those most allied to the Underworld. This will include daemons/demons, imps, vampiric spirits, many deities, and some spirits of the dead. The ways in which these types of spirits are framed and understood from a theological and cosmological perspective vary greatly depending upon the source, particularly in the case of demons and angelic beings. With this in mind, I won't attempt to define how they should be understood to the reader but instead encourage those who wish to work with these beings to research multiple sources regarding the folklore, mythos, and magic of the beings of the Supernal and Infernal realms. To this end, I have provided some resources in the recommended reading.

On "Trickster" Spirits

In the next chapter, I'll discuss discernment more in depth as well as ways to establish boundaries and verify the claims of spirits. However, I'd like to take a moment here to discuss what are commonly referred to as "trickster spirits," and more specifically, the way that they are often discussed in some broader magical communities.

I have regularly witnessed people within the magical community warn people about "trickster spirits," usually with the implication that these are spirits that only want to mislead and manipulate you in order to exploit you or cause you harm. Though such spirits do in fact exist, I'd like to set the record straight that they are more appropriately referred to as manipulative or parasitic spirits rather than "trickster spirits". The reason this matters is that true trickster spirits are some of the most powerful allies of the witch, as they often possess and mediate the very powers many of us wish to wield.

True trickster spirits are those that embody paradox, liminality, chaos, and change. They represent chance, luck, and the twisting of fate. Trickster spirits are generally mercurial by nature. They know the secrets of language and the power of word and song, and in many tales are credited with the power of all communication, particularly between the embodied world and the Otherworld. As such, they are the masters of divination and oracular prophecy as well.

Trickster spirits are found at thresholds, crossroads, and in all places betwixt. Throughout many of the world's stories, it is the trickster who is responsible for bringing us fire, teaching us to speak, and in some cases creating the world. Their ranks include Hermes, Anansi, Coyote, Raven, Prometheus, the Witch's Devil, and the manifold expressions of Eshu. They are often volatile spirits that challenge us and task us with overcoming the trials of the world. They ask us to grow, to adapt, to claim our power, so that we may either be tempered in their fire or reduced to ash and reborn. They create and destroy in a blink and, in short, *are* magic. As such, the witch would do well to meet them with neither trepidation nor hubris, nor to shun them entirely, as they are the catalyst for initiation, gnosis, and summoning us into our greatest exaltation.

On Defining the Maumet Spirit

Though this term is sometimes used synonymously with *poppet,* within the context of this book, a *maumet* should be understood not as a physical object, but as a kind of manufactured spirit.

A *maumet* spirit is created when an assemblage of magical *materia* is chosen and compiled to serve a specific magical purpose and combined in the form of an effigy, fetiche, or spirit vessel. The *maumet* spirit is a chimeric creation. It is a gestalt, which is more than the sum of its parts. It is all of the spirits and virtues of the elements of its making reorganized and reborn into a new collective form, which functions as a unique spirit.

In some ways, this may be viewed similarly to the creation of servitor spirits or egregores. Though the methodologies for creating those forms of constructed spirits are often quite different, as they tend to rely primarily upon the lending of personal power from the magician or a collective to birth them. They also tend to exist within different magical frameworks than the animist perspective my craft is rooted in. So though there are similarities and readers are welcome to employ the methods presented within this book to craft bodies for servitors and egregores, there are also some marked differences. Most notably, the initial primary power behind a *maumet* is the magical *materia* it is crafted from. In such creations, each element, whether it be a root, a bone, specific dirts, stones, or a man-made object, is contributing its own spirit and influence to the total design and collective spirit of the *maumet.*

Once it has been fully crafted, it undergoes the ritual process of death and rebirth and is given new life as a unique expression of spirit. The *maumet* is further kept empowered by being "fed" in various ways. This can include it being passed through the smoke of incense, dressed with oils, or sprayed with perfumes. Offerings of food, drink, flowers, or candles may be placed before it to help empower it. Or, similar to many servitors, it may be instructed to feed off of specific or ambient points of energy/power.

The term *maumet* is of Middle English origin and, similar to the word *Baphomet*, is believed to have originated from a corruption of *Mahomet/Muhammad* and was initially used to denote an idol or a false god. *Maumet* has, at various times, been used to refer to a figural effigy, puppet, or doll/poppet. In some cases, as an extension of the puppet idea, it has implied someone who does the bidding of another. However, if we search back even further and closer to its etymological origins, the term has variously referred to the image of a household god, a pagan or oracular idol, an item possessed by the devil, or a diminutive supernatural being.

For many of the points this word touches upon historically, I have adopted it as an operative term to simultaneously refer to both constructed spirits and their corresponding effigies/fetiches/vessels. This title was chosen in order to differentiate them from created spirits, such as the previously mentioned servitor, which exist within other magical traditions.

Maumet spirits are created around fairly specific areas of influence, such as protecting a location, aiding study, conveying messages to others, or the cultivation and generation of luck. As a part of this, the witch will speak conjurations over each element of magical *materia* that they are employing when crafting the *maumet* and request its assistance in the work. During the official birthing of a *maumet,* it is given a name, instructions, and the parameters it is meant to work within. These parameters may include how it is and is not to behave, the type of results desired, how and when it will be fed, and specifics around how and when its work will be concluded.

In some cases, a *maumet* may be crafted for a specific task which, once completed, concludes the witch's work with it. After which, they may be ritually released from service and their corresponding spirit vessel physically disassembled. This is all done with respect and gratitude to both the created and released *maumet* spirit as well as to the spirits of the materials it was initially crafted from.

In other cases, a *maumet* may be continually worked with over time. As a result, the *maumet* tends to become more powerful and a more autonomous and individualized spirit. Given enough time, attention, and development, a *maumet* may begin to fulfill broader roles as a magical assistant. In some rarer cases with enough development, a *maumet* may even begin to cross over into fulfilling similar roles to that of a familiar spirit.

Recommended Additional Reading

Walking with Spirits by Taylor Ellwood. Independently Published, 2020.

The Witch's Book of Spirits by Devin Hunter. Llewellyn Publications, 2017.

Spirit Work: A Guide to Communicating & Forming Relationships with Spirits by Sirian Shadow. Independently Published, 2022.

Ancestral Whispers: A Guide to Building Ancestral Veneration Practices by Ben Stimpson. Llewellyn Publications, 2023.

Spirit Beings in European Folklore (Volumes 1-4) by Benjamin Adamah. Vamzzz Publishing, 2022.

Encyclopedia of Spirits: The Ultimate Guide to the Magic of Saints, Angels, Fairies, Demons, and Ghosts by Judika Illes. HarperOne, 2009.

The Grimoire Encyclopaedia: A convocation of Spirits, Texts, Materials, and Practices by David Rankine. Hadean Press Limited, 2023.

The Tradition of Household Spirits by Claude Lecouteux. Inner Traditions, 2013.

A Study of Household Spirits of Eastern Europe by Ronesa Aveela. 2018.

The Plant Spirit Familiar by Christopher Penczak. Copper Cauldron Publishing, 2011.

Plant Spirit Shamanism: Traditional Techniques for Healing the Soul by Ross Heaven and Howard G. Charing. Destiny Books, 2006.

A New Dictionary of Fairies: A 21st century Exploration of Celtic and Related Western European Fairies by Morgan Daimler. Moon Books, 2020.

Faery: A Guide to the Lore, Magic & World of the Good Folk by Morgan Daimler. Moon Books, 2020.

A Dictionary of Fairies: Hobgoblins, Brownies, Bogies, and Other Supernatural Creatures by Katharine M. Briggs. Viking, 1976

Demons and Spirits of the Land: Ancestral Lore and Practices by Claude Lecouteux. Inner Traditions, 2015.

The Dictionary of Demons: Expanded & Revised: Names of the Damned by M. Belanger. Llewellyn Publications, 2021.

Encyclopedia of Demons in World Religions and Cultures by Theresa Bane. McFarland & Company, 2012.

A Dictionary of Angels: Including the Fallen Angels by Gustav Davidson. Free Press, 1994.

The Encyclopedia of Angels, Second Edition by Rosemary Ellen Guiley. Checkmark Books, 2004.

Chapter Five

Pactum: On Conjuring, Communicating, and Pacting with Spirits

On Why We Work with Spirits, and Them with Us

Through the witch's relationships with our spirits, we gain wisdom and insight into our magical practices. Being unbound by a material form, spirits easily travel throughout the Otherworld, and many spirits will have access to realms we may not. Whereas, as embodied beings, we may more easily interact with, influence, and manipulate things in the material realm, spirits more easily influence and manipulate things in the more subtle realms. A central belief of the witch is that the material world and the Otherworld are intrinsically linked, and influencing one has an impact on the other.

For instance, let's imagine that I am seeking to find quality reference materials for something I am writing. In the material realm, I may prepare a candle and a small offering for one of the spirits I work with who has proven itself to be good at these things. I might draw their sigil or symbol in front of an effigy I've created for the spirit and place the offering atop it. Then I could conjure the spirit by calling to it in whatever way reflects our relationship and ask for its assistance. I might follow this by performing divination to determine if the spirit accepts the work and what additional payment they might request in exchange. This is the planning and negotiation phase of the work. If we are both in agreement and clear on the terms, then we have made a simple pact. As an alternative to calling the spirit to me through evocation/conjuration, I might instead lay out the offering and meet the spirit via spirit flight to have our conversation/negotiation take place in the Otherworld.

During our conversation, either through mediumship, divination, or interaction in the Otherworld, the spirit might reveal a ritual working, formula, charm, fetich, or sigil that I should create to aid in realizing my goal. They may also offer counsel on the best ways to achieve the goal of finding reference materials, such as places I should visit or signs I should look out for. Once our work has concluded, they may ask for additional offerings.

The material components here include elements like the initial candle and offering given, the spirit's effigy/spirit vessel, any physical charms or fetiches I might make, rituals I might perform, and any additional forms of offering requested as payment. It also includes the physical act of going out into the world to find the materials I'm looking for. On a more subtle level, the spirit might pull upon the strings of fate, creating situations where I and others are in the right place at the right time. Sometimes, the manner in which spirits create an event in our world can seem rather commonplace, like coming across a post online about a relevant book or hearing an interview where someone begins talking about the subject I'm researching. In others, it might feel quite uncanny, such as having someone randomly and unprompted give me a book on the very topic I am researching.

Of course, spirits aren't incapable of directly influencing the material; it simply takes greater effort for them to do so. Witches are capable of influencing the subtle as well. However, this can also take a great deal of effort on the part of the witch and takes many years to become truly adept at it. Meanwhile, by their very nature, spirits exist in this state of the subtle, so they make excellent partners in both our learning and practice.

What the witch offers the spirit is our ability to have an embodied experience and to share that in a variety of ways with those spirits we trust. We accomplish this by doing something they are generally unable to do on their own behalf, such as dedicating material things to the spirit. The offerings we give provide them greater power and sustenance, the divination tools we dedicate to them give them a voice, the shrines we create give them a home, and the effigies, fetiches, and spirit vessels we create give them bodies. We also provide them with human attention and interaction, and through this process, spirits become more reified. As we have seen throughout history, many smaller local spirits, or even spirits of the dead, have eventually grown into fully realized folk saints or deities with many dedicated devotees. As the amount of human attention given to a spirit grows, so too does its realm of influence. This applies as much to personal relationships with familiar spirits as it does to the deities of world religions. There is a reciprocal relationship between the witch and the spirits/deities we work with, and to my mind at least, neither exists independent of the other.

On Evocation and Tradition-Specific Protocol

This book will, at times, present my own approaches towards the spirits I engage with within my witchcraft. This should not imply that my methods are intended or recommended as a default for approaching any and all spirits you may encounter and engage with, regardless of their cultural and historical origins. When seeking to work with tradition, culture, and sometimes even location-specific spirits, it is always best to make an effort and do the work of researching the most appropriate methodologies for respectfully meeting the spirits on their own terms.

Spirits may be categorized, defined, and ordered into hierarchies in incredibly diverse ways. By nature, this organization will be uniquely reflective of the traditions and cultures the spirits emerged from and exist within. Whenever engaging spirits from a specific cultural tradition, it is heavily encouraged that you approach them with all of the appropriate ritual protocols, etiquette, and taboos observed.

In contrast to transvection, which takes us to the Otherworld, evocation, conjuration, and invocation are approaches towards engaging with spirits in our realm. Evocation is the act of drawing the consciousness of a spirit to engage with us here in the embodied realm. The term implies a spoken element, such as the use of a prayer, verbal charm, or incantation to achieve this. Evocation, by its nature, is accomplished primarily through calling to spirits through empowered breath and voice.

Evocation could take the form of elaborate rituals like those found within classical grimoires. This often involves long prayers and conjurations, purification, and the crafting of specific ritual tools, as well as the creation of magical circles and a Triangle of Arte or some other device designed to contain the summoned spirit. Evocation might also look like a witch calling to the spirits of the four directions while laying a compass or casting a circle and asking that the spirits be present to lend their power and protection. Evocation could take the form of a *quimbandeiro* going to the crossroads, drawing a *ponto* in chalk upon the ground, and calling to an Exu with song.[35] Evocation might also look like a person sitting before an ancestral altar, lighting a candle, giving a simple offering, and speaking a few heartfelt prayers while asking for blessings.

There are many approaches to calling upon spirits, and each is shaped by the cultures and traditions they arise from. None of these approaches is more universally correct than another. There are, however, varying levels of correctness regarding our approach towards spirits as they exist within traditional and culture-specific contexts, including observing protocols demanded by those traditions, which exist for both the well-being of the spirit being called and the person calling them. For instance, it would generally be ill-advised for a person casting a Wiccan circle to call upon a spirit from an African Diasporic Tradition. Particularly if the ritualist had no prior experience with, or relationships to, these spirits within the context of their tradition. This is because the spiritual technology employed doesn't present an optimal experience for either the witch or the spirit they wish to call. In essence, you are attempting a meeting with someone you do not know, using symbolic languages they are unfamiliar with, within unfamiliar ritual terrain. This is not the behavior of a good host and not a good way to create a respectful relationship.

Each spiritual/magical tradition has developed its own methods of evocation and ritual protocols that allow for the best possible interaction with their own tradition-specific spirits. These methods have been developed, tested, refined, and adapted when necessary from within those traditions for optimal results. In short, there is less chance that a spirit might be made uncomfortable, become potentially dangerous, or simply not show up when we work from within the established ritual methods those spirits are familiar with. Just as traditions have developed around and adapted

35 A *quimbandeiro* is a practitioner of the Afro-Brazilian sorcerous tradition of Quimbanda and a *ponto* (point) is a seal/sigil usually drawn in chalk which is designed to conjure a spirit of that tradition.

to their spirits, so too have those spirits developed around and adapted to those traditions. Again, the human/spirit relationship is a reciprocal one. Please keep this in mind as you develop within your work with spirits.

On Conjuration

The word *conjure* has a somewhat varied usage within magical communities. In general, to conjure is often understood as calling forth a spirit by evocation or incantation. It finds its origin in the Latin word *coniurare,* which means "to swear together or conspire".[36] *Conspire* in turn originates in fourteenth-century France and implies plotting or agreeing to engage in a transgressive act, often accompanied by a spoken oath or pact. Bear in mind that at the time when the word "conspire" developed, by such a definition, witchcraft was very much qualified as a criminal and transgressive act. It is also interesting to note that breath appears again here as the word conspire draws upon the Latin *conspirare,* literally meaning "to breathe together." So by extension, conjure might further be understood as an agreement enforced by spoken oath.[37]

In many cases, the term *conjure* is similarly used by magical practitioners as *evoke* and is understood as meaning to call forth or summon. This usually implies the employment of prayers, incantations, the voice, and the breath. All this in mind, at its core the term *conjure* suggests an act of calling upon a spirit for purposes of forming an agreement or allyship.

In my own work, and throughout this book, when I speak of conjure, conjuring, and conjuration, I am speaking primarily about acts designed to capture the attention of a spirit. Primarily, when calling it forth in order to establish allyship and pacts. This sometimes takes the form of a more formal ritual; however, in many cases, such conjuration is incredibly practical and takes the form of speaking to the indwelling spirit tied to the magical *materia* I am working with. This form of conjuration is focused upon "awakening" the spirits of material items and aligning them to the work at hand.[38]

---

36 *Conjure* | *Etymonline,* www.etymonline.com/word/conjure

37 *Conspire* | *Etymonline,* www.etymonline.com/word/conspire

38 For more on this see the section on *Magical Materia.*

On Invocation, Possession, Transposition, and Embodiment

Before we begin here, it is worth mentioning that just as the terms conjuration and evocation have often been treated as synonymous, throughout much of the history of religion and magic, so too has the term invocation. The terms evocation and invocation are often treated as interchangeable by many magical practitioners. However, depending upon who you ask, the terms might imply separate ideas. Within contemporary witchcraft, *evoke* often implies calling or summoning a spirit *to* you, while *invoke* often implies drawing a spirit *within* you. Invocation in this sense is a form of trance-possession and a technique employed by many spiritual traditions, each with their own techniques and taboos surrounding it.

One such form of invocatory trance-possession is what is commonly referred to as *mediumship*. Mediumship is the ability to sense and communicate with spirits through sensory channels. This might appear as an image flashed within the mind, a faint whispering voice, or an image superimposed atop what we are seeing with our waking eyes. Though rarer, some witches might see or hear spirits as clearly as they might you or me.

Mediumship may also create other sensory phenomena, like feeling the temperature of a room change or having the hairs on the back of your neck stand up. Some might feel a tingling or pressure in certain points of the body. I have met several witches who experience certain tastes in their mouths or smells arising when different spirits are near them. How these experiences present for each witch are often as individual as we each are, and spirits will communicate through different means with different people. After all, each relationship has its own unique features. This is why, though it is beneficial to share our experiences of spirits with and learn from others, we should also temper this by avoiding an overemphasis on direct comparison with others while honing our own mediumship abilities.

In many forms of mediumship, such as when performing a seance or a *misa,* a medium might allow a spirit to move or speak through their body. Similarly, within both traditional witchcraft and contemporary paganism, invocatory rites where spirits or deities temporarily inhabit the body to confer initiation or provide oracular insights are not uncommon. There are also many traditions, such as within African traditional and diasporic religions, where ritual possession often forms a central pillar of the ritual experience.

Invocation and possession are interrelated terms and should be understood as existing on a spectrum. On one end are shared experiences with spirits where they might inform our words, offer revelation during divination, aid us in automatic writing, or, more germane to this work, guide the hand of the witch when crafting the fetich or effigy. Milder forms of invocation may also include those found within the *Greek Magical Papyri,* where the magician often identifies themself with a deity or within the grimoire traditions, wherein the magician assumes the authority of God in order to command spirits.[39] More recently devised examples include practices such as the Assumption of God Forms found within Ceremonial Magic traditions, or the Wiccan rite of Drawing Down the Moon, where the priestess acts as a vessel for the goddess on Earth.

One of the primary ways that invoked authority plays a role within my practice of crafting enspirited objects is what I refer to as the *Transposition of Power.* During certain points of ritual, I will incorporate wording that transposes the source or power responsible for performing important ritual actions. For instance, "It is not my hands which craft this image, but the hands of the creator"[40] or "It is not by my breath you are born, but by the first exhalation which enlivened all the world." By such a transposition, the witch acts as a conduit for spirits and power so that they may, in turn, bestow blessings, curses, or life through ritual action. Of course, it is highly recommended that the witch has a solid foundational relationship with and understanding of the spirits/deities they wish to invoke in this manner.

Such a transposition can, by extension, also be employed to invoke association with the focus of a magical working. For instance, "you are no longer a poppet of wax, but the flesh, the sinew, muscle, bone, and blood

---

39 The Greek Magical Papyri (PGM) is a collection of ancient texts from Greco-Roman Egypt, dating from roughly the second century BCE to the fifth century CE, containing spells, rituals, and invocations drawn from Greek, Egyptian, and other Mediterranean traditions, offering a syncretic glimpse into ancient magical practice.

40 As there are spirits that I work with whose areas of influence are directly aligned with sculpture and creation, in my own practice, I would more likely invoke their name. Should the reader adopt this practice in their work, I encourage them to call upon spirits and deities relevant to their own craft and the action at hand.

of [name]." Essentially, invoking a connection to the spirit of the targeted person that some aspect of them might, in effect, inhabit the poppet for the duration of the magical actions enacted upon it. In the case of enspiriting an object, this may take a form such as: "You are no longer an object of stone, bone, and soil. But the body and dwelling place of [spirit]." Here we are again invoking a link between a spirit and the material.

On the far opposite end of this spectrum, trance possession may fully ensnare the sensorium and overpower the body. Placing an external spirit in control whilst the body's owner is either partially or fully unaware of what is transpiring. Often, after a full possession, the possessed individual (sometimes referred to as a mount or horse within spirit possessory traditions) has no recollection of the events that occurred and is, in essence, unconscious during possession. In traditions that have an established protocol for possession and create intentional ritual environments designed for it, these forms of possession are often desirable. During such possessions, the mount behaves and speaks as the spirit and may display feats and abilities they would not otherwise be capable of. Embodied through the vessel of the mount spirits or deities important to the tradition are able to offer counsel, healing, or blessings to the community.

My aim here is not to encourage the reader to seek out possessory experiences. Particularly if they have not yet established a solid foundation in spirit work and have no access to experienced elders to aid them in the development of such abilities. Instead, it is to encourage us to consider the myriad ways in which bodies, human or otherwise, may be moved, influenced, or inhabited by spirits.

Possession is the foundation of working with enspirited objects. This doesn't mean that the witch must experience possession to perform this work. Instead, it means that this kind of magic relies upon an understanding that when the conditions are correct, spirits can inhabit material forms (bodies). Holy idols, haunted dolls, ritual masks, shrines of devotion, and all manner of fetich objects are examples of this. Each may serve as a *locus,* dwelling place, and a body to be possessed by spirits.

There are spirits that attend or encourage the full spectrum of emotions and experience, such as pleasure, anger, desire, hunger, satisfaction, affection, and attraction. I imagine many of those reading this have on at least one occasion been swept away by love, overtaken by hunger, or blinded by rage. These experiences might even be understood as forms of temporary possession. We are not constantly in love or enraged; we do not permanently possess these experiences, nor do they permanently possess us, but rather they pass through us, or are conjured up by us. We are regularly in contact with spirits, whether we are paying attention to them or not. For the witch, there exists great importance in widening our perspectives, truly knowing ourselves, and developing an understanding of both how we are influenced by, and how we may influence, the realm of spirits.

On Spirit Communication and Divination

In addition to invocatory/possessory experiences, another primary approach to spirit communication in the embodied realm is the use of *divination*. The word *divination* arises from the Latin word *divinare,* literally meaning "to be inspired by a god".[41] Divination may take many forms, such as cartomancy, sortilege, dowsing, and scrying. From my perspective, all forms of divination involve some level of spirit communication and mediumship. Though most forms of divination can be applied to working with spirits, there are two approaches that I'd like to highlight here. Each of these is relatively easy to approach whilst providing a historically grounded foundation for developing your spirit communication abilities.

On Scrying

Scrying as a spirit communication technique dates back to our earliest histories. In its simplest form, it involves softly fixing the gaze upon a focal point and allowing images and information to appear to us. The form of scrying that most will be familiar with involves gazing into a crystal sphere. Another common form of scrying utilizes a black glass or obsidian mirror in place of the crystal ball. Scrying may also be accomplished with a standard mirror and includes the creation of a simple ritual chamber known as a psychomanteum.[42] In some cases, the images received appear within the mirror or crystal as though they are arising from within it. In

---

41 *Divination | Etymonline,* https://www.etymonline.com/word/divination

42 A small dimly lit ritual chamber lined in black cloth with a mirror which is used for conjuring spirits.

other cases, softly fixing the gaze upon an object can distract the conscious mind so that images and information are instead received by the inner eye, inner ear, or other psychic faculties.

In addition to the techniques of transvection and mediumship, scrying has been one of the primary methods through which spirit communication has historically been accomplished, which is why it is a valuable ability for the witch to develop and employ in this work. When scrying for spirit communication, the witch will usually utilize some form of ritual protocol, such as laying a compass, creating a magic circle, and wearing protective amulets or oils. The spirits are usually evoked into a specifically delineated space, and in many cases, the spirit will be conjured directly into a scrying device in order to communicate with it. In these instances, the scrying vessel becomes, at least temporarily, an enspirited object. Within my practice, I will usually place the scrying device within a Triangle of Arte for this purpose.[43]

Scrying may be accomplished through a great diversity of approaches, such as looking for images and spirit forms in rising incense smoke, staring into a campfire or candle flames, gazing upon the surface of water or ink, scrying the leaves of a windblown tree, or seeking images in the clouds. It is an approach towards spirit communication that both heightens mediumship abilities and benefits from developing them. As with most skills, the more energy invested in developing scrying and mediumship, the greater the reward and, in time, scrying can develop into a methodology that becomes less reliant upon external focal points. Instead, it becomes a conscious shift of focus and employs the scrying sight to peer into the Otherworld at will.

On Simplistic Divination

One form of divination I frequently employ in the work of making fetiches and formulas is much simpler. Though the tools and answers involved are quite simple, calling this form of divination "simple" is a bit of a misnomer. Primarily because it takes time and practice to develop the discernment needed to analyze this type of divination. This form of divination involves using a tool that provides clear yes/no/maybe answers.

43 More on the Triangle of Arte in Chapter Ten.

For this method of divination, I recommend the use of coins, cards, or dice.[44] To work with these for divination, you should cleanse your chosen tools and dedicate them to the specific spirit they are meant to act as a mouthpiece for.[45] In lieu of this, if you have a trusted familiar or patron spirit you work with, you could dedicate a tool to them and allow them to speak on behalf of the spirits you wish to question. Just bear in mind that this is now a bit like having an interpreter between yourself and another person whose language you don't speak. After your choice of tools have been prepared, they should not be used for any purpose other than to speak with the spirit they are dedicated to.

When performing this method, you will want to use either:

- Three of the same coins, I prefer antique mercury dimes for this, but any coins you like will work.
- Three dice
- Or a new pack of playing cards

With these methods, we are looking at *affirmative* and *negative* responses from the pieces used to create varying degrees of yes, no, and maybe.

- For Coins: Heads is affirmative, Tails is negative. Coins may be flipped or cast upon a cloth or a tray to give answers.
- For Dice: Odd-numbered dice are affirmative, even-numbered dice are negative. Dice may be tossed upon a table or in a tray for answers.[46]

---

44 Though pendulums and spirit boards fall into this category, I believe that the likelihood of the diviner's expectations influencing the outcome is often too strong.

45 For this, you should consider employing the *Simple Object Exorcism and Cleansing* exercise listed in Chapter Ten as a starting point before dedicating the divination tool to a spirit.

46 This may vary depending upon the diviner; some will read even numbers as affirmative and odds as negative. When in doubt, test the dice to see how they are speaking for you.

- For Playing Cards: Red cards are affirmative and black cards are negative. The face value of the card does not come into play here; we are just looking at the colors. For each question asked, you will draw three cards.

Each casting or draw will utilize three coins, three dice, or three cards to give us our answer. Below, I will use A to represent an affirmative response and N to indicate a negative.

There are four possible answers provided by this method:

1. A-A-A: All affirmative - A solid "YES" response.
2. A-A-N: Two affirmative and one negative - A "YES, BUT..." response. This response falls into the "maybe" category. It should be followed by further questions and casts to determine more clarity of meaning.
3. A-N-N: Two Negative, One Affirmative - A "NO, BUT..." response. This response also falls into the "maybe" category. It should be followed by further questions and casts to determine more clarity of meaning.
4. N-N-N: All Negative - A solid "NO" response.

While seeking your answers through this method, it is important that you are clear with your questions and that they are phrased so that they can be answered with a yes/no/maybe. This approach will often become a conversational form of divination with the spirit. Below, I will give an example of such a conversion, the falls that might occur, and the ways they might lead to further questions.

Querent: *"I am seeking assistance in finding a new job. Is this work you are willing to help me with?"*
Spirit: A-A-N - *Yes, but...*
Querent: *"Yes, but you will require payment of some kind?"*
Spirit: A-A-N - *Yes, but...*
Querent: *"Yes, but I will also need to do some magical work as well?"*
Spirit: A-A-A - *Yes*
Querent: *"Okay. Will doing a candle spell work?"*

Spirit: N-N-N - *No*
Querent: *"Would creating a fetich I can wear or carry be a better approach?"*
Spirit: A-A-A - *Yes*
Querent: *"And you will assist in the making of this fetich?"*
Spirit: A-A-A - *Yes*
Querent: *"Will this help me get the job at the airport I am interested in?"*
Spirit: A-N-N - *No, but…*
Querent: *"No, but it will help me find something which makes me more fulfilled?"*
Spirit: A-A-A - *Yes*
Querent: *"If I make the fetich as instructed and find a job that I like. Will an offering of seven candles, a glass of rum, and a selection of fruits be appropriate payment?"*
Spirit: A-A-N - *Yes, but…*
Querent: *"Yes, but you would like something in addition to this as payment?"*
Spirit: A-N-N - *No, but…*
Querent: *"No, but you would like a simple offering now before you begin the work?"*
Spirit: A-A-A - *Yes*
Querent: *"Will some incense and a candle burned near your spirit vessel do?"*
Spirit: A-N-N - *No, but…*
Querent: *"Would you prefer that I leave a simple offering of fruit at the base of a tree?"*
Spirit: A-A-A - *Yes*
Querent: *"Will you be able to help me find a new job within the next six weeks?"*
Spirit: A-A-A - *Yes*
Querent: *"Excellent! I will give the initial offering. Is there anything else you wish to communicate right now?"*
Spirit: A-A-N - *Yes, but…*
Querent: *"Is it that I should communicate with you later on the specifics of what should be included in the fetich?"*
Spirit: A-A-A - *Yes*
Querent: *"I will partner with you on this later. Are we good to conclude for now?"*
Spirit: A-A-A - *Yes*
Querent: *"Excellent! Thank you for your assistance with this."*

This is just an example of the kinds of questions we might ask and the ways we might phrase them, as well as the ways we might get clarity when presented with "maybe" answers. The result of this conversation is that we created a simple pact with the spirit, we worked out a time frame, we established what forms of reciprocity would be appropriate, and we have committed to work with the spirit to create a fetich which will assist in the work as well. Afterwards, the witch might either go into the Otherworld via transvection to meet with the spirit and have it provide guidance on making the fetich, or they might let intuition guide them into creating a basic structure for the ritual creation of the fetich and the various *materia* used before confirming with the spirit by asking more questions, such as:

Will this fetich be effective as planned?
Do I need to add anything?
Do I need to subtract anything?

This form of divination is highly adaptable and may be applied to many situations, such as getting to know a spirit better, confirming the meaning of visions and experiences in the Otherworld, allowing trusted familiar spirits to have a voice in more commonplace divinations, and spirit-assisted creation of magical workings and formulas. For many witches, a close and trusted familiar becomes one of their primary sources for counsel and teaching. Having a yes/no/maybe method of divination dedicated to that spirit allows us to more easily verify our intuition and mediumship and can be indispensable in the process of developing our spirit communication.

On Exercising Discernment

It is difficult to teach discernment as grappling with personal sovereignty, critical thinking, self-doubt, appeals to authority, establishing healthy boundaries, and the power of saying no are something developed largely within the nucleus of our own lived experience. With that in mind, I cannot promise discernment fully formed and gift-wrapped at the end of some paragraph here for you. Instead, I believe exploring together what discernment might *look like* for us when working with spirits is a much more worthy pursuit. In addition to all that we have previously explored,

I believe some simple bullet points here will help provide some guidance on forming spirit relationships:

- Embody personal sovereignty, stand within your power as a witch, and be clear on your motivations, your personal boundaries, and your expectations.
- Behave with integrity and honesty and require the same in return.
- Effective communication and negotiation skills are indispensable when working with spirits.
- Practice good spiritual hygiene. This means performing regular spiritual cleansings, banishings, and exorcisms as needed and employing appropriate protective measures when engaging with unknown spirits. This will be explored a bit later in this chapter.
- When encountering a spirit you are unfamiliar with, approach the relationship as you would a meeting with any new person. Trust and alliance shouldn't be immediately granted.
- Simply because a spirit tells you so, it doesn't make it so. Do not take everything a spirit claims as truth until they prove they are able to clearly communicate and that they are a trustworthy and reliable source on the areas discussed.
- Test your spirits. If a spirit claims to be able to provide results or information, test this out on a trial basis. Give the spirit smaller tasks related to its claims and test the results.
- When it comes to working with and making pacts with spirits, start small and build up your trust and the relationship as they prove themselves.
- Just as it is ill-advised to rush into serious commitments like becoming business or romantic partners with another human, the same is true of spirits. Do not overcommit yourself or make promises that you may regret later.
- Sometimes, a spirit relationship is just not a good fit. You might really want to work with a particular spirit, but that spirit may be disinterested in you or provide poor results. A spirit may show a particular interest in you, but it may prove to be unreliable, dishonest, or simply leave you feeling unsettled. It is okay to disengage from these exchanges.
- Spirit relations, as with any other, should be reciprocal. Neither party should be benefiting at the expense of the other. Though it should

be said here that things we might consider small, like burning a candle or leaving simple offerings, can be received as very meaningful gestures by many spirits.

- Do not fall victim to flattery. Just as there are humans who will tell you everything you wish to hear to falsely gain your trust or manipulate you, some spirits might do the same. If a spirit is always telling you what you wish to hear, it is likely that you are either fooling yourself in your interpretation of messages or you are being fooled by the spirit.
- Be clear in your communication of expectations and boundaries. If you are only temporarily employing a spirit for a particular purpose, be clear about the transactional nature of the exchange, what your desired result is, the time frame, and what payment will be given.
- The ideal is a relationship where the spirits you work with will be honest with you, occasionally tell you no, and will respectfully accept no as an answer from you when necessary. This is a sign of honest communication, solid negotiation, and healthy boundaries.
- When developing deeper relationships and more serious pacts with spirits, always leave room for the possibility that the relationship may need to end, or it might simply run its course. In preparation for such possibilities, it is wise to have a mutually agreed-upon action or ritual of severance that can be performed to officially end the relationship.[47]

As previously established, the possibilities for harm to befall the average person engaging with the Otherworld exist in fairly equal measure in the embodied world. Experienced witches and sorcerers, however, will possess a greater knowledge regarding the dangers of the Otherworld and have developed skill sets surrounding personal power and necessary protections. As a result, the potential dangers of spirit work are often lesser than those that practitioners might face in the embodied world.

---

47 In the case of enspirited objects, such a contingency and rite of severance will be discussed in later chapters.

On Cleansing, Protection, and Exorcisms

When beginning spirit work, the witch should have established protocols for both protection and spiritual hygiene. As we develop more in our magic, and particularly our mediumship, we are more likely to draw the attention of a host of curious spirits. Some may become excellent partners in our work, others may be slight nuisances, and occasionally some are outright bothersome or parasitic in nature. Having established protections and a solid understanding of banishing and exorcism work will minimize the likelihood that you will encounter serious problems with troublesome spirits.

Establishing protections can take the form of wearing protective amulets or placing them near the entryways of the home or ritual space. You may also call upon your protector spirits and create spirit vessels, which will stand as a protector for the home. Oils of protection may be used to dress thresholds and windowpanes to keep unwelcome spirits at bay, added to mop water, or added to baths along with other botanicals that stand as protectors of the witch.

Additionally, it is always good practice to perform spiritual cleansings on yourself and your space when regularly engaging with spirits and spirit flight. This helps to cast off any undesirable attachments or miasma we may have picked up from encounters with spirits and grants us greater clarity in our own magical work. In many cases, the lines between spiritual cleansing, protection, and exorcism are intermixed, as most rites of cleansing are, in essence, banishings and exorcisms. The most common forms of cleansing I tend to engage in are suffumigation and spiritual baths/washes.

Suffumigation is the use of incense smoke to lend a magical effect to a person, object, or location by the spiritual virtue of that which is burned. In this case, it is employed to cleanse a space or our bodies. *Spiritual baths/washes* also partner with the spiritual virtues of botanicals and other *materia*, but use water as the medium instead of the fire and air of suffumigation. The difference between a bath and a wash is that baths are primarily for our bodies, whereas a wash is applied to other surfaces and objects. Washes may be employed for mopping our floors, wiping down the doors and window frames of homes, cleaning furniture, and cleansing spiritual tools.[48]

When suffumigating or washing the home, it is best to work from the top floors to the bottom and from the back to the front of the house. It is always advisable to crack the windows a bit when suffumigating the home to allow the smoke and what it is removing to more easily exit the home. Similarly, when using a wash to treat floors or other areas of the home for cleansing, it is best to use a bucket and discard any leftover wash water off of your property. When suffumigating or bathing, we work from our head to our feet, allowing the smoke or water to clear away anything that doesn't serve our greatest good.

I also highly recommend that those engaging in this work develop their own ritual protocols and practices around protection, cleansing, and exorcism reflective of their craft, or adopt them from traditions they are in alignment with. This might look like employing visualization techniques, establishing deep relationships with protector spirits and calling upon their aid, reading exorcisms from favored grimoires, or inscribing sigils in the air with a ritual knife. There are a diversity of options available to the witch in these realms. With this in mind, there is a basic *Ritual of Exorcism* provided and also basic instructions in the appendices of this book for creating ritual space. Though it is recommended that the reader avail themselves of the recommended reading in this book and develop their own confidence and abilities in these realms outside of this book, the exercises given can serve as a starting point for spiritual cleansing and establishing protections prior to spirit work.

On Exchange, Negotiation, and Spirit Pacts

When hearing the word *pact* in relation to spirits, many people will immediately jump to ideas around selling their soul to the devil. Though this is a popular trope in horror films and does exist in certain corners of the occult, such pacts are far from the most prevalent that witches and spirits

---

48 Examples of suffumigations and washes are found in the *Formulary* section and there are also workings for creating a protective hexentach and sentry *maumet* in the *Selection of Workings* section.

engage in. When approaching the idea of spirit pacts, it helps to establish that, in its most basic form, a pact is simply an agreement made between two or more parties. A spirit pact may be a one-time, simple transactional agreement or a long-term agreement. Though a pact usually involves some form of payment or exchange, this is not always the case. Additionally, pacts may be implicitly or explicitly agreed upon.

An *explicit pact* is when there are clearly communicated and defined parameters around the agreement. When working with spirits, this might take the form of promising an offering of some kind as payment for a spirit's assistance with a particular task, such as providing protection or securing employment. If it is an ongoing relationship, you might agree to provide an offering weekly or monthly to both fortify the spirit and retain their assistance. In the case of an explicit pact, the agreement is usually spoken or written by the witch and affirmed through communication with the spirit.

That said, when beginning spirit work, there are still ways to form pacts if you do not yet feel comfortable with your spirit communication skills. This could look like asking your ancestors to assist you in finding a new job within the next month and then promising you will prepare a special meal of some of their favorite foods in exchange. In this case, though you may not have the benefit of knowing they have accepted the terms of the agreement, if the new job presents itself in the time frame, you can still give them the promised offering. Ideally, as you develop more in your spirit communications skillset, you should be able to engage in a two-way conversation and negotiation more easily. The above would be considered an *implicit pact.*

An *implicit* pact is one where the exchange is more situational and less directly communicated and agreed upon. For instance, in the case of a longtime romantic partner, though it may not be explicitly stated, there is usually an implicit agreement that you will each consider the other when making large decisions that affect you both. In the case of creating spirit vessels, there is an implicit agreement that as a maker or caretaker of an enspirited object, you will attend to its needs and keep it from harm.

In the case of long-term relationships with spirits, there tend to be many things that end up falling into the realm of implicit pacts or expectations. In my relationships with familiar spirits, this takes many forms. Even if we have not agreed upon a specific routine, I will often give them regular offerings as a sign of appreciation, which in turn fortifies them and strengthens our bond. Because I care about our relationship, there is an implied expectation that I will show care and consideration for the spirit. In return, a familiar spirit might show up during divinations to provide information, appear in a dream to issue a warning, or help bring sales to my business without a previously negotiated payment. Ongoing spirit relationships are much like any other long-term relationship where two parties have a vested interest in each other. There is usually an implied expectation of continued attention, care, and communication from both parties.

Healthy spirit relationships, just as any other, should be built upon mutual respect, trust, and communication. A part of this communication involves negotiation. Be clear in your expectations and verify that the spirit you are working with can and does agree to them. Don't offer what you cannot give. Don't promise a spirit that you will burn incense for it every day for the rest of your life unless you are incredibly certain you can uphold this agreement. Similarly, if a spirit requests that you provide an offering you are unable to afford, or an act of devotion you are uncomfortable fulfilling, tell it that! I have had spirits request expensive offerings or tools that weren't within my means, and my response in such cases has been a counteroffer. Say, for instance, that a spirit requests a $200 bottle of liquor as an offering. I might instead offer it a $30 bottle of liquor and ask if that will suffice, or better, tell it that if it helps me make an extra $400 in the next month, I'll happily buy it the liquor it requests.

Additionally, don't promise needlessly excessive offerings when a spirit might be happy with a candle and a glass of water. If I offer someone $3,000 to clean my house for a day, they'll almost certainly say yes. However, they may have happily done it for $300, I wouldn't know, though, because I started with a high offer. Begin with smaller offerings and build up from there. Negotiate until you are both comfortable and agree upon the terms. If the terms cannot be agreed upon, then move on. There may be other spirits you can work with or other avenues for achieving your desires. In the spirit realm, just as in the embodied realm, it is always best not to negotiate from a place of desperation or greed.

Just as one-sided relationships amongst humans tend not to last long, the same is true with spirits. If you are constantly asking for a spirit to assist you but are not giving the spirit proper engagement, attention, or offerings. That spirit is unlikely to continue providing you with quality results, to have your back, or to remain in the partnership you've built. In contrast, as witches, we should not throw good money after bad. Meaning that if you are consistently keeping up with your end of the partnership and a spirit fails to provide satisfactory results, it is important that you reassess or end the relationship.

In such cases, we should communicate with our spirits either through conjuration, transvection, or divination in order to determine why we are not seeing promised results. This might be a matter of patience, a matter of payment, a matter of circumstance, or a matter of a spirit simply not being able to provide what they agreed to. In any case, we should always use our discernment to determine if the relationship continues to be one that is still beneficial for all parties involved.

Spirits can vary wildly. Therefore, the things they ask for in exchange for their help will also vary quite a bit. In my experience, land spirits often respond well to offerings of tobacco, song, or stewardship and cleaning litter from the land. Many familiar spirits will be happy with a bit of cream, butter, honey, or bread in exchange for work well done. Others might prefer incense smoke, alcohol, or candles burnt for them. Some spirits might ask for a bit of the witch's own blood as payment.[49]

We will revisit the idea of offerings later on in the *Domestic Spirits* chapter. For now, I think it's best to once again emphasize the idea that, in any healthy relationship, both parties should have agency and a say in the terms of that relationship. If you find yourself in a situation where you are not receiving an equivalent return on your investment, feel uncomfortable, or feel you are being taken advantage of, it is best to either seek a remedy to the issue or terminate that relationship altogether.

PRAXIS: Creating a Formal Pact

In order to avoid situations where our spirit relationships are not what we hoped they would be, it can be helpful to create a formal written pact with spirits to establish clearly communicated and enforceable agreements when appropriate. This is particularly applicable when the agreements include long-term arrangements with a spirit or workings of greater risk or importance. This is essentially an enforceable contract with explicit terms

49 Though there is great historical precedent for such an exchange between the witch and their familiar, here the witch is heavily cautioned in making such an agreement without establishing a long-standing trust and considering all possible implications of such an offering.

spelled out. Creating a formal pact can sometimes be a helpful addition when creating spirit vessels to ensure that the nature of the relationship is very clear and agreed upon by both parties. A formal written pact should include the following:

Establishment of Authority and Enforcement
Under whose authority will this contract be enforced? This will vary for each witch, and often for each class of spirit worked with. For many witches, the authority invoked will be a patron deity or spirit who is more powerful than both the witch and the spirit in question. For example, a formal pact might be created and signed under the authority of Hekate, the Witches' Devil, or the Queen of Elphame.

Contracts with spirits beholden to planetary rulership may be created under the authority of a deity, an Olympic spirit, or the angel of that planet. Many spirits of the grimoire traditions fall within hierarchies enforced by the authority of higher spirits, angels, or 'God'. The guardian spirits of certain lands, such as the guardian of the forest or the cemetery, may serve as authorities over the spirits they oversee. And in cases when a spirit familiar is 'given' to the witch by another spirit, it is that gifting spirit who can be invoked as an authority to enforce the formal pact.

Payment
What does this spirit want in exchange for its work, and how often does it want it? Will there be some form of regular offering/engagement expected by the spirit? Will payment occur and be negotiated on a case-by-case basis? Or will it be a mixture of the two? Perhaps a monthly or yearly offering to maintain the relationship and additional offerings for specific workings? In many cases, the spirits I work with will receive a small token offering at the time of establishing a pact. This is then followed up with the agreed-upon payment after they fulfill the requested work.

Taboos and Boundaries
Are there any taboos established in this relationship? In some cases, spirits might ask you to refrain from certain foods or activities. This is not uncommon for those who have pacts with the faerie spirits. Spirits may wish for you not to use certain herbs or incense around them. They may be averse to certain types of magic, or they may wish only to be called upon in certain

locations or times of day. In some cases, they might even request that you avoid certain kinds of situations, relationships, or people. Again, you have agency, and just because something is requested doesn't mean it needs to be agreed to.

In contrast, you may have boundaries you wish to enforce, such as that spirits should not meddle with your personal relationships unless expressly requested of them. Or that they are only to congregate in certain areas of the home when others are around. Perhaps you prefer them not to appear in your dreams unless they need to convey emergency information. Or that they don't distract you while you are at your job. There are any number of things which may be requested by the witch or the spirit. These should all ideally be negotiated beforehand and then included in any formal pact.

Particularities on How the Work Should Be Done

If this contract is for a specific working, or a specific kind of work, you may wish to have clarity about the boundaries within which it will be accomplished. It is not uncommon to establish an agreement that the spirit does not intentionally harm anyone in the course of its work, or that it does not attack or expel any other spirits that the witch is working with unless it is specifically requested to do so.

For example, it would be wise when asking a spirit to assist you in finding a new job or new place to live that you specify that you wish to keep your current job or living situation until the new opportunity has been established and is secured. I have seen numerous people make such a request without a clarifier of this sort, only to find their lives upended, forcing them to make a change. Their spirits did have their best interests in mind, and in fact were often employing the most expeditious methods to enact the requested result.[25] In the end, most of the folks I've seen experience things like this ended up very happy with the final result and found much better jobs or living situations. Though I'm sure they would all agree they would have preferred a less dramatic and stressful transition.

Specificity of Result

Formal pacts are excellent and important for establishing clarity around an agreement. In order to do this, we should choose our words wisely. Not because all spirits are out to trick us, but because we want to ensure that both we and the spirit are crystal clear on the terms so that there is very little room for either party to be left unhappy. If you wish for prosperity, it is helpful to be clear on what you mean by that. Instead of just saying "I want money" it may be better to state that you wish for a spirit to help ensure that your bills are paid, that you have a reliable income at a job you like that provides comfort and fulfillment, and that it provides you with enough extra income to indulge in occasional luxury items and extravagant vacations.

When it comes to specificity, it is valuable to consider when it's helpful to be specific and when it may be a hindrance. For instance, I could ask a spirit to help me generate twenty new clients in a set time period. If it agrees, this could be a good test to see if the spirit can and will provide what it says it can deliver. Alternatively, by tying its action to a specific number, I might have limited the ways things unfold. Perhaps if I specified that I needed enough paying clients to provide stability for the next year the spirit might have been happy to assist me in generating fifty new clients and greater revenue. These are all valuable points to consider when forming our requests and our pacts.

Timing

Including a timeframe in your pacts is important. If you are contracting a spirit to assist you with a specific goal or project, say starting a business or writing a book, set a timeframe for the work. This should include considerations for when you would like to receive the agreed-upon results. Will you expect to see results within a month? A year? Additionally, you might include the length of the working relationship with the spirit. I have known witches who will create contracts anywhere from six months to a couple of years with a spirit in order to keep it on retainer with monthly offerings so that it might perform workings as requested. This kind of arrangement can be helpful when you are deciding if you'd like to create a more long-lasting or enduring relationship, such as taking a spirit on as a primary familiar or gifting it a dedicated shrine or elaborate spirit vessel in your home.

Establishing a Severance Clause

As mentioned earlier, if the arrangement is no longer one that serves both the witch and spirit, it is always good to be prepared and to have specified an agreement for terminating the pact and/or the relationship. This can be established as a specific ritual action, such as intentionally disassembling a spirit vessel and returning it to the Earth. Or it could be established that a small final offering be given to the spirit somewhere away from the home, that the witch verbally states aloud that the relationship is severed, and that the contract be destroyed in a ritual fire under the authority of the enforcing spirit mentioned earlier.

Such dramatic actions may not always be required. For instance, if the scenario is one where the spirit simply fails to provide the services it committed to. This is a breach of contract that nullifies the agreement. So long as this is spelled out in the written pact, you wouldn't be required to provide payment. In other cases, it may be a decision that, either due to your own reasons or life situations, you wish to end the pact. In these situations, it is always best to negotiate if any form of final payment/offering is required, respectfully thank the spirit for its efforts, and perform the agreed-upon rite of severance.

Though I have generally found that so long as honesty, respect, and communication are maintained, these things tend to go fairly smoothly. If a spirit seems resistant to ending the pact or relationship, call upon the enforcing spirit and/or other protector spirits to escort them off the premises if necessary. Follow up with any forms of spiritual cleansing, protections, or exorcisms you feel are appropriate. It is important to avoid entering into formal pacts with spirits that you do not have an established understanding of, and without having the ability to forcefully cut ties with if necessary

Completing the Formal Pact

Consider all of these points and include them within the written agreement. Feel free to rework it as many times as needed before formally signing it. You may wish to handwrite the pact in magical ink on fine parchment, or you might simply print it out on a sheet of paper.

At the top of the sheet, it should state something to the effect of *"As Witnessed and Enforced Under the Authority of [insert enforcing spirit/deity here]"*[50] and include any appropriate symbols or sigils associated with that enforcing authority. What should then follow is all of the information

50 This might be as simple as saying "The Witch's Devil" or "The Lineage of Witches Who Came Before Me". Where does your authority come from?

listed above. When the physical pact is created, you should establish ritual space as is appropriate to your practice. In some cases, you may wish to go to an appropriate location, such as a crossroad, the forest, or a cemetery, to perform the signing. You should call upon and conjure both the enforcing spirit and the spirit being pacted with. Once this is complete, you should verify through divination or other means that the spirit is in agreement with the contract as written.

When you are ready, the document may be signed by you and the spirit. In most cases, I have signed with both my legal name and any magical names I have. I have also included personal sigils made specifically for the purpose of signing pacts. On occasion, a pact might be signed by the witch by fully reading the pact aloud and then spitting upon their thumb, or pricking their thumb to draw blood, and then signing by stamping their thumb upon the paper. Using your spittle or blood in this way becomes both a mark of your word and ties you to the pact. This is usually reserved for more formal pacts like those establishing a relationship with a familiar spirit.[51]

The spirit's signature is often accomplished by receiving a sigil from the spirit via transvection/scrying/mediumship, which is then drawn upon the paper during which the witch should state aloud *"It is not my hand which signs, but the hand of [insert pacting spirit's name] as granted and witnessed under the eye and authority of [insert enforcing spirit's name.] The pact has been sealed."* Next, the pact should be signed in the same manner on behalf of the spirit that will stand as the authority and enforcer of the pact. The written pact should be dated, the spirits thanked and given license to depart, and the form kept safe as a material expression of the agreement. In some cases, a copy of the pact may be added in some form to a fetich or spirit vessel, though you should always keep the original for yourself. For an example of a written pact that you can use as a template for creating your own, please see the appendices section at the back of the book.

---

51 For more on the use of spittle see Chapter Eight and for some thought on the use of blood in this work see Chapter Twelve.

Recommended Additional Reading

Titles on Spirit Work:

Consorting With Spirits: Your Guide to Working with Invisible Allies by Jason Miller. Weiser Books, 2022.

Living Spirits: A Guide to Magic in a World of Spirits by BJ Swain. Independently Published, 2018.

Spirit Speak: Knowing and Understanding Spirit Guides, Ancestors, Ghosts, Angels, and the Divine by Ivo Dominguez, Jr., New Page Books, 2008.

Communing with the Spirits: The Magical Practice of Necromancy by Martin Coleman, 2005.

Spirit Allies: Meet Your Team from the Other Side by Christopher Penczak. Weiser Books, 2002.

Titles on Scrying and Psychic Development:

Through a Glass Darkly: The practice of Catoptromancy or divination by mirrors in Traditional Witchcraft by Oscar Tusk. Troy Books, 2024.

Scrying for Beginners: Tapping into the Supersensory Powers of Your Subconscious by Donald Tyson. Llewellyn Publications, 1998.

The Art of Black Mirror Scrying by Rosemary Ellen Guiley. Visionary Living, Inc, 2016.

Psychic Witch: A Metaphysical Guide to Meditation, Magick & Manifestation by Mat Auryn. Llewellyn Publications, 2020.

Titles on Spiritual Protection & Cleansing:

Spiritual Cleansing: A Handbook of Psychic Protection by Draja Mickaharic. Weiser Books, 1982.

Protection & Reversal Magick: A Witch's Defense Manual by Jason Miller. Weiser Books, 2023.

Traditional Magic Spells for Protection and Healing by Claude Lecouteux. Inner Traditions, 2017.

Part Two:
On Enspirited Objects

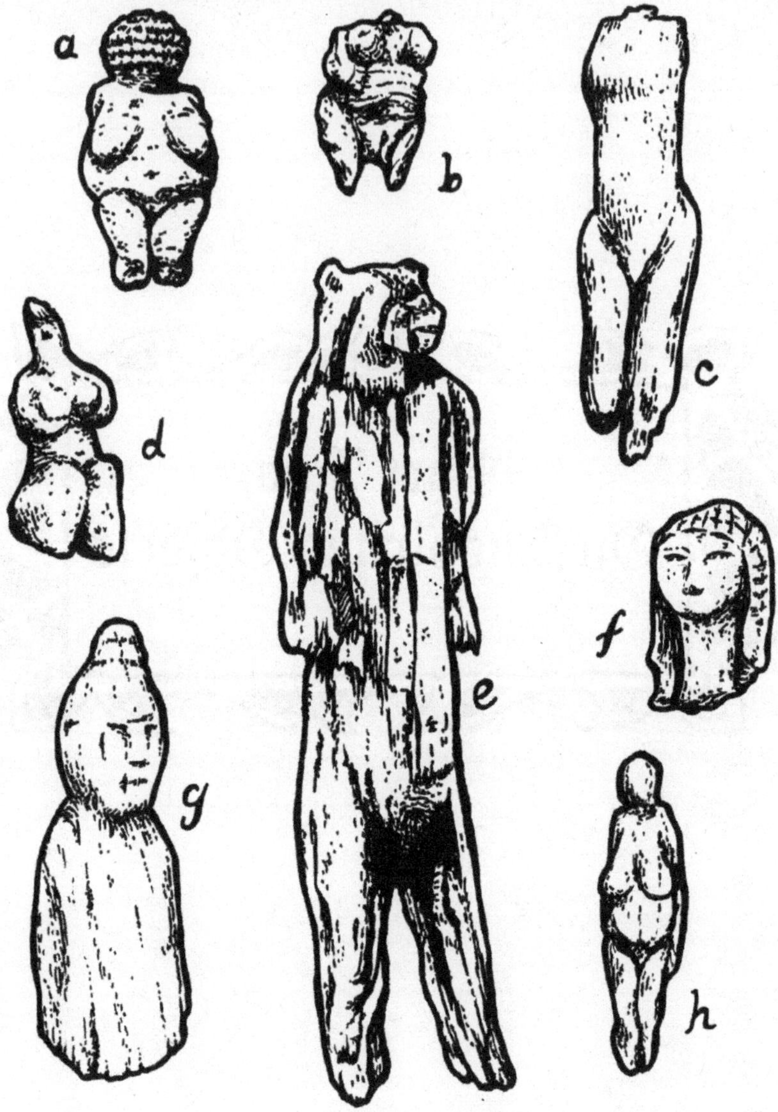

a. The Venus of Willendorf b. Venus of Hohle Fels c. Vénus impudique d. Mesopotamian fertility figurine e. Lion-man of Hohlensteine-Stadel f. Venus of Brassempouy g. Ancient American human effigy h. Avdeevo venus figurine

Chapter Six

Imitatio Dei: On Inspiration, Effigies, and Being Like Unto the Gods

A truly unique aspect of humanity is our drive towards inspired creation and our talent for transmuting the imaginal and conceptual into the material. We see this on a pragmatic level when creating tools and material solutions to assist with everyday challenges and tasks. But what of humanity's drive towards creative expression, ornamentation, symbolism, and allegory? What leads us to transform ephemeral ideas into objects, writing, music, and other forms of art. What is to be made from chasing the fleeting light of inspiration, and how might this relate to the work of the witch as crafter and conjurer?

Here, it is helpful to explore the often-overlooked origin of the term *inspiration*. Born from the Latin root words *in* (literally within) and *spirare* (meaning to breathe), in the most literal of senses, *inspire* refers to the breath and references inhalation specifically, but might also be extended to mean *breathing into, breathing upon,* or *being breathed into* by someone or something.[52]

In a more figurative sense, it assumes a much broader application, and the terms *inspire* and *inspiration* have been applied in reference to receiving the breath of life, the force which unites the immaterial spirit

52 *Inspiration* | *Etymonline,* https://www.etymonline.com/word/inspiration

to the physical form and animates things. This is demonstrated in the *Book of Genesis 2:7,* where it appears in Latin as "*formavit igitur Dominus Deus hominem de limo terrae et inspiravit in faciem eius spiraculum vitae et factus est homo in animam viventem*" (*Therefore the Lord God formed man from the clay of the earth and breathed into his face the breath of life, and man became a living soul*).

Our inspirations (breathing in) grant us life and agency in the material realm until our final expiration (breathing out) when the spirit departs our body. In some usage, inspiration becomes further understood as receiving the direct influence of the unseen or the divine. To be breathed into, whispered to, guided, invigorated, and empowered by the gods, the spirits, the Others. In this, each inhalation, from our first to our last, offers the witch a possibility for greater forms of creation, connection, and magic. To inhale is to receive life, vision, and spirit; to exhale is to gift the same unto the world.

In such a meditation lie greater revelations to be touched upon. On the nature of air, of words, of conjuration, incantation, charming, and of song. On speaking our magic forth into the world, and of the power of breath in the passing of life and spirit. In this examination, a consistent theme arises when we note that additional terms such as the Greek *pneuma,* the Latin term *spiritus,* and the previously mentioned *anima* all contain similar associations with breath and air, whilst also referring to spirits.

In addition to the pneumatic, airy, and conceptual natures associated with inspiration, greater illumination arrives when we examine some of the term's more incendiary associations. When we speak of becoming *inspired,* we often refer to the "spark" of inspiration, of having a "brilliant" or "bright" idea, and discussions around the act of becoming inspired commonly include such terms as being *ignited* towards action or having our passions *inflamed.*

Inspiration provides a potential, a possibility, a moment to be seized. It comes to the witch as a flickering firefly which we must chase after, claim, and tend to, or else watch as it flits away to alight the eager eyes of another. When we pursue the fire of inspiration with a witching gaze, we are led by a desire for the Others to create with and through us. To capture the fleeting, Luciferian spark of a falling star, tend to its care, and build for ourselves a brilliant Promethean fire from it. To find what might be illuminated, revealed, realized, reified, and born forth into the embodied realm by allowing ourselves to become inflamed by inspiration and foster the immaterial into the material. To be breathed into and through, letting our work be the bellows that feed the co-creative fires of inspiration that birth forth forms from the Otherworld into our own.

On Our Beginnings

It is difficult to trace the earliest examples of what we might classify as art crafted by human hands. As with most discussions related to art and archeology, it's a matter of vigorous debate. The oldest example we currently have of drawings from early humans is found in Blombos Cave, South Africa, and is dated to the Middle Stone Age. It is a simple series of lines, drawn in red ochre, and believed to be approximately 73,000 years old. Though this is impressive in its age and potential implications, it is simply the oldest *existing and discovered* example of an image created by human hands. Given the largely nomadic hunter-gatherer nature of early humans, it is more than reasonable to assume that we may have been creating images which were less easily preserved for quite some time prior.

There is evidence which suggests that earlier ancestors, *Homo erectus,* were carving and etching simple markings upon natural materials such as shells as much as 540,000 years ago.[53] As with many ancient markings, there is much debate around what intention and meaning we should ascribe to these acts of simple engraving. Through contemporary understandings of art and inspiration, we might view such artifacts as early examples of intentionally performed alteration and artistry. Perhaps they are echoes of an inspired desire to etch ourselves upon the embodied realm for the sake of expression, to quite literally make a mark upon the world and to proclaim I exist, I am, and I was.

On Effigies

Though enspirited objects appear in incredibly diverse forms, we'll begin here with an examination of this book's namesake: the Effigy. For the

53 Helen Thompson. "Zigzags on a Shell from Java Are the Oldest Human Engravings." *Smithsonian Magazine,* 2014, www.smithsonianmag.com/science-nature/oldest-engraving-shell-tools-zigzags-art-java-indonesia-humans

purposes of this work, an effigy should be understood as any sculptural representation of a human or humanoid form, with a particular emphasis here upon those intended for use in magical and spiritual practice.

Though we can't know for certain when we began creating sculptural forms in our own image, some believe we may have been doing so as much as 500,000 years ago. Two figures, the Venus of Tan-Tan (500-300K years old), and the Venus of Berekhat Ram (280K-250K years old) are interesting examples of potential effigies.[54] Both are small figures that appear to have been formed from pebbles that resemble the human form. Whether these pebbles were altered with the intention of making them appear more human or if they were simply naturally occurring forms that were collected by early hominids due to their similarity in appearance to humans is largely contested by archeologists.[55]

In contrast, the earliest undisputed intentionally crafted humanoid forms that we have encountered so far date to at least 40,000 years ago. The primary examples are the Löwenmensch (Lion Man) found in Hohlenstein-Stadel cave, mentioned in the first chapter of this book, and the Venus figure found in the Hohle Fels cave, both of which were discovered in what is now modern-day Germany.

Similar to the *Löwenmensch,* the Venus of Hohle Fels was carved of mammoth ivory. It is roughly 5cm tall and depicts the body of a woman with large breasts, hips, and buttocks, and much smaller appendages.[56] The figure is headless, with a small loop carved where the head would be, indicating that it was likely worn as a talisman or amulet. Within the same cave this Venus figure was located in, archaeologists found another lion/man hybrid carving, as well as remnants of several bone flutes which, to date, are the earliest examples of musical instruments we have encountered.

---

54 Robert G Bednarik. "A figurine from the African Acheulean." *Current Anthropology,* vol. 44, no. 3, (2003). 405–413.

55 Francesco D'Errico and April Nowell. "A new look at the Berekhat Ram Figurine: Implications for the origins of symbolism." *Cambridge Archaeological Journal,* vol. 10, no. 1, (2000). 123–167.

56 Nicholas J Conard. "A female figurine from the basal aurignacian of hohle fels cave in southwestern Germany." *Nature,* vol. 459, no. 7244, (2009). 248–252

It feels appropriate here to explore the prevalence of the sculptural forms, which are commonly referred to as "Venus" figures, and their continued presence throughout our history. Venus figures are smaller portable effigies that represent female bodies, often with exaggerated hips and breasts. There are some two hundred plus examples which have been found throughout the world and that date from between 40,000-10,000 years ago.[57] Though there is no absolute consensus on what purpose these figures were meant to serve, many believe them to be talismanic or devotional items tied to fertility, prosperity, and survival.

Some maintain that the prevalence of these figures indicates the possibility of a widespread prehistoric matriarchal religion. As there is little beyond the figures themselves to provide context, this is difficult to prove with certainty. Nevertheless, these diminutive sculptures, which have been carried throughout our history, exist as powerfully evocative enigmas that inspire both awe and curiosity around the recurrent motif of the feminine form in sculpture. With this in mind, it is unsurprising that more well-known examples, such as the Venus of Willendorf, have often been embraced by contemporary witches and pagans as representative of the Earth goddess. Within my own practice, I have worked with such Venus figures, employing them as idolic effigies to call upon the primeval divine creatrix and conjure forth crafters among our ancient ancestors, as well as to connect with the spirits of the land, the earth, and the clay.

These early examples of humanoid sculptures begin to point us toward something deeply embedded in our own nature: a desire to reflect and replicate ourselves through our own artistry in an act of *breathing back* into the Universe. In this case, they likely convey a desire to idealize an imprint of our human form upon idols and talismans of fecundity, beauty, and security that we might in turn be possessors of such things. Our prehistoric effigies once again illustrate the human urge to anthropomorphize the spirits, as well as the desire to craft bodies which might be offered up to them, so that they may be embodied, drawn nearer to us, and more presently into our lives. Merging the human and the Other, that we might give breath to them, and them to us in an atavistic embrace of both remembering and becoming.

---

57 Jessica Liew. "Venus Figurine." *World History Encyclopedia*, www.worldhistory.org (2017)

On the Crafting Gods

Our very earliest written myths contain preserved accounts of how human beings came to be fashioned from clay. In the Sumerian *Epic of Gilgamesh,* the goddess of creation, Aruru, creates Enkidu from clay. Though we are missing parts of the text, it is at least implied that all of humanity was created from clay and that upon death, we will return to clay. In other Sumerian and Babylonian myths, the mother goddess Ninhursag/Nintu creates humans from clay and the blood of the god We-Ilu, who willingly sacrifices himself to give them life. In variant myths, it is not Nintu, but her husband, the crafter god Enki/Ea, who fashions humans out of clay. Later, it is Marduk who is credited with creating the first humans with clay and the blood of Kingu, the slain consort of Tiamat.

In Egyptian mythology, the god Knum fashions each person from clay, after which his spouse, Heqet, the goddess of childbirth, gifts the breath of life to them. Similar myths from different periods in Egyptian history attributed the creation of humans from primordial clay to the god Ptah. In Greek mythology, the titan Prometheus is said to have crafted the first humans from a mixture of water and earth, which were then given the breath of life by Athena. In Chinese mythology, it was the mother goddess Nüwa who created humans from clay. Several origin stories from indigenous peoples of Turtle Island (North America) also tell of humanity being fashioned from mud or clay as well.

Yoruban stories tell us it is Obatala who skillfully sculpts each person from clay, giving them each their unique features. While the water and clay he chooses for sculpting each person informs which Orisha will likely own their head, river water belonging to Oshun, saltwater belonging to Yamaya, crossroads clay belonging to Elegba, clay from the mountain belongs to Obatala himself, etc. In this way, as beautifully stated by Jesse Hathaway-Diaz when discussing Obatala, we see a mythic expression of how "the materials employed during the process of creation influence the destiny of the person in their life here on Earth."[58] A point worthy of carrying with us as we begin our own work in the crafting of bodies for spirits.

58 Jesse Hathaway-Diaz, in discussion with author, March 2024.

The creation of humans from clay is equally present in Abrahamic traditions, wherein the name given to the first human Adam אָדָם is derived from the Hebrew אדם, implying *redness and blood,* and has further entomological links to the word Adamah אדמה, which means *earth.* This leads to an understanding of Adam's name, meaning both "man" and "red earth," an allusion to the substance he was formed from.[59] As we have seen, this motif of humanity originating from clay, fashioned by the gods in effigy and given the breath of life in order to animate it is shared by cultures across the globe.

Whether we began crafting human forms from clay because it is how the gods created us, or if it's the other way round, and instead our stories have deified the sacred magic of effigy crafters, is a question to which no definitive answer need be sought. Instead, I believe it provides greater nourishment and guidance to sit within such a paradox. Honoring both possibilities as equal in a way that informs and is reflective of the co-creative processes at play when crafting vessels of spirit.

On Our Crafting of Gods

Long before our stories of the gods were preserved in writing, we were crafting their forms from clay, stone, wood, and bone. Bringing them to life through the sculptural work of the hands, sanctifying their forms by our breath and invocatory incantations, that they might serve as a devotional *locus.* Our temples, churches, domestic shrines, and our museums are populated by bodies of artifice rendering ineffable deities and spirits into familiar, tangible, terrestrial, and humanoid forms.

Artistry is a mirror that echoes back an inspired understanding of our world. Again, a breathing of spirit back into the embodied realm. In essence, the work of the witch as effigy-maker is to materialize and anthropomorphize the spirits that we may be guided towards them and draw them nearer to us. Far from being a mirror of vanity, this work is both an act of devotion and an effective approach towards creating a bridge between ourselves and the Otherworld. The union of material art and the

59 *Adam | Ancient Hebrew Research Center,* https://www.ancient-hebrew.org/names/Adam.htm

magical arte of envisioning, engaging, and materializing the intangible. The result of which creates a metaphorical scrying mirror which allows us to conjure forth the other-than-human and, through our devotion, reify it into an embodied reflection, as something not so terribly unlike ourselves. The spirit envisioned in human form offers us eyes to witness us, a face to look upon, ears to hear our prayers and conjurations, hands to bestow blessings and aid us in our burdens, and feet to lay our offerings before.

As explored in the first part of this book, the overlay of forms and symbolism that we relate to and connect with is an integral part of the process of engaging spirits. Easily evidenced by the innumerable catalogs of spirits and deities bestowed with humanoid forms and characteristics. In short, the gods created us in their image, and we in turn have created them in ours.

On Holy Idols and Enspirited Effigies

The differentiation between what serves as a devotional idol versus what functions as the material embodiment of spiritual power is not so easily distinguished. At what point does a properly consecrated statue placed upon our altar cease to be only a representative icon of a spiritual force and instead transform into a physical storehouse that preserves and radiates that same influence and power? What we feed feeds us in return. With regular devotional practice and by ritually engaging with sacred icons as a spirit *locus,* such a transition is one that often occurs quite organically. Though there are various methods by which we might quicken this process, which will be explored later on. Let us first examine a small but relevant sampling of cross-cultural examples of effigies. Specifically, those crafted for the purpose of serving as active conduits for deities and spirits so that they might illuminate and inspire us in approaching this work.

Within Kemetic tradition, the statues of *netjeru*[60] intended to be housed within the temple were ritually prepared in a ceremony known as the *Opening of the Mouth.* As a result of this ritual process, the statue was transformed from a sculptural icon into an enspirited effigy. Within the magical processes performed upon the statue, the eyes and mouth would be symbolically opened in order to give life to the statue as a physical

60 Deities.

embodiment of the deity. As such, this granted the statue the ability to see, hear, and speak, as well as to directly receive offerings on behalf of the netjeru. Similar rituals were performed upon the funerary statues and mummies of pharaohs as a part of the ritual processes intended to transition them from earthly to divine status. Parallels to this ritual enlivening of religious icons can be found in ancient Sumeria as well.

Among the Kongo people of Central Africa, the making of *nkisi* presents an approach to spirit calling enacted through effigy/fetich crafting which is worthy of highlighting in relation to some of the themes present within this work. The term *nkisi* (plural *minkisi*) is of Kikongo origin and is often understood to mean "sacred medicine".[61] It is a term which is equally used to refer to both the spirits themselves and to the objects which act as reservoirs and transmitters of their power, medicine, and influence. Often, with little distinction or differentiation between spirit and object.

Though most will be familiar with the evocatively carved wooden figures studded with nails as examples of *minkisi,* the physical expressions of *minkisi* may take many forms outside of the figural. *Minkisi* might also be created as cloth bags, shells, or animal horns packed with various magical *materia* and intended to be carried on the person. European encounters with this form of African sorcery *heavily* informed early ideas around what constituted a fetich.[62] When *minkisi* are created as wooden effigies, they are often constructed for purposes of defense and protection and usually outfitted with a chamber in the stomach area that is loaded with various botanical, mineral, and animal *materia. Minkisi* may also have cloth bundles, horns, or other items containing magical *materia* affixed to the effigy in order to empower them.

The process by which *minkisi* are made is a formulaic one. The disparate material components that come together during the making of a *nkisi* are both links to the spiritual medicine represented by the *nkisi,* and the necessary elements required for its proper construction and empowerment. With each unique medicine lending its own virtues to the finished object. It is the skillful construction of spiritual medicines (*materia*), coupled with ritualized action, and singing to call forth the spirit, which collectively creates a *nkisi.* Note that here we see the coupling of ritual, *materia,* and the

---

61 *Nkisi* | *Brittanica,* www.britannica.com/art/nkisi

62 As well as later philosophical/psychological ideas around fetishism.

voice working to birth an enspirited object. Once a *nkisi* is completed it will be worked with, asked to provide protection or blessings, fed with offerings, and very much approached as the earthly expression of a spiritual being.

On The Effigy as Prayer

In cases where the faithful desires to provide a token of devotion or of a spiritual request, an effigy may be employed. Such items are more broadly known as votary figures and stretch back at least to ancient Sumeria where they were often made of clay or stone. These statues were usually depicted in a stance of devotion and were meant to represent, and function as an extension of, the person who left them. Votary figures would be placed within temples and sacred sites so that those who left them would receive the benefits of their devotion whilst they went about their daily work and responsibilities. Similar votary figures are found amongst the koros/kore statues of ancient Greece which were placed in temples and sanctuaries as offerings of devotion to the gods.

More recent examples of such can be found in the figural ex-votos left by Catholics at cathedrals and shrines of the sainted as tokens of prayerful request or given in gratitude of a prayer answered. These may represent a fully human form but are also made to resemble certain body parts which require healing: an ex-voto in the shape of lungs for respiratory concerns, in the shape of a heart for pulmonary illness or heartbreak, etc. Ex-votos have traditionally been made of wax, ceramic, or metal and may also take the form of animals or everyday objects that represent the nature of a request. Within Mexican Catholicism and folk traditions, these take the form of metal charms known as *milagros* (miracles) and often are affixed to statues of saints or carried as charms. It is this same general concept of prayerful request and offering that lends itself to the popular use of glass-encased votive candles employed in both religious devotion and magical practices. The terms *votary, ex-voto,* and *votive* all find their origin in the Latin *votivus* and relate to the fulfillment of a vow.[63]

63 *Votive | Etymonline,* https://www.etymonline.com/word/votive

On Dolls as Spirit Vessels

Though establishing a distinction between what qualifies as a doll, a statute, or a figurine is one we needn't trouble ourselves with too much in the course of this work, I would like to specifically highlight some examples of children's playthings as enspirited objects. For many children, playing with dolls, action figures, or stuffed animals becomes a very early exploration of animistic sensibilities. It is through such interaction, coupled with the imaginal capabilities of the child, that a doll occasionally becomes an active spirit vessel. Here we enter the territory of so-called "haunted dolls".

In many cases, when a child loves, cares for, and projects a personality upon a doll, this can, in effect, conjure that personhood as a spirit. This could be viewed as what some magical traditions refer to as a *thoughtform* or *servitor*. In some cases, long after the child has moved on from their relationship with the toy, it maintains an element of that personhood. In other cases, existing spirits who have an affinity towards protecting and comforting children and who respond well to their innocence and joy might take up residence within a doll or toy. Unsurprisingly, these sorts of occurrences crossover quite a bit with the territory of "imaginary friends".

Recalling our earlier discussion about a cultural fear of spirits, it is not surprising that when the average person encounters any sort of enspirited doll, their first response is often one of fear. There is an uncanny aspect to most children's dolls, which may become rather unsettling when people sense something peering back at them from behind those little glass eyes. Particularly in the current era of horror films, which frequently employ dolls as a trope for expressing the subversion of innocence to inspire both fear and unease. Though there are certainly very rare occasions where a doll might be inhabited by a spirit that is parasitic or harmful toward humans, this is generally the exception rather than the rule.

It is much more common that the spirit tethered to a forgotten or lost doll is simply confused and acting out in strange ways as a result. I have known several witches, including myself, who have worked with such dolls to either release the attached spirit and allow it to move on, or worked to acknowledge, calm, and comfort the spirit, and have eventually befriended it and successfully worked with it as a spirit ally. In many of these cases, when properly approached, these orphaned spirits are effective in helping cultivate laughter, joy, and creativity. That said, this is generally not the kind of work recommended to those who are quite new to working with spirits.

Within some spiritual traditions, children's dolls are the preferred vessel for certain spirits. For instance, though the Orisha Ibeji, who are the divine twins within Yoruban belief, are usually housed within wooden statues in African expressions of the religion, in the Afro-Cuban tradition of Lucumí, they are very commonly housed within two plastic baby dolls. The Ibeji are viewed and treated as children and are often credited with bringing good fortune and happiness. The baby dolls for the Ibeji are ritually prepared and washed in sacred herbs, fed, and dressed in appropriately colored clothing. Once they have been spiritually prepared, they become an embodiment of the Orisha. Similar forms of working with dolls are found within the adjacent Afro-Cuban mediumistic tradition of Espiritismo, where dolls are often employed for the housing of spirit guides.

Among the sorcerous traditions of Thailand, which present a wide array of beautiful and skillfully crafted animistic talismans and effigies, one may encounter the *Kuman Thong* or *Golden Child.* These are child spirits of those who were most often stillborn babies or died as a result of their mothers' passing. As a result, their spirits are full of potential and a desire to engage in and experience human life. They are commonly worked with to bring happiness, good fortune, and prosperity to those who care for them. When working with *Kuman Thong,* they are adopted by their caretaker, and often given toys or sweets as an offering.

In recent years, an incredibly popular variation of *Kuman Thong* has appeared in the form of the *Luuk Taep* (Angel Child). Like more traditional *Kuman Thong,* these spirits are conjured by a professional Thai sorcerer known as an *Ajarn* or *Luang Phor.* In the case of *Luuk Taep,* the spirits are housed within baby dolls. Some of which are incredibly costly and very much resemble a real human baby. In contrast to other *Kuman Thong,* the *Luuk Taep* does not usually contain any *prai*[64] and is viewed as a more "angelic" type of spirit. These baby dolls are treated very much like real children by many of their owners. Some of whom go so far as to provide them with babysitters or purchase seats for them on airplanes when traveling.[65]

---

64 Necromantic *materia.*

65 Jenx. *The Thai Occult.* (Timeless, 2018) 351

Within contemporary streams of traditional witchcraft, enspirited dolls may serve as a *locus* for ancestral spirits, they may house familiar spirits, or they may be the home of household spirits. Common examples of this are found in the House Hag, House Doll, or Kitchen Witch. These effigies, often crafted in the guise of a crone, house a spirit tasked with protecting the home as well as bringing good fortune and blessings. Such dolls are commonly kept in the kitchen or near the hearth. They are to be given regular offerings, kept informed about familial and household events, and approached for their assistance when needed. An example of such a doll is preserved in the collection of the Museum of Witchcraft in Boscastle, England.[66] In this case, the soot-soiled doll is referred to as a Chimney Doll, and it was found hidden away within the chimney of a cottage. According to the doll's recorded history, it was known as Mother Shipton[67] and previously served as the protector for a pub located in Bodmin.[68]

On Poppetry

When discussing the magic of effigies, most people's minds will immediately veer towards the work of poppets. A poppet is, quite simply put, a doll that is meant to be worked magically and represents a living human, or in some cases, an animal. Poppetry is a form of sympathetic image magic where what is enacted or imposed upon the symbolic form (the representation of a person) is meant to occur to that which is symbolized (the person themself).

The term poppet dates from the 1300s and was initially used to reference any small effigy, doll, or puppet. It later gained popularity as a term of endearment to refer to young children. In the vernacular of contemporary magic poppet has become embraced as a term broadly understood to imply a doll intended expressly for magic and ritual. It is generally preferred over the term "voodoo doll," which often carries the baggage of racist tropes and allusions to sensationalist horror movies. Considering that employing magical effigies to cause harm and sticking them with pins does not originate within, nor is it exclusive to voodoo/voudon, the term

66 Accession number 1465.

67 Named after the English seer and prophetess.

68 *Doll: Chimney Doll | Museum of Witchcraft & Magic,* www.museumofwitchcraftandmagic.co.uk/object/doll-chimney-doll/

is both insufficient and inaccurate for use within the broader context of effigy work. With this in mind, "poppet" serves our purposes here as a more appropriate and accurate term. Though it is worth bearing in mind that practitioners from within different traditions will have their own preferred and unique terms. For example, many hoodoo practitioners will refer to such effigies as "doll babies".

Poppets, as with any effigy, may be crafted from all manner of materials, take a myriad of forms, and be made for a wide range of purposes. Though we often think of them for works of hexing and causing harm, poppet magic works just as effectively in matters of healing, love, protection, fertility, and more. Poppets may serve well for binding a threat, influencing others, or performing prolonged and remote rituals of healing or cleansing. They may also be fashioned as representations of ourselves to stand in as a form of decoy against magical attacks, to act as a votary figure, as mentioned earlier, or even worked with to grant ourselves greater magical, physical, and cognitive abilities.

Some of the most prevalent examples of poppetry in the ancient world involve *execration figures;* effigies designed for cursing and inflicting pain or death upon an enemy. The remnants of such figures have commonly been found in archeological digs of Egyptian burial sites from the Old and Middle kingdoms. They usually take the form of sculpted clay figures with their hands bound behind their backs that may also have the name and identifying details of the target written upon them, along with a litany of curses. The figures would be ritually smashed to pieces or otherwise injured and destroyed in order to enact the curse upon its target. The remnants left among the dead with the intention that the target would soon join their ranks.

Similar figures from Ancient Greece were crafted from clay, wood, metal, or wax and known as *kolossoi.*[69] These figures often share similar postures to the Egyptian examples, with their hands or feet bound behind them. They may also have their heads or feet twisted backwards to incapacitate them and be bound with wire. The figure's eyes, ears, mouth, etc., are sometimes pierced with pins to capture and eliminate the target's ability to behave autonomously. The primary purpose of these sorts of figures was not for

69 A term often applied broadly to Greek effigies, but more commonly used in reference to figures employed in magic.

cursing, however, and was more often used for binding people, spirits, or even deities. They may be crafted to bind a potentially dangerous person, spirit, or the more harmful aspects of a deity. Or in some cases, created to bind a benevolent spirit or person to ensure they keep an oath or to keep them from leaving. These figures were often secured within boxes or clay jars to further contain them and were also sometimes buried amongst the dead, dropped into wells, or put into the walls of buildings.

Though I'm personally unable to imagine the dismissal of a person's autonomy as an acceptable expression of love, a working of historical interest known as the *Wondrous Spell for Binding a Lover* is found within the *Greek Magical Papyri* and follows a similar template to the above.[70] Two figures are crafted of wax. A female target is made in the form of a figure kneeling with her hands behind her back, and another figure made to represent the man wishing to subjugate her in the form of the god Ares, threatening her with a sword. Thirteen pins are used to pierce the figure's orifices, genitals, and extremities. In addition to this, a host of chthonic deities and spirits are summoned, and as a part of the greater ritual, a lead curse tablet is then made, which reads in part:

Let her be in love with me, NN whom she, NN bore.[71]
Let her not be had in a promiscuous way,
let her not be had in her ass, nor let her
do anything with another man for pleasure,
just with me alone, NN, so that she,
NN, be unable either to drink or eat, that
she not be contented, not be strong,
not have peace of mind, that she, NN,
not find sleep without me, NN, because I
adjure you by the name that causes fear and trembling,
the name at whose sound
the earth opens, the name at whose terrifying sound
the daimons are terrified, the name at whose sound rivers
and rocks burst asunder.[72]

70 *PGM IV.* 296-466

71 NN here indicates where a name is meant to be inserted.

72 Hans Dieter Betz, ed. *The Greek Magical Papyri.* (Chicago Univ. Press, 1986) 45

Another well-known example of this sort of figure closely mirrors the above instructions and is found within the collection of the Louvre. This example was donated to the museum and is said to have come from Egypt. It is a small clay figure depicting a woman with her hands and feet bound behind her back with pins piercing her. It is accompanied by a terracotta vessel that it had been placed within along with a lead curse tablet which has been inscribed with a strikingly similar spell to the one in the *Greek Magical Papyri.*

These workings from antiquity represent a form of "love none but me" binding magic which is as pernicious as it is persistent throughout the history of magic. Such workings designed to force the target (usually a woman) to be romantically/sexually involved with the person crafting the spell (usually a man), or else be tormented and tortured, are some of the more insidious forms of magic. Though the consistent appearance of such magical working throughout history is worthy of note, so too are their utter disregard for consent, perverse understanding of love, and their often-misogynistic perspective.

Though we have fewer material examples of waxen effigies preserved from the ancient world, there is no shortage of written attestations to the popularity of wax as a medium for sculptural images. In many cases, wax execration figures would be named for a target and then slowly melted over a fire to diminish their power or cause them to waste away and die. This method of working has been maintained throughout history and a version of it was said to have been performed by Agnes Sampson, a sixteenth century cunning woman accused of witchcraft during the North Berwick witch trials of Scotland. At the behest of a client, Agnes fashioned an effigy from yellow wax and conjured it by naming the target, and placed near the hearth fire to melt so that as it dwindled away "so should that man whose picture it was consume and pine away."[73]

On the Effigy of Healing and Exorcism

Less nefarious practices surrounding the surrogate effigy can be found in cases where a figure is crafted with the intent of healing the. An example

73 Emma Wilby. *Cunning-folk and Familiar Spirits: Shamanistic Visionary Traditions in Early Modern British Witchcraft and Magic.* (Sussex Academic Press, 2013).

of this can be found within the tradition for treating *xib'iril* or "soul loss" among the Kaqchikel Mayas. In instances when an individual cannot be physically present for this spiritual healing ceremony an effigy known as a *k'al k'u'x* is crafted to take their place. Personal belongings of the person are attached to an armature made of things such as sticks or a broom. This is dressed in worn and unwashed clothing from the person it will represent to link them with it. The *k'al k'u'x* then undergoes a ceremonial process which makes it an enspirited extension of the person. Once awakened in this way ceremonies for calling back the soul fragment may be performed upon the effigy so the patient may receive the ritual benefits without being physically present.[74]

Effigies may also serve in rituals of personal or collective purging and exorcism. An example of this is found throughout Christendom in the ritual burning of an effigy representing Judas Iscariot. These rituals usually occur as a part of Easter celebrations wherein an effigy representing Judas is hanged on Good Friday and then burned on Easter Sunday. In some cases, the effigy may be beaten, drowned, or blown up with fireworks as well. Through this act the community enacts a casting out and condemnation of the actions and influence associated with the individual represented, in this case Judas's betrayal of Jesus.

Such effigy burnings are not resigned to religious observation and are found throughout the world where political, religious, or historic figures are fashioned in effigy and destroyed through various acts of violence. In this manner, though the figure may be long dead or out of reach for the community, they may unburden themselves by enforcing a collective judgement upon the effigy as a surrogate.

These sorts of effigies needn't be resigned to representing only human beings but may be fashioned to act as the embodiment of spirits of illness or misfortune. Throughout Latin America exists the New Year custom of the *Año Viejo* or "Old Year" effigy. These effigies may have incredibly diverse appearances, sometimes appearing as an old man in the tradition of "Father Time," but they may also include references to politics, pop culture, or anything else that the crafter feels is representative of the troubles of the previous year. These effigies are often paraded through communities before

---

74 Servando Z Hinojosa. "Ritual Effigies and Corporeality in Kaqchikel Maya Soul Healing" *Ethnology 50,* no. 1 (2011) 79–94.

they are burned or blown up with fireworks at midnight on New Year's Eve. Such collective effigy rituals function as a form of social exorcism and provide a vehicle for catharsis while also, in the case of representations of living people, providing a warning to those whose sympathies might align with the target of the effigy.

On the Two Primary Forms of the Effigy

Here, we have covered only a small portion of humanity's incredibly rich spiritual and magical relationship with effigies. I highly encourage the dedicated seeker to peer more deeply into the vast and varied history of effigies and consider the many ways it may inform your own practice. To summarize, let's revisit the themes found throughout this chapter so that we might arrive at the two primary roles served by the effigy:

1. **As a Surrogate for an Embodied Being**

Here, examples such as the votary figure, the execration figure, and *k'al k'u'x* demonstrate the sort of sympathetic image magic that effigies are incredibly well suited to. In such cases, the effigy serves as an extension of the spirit of the person represented. In most cases, the effigy will undergo rituals designed to link it with the target. In some instances, this may take the form of naming, birthing, or baptism rituals, while in others, a portion of the individual's spirit may be ritually conjured and tethered to the effigy.

2. **As a Spirit Vessel or Body**

We possess a deep desire to give form to the formless and materialize the imaginal. Through the witch's art of the effigy, we provide an offering to spirits and gift them a tangible anchor for greater interaction and expression in the material. Creating a spirit vessel invites greater presence and agency for the spirit, allowing for ritual engagement through offerings and other acts of devotion.

Though there is often great overlap between these, it may be helpful to highlight the two primary ways a spirit vessel may be approached:

As a Physical Body and Anchor

Some effigies are regarded as a spirit's material body, meaning their condition directly affects the spirit. So, should the body be harmed or destroyed, the spirit will likewise be affected. In some cases, effigies may be employed to bind and restrict troublesome entities. In others, much like the witch engaging in transvection, spirits will have the freedom to come and go from the effigy in order to do their work. Through pacting and elements of ritual construction, we may establish boundaries and restrictions on how the spirit is tethered to a spirit vessel, as well as the implied consequences of altering or destroying the effigy.

This approach towards effigies is best applied when working with a spirit, such as a temporarily employed *maumet*, where the effigy will be ritually dismantled at the conclusion of the work. Or in cases where a trusted spirit requires/desires greater influence in the material, and we wish to have its influence regularly present. It may also be employed when working with untrustworthy spirits whom we might desire greater control over, should we need it. In such cases, an effigy may be ritually bound or destroyed should the spirit become unruly.

As a Locus for Spirit Work

More commonly, effigies act as ritual focal points serving as places our spirits may inhabit when called. This is especially relevant for spirits which exist in forms much greater than the scale of an effigy, such as deities or those who are otherwise already tied to physical locations, such as a river spirit. In this case the effigy acts as an anthropomorphized representation, facilitating personal engagement and devotion. Some effigies may be created with the intention that they are only inhabited when summoned, while others allow the spirit to come and go freely. This method is suitable for many spirits, including land spirits, plant spirits, deities, daemons, ancestors, and familiars.

Though the effigy may serve all the above purposes, it is far from the only possible methodology we might employ when creating enspirited objects. In the next chapter, we will begin exploring broader categories of spirit vessels and consider the ways they each might serve within our craft to strengthen our bonds with the Otherworld.

Recommended Additional Reading

Effigy: Of Graven Image and Holy Idol by Martin Duffy. Three Hands Press, 2015.

On Needles & Pins: A Witch's Book of Poppetry and Figure Magic by Kamden Cornell. Acorn, 2021.

Idolatry Restor'd: Witchcraft and the Imagining of Power by Daniel Shulke. Three Hands Press, 2023.

Astonishment & Power: The Eyes of Understanding: Kongo Minkisi / The Art of Renee Stout by Wyatt MacGaffey, Michael D. Harris, et al. Smithsonian, 1993.

Shaping the World: Sculpture from Prehistory to Now by Antony Gormley and Martin Gayford. Thames & Hudson, 2020.

Chapter Seven

Where My Beloved Dwells: On Spirit Vessels and Fetiches

The humanoid form of the effigy represents only one of the incredibly diverse forms a spirit vessel may take. Though this type of witchery does often involve working with boxes, bags, and bottles, the term *spirit vessel* refers to any object that houses a spirit and needn't be an actual container or vessel. A spirit vessel may act as a body/home to fortify and protect the spirits we have conjured into it or as a prison for binding or trapping harmful spirits.

On the Fetich

Much like the term *animism,* the history and usage of the term *fetich* is one that is multilayered and not without its problems. Before we explore the term's broader origins and implications, I first wish to define it as it is applied within this book. Within the context of this work, a fetich should be understood as a portable material object meant to serve as a spirit vessel and object of magical power. Though the term may occasionally be applied to singular objects such as a root, stone, or animal paw, in its most proper usage, a fetich should be understood as a fabrication created from an assemblage of materials.[75] Though there are exceptions, the fetich is

75 Wyatt MacGaffey. "Fetishism Revisited: Kongo Nkisi in Sociological Perspective." *Africa: Journal of the International African Institute* 47, no. 2 (1977) 172–84.

commonly an object intended to be carried or worn on a person so that they may benefit from its influence. Such an action may be viewed as an augmentation of one's own spirit(s). As we are in essence, bringing the fetich and its associated spirit/power within the spiritual ecosphere of our body.

Though throughout this work fetich is often used to denote any enspirited objects that do not fall into the category of effigy or shrine, a fetich is not defined by its form but by its function. The fetich is distinguished from icons and idols in that its purpose is less related to devotion or worship. Instead, its existence is centered upon creating a particular result, such as healing, protection, empowerment, or prosperity in partnership with its indwelling spirit. Such objects are not simply magically powerful, but more specifically house a spirit that acts on our behalf. Though there are wider applications, by their nature fetiches lend themselves very well to the crafting of *maumet* spirits.

The term fetich finds its early origins in the Latin term *facticius,* meaning something made by art or something artificial/fabricated. From this is derived the Portuguese word *feitiço,* which was understood to mean a charm, bewitchment, or sorcery. A similarly derived term is found in the Spanish word *hechizo.* Again, we find a connection here that ties the crafting of objects directly with the concept of witchcraft and sorcery. As a result, practitioners of witchcraft and sorcery, particularly those who craft or bewitch objects, were often referred to as a *feiticeira/feiticeiro* or *hechicera/hechicero* in Portuguese and Spanish, respectively.[76]

When Portuguese sailors began arriving along the West Coast of Africa during the sixteenth to seventeenth century, this term became pidginized as *fetisso* and was heavily applied to the crafting of *minkisi* by Kongo people. The term was adopted into French as *fétiche* and English as fetich/fetish and was largely popularized by people such as the French historian Charles de Brosses and the English anthropologist Sir Edward Burnett Tylor, who we mentioned in Chapter One. As is common in cases when an imperialist power grafts its own vocabularies and worldviews upon indigenous practices, early anthropologists' use of the term fetish

76 Given here with their feminine/masculine forms.

in explaining the *minkisi* of indigenous Africans often exhibited a lack of understanding for the metaphysics and cultural role of these practices. Unsurprisingly, Tylor and other anthropologists of his generation regarded such practices as primitive animism and therefore as lesser expressions of spirituality than their own. In time, the term became more broadly applied to many indigenous traditions throughout the world.

From here, the terms fetish and fetishization become stretched further in meaning and associated with concepts more distant from their origin. Particularly, the use of fetishization as introduced by Freud within the realm of psychology and sexuality, or within Marxist philosophy and economic thought. To more broadly explore the incredibly complex and often challenging history of the term fetish goes well outside the scope of this work.[77] Suffice to say that the spelling of fetich here intentionally employs an archaic form of the word fetish in an effort to more clearly establish our use of the word here in relation to enspirited objects and differentiate it from philosophical or psychological applications of the term.

On Magical Materia

I have already mentioned the idea of magical *materia* several times throughout this book, and we will spend more time exploring diverse forms of magical *materia* and how to work with them in a later chapter. Before moving on, though, I want to more thoroughly establish what is meant by this term. In general, *materia* refers to matter or the material components from which a thing is constructed or compiled. Within this work, it primarily refers to the *materia magica* we employ in crafting spirit vessels. This includes all of the botanical, mineral, animal, and other elements that we recognize as being magically active and spiritually powerful allies within our rituals and spellwork. This can also extend to include the formulas, oils, powders, candles, etc. that we are employing in our craft. In the case of creating effigies and fetiches, it may refer to all of the materials we have worked with to craft the final object, so long as we are engaged with their indwelling spirits, magical virtues, or symbolism.

---

77 For those interested in such an exploration, I recommend *The Problem of the Fetish* by William Pietz.

On Spirit Pots and Container Spells

The use of bottles, boxes, pots, and other containers as spirit vessels appears almost as often as the use of effigies. Tales abound of Djinn spirits kept within lamps and other vessels. Within Afro-Cuban Lucumí and similar traditions, the stones and tools that become the material form of the Orisha are housed within urns, *soperas,* or other vessels that become a part of that spirit's house by extension. In Kongo-derived traditions like Palo and Quimbanda, spirit vessels, such as cauldrons or terracotta bowls, house spirits through the use of various dirts and animal, plant, mineral, and necromantic *materia,* echoing the making of Nkisi. Similarly, in traditional witchcraft, familiar spirits often dwell in pots, bottles, boxes, or baskets lined with wool, sometimes filled with stones, bones, or left empty. These vessels are not merely containers but physical embodiments of the spirit, requiring ongoing care, protection, and attention to keep the spirit fortified and effective.

In recent years, bottle and container spells seem to have become increasingly popular, and books have been devoted exclusively to the topic. Unfortunately, in many popular approaches, there is often little to no discussion of the conjuration of *materia* or of approaching such workings as a form of spirit vessel. To the animist witch, however, all bottle spells essentially serve the purpose of containing spirits.

This is sometimes done to capture aspects of a living person to exert influence upon them for good or ill. In conjure traditions of the American South, this is seen in sweetening and souring jars, where personal taglocks (hair, nails, photos) are combined with sweet substances like sugar or honey, or sour ones like vinegar and alum, alongside relevant botanicals and other *materia.* In these workings, the awakened spirits of the ingredients act upon the spirit of the individual bound to the jar. A key advantage to such container spells is the vessel's portability, allowing it to be actively worked through prayer, agitation, and shaking, or by burning candles atop it. This approach of binding a target's spirit through taglocks and creating influence through allied *materia* can be adapted by the witch for diverse workings of blessing or bane.

On Witch Bottles and Spirit Traps

The results of malefic magic can be devastating. Many who have feared that their neighbors might be passively casting the evil eye, or more actively cursing them, have turned to the witch bottle as a measure to protect themselves and fight back. In this case, the use of the term "witch" is not intended as an identifier for the bottle's maker, but for its target—a witch who has cast malefic magics. Though this aspect of witch bottles tends to be overlooked by many modern practitioners, the historical witch bottle is, in essence, a form of spirit trap which functions on the basis of contagion. The purpose of these bottles was primarily to contain and cause harm to a part of the spirit of the witch who worked magic against the person for whom the bottle was made.

Witch bottles were a popular apotropaic magic throughout the Early Modern period and are still employed today. Though they take many forms, they are most commonly identified by three recurrent elements:

- Being crafted from a bottle or sealable vessel.
- The inclusion of urine from the afflicted.
- The inclusion of some sort of iron objects, such as nails or pins, and other sharp objects, such as broken glass.[78]

The concept here is that the urine of the afflicted person or animal will carry some link to the witch who is causing harm. In a similar way that our urine expels toxins from the blood, it also expels some of the spiritual poisons linked to the witch, affecting the person who has been under their attacks. As a result, causing harm to the urine can, in turn, cause harm to the witch.

In practice, this often took the form of the victim's urine being heated or boiled, having red-hot iron plunged into it, or being stopped up in a bottle along with sharp objects and iron to torment the witch. Some witch bottles would be worked by placing the urine/iron-filled vessel upon a fire until it exploded. There are quite a few folktales and testimonies of people having done just that, only to find that a suspected culprit suffered burns or died as a result of the working.

78 Daniel Harms. Witch bottles: History, Culture, Magic. (Avalonia, 2022).

Witch bottles may also be buried in one's yard or bricked up inside of a chimney so that they are regularly being exposed to heat as a preemptive measure against possible attack. In crafting a witch bottle, any vessel of appropriate size will likely suffice. Several historical examples have been found made from glass bottles. However, most examples of witch bottles that we have in the archeological record are made from Bellarmine/Bartmann jugs.

Bellarmine jugs originated in Germany and were made of thick, durable stoneware that was salt-glazed. The jugs were often decorated on their neck with the grimacing face of a bearded man. They were quite popular throughout the sixteenth and seventeenth centuries for the storage and transportation of liquids, particularly wine and other alcoholic beverages. As a result of their availability and distribution, they have been found throughout Europe and the Americas, and many examples of their use for witch bottles exist. It is believed that these were so commonly employed for this work because of their durability, and that the frightening faces found upon them served as a form of grotesque,[79] which contributed to the bottle's apotropaic function.

In other cases where an individual feels they may be plagued by malicious or parasitic spirits, bottles may be fashioned into quite effective spirit traps. The essential design of a spirit trap usually includes elements that will capture a spirit's attention as well as items that will cause it to remain imprisoned within the bottle. For instance, many spirit traps will have an element intended to draw a spirit in, such as items it may feed on or become transfixed by. For this purpose, some contain bits of multicolored glass or a large number of seeds or pebbles. This is based upon spirit lore that attests to spirits being attracted by colorful glass items, such as the Witch Balls hung in windows throughout New England. As well as stories found throughout Europe and the Americas that attest that, when encountering a large number of small granular objects (seeds, pebbles, beads, grains of sand, etc.) nocturnal spirits as diverse as vampires, boo hags, and werewolf creatures such as the *rougarou* will be stopped and must count them before entering a home. They are believed to regularly lose count and become distracted, leading them to never finish, forcing

79 An ugly or distorted face or image often believed to frighten away harmful spirits.

them to either leave or become destroyed when the sun rises. In some cases, these items have been scattered upon the threshold or windowsills of the home. However, in the case of a spirit trap, they are placed within a bottle which is kept by a door or window.

Spirit traps may also include elements meant to confuse and tangle up a spirit so that it cannot escape the bottle. In some cases, this may be knotted up, tangled, or multicolored bits of thread. Mirrors and other reflective materials may be placed within or around the bottle, as many spirits are said to become transfixed or confused by these items. Botanicals known for tripping up or binding spirits, such as Devil's Shoestring (*Viburnum sp.*) or Bindweed (*Convolvulus sp.),* may also be employed in these vessels.

Occasionally, spirit traps may contain nothing at all. An example of this is found in the bottle trees popular throughout the Southern United States. Bottle trees largely emerged from African American spiritual traditions and consist of a tree that has had colorful glass bottles placed onto it by feeding the tree branches into the mouth of the bottle. Over time, as this inhibits leaf growth, this usually leads to the death of the tree. The bottles are usually a single color, the most traditional being blue. The belief being that during the night, any haints, hags, or other malicious entities will be drawn into the bottles, captured and destroyed by the morning sun.

In cases where a spirit trap is inside the home near a window or door, so long as it receives sunlight in the morning, it will be cleansed of its inhabitants. In place of, or in addition to this, some folks will take the bottle outside of the home and expose it to the sun more directly. Though these traps may be used fairly indefinitely, I have known a few witches who prefer to create a new one each year and discard the old one by burying it in the woods or a cemetery away from their home.

Spirit traps may also be created by intentionally conjuring a spirit into a vessel and capturing it within. These may be fashioned in some of the manners above; however, they can be quite diverse and, at the witch's discretion, additional elements may be included. This could include the use of a lodestone, washing the vessel with appropriate herbs, or adding other items allied to the spirit we wish to draw into it. When creating a spirit trap meant for the long-term binding of a spirit, if a bottle or vessel is clear, I personally prefer to wrap it in black cloth or paint it black so that no light may enter. This type of trap is used for imprisoning a spirit in order to keep it from doing harm, or for capturing ambient, unknown spirits who may be drawn to the witch. Such traps may be employed as a temporary holding cell so we might interrogate a spirit and determine whether it should stay bound to the vessel, released, exorcised, or possibly even partnered with. Within the Solomonic grimoire tradition, we see a somewhat similar example of this in the brazen vessel employed by the magician for the keeping of spirits.

On Spirit Crafting and Conjured Bags

The gathering of spiritually significant *materia* and medicines within portable bags and bundles is found within many traditions. Within my craft, such bundles function as a fetich that houses its own unique spirit. I often refer to these as *Hexentaschen,*[80] or simply *Witch Bags.* When crafting a *hexentache,* the material used for the bag itself will be dressed with tinctures, oils, or perfumes to further empower it and align it to its purpose. I will also draw or paint appropriate sigils and seals upon the bag. This approach towards creating enspirited bags was passed on to me by one of my teachers in the craft, and instructions can be found later in this work for the crafting of such a witch bag for protection.

A somewhat comparable practice is found in Hoodoo and Southern Conjure, with varying degrees of explicit animism. As I was taught by my elders in those traditions, each conjure bag[81] houses a unique spirit. When we craft the bag, the spirit of each element we are adding is "woken up". Once all of the various elements that make up the bag are added, we will conjure the spirit of the bag as a whole. The spirit is often given a name by the conjuror and then periodically "fed" with oils, perfumes, alcohol, incense, or cigar smoke to keep them strong and working. In essence, the conjure bag is a spirit that is constructed through the act of crafting its material form.[82]

---

80 This is a German word which translates to witch bags. The singular form is *hexentache.*

81 Also commonly referred to as a mojo hand, gris gris, *wanja,* or in some cases a toby/tobie depending upon regional variations.

82 This approach towards crafting conjure bags displays a continuity of spirit construction techniques, such as the making of *nkisi* found within the West African traditions from which Hoodoo arises.

Though *maumet* isn't a term applicable in Southern Conjure or Hoodoo, constructing new spirits through conjuring and joining together the spirits of disparate magical *materia* as displayed in the above hexentashen and conjure bags is essentially comparable and equivalent to the process of creating the *maumet spirits* mentioned earlier.

On the Spirit of Masks

From their earliest origins, masks have been associated with spirit work. Our oldest known examples of masks are from roughly nine thousand years ago during the Neolithic period and were carved from stone. Eleven such examples were unearthed near Jerusalem, and they are believed to represent ancestral spirits. Though it is uncertain if these masks were ever worn by people, it is believed they may have been hung upon poles during ceremonies meant to honor the dead.

Masks interweave the realms of spirit vessels, ritual apparel, and spirit possession. The hollowness of the mask demands that it be filled, and this role may be taken on by the spirit it represents, the witch, or both simultaneously. As devotional objects and spirit vessels, masks may be hung above altars and placed within shrines. And many life-sized effigies have been fashioned from makeshift armatures, stuffed clothing, and a mask serving as its face. For instance, the Guatemalan folk saint Maximón is often depicted in this manner and then decorated with strips of colorful fabric.

The god Dionysus was often depicted quite simply by a mask hung upon a pole. And the implications of choosing a mask to depict a god associated with the subversions of social norms, diminished inhibition, and liberation, should not be lost on the reader. Within the act of masking, we are taking off one face and putting on another. By obfuscating our identity with the anonymity afforded by the mask, we are released from many societal expectations and the confines of the persona we have crafted for ourselves. Instead, we are invited to embody and be embodied by that which is personified by the mask.

Ritually enspirited masks provide the opportunity for a palpable union which naturally encourages various levels of spirit possession. This is the realm where ritual, theater, and possessory spirit work reach a collective pinnacle and afford an opportunity for powerfully transformative magics. This is the role that masks have played within broader cultural contexts throughout our history. The ability to "put on" a spirit allows our own sense of self to drift into the background and instead invites the spirit of the mask to step forth and work through us. To move, to dance, to speak, and to sing. The masked ritualist becomes the spirit-embodied and may provide oracular revelation, give blessings to the community, conjure the dead, or act as a representative of illness or misfortune to be punished and chased away.

Enspirited masks may be sculpted from sacred wood or incorporate various botanical and animal elements into their composition to lend their power. I often sculpt masks from clay embedded with powdered botanicals, dirts, and ashes. Alternatively, a fetich bundle or bag may be affixed within the mask to act as its central *locus* of power. In some cases, the mask will never be worn and is solely intended as a spirit vessel in the form of a visage.

The crafting of masks and the art of masking are aspects of ritual and magical practice too often overlooked by many practitioners. In wearing ritual masks, we are in mutual exchange with our spirits, wearing each other and dancing within the same space in a form of intimate communion that is transformative beyond the scope of the rite itself. Whether the spirit provides blessings of protection, healing, charisma, or wisdom, through the work of the mask, we are directly empowered by these very blessings. I must attest that I find the mask to be a terribly appropriate choice for the depiction of spirits and gods, as all images we craft for the spirits are, in truth, only masks they might inhabit.

On The Use of Skulls

The skull stands as the crucible of spiritual transmutation. Though theories of consciousness and multiple soul models can vary, our heads are the part of our bodies that most people align with the concepts of mind, spirit, and identity. This ties a bit into our previous topic as our skull provides the structure for each of our unique faces. The masks of flesh, which become synonymous in many ways with how we define and, quite literally, express ourselves. As well as how we are recognized and perceived by others. The skull of each creature is, by its very nature, a spirit vessel that may be worked with in a post-mortem extension of that role.

Skulls have been worked in this way since at least the Neolithic period. Artifact skulls dating from eight to ten thousand years ago have been found throughout the ancient Levant, with a high concentration being found in the city of Jericho in Palestine. These skulls were covered in a form of plaster, which was sculpted into crude faces. In some examples, the plaster was used to plug up the eye sockets of the skulls, which would then have seashells such as cowries inserted in place of eyes. Remnants of pigments have been found on many of these plastered skulls, suggesting that they were further decorated and treated as sacred objects. Though we cannot say with certainty what role these skulls served, considering that they were not interred at the time of death, they likely functioned as a form of spirit vessel used for the honoring of ancestral spirits.

Similar use of skulls can be found among the Asmat people of New Guinea, who have been known to preserve and decorate the skulls of both ancestors and conquered enemies. In the case of enemies, the skulls are worked with as a method for absorbing power and enslaving the spirit of the conquered. This use of skulls to put spirits to work, either willingly or otherwise, is one echoed in diverse necromantic traditions throughout the world.

In the case of traditional craft, the skull is primarily worked with in one of two ways. Firstly, we may work with the spirit that the skull belonged to in life. Generally, this is a mutually beneficial partnership where the spirit functions as a sort of familiar to the witch and receives attention and offerings in return. Such spirits may work in a diversity of ways, from protection to aiding in divination. All of which is dependent upon the knowledge base and skill set of the spirit, as well as the type of work it is willing to do.

I should note that I am absolutely not advocating for grave robbing here. Instead, many industrious witches may find themselves in possession of a human skull by perfectly legal means. Though it is highly recommended that each witch does proper research into the sourcing of such skulls to determine if it aligns with their ethics, and that they understand applicable laws regarding the possession of human remains in their location.

This work requires the witch to employ methods of divination, mediumship, or conjuration to determine if there is still a spirit attached to the skull, and if so, who that spirit is, what they desire to be called, and the nature of what, if any, work you may be able to do together. For instance, I am the caretaker of a female skull. A part of our work is that she helps mediate other spirits within the ritual space and particularly works as a sort of guardian against any intrusive spirits of the dead. She often plays the role of "holding" spirits of the dead and allowing them to speak through her when they are conjured. She also assists in removing any unruly or hungry shades that might appear during necromantic works. She is given a place of honor in the ritual space and offerings when appropriate.

The second manner of working with skulls, as touched upon above, involves employing them as a vessel for the temporary or permanent housing of spirits other than the one who owned the skull in life. Most appropriately, this applies to spirits of the dead, though not exclusively. This is incredibly common within traditional craft, and skulls are often worked with as a vessel for calling upon ancestral spirits and spirits of craft lineage. An excellent example of this can be found in a working presented by Doreen Valiente and Evan John Jones in *Witchcraft: A Tradition Renewed*, wherein a human skull is exorcised of all previous spirits and then a new spirit with craft lineage is invited to inhabit the skull. This spirit then serves as a sort of familiar to the coven who is working with it.[83]

Alternatively, the skull may stand as an empty vessel when not in use and instead become a *locus* with which spirits may be temporarily conjured to communicate with and question them. In this case, they are often worked with to interview or interrogate spirits of the dead in order to obtain information or determine their nature and intentions.

For any of these purposes, a real human skull, though an ideal vessel, is not entirely a necessity. Many witches will employ skulls crafted from clay, stone, or wood for this sort of work. Usually, these skulls require a bit more ritual preparation and are often washed in necromantic herbs and loaded with appropriate material such as graveyard dirts and powdered bone. Though often conflated with rather questionable new age ideas and extraterrestrials, crystal skulls, particularly those made from quartz, serve well for the temporary housing of spirits of the dead. They also quite readily serve as scrying tools as well. Oftentimes, the face of the crystal skull will be turned away from the witch, and the spherical back of the skull will be worked with for this purpose.

Lastly, animal skulls may be worked with to call upon the spirit of a specific animal, or to enlist the spirit virtues of that entire species. They

---

83 Doreen Valiente and Evan J. Jones. *Witchcraft: a Tradition Renewed* (Hale, 1990) 134-146.

may also lend themselves well to housing various land spirits and familiar spirits, or be employed as a central vessel for crafting a fetich around. We will explore this in greater detail in Chapter Nine.

On the Liber Spirituum

Books are often inhabited by spirits, and I would argue that each grimoire and handcrafted magical book is very much its own entity. The collection of varied spirit names and their associated sigils and seals essentially draws upon and calls to those spirits. In certain cases throughout history, some books of magic were believed to be so cursed or contain spirits so volatile that they were kept locked up to keep them constrained.

An excellent example of such an enspirited book which might inspire our own efforts in this arena can be found within the *Fourth Book of Occult Philosophy*, spuriously attributed to Heinrich Cornelius Agrippa. In it are given instructions for the creation of a *Liber Spirituum* or Book of Spirits. The working as presented within the Fourth Book is an involved process, which I encourage the reader to examine for themselves for greater context. In essence, it describes a method by which a book is crafted from virgin parchment with seals of protection placed at the front and back of the book. It is designed in a manner that at each opening, an image of a particular spirit is presented on the left page and the spirit's appropriate character or sigils upon the right. The book will be populated with entries for all of the spirits that the magician endeavors to employ within their magic. The implication here is that these are spirits with whom the magician has previously made acquaintance through the conjuration methods common to such grimoires as the *Fourth Book.* Each spirit entry is accompanied by a written oath (pact) by which the spirit will be bound to the book and be obedient to the magician when called.

To consecrate the book, it is placed within a Triangle of Arte outside of the magician's circle, and each spirit who has been given an entry in the book is conjured and "compelled to impose their hands where their images and characters are drawn, and to confirm and consecrate the same with a special and common oath."[84] An alternative manner of consecrating the book involves creating a magical circle at a crossroads, wrapping the book in cloth, and then burying it at the center of the crossroads. It is left for three days before returning to create another circle and retrieve it. Over the course of the three days, in the magician's absence, the spirits within the book are said to arrive and bind themselves to the book. The location of the crossroad here is quite relevant as it is almost universally viewed as the place where one goes to meet with spirits. Particularly those of a sub-lunar nature.

Upon its completion, the *Liber Spirituum* is worked with in such a manner that all the magician needs to do is open it to the entry for the appropriate spirit and call upon the spirit to conjure it forth from the book. The magician may then engage with and employ the spirit as they desire. Though the reader may not choose this specific approach for crafting an enspirited book, it does provide fertile ground as a starting point for one's own experimentation.

On the Spirit of Magical Tools

Though witches often possess an arsenal of magical tools and ritual implements, it seems much less common that they view their tools as possessing a unique spirit. Quite often, within contemporary craft, ritual tools are relegated to the realm of being little more than props valued only for their symbolic virtues. I am here to argue that the wand, the knife, the cauldron, the stang, and all other such implements can and should be engaged with as spirits. In some cases, the witch may desire to intentionally place a spirit within a ritual tool. In others, our tools will develop their own spirit over time, so long as they are engaged as such. In this, the spirit becomes the personified reflection of all that the tool has enacted and been imbued with.

The processes through which most ritual tools are hallowed (made sacred) is not dissimilar to the vast majority of initiation rituals a person might undergo when entering the craft. The tool is usually cleansed of any previous associations and influences. This mirrors many rites where an

84 Henry Cornelius Agrippa, *Fourth Book of Occult Philosophy: The Companion to Three Books of Occult Philosophy*, Donald Tyson, ed. Robert Turner, tr. (Llewellyn Publications, 2009) 94.

initiatory candidate undergoes ritual cleansing and often a symbolic death. Leaving their previous state of being behind so that they may make way for this next life. The tool is then introduced to external spiritual forces that might provide empowerment. This may take the form of passing it through incense smoke and sprinkling it with consecrated water to bless it by elemental forces. Again, in parallel to many craft initiations, the tool is then dedicated to its new role as an agent of magical change and may further be dedicated to a particular deity or spirit.

Ritual tools may also be given or reveal a unique name. This is a name by which the spirit of the tool may be conjured even in its absence. In such cases, should the witch find themself in need of their ritual knife but be far away from home, they might call upon the spirit of their knife and ask that it inhabit a rather ordinary kitchen knife so that it may be momentarily transformed into an empowered ritual implement. Additionally, should a name be known and a relationship well established with a ritual tool, if that tool is ever in need of replacing, either because it has broken or because a more suitable one is found, a ritual of transference can be constructed and the spirit housed within the new form.

On Spirits Enshrined

A shrine is any structure, usually one of a smaller size, that functions as a home for spirits. Shrines may be quite simple or beautifully extravagant, but they are always a place where we go to commune with and give offerings to spirits. Many shrines are small areas within a home or business that function as a house within a house. A place dedicated and devoted specifically to that spirit. Shrines sometimes take the literal form of a small house. An example of this is in the Thai tradition of creating outdoor spirit houses for the land spirits so they might, in turn, provide the people living there with blessings. Shrines may, of course, be much larger affairs created for public engagement. This allows for those who lack either the desire or the resources for housing a spirit within their home, a place to give honor to that spirit. Shrines will also be outfitted with various tools dedicated to the work of that spirit and decorated in a manner reflective of and appealing to whomever it is dedicated to.

As shrines are often constructed around an effigy, mask, or spirit pot as the central focus, much of what we have previously discussed will be easily incorporated within larger shrines. Oftentimes, the witch's altar becomes both a working area and a shrine to the spirits with whom they work. However, some spirits will prefer their own space if possible. This in mind, depending upon your resources and relationships with spirits, home shrines can be as simple as a small box which can be stored away as needed or as involved as dedicating a closet or even an entire room to devotion and working with a spirit.

On Amulets, Talismans, and Jewelry

In the infinitely vast realm of what might be classified as amulets and talismans, most will be understood by the witch as being, at least tangentially if not directly, enspirited. Various historical accounts speak of magicians, witches, and cunning folk housing familiar spirits within rings or pendants so that they might be close at hand and easily conjured. In some cases, these were filled with magical *materia* and engraved with appropriate sigils and seals relevant to the spirit in question. Most lockets, brooches, and small portable vessels lend themselves to this and may be easily loaded with appropriate *materia*, conjured, and serve as the home for a spirit.

In the realm of talismans created using traditional astrology, both the crafting and the consecration of a talisman often make use of auspicious celestial occurrences to empower a talisman. This is performed in collaboration with spirits allied to the planets and stars in question. Though this aspect may be more or less explicit depending upon which sources one relies upon, I would argue that the crafting of astrological talismans primarily occurs as a pact between their crafter and the celestial spirits conjured to empower the talisman. All done at times when those planetary and stellar spirits are believed to be at their height of power for the work at hand.

Depending upon the inclination of the one crafting such a talisman, the spirits of any *materia* utilized in creating the talisman may also be conjured and more intentionally allied to the work. The resultant talisman becomes a material object by which the influence of supernal spirits might be drawn down and directed by the magician or witch who calls upon their aid. We might take this a step further and argue that through an animist lens, the completed astrological talisman could be viewed as being inhabited by a spirit which is a wholly unique amalgamation collectively drawing upon the virtues of the *materia* of its construction, the influence of the patron spirit through which it is born, as well as the nativity of its conception (crafting), birth (consecration), and ultimately the manner by which the magician or witch engages with and directs its attentions.

Amulets and talismans are often bolstered by other methods for calling upon the presence of spirits, such as emblazoning them with sigils and images that represent the spirit. They may draw upon and incorporate symbolic elements such as shapes, numbers, and colors sacred to the spirits to further ally both object and spirit. In other cases, an amulet or talisman may be centered around a singular object such as a gemstone, a root, a bone, etc. Within these examples, the talisman is calling upon the spirit and virtues of the specific material it is made from. As we begin to explore the realm of talismans and amulets of more complex compositions, we again enter the realm of the fetich and find that this also begins to cross over into the territory of conjure bags and the like. As with most things in this work, the lines that separate one form of magic or spirit vessel from another are ever shifting and mutable.

On the Diversity of Spirit Vessels

Though we have explored numerous examples of what might serve as spirit vessels, in truth, we are regularly surrounded by enspirited objects, though we seldom awaken and engage with them as such. That said, a few other items worthy of consideration here include the use of boxes as a spirit locus. Much like other containers, boxes may be filled with magical *materia* and given an indwelling spirit. Smaller boxes also serve very well in the creation of easily portable shrines.

Though we will revisit this in chapter nine, I would be remiss if I didn't briefly mention working with animal and botanical materials which naturally lend themselves to being crafted into fetich objects. Animal horns and seashells serve very well in the making of spirit vessels. Bones may be sliced and have their marrow removed so that they may be filled with *materia* and crafted into a fetich. And naturally occurring botanical containers such as walnut shells may be worked quite the same.

There are countless options for the manner in which this work may be accomplished. I have created fetiches from antique leather pistol holsters and loaded *materia* into spent bullet casings. I have made spirit houses from old wooden shoes, pill boxes, and tobacco tins. Here, the witch is encouraged to employ their cunning and craft when exploring the limits by which they might create bodies for spirits. In the work of enspiriting objects, we are limited only by our ingenuity, imagination, and the inclinations of our spirits.

Recommended Additional Reading

Witch Bottles: History, Culture, Magic by Daniel Harms. Avalonia Press. 2022.

Container Magic: Spellcraft Using Sachets, Bottles, Poppets & Jars by Charity L. Bedell. Llewellyn Publications. 2023.

Bottle Up and Go! The Magic of Hoodoo Container Spells in Boxes, Jars, Bags, Bowls, and Buckets by Catherine Yronwode and Lara Rivera. Lucky Mojo Curio Company. 2020.

The Art of Making Mojos: How to Craft Conjure Hands, Trick Bags, Tobies, Gree-Grees, Jomos, Jacks, and Nation Sacks by Catherine Yronwode et al. Lucky Mojo Curio Company. 2018.

The Hand Book: Hoodoo Mojos, Gris-Gris, Medicine Bags, Jackballs and Paquets by Talia Felix. Independently Published. 2014

Sacred Mask Sacred Dance by Evan John Jones and Chas S. Clifton. Llewellyn Publications. 1997.

The Spiritual Power of Masks: Doorways to Realms Unseen by Nigel Pennick. Destiny Books. 2022.

The High Magic of Talismans and Amulets: Tradition and Craft by Claude Lecouteux. Inner Traditions. 2014.

Witchcraft: A Tradition Renewed by Doreen Valiente and Evan John Jones. Phoenix Publishing. 1990.

Amulets: Sacred Charms of Power and Protection by Sheila Paine. Inner Traditions. 2004.

The Ancestral Power of Amulets, Talismans, and Mascots: Folk Magic in Witchcraft and Religion by Nigel Pennick. Destiny Books. 2021.

Chapter Eight

Born of Breath, Born of Clay: On the Crafting of Effigies

Here we begin the more practical work of joining spirit and material form by examining some materials and methods for creating, or sourcing, the body which will become the effigy. Though this chapter is largely framed around the making of effigies, the materials, suggestions, and magical considerations mentioned here apply equally to the making of fetiches and other spirit vessels.

Once we have established a clear idea of the role and spirit we wish our vessel to serve, we can begin to consider the various approaches towards crafting its form. The mediums we choose for our effigy might be guided by their spiritual virtues, ease of use, symbolism, accessibility, and affordability, or based upon how permanent of a form we wish to make. There are many options available to us, and though the following certainly isn't an exhaustive catalog of all available options, I believe it offers a decent overview for those beginning this arte.

On Clay and the Clay Mother

With the prevalence of creation myths in which humanity was birthed from the earth, it should come as little surprise that clay is one of the most common materials effigies have been, and still are, crafted from. Coaxing spirit forms out of the earth with our hands is one of humanity's most primeval art forms. Our earliest extant example of a sculpted and fired ceramic figure is represented by the Venus of Dolní Věstonice (29,000 BCE).

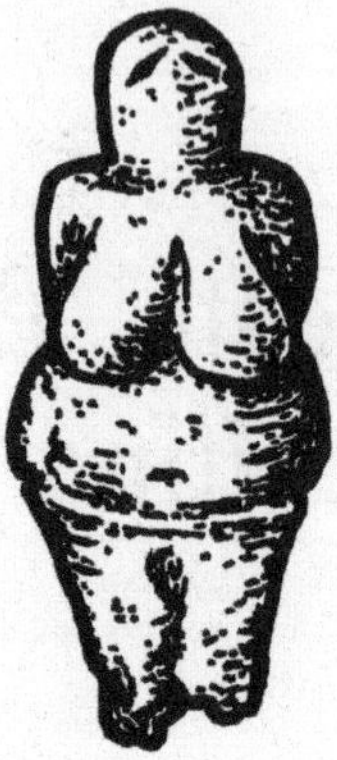

A female form with exaggerated breasts, hips, and buttocks sculpted of earthen clay unearthed in what is now the Czech Republic. In the same location where she was discovered were found ceramic figures representing owls, bears, horses, foxes, lions, mammoths, and rhinos. In a fascinating contrast, our earliest evidence of humans creating ceramic food vessels isn't present in the archaeological record until over ten thousand years later! Indicating that our early ancestors' first encounters with clay, and the alchemical process of firing it, were devoted to replicating the human form in effigy and the crafting of animal forms.

Employing a mythic gaze, we might imagine these earliest clay effigies as representative of the life-sustaining gifts of the land, a personification of the Clay Mother. An aspect of the bountiful and nourishing Earth who has been a steadfast companion to humanity throughout our development. Long before we crafted our sculptural forms of her from her, we conjured her through the ochred blood of the Earth. The pigment of life and resurrection, of tomb and womb. The ruddy color of our earliest magics, raised from the earth alongside her yellow ochres and white kaolin clay. Sacred pigments painted across the ages as petroglyphs hidden in caves, smeared upon talismans and tools, and adorning the bodies of the living and the dead. Her red, yellow, and white minerals, accompanied by the blackness of her deeply fertile soil, are our earliest palette and are still to be found within the colors of the Kongo cosmogram and the Medicine Wheel.

There is an intimacy involved in the working of clay, a co-creation which echoes back to our earliest imaginings of our origins. It is from the Clay Mother we are formed, and to her we shall be returned. So it is that we too might, by the work of our clumsy, impassioned hands, and by her blessing grace, sing in concert with the Earth, give life to new forms, and render bodies unto spirits.

Our mythic understanding of the Clay Mother is, quite literally, given greater grounding when we consider recent ideas championed by biologist, biochemist, and biophysicist Helen Greenwood Hansma. Her hypothesis, which has gained some greater support, suggests that the necessary conditions that allowed for the genesis of life on Earth were made possible by the existence of micaceous clays.[85] Raising a possibility that recognizing clay as our point of origin may one day no longer be resigned only to the echoed mythos of our ancient ancestors, but instead, embraced more broadly in our understanding of the animate world.

As a sculptural medium, the plasticity of clay allows for nearly limitless possibilities. Making it one of the more versatile and easily workable options when crafting an effigy, while also allowing for high levels of detail and providing various levels of durability. For our purposes here, we will extend the classification of clay beyond that which is sourced directly from the Earth, and include all forms of clay-like substances, such as dough and more modern mediums, such as air-drying paper clays and polymer clays.

Types of Clay

Earthen Clay

As its name implies, earthen clay is any clay sourced directly from the earth and is one of the most common mediums I use when crafting effigies. This is the clay we are speaking of when discussing the art of ceramics. Depending upon the minerals present, earthen clay comes in an incredible array of colors and may be purchased readily prepared for use.

For the more industrious artisans, wild clay might be sourced directly from the land itself. Such a direct sourcing allows us greater possibility

85 Helen Greenwood Hansma, "Potassium at the Origins of Life: Did Biology Emerge From Biotite in Micaceous Clay?" *Life,* vol. 12, no. 2, 17 Feb. 2022, 301

for engaging with the spirit of place, giving offerings, and requesting that spirit's influence upon the effigies born from its earth. In exchange, wild clays require greater work to refine and prepare for sculpting and firing. The results can be much less predictable than when using clays that are sourced from pottery supply houses. However, working with wild clays can provide an incredibly rewarding practice of directly engaging the Clay Mother.

When creating with earthen clay, there is a spectrum of durability that it may be worked to. Clay that has air dried (meaning that all the water content has evaporated) has reached a state referred to as *bone dry.* In this state, it is often referred to as Greenware. It is solid and no longer malleable; however, it is still very porous, quite brittle, and can easily be broken. Through the reintroduction of water, greenware can be returned to a soft, malleable form of clay. It is only when bone-dry earthen clay is fired by being heated to incredibly high temperatures that it becomes much more durable. This fired form of clay is what transforms it into a ceramic. The two primary forms of which are Earthenware and Stoneware.

Earthenware accounts for much of humanity's earliest ceramics and refers to clay that has been fired at temperatures under 1,100°C. Achieving these temperatures was much easier for our early ancestors, as it could be accomplished through methods such as pit-firing.[86] Earthenware is much more durable than unfired clay. Still, the finished pieces remain very porous and absorb water easily. Though finished earthenware pieces may be waxed to give an additional layer of protection and water resistance. An example of an earthenware ceramic many of us are familiar with is terracotta.

Stoneware is fired to a much higher temperature and, as a result, is more durable and substantially less porous. As the heat required for achieving stoneware is so high, its production didn't become common until around 6,000 BCE, when we began using kilns. Kiln firing allowed us to maintain higher temperatures for sustained periods. In most cases, stoneware is fired twice. Its first firing takes it to an earthenware state

86 Pit-firing is one of the earliest methods of firing ceramics and involves digging a pit in the ground and placing greenware pieces surrounded by combustible materials such as grasses and leaves within. A fire is created and allowed to die down to coals. The pit is then usually covered in some fashion to keep the heat within and raise it to the required temperature.

usually referred to as a biscuit or bisque firing. It is then removed from the kiln and cooled. In this still porous form, a glaze is often applied to it.

Glazing involves painting a piece with a variety of minerals that provide color and essentially melt into a glass-like surface upon the clay body, making it relatively impermeable to moisture. Glazing offers endless possibilities for finishes and adds to the durability of a finished effigy. Once glaze is applied to an earthenware piece, it is returned to the kiln. The temperatures reached in this second firing bring our effigy to the hardness of stoneware. Most everyday dishes, drinkware, and ceramics we encounter today are made of stoneware.

Some drawbacks to consider when working with earthen clay are that it does not always lend itself easily to the direct incorporation of powders, botanicals, and other *materia* into the clay body, as this may cause difficulties in firing. However, I have successfully incorporated ashes and a variety of infused waters, botanical tinctures, and oils into the process of sculpting earthen effigies to very good effect.

Additionally, though more durable than some alternatives, even fired ceramics are likely to shatter when dropped or impacted. Also, earthen clay does not allow for the addition of fresh clay to already dry clay, as the differences in moisture will lead to cracks and breakage. Pretty much any ceramic artist will tell you that it is a delicate dance when dealing with the various states of moisture in clay before it reaches the bone-dry state and is ready for firing.

Even afterwards, among all the possible variables encountered in firing and glazing, there are ample opportunities for misstep. For this reason and many more, the working of earthen clay has a relatively easy point of entry, but a steep learning curve towards mastery. However, as any ceramic artist is likely to tell you, this is all a part of the unpredictable, yet incredibly rewarding, journey of working with the Clay Mother.

In revisiting the states of greenware, earthenware, and stoneware, we see a variability of permanence which might be both practically considered and meditated upon to provide deeper revelation. From a practical perspective, bone-dry clay might best serve for effigies that are intended to be easily broken apart by hand or eroded away through submersion in water or burial in the earth. This lends itself to execrations, spells of wasting, or those in which an effigy is otherwise intended to be integrated into the land.

In contrast, earthenware might serve well if we desire to create an effigy that can be fired in a highly ritualized form. Employing a pit-firing method or similar allows the witch an opportunity to engage directly with the elements and also enact the very same ritual processes developed by our Paleolithic predecessors. To witness an effigy which has been drawn from the earth, crafted by our hands, interred back into the tomb/womb of earth, and phoenix-born anew from fire and ash, stronger than before, is itself a deeply magical act. Pit-firing also allows for the easy inclusion of sacred herbs, woods, and various minerals into the process to further align the entire working with the nature of the effigy. Given its porous nature, earthenware might also be a desirable option for producing an effigy that can absorb and accumulate the power of unguents, oils, and liquid offerings applied directly to its body.

Finally, stoneware creates the most lasting ceramic form as it is the most durable. It provides more opportunities for glazing pieces in a diversity of finishes. By strengthening the form and creating a less porous body, it gives greater permanence to an effigy. This lends itself to a spirit *locus* that might withstand many generations.

It's worth mentioning that within certain streams of traditional craft, those who are unawakened or unwitched are sometimes referred to as the clay-born. Brittle, impermanent, and destined for a return to dust. Again, a reference to Genesis 2:7[87] and to 3:19.[88] It is not until the witchfire is awakened, stirred, tended to, fed, and strengthened that our otherwise brittle impermanent forms become fortified. When ignited by the flame betwixt the horns, through the pit and pyre, much like our effigy, we experience our death, transmutation, and resurrection into a creature which is no longer the child of Adam but who is the Other incarnate, the Witch.

To work an effigy by the clay of earth is a primordial conjuration of spirit. It is an act that reaches into our earliest ancestral memories to grasp at and be grasped by the reddened hands of all who shaped the earth before us. A work of devotion to the Clay Mother. An entry into her art wherein there exists no shortage of primeval caves and lamplit corridors to offer revelation for those whom she welcomes into her mysteries.

---

87 "And the Lord God formed man of the dust of the ground, and breathed into his nostrils the breath of life; and man became a living soul." KJV

88 "for dust thou art, and unto dust shalt thou return." KJV

Paper Clay

Another of my preferred mediums for creating effigies is air-drying paper clay.[89] This is a somewhat broad term that can include refined forms of paper-mâché. This largely cellulose-based clay easily accepts the inclusion of botanical powders, dirts, tinctures, sacred or botanically infused waters, and other *materia* into the body during the sculpting process. Though working with it has a bit of a learning curve, this type of clay requires no firing, and when it dries, it is quite durable and easy to paint with acrylics. Another advantage that this medium provides over earthen clay and polymer clays is that fresh paper clay can be added to already dried and hardened parts with relative ease. Dried forms can also be easily sanded or carved after hardening. Drawbacks with this clay are that it remains porous after drying unless otherwise sealed, and it is not as durable and long-lasting as some alternatives, such as fired earthen clay or polymer clays.

Polymer Clay

Polymer clays are a plastisol that combines a liquid plasticizer with PVC resin. Common commercial brands include Sculpey and Fimo. These are readily available at most art and craft stores and are, in essence, a form of plastic modeling clay that remains malleable until it is heat-cured and hardened. A specialized kiln is not required, and curing can be achieved with most conventional ovens at relatively low temperatures of around 270°F.

My own inclination tends towards mediums that are more organic and ecologically benevolent in composition. However, due to their versatility, durability, and availability in a wide range of colors, polymer clays have found increased popularity amongst many magical creators, statue makers, and art doll enthusiasts alike. They retain a high level of detail and yield striking results for artisans skilled in their use. Polymer clay figures may also be painted with relative ease.

Some of the drawbacks of this medium are that it doesn't easily lend itself to the inclusion of powdered *materia* and dirts into the clay. However, due to its low curing temperature, it does allow for the inclusion of internal armatures made of wire and/or aluminum foil. Some of the witches I have known who work in this medium incorporate magical *materia* into their effigies by creating a bundle or load of appropriate botanicals, bones,

89 The specific brand I prefer is called Creative PaperClay.

stones, etc., wrapped in a packet of foil, which is then housed within the body of the effigy. This form of clay also has a reasonable learning curve to truly master. Additionally, some sources recommend that you not use the same oven you cook with for curing polymer clays, as there are some concerns about cross-contamination.

Epoxy Clay/Putty

Epoxy putty refers to a variety of clay-like substances that consist of two parts. Each part is soft and malleable at room temperature, but when combined, they create a chemical reaction and will harden fairly rapidly. It presents similar advantages and challenges to polymer clay with the addition of a shortened work time. However, fresh putty can often be added to cured pieces, allowing for an effigy to be crafted in stages as needed. Similar to polymer clays, epoxy isn't the most ecologically conscious option for working with, and this should be considered when selecting it as a possible medium.

Dough

There are a variety of doughs, both edible and otherwise, which might be employed in crafting effigies. For those kitchen witches with a knack for baking, there are countless opportunities for crafting edible effigies for ritual workings in which ingesting the power or blessings of a spirit is required.[90] Dough effigies might also be left in the wild as offerings to the land, or to represent a person, quality, or situation we wish to see devoured and returned to the earth.

Salt dough, though not really edible, is easy to create and can also be an excellent option for protection and cleansing work, and utilizes ingredients found in most kitchens. Cinnamon dough creates a truly potent vehicle for effigies and charms in works of prosperity and arousing amorous attentions. Additionally, a wide variety of doughs can be created by combining powdered herbs and woods, with resins and gums to bind them.[91]

---

90 I also can't help but encourage the animist kitchen witch to explore working their sourdough starter as a spirit vessel here.

91 See the Formulary for salt, cinnamon, and herbal dough recipes.

On Waxen Images

As exhibited in earlier examples, waxen effigies have a long history in magic. Beeswax is often preferred as it evokes the vast arcanum of lore surrounding both the bee and her honey. More practically, in contrast to less ecologically mindful waxes such as paraffin, when slightly warmed, beeswax becomes fairly malleable and may be formed and sculpted with the hands. I have crafted quite a few effigies in this way and find the process to be one that easily lends itself to a meditative and focused approach, which aids in the work.

Such malleability lends itself to the addition of powdered pigments, botanicals, taglocks, and other inclusions directly into the body of the effigy while kneading beeswax. Further, as with the working of clays, this state of mutability between forms might be leveraged to provide points of vulnerability and receptivity in the target of the effigy.[92] As the work of the hands imposes itself upon the body of the waxen effigy, similarly, charming and cursing might more readily be kneaded into the life of the one it represents and remain fixed there upon the wax's return to a more solid state.

For those fortunate enough to have access to apiaries, we might also take the opportunity to more directly engage through acts of devotion and offering with those blessed spirits of the hive: the bees, their queen, and by extension the fields they feast upon, so that they might aid in our work. As Martin Duffy puts it:

> *Being emblematic of living spirits, bees are oft treated with great respect, exemplified in such folkloric practices of 'telling the bees' of significant events, especially those of birth and death. Considering its 'living' quality, it is unsurprising then that beeswax has great tradition in the shaping of magical effigies and talismans, it being as a living nexus capable of housing spirit.*[93]

In lieu of working wax by hand, it may also be melted and poured into appropriately shaped molds for our effigy. Still easier, many occult suppliers

---

92 Martin Duffy. *Effigy: Of Graven Image & Holy Idol.* (Three Hands Press, 2015) 72

93 Duffy, *ibid.* 74

and botanicas offer candles in a plethora of forms that might readily be employed as effigies. In such cases, the witch might carve a cavity into the candle base or elsewhere that might be loaded with appropriate *materia* and sealed. Waxen effigies of all kinds are also easily inscribed with names, sigils, and further identifying characters related to the person or spirit they are meant to be bound to. Effigy candles may be dressed with oils, botanicals, and powders, and then be worked with as any other effigy. Or they may be burned as originally intended, should it be appropriate for the working. Here we find the fortunate crossing of effigy work and candle magic.

On Cloth and Thread

Working with cloth when crafting effigies is another incredibly common approach and offers a variety of ways we might incorporate other *materia*, symbolic, and decorative elements into the work. Personally, I tend to prefer working with natural plant-based fabrics such as cotton and linen when possible. However, there are a tremendous diversity of options for colors, patterns, and fibers available when working with fabrics. Additionally, finding fabric with symbolically relevant patterns (such as fabric printed with images of money or tarot cards) or having fabrics custom-printed has become quite accessible as of late. This allows the option for personalized fabrics to be made that display sigils or other symbolism appropriate to your work.

Working with fabric allows us an excellent opportunity to further align a poppet we are crafting with the individual it is meant to represent. When possible, I will usually make a poppet at least in part, with fabric from a piece of clothing the person has worn. This serves as an effective taglock, or link to the target of the poppet. Though any piece of a person's worn clothing will usually suffice, depending upon the purpose of the poppet, different types of clothing may be better suited than others. For instance, undergarments are very personal and may be used very effectively in this work, but particularly when doing work to affect desires, lust, fertility, or passion. The socks might be better suited if you wanted to cause movement, to banish a person, provide road opening, or keep someone in place. Using pieces of headwear or a pillowcase someone has slept upon may better serve in works dealing with mental health, influencing thoughts, and all areas related to the mind.

On Botanical Dyes

I often like to incorporate herbs and botanicals relevant to the work by either dyeing my fabric with them or by soaking or painting my fabrics with herbal tinctures aligned to the work. In effect, infusing the skin of the effigy with the virtues of these plant spirits. Dying fabrics can be a very effective and incredibly enjoyable way to partner with plant spirits in this work.

Though this is far from an exhaustive list, some fairly common botanicals that can be easily found in most kitchens and which produce some excellent results both visually and magically include:

- **Onion Skins (*allium cepa*):** Red Onion skins produce tans, browns, and greens when used as a dye. Yellow onions usually produce a yellow ochre tone. Onions are generally seen to have Martial alignments, and so they are commonly worked with for protection. Onions are also often employed in works of cleansing and healing, as well as those related to fertility and prosperity.
- **Turmeric Root (*Curcuma longa*):** The dye created by turmeric creates beautifully bright yellows to golden orange colors. The traditional saffron robes worn by many Buddhist monks have historically been dyed with turmeric root for their color. When considering its applications, turmeric is nearly limitless, as it has an incredibly long history of religious and spiritual use. Just a few of turmeric's magical associations include prosperity and good fortune, protection from the evil eye, strengthening love and fertility, as well as calling upon and honoring the sacred.
- **Red Cabbage (*Brassica oleracea*):** Red cabbage will produce light blues or purples when dyeing. When worked magically, cabbage has long been seen as a symbol of prosperity and health. It is also commonly associated with love and works of protection. Through the doctrine of signatures, cabbage is linked to the brain and may also be employed in works of the mind. As it is also aligned with the influences of the Moon, cabbage-dyed fabrics might be well-suited to effigies having to do with dreams, intuition, and the development of psychic faculties.

- **Beets (*Beta vulgaris*):** Beetroot creates pink and red dyes. It is said that the goddess Aphrodite consumed large quantities of beets to enhance her beauty and allure, and by extension, beets are often employed in works of beauty and amorous attention. Additionally, beets have often been regarded as an aphrodisiac in a variety of cultures. Fabrics dyed with beetroot may serve well in works of love and sex magic, as well as those designed to enhance our general allure to others.
- **Coffee Grounds (*Coffea*):** Light browns and tans are achieved by dying with coffee. Understandably, the nature of coffee lends itself well to works and effigies aligned with focus and alertness, as well as those we wish to work rapidly. Coffee is also aligned with works of prosperity and bounty. Within my practice, coffee is a common offering given daily to ancestral and household spirits, so it is not uncommon for me to use it as a dye when creating effigies related to these types of beings.
- **Black Beans (*Phaseolus vulgaris*):** Black beans produce light grays, lilac, or pale blue tones. Beans in general tend to have associations with prosperity, fertility, and the dead. Within some spiritual traditions, black beans in particular are associated with the dead and the ancestors. I have found them to be an incredibly effective dye to work with when creating necromantic effigies and fetiches.
- **Black Tea (*Camellia sinensis*):** Black tea creates light browns and tan tones. When an iron mordant is added, it can create grays and blacks. Tea has some similar associations with coffee. Historically it has also been heavily tied to commerce and trade. So, it may be good to work with when crafting effigies related to those areas or concerns. Additionally, tea is often related to hospitality, leisure, communication, and prophecy.

In addition to the above, there are endless options for incorporating the botanicals that we have growing in our gardens or have wildcrafted into dying fabrics. I enjoy working with mugwort for crafting effigies and charms for dreaming and divination, and black walnut is a wonderfully effective dye for works involving powerful protection, memory, or works of a more diabolical nature. Berries may also make effective dyes. I have enjoyed working with blackberries and elderberries in the past, both of which create results in the pink/purple/blue range.

The process of dyeing can be somewhat involved for those new to it and is, unfortunately, not a topic we can thoroughly explore here. I encourage you to look deeper into this art, should it call to you. For an introduction on working with natural botanicals for dyes, I recommend *The Wild Dyer* by Abigail Booth as a starting point. And if working with dyes feels a bit daunting, keep in mind that in lieu of this, we might also empower our fabrics by soaking them in botanical tinctures and infusions, washing them in sacred waters, dressing them with oils, or spraying them with perfumes.

On Bestial Skins

Leather, pelts, and rawhide may all be worked with similarly to cloth when creating effigies. With the added effect of incorporating some level of alignment to the spirit of the associated animal into the greater whole of the effigy. For instance, we might work with the spirit of a rabbit and its skin if we wish to call upon the aid of its swiftness, alertness, or fertility. For effigies meant to call upon the witches' devil, or those related to lust, we might work with goatskin. For works of cunning, we might work with coyote. There are certain spirits I work with who appear as specific animals; in such cases, incorporating elements of those animals into the effigy serves to better align the body to the spirit it is meant to house. However there are a number of considerations when employing animal parts that should be examined before beginning our work with them. This will be addressed in greater detail in the next chapter.

On Stuffing and Fillings

When creating cloth or leather effigies, we have an opportunity to fill the body with whatever we choose. This can include appropriate herbs, roots, stones, and bones. Or in the case of a poppet representing a person, we might also fill it with cut-up strips of clothing worn by the target, their hair, or any other items to link them to the doll.

As we are often left with quite a bit of extra space in these dolls when this is done, there are several stuffing options worth considering to complete the doll. Cotton stuffing is quite easy to come by in most craft and fabric shops and works very well, as does bamboo fiber, which is a somewhat more sustainable option. I have even used shredded up money in the past when making effigies for prosperity, or pages from old books to lend their character or wisdom to an effigy. Any natural fiber or material of your choosing may work; however, it's wise to consider what it brings to the composition of your effigy.

My preferred choice for effigy stuffing these days has been kapok. Kapok is a sustainable natural fiber that comes from the seedpods of several tree species. It is somewhat similar to cotton in texture but silkier and more lightweight. When sourcing it, I usually look for kapok that has come from the Ceiba (*Ceiba pentandra*) tree. This is largely because the Ceiba is a sacred tree found both in parts of Africa as well as in the Americas, and in many cultures where it grows, it is regarded as the World Tree and the dwelling place for a host of spirits. Effigies might also be filled with sawdust, Spanish moss, or sand. Wool or other types of animal fur are also valid options, depending upon the nature of the animal and the purpose of the effigy. The body might also be filled with beans, seeds, or rice, particularly if they are designed around creating prosperity and fecundity.

On Threading and the Witch's Spittle

When working with fabrics and thread, we are further able to entwine our desires into our creation process through the act of sewing. We need only to turn to tales of the Moirai (Fates) who spin, measure, and cut the thread of life as one example of the deeper mysteries of thread within magical works. The nature of thread is joining, binding, weaving, and strengthening. When worked by the witch, thread may be enchanted into an effective addition to the process of effigy creation that lends greater power to the finished piece.

I will often slip into a meditative rhythm and mutter charms, blessings, or curses whilst sewing a doll. Here we are literally stitching our utterances into the fabric of the effigy; we are joining, binding, and tying into the skin of the thing, and doing so by the power of verbal charms. On occasion, I might instead simply hum while intently focusing my mind upon the work of the effigy and its associated spirit.

When the final stitches are made in the effigy, we have an opportunity to speak aloud the intended work/purpose of the doll and align it with the spirit it will represent. Directly after this, the witch's spittle is then spat upon the ends of the thread before the final knots are tied to complete the sewing of the figure. Thus, binding that which was spoken and the will of the witch into the very body of the effigy.

I have occasionally taken a different approach and muttered full incantations over the cloth and thread before beginning the work of the doll. This is then immediately followed by dragging the length of thread I intend to use for the effigy through my lips and moistening it with my saliva. In this case, as well as in the previous example, the spittle of the witch becomes the mark of our empowered word. It carries a remembrance of the magics uttered and embeds them within the effigy.

The witching arts of spoken charms, incantations, and employing our spittle as a vehicle for them are deeply rooted in our histories. As such, it may be further employed throughout the work of crafting enspirited objects in highly effective and inventive ways. For instance, we might whisper a call to a certain spirit or a charm for protection and then spit upon the clay we are working. Or we might speak instructions, requests, or commands and then use our spittle to anoint the head of an effigy. There is much here to explore and expand upon for those with such inclinations and ingenuity.

Finally, the thread we employ may additionally be treated in any number of ways to further imbue it with greater power. I have often soaked thread in botanical tinctures and infusions before sewing poppets. Magical oils or ointments may also be applied to the thread. Thread can also be easily infused with diverse powers by washing it in waters from sacred sites, rainstorms, or from local springs.

On String and Rope

String and rope lend themselves to easily crafted, simplistic forms, which are readily infused with oils, tinctures, waters, and washes. In choosing the materials, you might simply draw from what is immediately available or employ specific ropes in your work. For instance, a piece of thin rope might be used to measure the length of the person an effigy is meant to represent and then fashioned into the effigy itself. Or the string might be wrapped around certain parts of their body, such as the head, before crafting it into a poppet for healing or fortifying the mind.

In conjure traditions of the Southern United States, there exist workings of domination and control in which a man's penis is measured with a string, which is later dressed in his sexual fluids. Similar approaches might be employed in this work as well, wherein the resulting string is fashioned into the body of a poppet that might be worked for control, fertility, libido, or sterility. In necromantic pursuits, rope from one who has hung themself has traditionally been greatly valued, and it is not difficult to see how such *materia* might be put to good use here.

Similar methods to those suggested in reference to the working of thread may be employed here, where knots are tied into the body of the effigy and fortified with verbal charms and spittle applied to literally tie our words into the work. We might also introduce color into the string effigy by selecting a variety of embroidery threads in colors representative of the work we wish to do or allied to the spirits conjured. String and rope bodies also allow us the ability to incorporate braiding into our fashioning of the effigy. As with sewing, such repetitive actions invite us to slip into a light trance and employ incantation in order to further empower the effigy during its creation.

On Arboreal Allies

Here, we are able to partner with the spirits of the trees and ask that they each lend their unique virtues to the effigy we are creating. Additionally, this approach offers endless opportunities for crafting diverse forms to anyone who is inclined towards developing their skill in carving. In much of this work, we are best served when we can source our wood from local tree species so that we might more easily work with them as allies and representatives of the land we live upon. With permission sought and offerings given, wood may be mindfully and respectfully collected directly from trees with which we have formed relationships. Of course, we may not have direct access to the trees we wish to work with, so turning to suppliers of wood prepared for carving may be necessary and is perfectly good. We can still give our offerings and conjure the spirit of the tree to aid us in our work.

Simple effigies are easily crafted by binding together sticks and twigs in roughly human forms. These rough armatures may stand alone or serve as a frame that we might wrap with cotton, cloth, and other items. A very popular form of effigy of this sort is often sold in New Orleans to tourists as a "voodoo doll" and takes the form of crossed sticks wrapped with Spanish moss and then wrapped with cloth.

When gathering sticks for our work, we might choose to search for fallen sticks in places of power, such as forests and parks we have come to know well, and around local cemeteries. We might also harvest branches and sticks directly from trees we wish to work with. When fabricating such effigies, we also have an excellent opportunity for drawing together disparate influences and spiritual virtues by incorporating sticks sourced from several tree species into one effigy.

On Botanicals and Bodies of Root

Similarly, to crafting effigies from twigs, there are a great number of possibilities for tying and braiding herbs, grasses, and other botanicals in human forms to serve as an effigy. Examples of this can be found in various parts of Europe, where dollies are traditionally fashioned from the last sheaf of wheat to carry over the spirit of the field. These were traditionally kept through the winter and then returned to the soil of the field during the first planting of the new season. Of course, many of us will be familiar with corn dollies crafted from the husks of corn, which have also served a similar purpose.

In North America, we have traditions of apple head dolls, which are created by peeling and carving faces into fresh apples and allowing them to dry and shrink. This often results in faces that appear endearingly wrinkled and aged. These dried apples may then be attached to a body fashioned from whatever materials the maker desires.

There is perhaps no greater-known root in all of magic than the *Mandragora* or mandrake. The roots often appear in vague, or occasionally rather striking, humanoid forms. There are volumes of lore surrounding the mandrake, and here it is the spirit of the root itself that we are seeking to work with. Traditionally, it is said that the spirit does not fully awaken or enter the root until its third year. Prior to this, the manner in which it must be planted, tended to, and harvested for best results is usually quite specific, though what those specifics are tends to vary. Depending upon the source, it is said that the mandrake will only grow beneath the gallows, that it must be watered with blood, and that removing it from the ground will cause it to emit a terrifying shriek which will kill whoever hears it. *Mandragora* serve as powerful familiar spirits to the witch and are known to be equally effective in works of love and cursing alike. Though *Mandragora* roots are often worked with in their natural form, some witches will carve faces into the dried roots. Several examples of this can be found in the collection at the Museum of Witchcraft in Boscastle. It is claimed that some witches will work to coax the roots throughout their growing into more humanoid shapes, though sadly, this is something I have yet to personally see very successful examples of. In cases where alteration or carving of the roots occurs, the mandrake straddles the line between a naturally occurring fetich and the intentionally crafted effigy.

Plenty of other roots may be employed in the work of the effigy. For instance, white bryony root has been worked with similarly to mandrake and served as an effigy to the witch. Such root effigies were referred to as *alrauns* in Germany, which essentially translates to *witch.* They were so feared that during the seventeenth century, the possession of an *alraun* was enough to see you charged as a witch and executed.[94] In my own work, I have enjoyed growing angelica plants, harvesting their roots, and once dried, carving grimacing faces into them to serve as protective fetiches. I have known other witches who have similarly carved roots of High John into faces to serve as the heads of effigies.

On the Stone Bound Spirit

Should a witch be skilled in this craft, stones may be carved to serve as effigies that we wish to have an enduring presence. Of course, this includes the exceptionally carved masterpieces of classical gods rendered in marble that still grace the halls of museums and temples today. This also extends to more crudely carved figures meant to represent household spirits and to simple pebbles which have been worked to display humanoid characteristics.

94 C.J.S. Thompson, *Mystic Mandrake* (Kessinger Pub Co, 2003)

As with carving from wood, stones will each bring their own unique virtues to the effigy based upon their mineralogical makeup. They might also carry allyship to the land they were sourced from. If by some good fortune we find naturally occurring stones, similar to the Venus of Tan-Tan, that already bear a human likeness, we might explore them and determine if they possess an already active spirit we wish to work with, or if they might work well as a potential vessel in which to house a spirit. The working of magical stones will be further expanded upon in our section on magical *materia.*

On Diverse Metals

Working with metals for our effigies allows for a range of possibilities of greater or lesser durability. Thinner sheets of metal, such as copper, lead, or tin, may be cut into human shapes with relative ease and inscribed or etched with appropriate features or symbols. I have also seen some resourceful witches create effigies from metal wire or aluminum foil for their work. Additionally, as planetary powers are often allied to certain metals, when working with this medium, we might also elect to incorporate planetary influences into our effigies.[95]

Certainly, the work of the forge and foundry comes to mind here. Effigies might be cast in bronze to serve as enduring spirit vessels that will last for centuries. Alternatively, effigies cast in lead, pewter, or tin are often more easily created due to the lower melting point of these metals. However, they result in a more brittle or malleable body, so they may be better suited for shorter-term works or the crafting of execration figures. For those with the means and desire, the alchemical processes at play in metalsmithing allow the skilled metalworker ample opportunities for the inclusion of diverse magical *materia* when crafting the metal effigy. This may take the form of sacred botanicals added to the forge fire, the quenching of metals in blessed waters and botanical infusions, or the finishing and seasoning of pieces with oils and unguents. There are many paths the witch turned blacksmith may employ to enhance the constitu-

95 See the appendices section at the end of the book for an overview of planetary metals and magical associations.

tion of their effigy with enough to provide for a lifetime of practice and growth within such an arte.

On Paper Dolls

Paper dolls work well when we need to create a poppet or effigy quickly or inexpensively. They are particularly of use when creating poppets we wish to burn or tear with ease. Paper figures can be easily dressed with magical oils and infused with waters, tinctures, and perfumes. They may be dusted with powders and dirts. And should one desire, sigils can be drawn upon them with magical inks or colored pencils/pens. For those who are skilled at origami, there are interesting possibilities presented for crafting figures from paper. Such papers might even be made from appropriate botanicals aligned to the work, or have petitions or charms written upon them before forming them into the desired figure.

Photographic images are an easily obtainable yet incredibly appropriate form of image magic that we might work with. Here, it almost goes without saying how effective an actual captured image of a person is as a stand-in for them in poppet work. In some cases, a photograph might function as a readymade paper poppet. In others, the face of the intended target might be affixed to a body crafted in cloth, clay, or other medium.

On Assemblage Effigies

Assemblage art is a form of sculptural collage where diverse objects are pieced together to create new forms. In essence, whenever we create an effigy from more than one material, it becomes a form of assemblage. An assemblage doll or effigy can utilize any combination of the elements previously mentioned in this chapter, as well as anything else we desire. The possibilities are limited only by the creativity of the witch.

Here, the animist is at an advantage, as when we recognize the inherent spirit and virtues of an object, we might then more mindfully consider how they can be incorporated to lend that power to the work of the effigy. For instance, an old and well-used pair of scissors might serve as the body of an effigy that is meant to cut away unhealthy attachments. Or we might utilize old skeleton keys as the arms of an effigy that assists in opening new doorways to opportunity. For an effigy aligned with money drawing, we might use old coins for its eyes or make a doll using actual paper money for its hair or clothing. Each of these items holds a form of spirit and a memory of its function that might be conjured and integrated into the work of crafting the effigy as a whole. With this in mind, it should be clear here how well-suited the crafting of assemblage effigies is to constructing created spirits such as the *maumet*, and I encourage the reader to do a bit of research on assemblage art and assemblage dolls for inspiration in their work here.

On Ready-made Effigies

Within all of this, we should not overlook the option of employing premade figures such as statuary, figurines, and dolls that might be used as is or further altered to suit our desired purposes. Though I find great fulfillment in the act of creating an effigy entirely myself, I have also had great success with repurposing store-bought figures and dolls for this work.

The store-bought statues of pagan gods that many witches employ as sacred icons are an excellent example of the ready-made effigy. However, I've found people often do little more than simply unboxing and placing such statuary upon an altar without much else in the way of preparations. In doing so, we are denying ourselves an excellent opportunity to ritually prepare, empower, and enspirit these statues so that they might serve as even greater devotional items, reservoirs of power, and transmitters of influence for their allied spirits and deities.

Some approaches to this work include washing statuary in hallowed waters and herbal infusions, suffumigating them with incense smoke, dressing them with perfumed oils, and loading the statue with a bundle of magical *materia* in order to give it a "charge" aligned to the spirit and work it is meant for. Further on in this work, we will explore the praxis of both loading a statue with magical *materia* as well as ritually creating enspirited statuary.

As in some earlier examples, premade dolls and figurines may be purchased new or used and crafted as spirit vessels. It is always a good idea when working with previously owned items to get a sense for what kind of spirits may already be attached to them and determine if the current resident will be a beneficial addition to the work. If not, you may need to either respectfully assist it in moving on or forcibly exorcise it. Premade dolls and figurines can be prepared much like the suggestions for statuary above.

I encourage the reader to be creative in their craft and consider innovative ways we might approach existing materials in magical ways. For instance, a favorite quick trick of mine is to work with those sets of tiny "worry dolls" made of cloth, paper, and string that are sometimes found in gift shops. I will often employ these diminutive effigies by enlivening them with breath and then speaking a prayer or command to them. They can then be dressed with a bit of bewitched spittle or a magical oil and then carried or secreted away somewhere. These little figures function quite well for short-term *maumet* spirits that are meant to provide protection, alert us to danger, bring quick bursts of luck, and so forth. Their tiny size makes them excellent for carrying in a wallet, purse, or even a locket. And they can easily be added to conjure bags and bottle spells, or stealthily hidden in areas where you wish for them to exert an influence.

On Designing the Effigy

How we wish to design and embellish our effigies will be largely dictated by their intended purpose, our personal tastes, and the influence of our spirits. Here, you are encouraged to let such inspiration move through you. When creating an effigy meant to serve as a spirit vessel, let yourself be guided by the spirit it is being crafted for. You should incorporate symbolic elements, botanicals, colors, etc., that align with or have been requested by the spirit. You may also wish to consider the posing and gesture of the effigy when designing it. Perhaps a protective effigy is best represented as standing at attention, whereas an effigy for a spirit of prosperity might be depicted sitting upon a bag of money with its hands extended and offering handfuls of coins.

If the goal is to make a poppet representing a person, we might choose to invest a great deal of time and effort in ensuring its appearance is very similar to the person it represents. However, this is not necessarily required to create an effective poppet, particularly if we are employing other links (taglocks) in its creation. The choice here lies with the maker.

Effigies may be further outfitted with clothing, accessories, and tools that match the nature of their intended spirit. For instance, if the spirit we are working with expresses an affinity with amber, we might create a tiny necklace of amber beads for it. If it is meant to serve as a protective spirit who watches for danger, we might craft eyes for it from pieces of onyx or *nazar* (evil eye) beads. We might also give it a tiny sword and shield to arm it in fighting against danger. If we are working with a spirit with lunar associations, we might design it with a crescent crown, moonstone eyes, and a silver chain around its neck, and we might fill it with lunar herbs like willow and mugwort. If the spirit is meant to assist us in gathering knowledge and information, we might give it a small satchel that represents this ability to collect and store knowledge or place a miniature blank book in its hands. If it is a spirit aligned with assisting in divination, we may wish to give it a tiny tarot deck or other divination tools.

In doing these things, we are further aligning the created material body of the spirit to its nature and areas of influence and better preparing it to work with us in the material realm. The clothing, accessories, and tools we give to these effigies needn't all be present at their creation either. These are all items that we may offer to spirits as gifts of devotion or forms of payment for their work. I have often found that over time spirits will make requests for certain items so that they might be better equipped to do their work in our realm or as an exchange for their assistance on magical workings.

In your process of crafting an effigy, you may begin with a very specific vision of what form the effigy will take and wish to sketch it out first in order to meticulously plan each element you'll incorporate into its design. Or you might instead wish to approach the act of creation as an evolutionary one that allows for adaptation, improvisation, and revelation throughout the process. Allow yourself to develop an approach that feels organic to you and provides the best results.

In much of the work I do, the acts of crafting, communion, and conjuration become so incredibly intertwined that they are indistinguishable at times. In these moments, the process of creation informs both the material form of the effigy and reveals deeper understandings of the spirit it will serve.

For example, when I am creating with clay, I might begin with a vague idea of what I wish my sculpture to look like or the type of spirit I wish to call forth. Once I begin sculpting, I allow my spirits to quite literally move with and through me. An example of how this might look within my own practice begins with a familiar spirit that I have worked with for many years and have built a foundation of trust with. One of his roles in our partnership is to bring forth and connect me with other spirits who are willing to serve as workers and familiars for myself or my clients on either a short-term or more permanent basis.

In my work with him, I begin with a lump of clay which has had simple conjurations whispered over it, and at times, sacred waters or magical oils worked into it. I will then engage in a form of half-trance/possession wherein I allow my hands to work the clay with the guidance of this trusted familiar spirit. Throughout this process of crafting and creation, I am receiving greater information and understanding of the spirit as it slowly emerges, reveals itself, and is born from the clay. Such an approach reinforces the co-creative dance we are courting when drawing spirits forth from the Otherworld and into embodied forms.

PRAXIS: Conjuring Through Clay

This is a fairly simple exercise that may provide some truly powerful results. The purpose here is to treat the art of crafting as a vehicle for the arte of mediumship. In this example, we are using clay as our material to craft a *maumet* spirit. However, this can be adapted as needed for other kinds of work. It is a co-creative conjuration where we allow the act of sculpting to be the vehicle through which spirit communion may occur. You should begin this work with a fairly clear, but not rigid, idea for a desire you seek to achieve or a kind of spirit you wish to create/conjure and work with.

Items Needed:

- Clay of some kind
- Tools for sculpting

1. In a place where you will not be interrupted, begin by preparing your space however best suits your needs to do this sculpting work and your personal practice. For these purposes, an art studio or even your kitchen table may become the ritual space, but you can certainly do this in a more formal setting, as preferred. If desired, you should ritually prepare yourself and the space as feels most

appropriate, such as by laying a compass, casting a circle, and wearing a protective oil such as the *Oil of Protection* listed in the Formulary section.

2. Do the basic alignment from Chapter Three, then state:

> *"I call now to those spirits who serve as both protectors and allies. I call to my ancestors and to the spirits who walk with and watch over me, both known and unknown, named and unnamed, and ask that you guide my hands in this work and aid me in this conjuring of clay. Bring forth form from spirit and grant revelation in the crafting of this maumet for the purposes of [insert your desire or need here]."*

3. You should begin working your clay now. I will often begin by adding a small amount of consecrated water to the clay to slightly moisten it and also by working a bit of Spirit Summoning oil into the clay.
4. With your magical desire in mind, allow yourself to work the clay into whatever shapes and forms you feel inspired towards. Allow for this to become a bit of a conversation between yourself and this *maumet* spirit which seeks to be born and aid you in your work. The spirit vessel you are creating may be humanoid in appearance or something entirely different.
5. In your crafting, if the type of clay you are using allows for this, you may feel guided to work dried herbs, additional powders, dirts, or other items into it, which will help empower the *maumet.*
6. As you are sculpting this figure, consider what is being revealed. Are you receiving images and inspiration towards its form, or perhaps for incorporating any sigils, colors, or other material into this item? Are you receiving any further insights into the nature of the spirit being crafted, such as its likes and dislikes, offerings it may prefer, or what name it may be called? This is an excellent time to allow such insights to flow, as they will contribute to a greater understanding of the connection to the creature you are bringing forth.
7. Continue this until you are done or reach a reasonable stopping point, and conclude by saying:

> *"I give deepest gratitude to those spirits who serve as both protectors and allies; to my ancestors and to the spirits who walk with and watch over me, both known and unknown, named and unnamed, and thank you for guiding my hands in this work and aiding me in this conjuring of clay."*

Notes on this Practice:
This is often only the first step in a process of crafting with clay, as once it dries, it may need to be fired, but it will inevitably be given further decoration and embellishment with paints, glazes, and such. When crafting spirit vessels from clay, I almost always include a cavity in the base or the back that can be further loaded with magical material relevant to the spirit/working and then sealed in some way. This exercise serves as a basic template for approaching the act of crafting as an opportunity for spirit communication and revelation, and it may be altered and adapted as suits you best.

Recommended Additional Reading

The Wild Dyer: A maker's guide to natural dyes with projects to create and stitch by Abigail Booth. Princeton Architectural Press. 2019.

Anatomy of a Doll. the Fabric Sculptor's Handbook by Susanna Oroyan. C&T Publishing. 1997.

Designing the Doll: From Concept to Construction by Susanna Oroyan. C&T Publishing. 2010.

Secrets of Rusty Things: Transforming Found Objects into Art by Michael de Meng. North Light Books. 2007.

Carving the Little Guys: Easy Techniques for Beginning Woodcarvers by Keith Randich. Fox Chapel Publishing. 2013.

Mastering Sculpture: The Figure in Clay: A Guide to Capturing the Human Form for Ceramic Artists by Cristina Córdova. Quarry Books. 2022.

Powerful Clay Spells: Manifest your desires with the oldest magical tool by Leopoldo Thompson. Independently Published. 2021.

Chapter Nine
Stone, Bone, Relic, and Root: On Materia Magica

By this point in our journey, it should be well established that, from an animistic perspective, each element employed in the practice of witchcraft, such as herbs, clay, cloth, stones, and bones, possesses a facet of spirit and consciousness. A personhood that can be awakened and aligned with our desires, enabling us to coordinate each unique component of our fetich towards the greater objective. Although we will soon discuss methods of conjuring and forming alliances with the spirits of our materials, such work often begins with our initial approach to gathering magical *materia.*

On the Collection of Materia

When entering a place where there are spirits and their associated *materia,* that may be beneficial partners within my magical work, or if I happen to stumble upon a plant, stone, or some animal bones I'd like to collect, I will usually announce both my presence and intentions to the spirits of the place verbally. This needn't be a shouted declaration. It might be a simple whisper. But, as with most things magical, I believe the inclusion of spoken word and breath is important here. Afterwards, I will wait and see if I receive a feeling or sign of approval from the spirits to gather the requested materials before moving forward.

This sort of intuition takes time to develop in order to ensure that we are informed by the desires of the land and its spirits and not led by our own wishful thinking. This is where divination comes in as a helpful way to verify if permission has truly been granted. In such cases, the simple divination methods mentioned earlier may be of use. Occasionally, I will instead take a moment to sit and briefly slip into the Otherworld via simple spirit flight or scrying techniques. From here, I attempt to connect with the spirits of place, particularly the guardian of the land or *Genius Loci,*[96] to get a greater sense of their nature and commune with them.

Through the above actions, I am seeking to build rapport, and give acknowledgement and respect to the local spirits, as well as gain permission to gather *materia* from this place. I have consistently found that getting on the good side of the local spirits and showing them respect tends to encourage them to reveal greater mysteries and blessings to the seeker. In some cases, when searching for elements for our craft, it can be rewarding to go forth into a place without seeking a specific type of *materia* and instead open yourself to whatever might present itself as an ally in your work. Doing the work of establishing respect and connection upfront will often provide some incredibly fruitful and unpredictable results.

Once I feel I've established contact, I will then work to determine through divination or intuition what, if any, offerings the spirits of that place might request in return for their aid. When I go out into the world to collect *materia,* I usually carry a satchel that includes: a trowel, a harvesting knife, plastic and paper bags, permanent markers for labeling bags, tools for divination, and various items for spirit offerings. These offerings may take many forms, but I find that carrying coins, tobacco, whisky, and fresh water tends to serve well for most of the spirits I encounter. I also usually carry a wind instrument of some kind. Usually, this is a flute crafted from elder wood or a ceramic ocarina. I often play these as a form of spirit calling and as an offering of breath and song to the spirits of place. In my own work, I have generally received very positive responses from land spirits with one or more of the offerings listed above.

To be given guidance from a spirit, agree upon offerings, and to be granted permission to collect *materia,* is to form a simple transactional pact with the spirit of that place. This might be a one-time interaction or it may grow into an ongoing relationship with that spirit, should you both desire it. Once permission and pact are secured, any agreed-upon offerings will be given. For me, this often takes the form of a bit of tobacco

---

96 Spirit of Place

crumbled and sprinkled upon the earth. Offerings may also take the form of coins being buried, or fresh water or whisky poured upon the land and accompanied by prayer. In some cases, the spirit might request that I offer up a song or spend time tending to the land and removing litter from the place. In other cases, they may request nothing at all.

I will then collect or harvest the necessary *materia,* taking care not to take more than needed and to be as respectful to the land as possible. The items are then placed into individual bags and labelled with the date and place they were gathered with a permanent marker. Upon returning home, I will likely find a more appropriate option, such as a glass jar, for storing whatever I have gathered until it is to be incorporated into a fetich or effigy.

On The Conjuring of Materia

When conjuring our *materia,* we are stirring, rousing, and calling the spirit to attention and action by speaking aloud to it or praying over it. The goal is to respectfully awaken the spirit, form a partnership, and better align the virtues of the spirit with our desires. When I speak of awakening the spirit of *materia,* it is not viewed as literally asleep. However, such spirits are often not used to engaging with humans in a personified and anthropomorphized manner. So, we are taking actions to awaken its attention/consciousness in these ways in hopes that we might more effectively engage and partner with the spirit.

Though recognizing the spiritual personhood and applying methods of conjuration to the store-bought paints, cloth, or clay we work with may feel odd to some, I assure you, it can be done. That said, many witches will find it more organic to first apply this approach towards engaging with the spirits of botanical, mineralogical, and animal *materia.* Let's begin with botanicals as an example for the ways we might approach stirring the spirits of magical *materia.*

When we turn to lists of magical correspondences for understanding herbs and botanicals, what is being presented for us is often a condensed understanding of plants informed by folklore, history, and sympathetic associations that have been collected from any number of sources, ancient or contemporary. Though it might prove somewhat effective to look through a book of herblore and choose, say, seven Venusian herbs to work into a love fetich, I would like to make an argument here for the benefits and effectiveness of actively working *with* and conjuring our magical *materia* as opposed to simply *using materia*.

Whereas *using materia* tends to look like collecting ingredients, combining them based solely upon their collected lore, symbolism, and correspondences, and then hoping they might work as we wish. Working *with materia* initially takes the form of truly contemplating what we are working with and making efforts to better understand its spirit and nature. One of the ways I suggest when beginning this process is to contemplate some or all of these questions:

- Where is the *materia* native to?
- What are its unique or defining properties?
- What environments does it thrive in, and what are its needs for survival?
- What can I learn from its life cycle and/or growing patterns?
- What can I learn from its biology or phytochemistry?
- What has its relationship been with humans and what roles has it played?
- How have we worked with it in the realm of magic, sustenance, medicine, artistry, and industry?
- What folklore and mythology is there about it? How is this relevant to my practice, location, or ancestry?
- What psychic impressions do I get from handling it, being in its presence, and attempting to communicate?
- All this considered, what is the nature of this *materia?* What does it do?

Regardless of whether we are attempting to connect with the spirit of an animal through working with its bones or seeking to ally with the spirit of an antique deck of playing cards. Beginning from a place of curiosity and having done at least some basic contemplation upon the nature of the *materia*/spirits you are working with will provide a much more solid foundation for the work of conjuration, which follows.

The more materialistic approach of simply *using materia* misses an opportunity which invites us to strengthen our arte through developing reciprocal relationships with spirits who might, in time, become valuable allies in our endeavors. In essence, working *with materia* is creating a partnership.

To better illustrate this, allow me to give an example: Imagine you wish to craft a charm for protection, and while selecting herbs, you choose to include Rue *(Ruta graveolens)* because you saw it mentioned in a book as a protective botanical. Because it is indeed a plant of protection, Rue will likely do some protective things on your behalf. However, how much better might you know Rue, and how much better might it work as an ally, if you studied more deeply into its lore and learned how it has historically been worked with by people? What if you studied its folklore and learned that it has been said to work against the venom of snakes and the dreaded basilisk? That it has been said to dispel the evil eye and malefic magic? Or that it has traditionally been known as "herb of grace"? How much better might you know Rue if you were to learn where it grows best, and perhaps grow it for yourself and witness its patterns? What about communing with the spirit of Rue in the Otherworld to become better acquainted and establish a relationship with it?

Through such understanding and relationships, we are better able to effectively partner with the spirit of things towards our intended goal. Using another protective plant as an example, let's say you wish to use chili pepper in a protection effigy or fetich because you saw it listed as a plant of protection. So, without much thought for the spirit of the plant or conjuring its aid, you toss it into a conjure bag and start carrying it for protection.

Now, much like all dogs will have dog-like qualities, chili peppers will indeed have protective and martial qualities by nature. A dog, when left to its own devices, will likely do dog-like things. In a similar way, chili pepper will do chili pepper-like things, and that might include providing protection. However, we aren't guaranteed that.

How much more loyal might a dog be if we spend time with it, get to know its personality, care for it, and befriend it? How much more likely is it to protect us? Particularly if we begin to work with the protective instincts and nature of that dog, and encourage it to bring those behaviors forward when commanded? Building upon this, it's worth noting that most magical *materia* can be conjured for blessing or bane. So, as much as chili peppers might be used for magical protection, they can also be worked with for hexing to cause discord and harm.

Next, let's imagine that I don't particularly like you. Perhaps I'm the reason you're carrying that protection bag to begin with. Let's also imagine that I've already established a strong relationship with the spirit of chili pepper, and I'm currently working malefic magic upon you. If I'm already working with the spirit of the chili pepper to cause difficulty and discord in your life, you've just unwittingly amplified that influence by bringing the spirit of chili pepper into your spiritual ecosphere.

Further, if I happen to find out that you are carrying it on you, it gives me even more opportunity to directly conjure the spirit of the "protection" bag you have crafted and turn it against you. Why? Because that "dog" loves me more. We know each other. We're friends. I've shown more care, attention, and respect to it and built a relationship. I've tended to it in my garden and worked magic alongside it many times. It's a welcome ally in my home. Who do you think that dog is more likely to come to when it's called?

These examples may seem harsh, but I assure you, they are very real amongst witches. Though I've used the example of a dog here, the reader should not mistake my usage here as disparaging either dogs or chilis, but instead highlighting the nature of relationships, respect, and the reciprocity with which we should approach spirit work. As well as some of the pitfalls of simply *using materia.*

Is it possible to connect fully and form tight relationships with *all* of the *materia* you will use? Depending upon how many elements you are incorporating into your arte, perhaps not. However, it is highly advised that you have a solid selection of at least ten or so botanical/animal/mineralogical spirits with which you have taken the time to form a close relationship. Investing the effort and time in forming these relationships can prove invaluable and richly rewarding to the witch. In part because once you have built this rapport, these allies can help bring all of the other diverse spirits of *materia* you include within the crafting of effigies, fetiches, etc. in line with your goals. Additionally, the more we engage with and research the spirits of the *materia* we work with, the greater the likelihood is that they will reveal themselves and work with us in some truly exceptional and unexpected ways.

Continuing with our protective examples, let's explore what conjuring the spirit of *materia* might look like. If I wished to add an Angelica root to a protective effigy I was crafting, I might take the root in my hand and knock it gently upon a table three times in order to wake it up. Others might simply whisper "wake up" to the root. From here, I will speak aloud to the root. Something to the effect of:

"Awaken and be stirred, spirit of Angelica, Holy Ghost Root, you who are beloved of the Archangels and whom no malefic spirits, calamity, illness, or injury may prevail in the presence of. I call you forth and seek your aid that you might lend your protective virtues to the work of this effigy."

You can create something more specific, elaborate, and poetic if it suits your craft. Though such conjurations needn't be terribly wordy to prove effective. Your conjuration might be as simple as holding the *materia* in your hand and saying something like, "I awaken you, spirit of Angelica, and ask that you lend your virtues of protection to this effigy." I often find that speaking extemporaneously and from the heart during this process is the best approach to our work. What is most important is that you create some form of meaningful connection and partnership with the spirit of the things you wish to work with.

If, during the conjuring of *materia,* you find that you feel a sense of resistance or a message from the spirit that it is not inclined towards assisting you, it is best to avoid including that particular item as a part of the fetich or effigy you are working on. Instead, utilize spirit flight, divination, or other methods to connect with that spirit at a later time if you wish to determine more about how it will or won't assist you in your future magical endeavors. Not all spirits want to work with all people, and that is okay. There are plenty of other spirits we might find to partner with in accomplishing our goals.

On Purchased Materials and Found Objects

It is unlikely that all of the materials we will use in our arte will be found whilst strolling through woodlands, swamps, and cemeteries. Many of the things we use in our craft, from paints and pigments, clay and cloth, and even the botanical, mineral, and animal *materia* we require might need to be purchased. This should not imply that they are necessarily lesser, unpossessing of a powerful spirit, and unable to be conjured just as effectively.

Within much of my work, I purposefully employ vintage, antique, and everyday objects so that they might lend their virtues to the arte. Under a witching gaze, these items have a history and a spirit that may be effectively conjured and partnered with to craft spirit vessels. For example, an old used horseshoe is not only allied to the spirit of the horse but also to work and travel. An antique thimble is allied to the work of crafting, mending, and protection. An old cooking vessel may be allied to the work of providing sustenance and comfort.

To connect with the spirit of things, whether they be old or new, we need only to gaze upon them with a curious and animistic eye and ask ourselves questions about them:

- What is the purpose and nature of scissors? How is the nature of a new pair of scissors different from a well-worn and well-used pair of scissors?
- What is the nature of a mirror? How might I work with the spirit of a mirror in the work of crafting a fetich, and for what purpose?
- What is the nature of an old telephone? Might parts from it be well-suited for crafting a fetich for enhancing spirit communication?
- What is the nature of thread? Or a button? Or beads? What do they do?
- If it is a previously owned object, how was it previously used? Does its history help or hinder the type of magic I'm considering using it for?
- If it is a newly purchased object, what is it intended to do? What was it made for? How have human beings traditionally interacted with it?

What the average person disregards as everyday inanimate objects, the witch possesses the ability to ally with, conjure, and bewitch. Where some folks may see an old set of casino dice, I see a spirit I may call upon and work with for turning luck for good or ill. Where some might see an old pair of shoelaces, I see a spirit I might call upon for securing safe travels or tripping up enemies. We do not live in a disenchanted world; it is instead our own perspective that must become bewitched into allowing us to recognize the ways we might partner with the diversity of spirits around us.

PRAXIS: The Path of Revelation - A Found Materia Journey

This exercise is designed to act as a bit of a revelatory experience which provides guidance, inspiration, and assistance from the Otherworld when we are sourcing *materia* for crafting spirit vessels. It is designed to be approached from a place where you have not yet determined all of the *materia* that may be employed in your work, and is intended as a co-creative experience where unexpected *materia* may be revealed and granted as unique gifts whilst informing your work.

1. To begin, you will want to have established a purpose for which you are crafting a fetich, effigy, etc. Depending upon where you imagine you might end up you should pack your bag with any tools you may need, such as shears, a trowel, or gloves. You should also bring bags or some other way to store and organize any *materia* you might gather. Lastly, be sure to bring items for simple offerings to the spirits of the places you may go.
2. Standing before your front door, do a quick Basic Ritual Alignment as given in Chapter Three.
3. Next, keeping the intention for your spirit vessel in mind, state:

   "I stand at the threshold of this world and the Otherworld, and I call upon the ancestors and the spirits who walk with and watch over me, both known and unknown, named and unnamed. I embark upon a journey with my spirits as companions and ask that you may reveal to me that which will grant power and potency to my work. I go forth into the world with eyes alight and shall move in silence that I might truly hear".

4. You will then leave your home silently and go where you feel you are led to. This is treated as a sacred journey, somewhat akin to a walking meditation.
5. I find it best if you can travel there on foot, but this is not entirely necessary. The places you end up at could be incredibly varied. You may travel to a beach, to a crowded city street, to a nearby park, a junkyard, or even a local thrift store. There are no set rules here.
6. Ideally, when doing this exercise, you will remain as silent as possible. The exception to this is when you are speaking to spirits, either to ask permission, give offerings, or engage in charming or conjuration.
7. As you are out and about, allow yourself to be receptive to the places you feel led to. You may come across a particular plant, stone, or bone that wants to be included in your work. You might also find yourself in excellent places for gathering dirt. The items

you find may also be inorganic objects. I have done this exercise quite a few times and have returned home with items as diverse as old rusted bottle caps, railroad spikes, discarded glass bottles, and antique rat traps. Keep an open mind about what you may encounter and be creative when imagining how these things may be incorporated into your work.

8. Where appropriate, give offerings when collecting your *materia.* If you happen to find yourself in a shop, simply paying for the item might suffice as a form of offering.
9. When you are ready, return home. When approaching your door, leave a small offering in front of it and state:

> *"I stand at the threshold of the Otherworld and my own. I offer gratitude to the ancestors and spirits who walk with and watch over me, both known and unknown, named and unnamed, for your guidance, wisdom, and revelation."*

10. You may then enter your home, and the journey is concluded.

On Botanical Materia

Of course, the work of developing skill and wisdom in the realm of plants can easily become a lifetime of incredibly rewarding study. As there are many resources available that focus exclusively upon the magic and folklore of plants, I will not delve deeply into all possible realms of botanical witching here. I encourage the reader to avail themselves of some of the titles suggested at the end of this chapter for greater exploration in this realm. Instead, I wish to highlight a few additional considerations here that are somewhat unique to working with plants.

When we are able to directly harvest plant *materia* for our magic, in addition to the same considerations mentioned around collecting *materia* earlier, we should also seek the permission of the plant spirit itself. This may be worked into the same processes we discussed previously for gaining permissions from the spirit of place. Another aspect that we may wish to employ when gathering botanical materials is the often-underexplored use of verbal charms.

Employing verbal charms at the time of harvesting is its own form of conjuration. In the process of plant charming, we are calling the spirit to attention, speaking of its magical virtues, and by extension stirring them up, and then requesting its aid. Throughout history, we find diverse examples of such plant harvesting charms that we might borrow from or alter to make better suited to our use. One such example is this verbal charm meant to be spoken when harvesting plants just before sunrise that originates in the *Greek Magical Papyri:*

> *"I am picking you, [name of plant], with my five-fingered hand, I, [name], am bringing you home so that you may work for me for/ to [state purpose]. I adjure you by the undefiled [name of the god]: if you pay no heed to me, the earth which produced you will no longer be watered as far as you are concerned - ever in life again, if I fail in this operation, MOUTHABAR NACH BARNACHŌCHA BRAEŌ MENDA LAUBRAASSE PHASPHA BENDEŌ; fulfil for me the perfect charm."* [97]

Personally, I am not a fan of the often unnecessary tactics of threatening and bullying spirits that are so often present within the *Greek Magical Papyri.* That said, the first line within the text is an excellent template for how we might approach harvesting a plant. This is a simple and straightforward approach to showing the spirit of the plant respect as well as explaining what you are doing, and for what purpose. Instead of a threat, I am much more inclined to say something more to the effect of:

> *"If you aid me in this work, I will sing praises of you upon the wind, that my breath might strengthen and fortify you,"* or *"If you lend your power to this work, I promise to return to this place and offer water to the land that it might nourish you and your kin."*

Another example of such an herbal charm is recorded in Reginald Scot's *The Discoverie of Witchcraft* and is said to have been used by witches when gathering medicinal herbs:

97 *PGM IV.* 286-95

"Haile be thou holie hearbe
growing on the ground
All in the Mount Calvarie
first wert thou found,
Thou art good for manie a sore,
And healest manie a wound,
In the name of sweete Jesus
I take thee from the ground."

Again, the above might be used as is or altered for our own use as suits our arte. We might also speak simply and extemporaneously from the heart to plants as we harvest them and say something to the effect of:

> *"Oh, ancient, mighty, and powerful oak tree, you who are king of the forest. I gift you my breath by the speaking of this charm and ask that you grant me permission to gather your leaves and acorns that they and you may assist me in works of strength, protection, and prosperity."*

On the Sourcing and Use of Dirts

Dirts (earth/soil/mud) are a bountiful, accessible, and incredibly effective *materia* that we can employ in a vast number of magical operations. Conjured dirts may be easily incorporated into magical formulas such as oils and powders. They may be worked into our clay and wax for the crafting of effigies, and they may be incorporated into fetiches, conjure bags, and spirit vessels.

While the use of dirts in magic does appear to greater or lesser degrees across various magical traditions, it is worth noting that much of the dirt magic found within modern magic finds its primary inspiration from living African diasporic traditions. Some more notable examples being the traditions of Hoodoo, Quimbanda, and Palo, where various dirts are ritually collected and employed in a diversity of works. Due to a growing popularity within certain circles of contemporary witchcraft, it seems more than appropriate that we pause to give acknowledgement to these origins, as the African roots of this practice are often overlooked in popular explorations of this arte.

As we begin to think about dirt as a link to the power, history, and spirits of a place, the industrious witch will find appropriate locations to gather dirts for any and all purposes. When collecting dirts, we might choose locations based on their spirits, folklore, historical significance, or the current activity happening on that land.

Examples of historical dirts might include those collected from sites of ancient temples or where historical battles occurred. These might, in turn, be allied to the spirits and history of devotion at those temples, or to the violence, triumph, and turmoil of the battlefield. Remembering that our craft is often a mythopoetic one that finds great power undulating between the twin serpents of the historical and the mythological, we should treat the places of myth with equal consideration. For example, when creating formulas meant to call upon the witches' devil, I have included dirt from Dimmuborgir, a location in Iceland said to be where the devil landed when he was cast down from heaven.

Any places of business, or locations where people gather for a purpose, may be conjured to call upon the diverse spirits associated with the activities that happen there. Casinos are an excellent place to gather dirts for working luck magic. Dirt gathered from event halls and nightclubs can be worked effectively for magic related to community, revelry, or entertainment. Dirt from a marketplace may be worked with in matters of commerce and business. Dirt from a garden may be worked with for growth, life, beauty, and bounty. And dirt gathered from prestigious universities or libraries might be employed to aid in crafting fetiches for study and knowledge retention.

Dirt from the crossroads may be worked with for magic associated with travel, communication, and commerce. It is also appropriate for connecting with and calling upon the myriad of spirits related to change, chance, catalyst, and chaos associated with the crossroads in various cultures. Crossroads are where spirits meet, so dirt gathered there may assist us in a variety of works of spirit conjuration and communication. That said, the type of crossroad will have an impact on the spirits present. A cemetery crossroad is quite different in the sorts of communication and magical virtues it offers when compared to the dirt gathered from a woodland crossroad or a busy urban center.

We may also gather dirts to exert influence upon a person or place for good or ill. This sort of work might look like gathering dirt from the four corners of our home and working with it to connect to the *genius loci* to ensure domestic protection and peace. Similarly, dirt gathered from your place of employment might serve in works for drawing business or securing a promotion. Dirt gathered from another person's home, or carefully gathered dirt from their footprint, may be worked with to influence the target for blessing or bane.

We might also gather dirt from the tracks left by animals to call upon their spirits for aid. The dirt from an anthill may assist us when we wish to inspire teamwork or when doing ancestral work. We might collect dirt from a riverbank for movement and flow. Whereas dirt from the opening of a cave or an animal's den might serve us well in fetiches centered on chthonic works. We might also choose dirts from locations that radiate planetary virtues. In this case, it is most appropriate to gather such dirts during the associated planetary day and hour and call upon the aid of any deities or spirits that you associate with those planets in your craft. For inspiration in the area, please see the appendices at the back of this book for a listing of planetary associations and places commonly associated with the seven classical planets.

As with much of the materia we might work with in our craft, the only limitation to the types of dirt we may gather and the spirits we may work with by extension is our own ingenuity. I encourage the reader to more frequently shift their gaze downward and look upon the land they walk upon with witching eyes. Sourcing points of power and allying with the spirits of those places so that they may become allies in this arte.

PRAXIS: Crafting Dirt Clay

This is a method for working with ritually collected dirts and other *materia* which creates a claylike substance that may be used for filling spirit vessels such as shells, horns, and the like as well as for loading statues. Depending upon what your purpose is this can be highly tailored to suit the work.

For this, you will need:

- Enough of your chosen dirts to serve as the bulk of the dirt clay. These should be mixed and sifted to remove any stones or random plant material.

- Any additional powdered herbs, bone, ash, or other *materia* you may wish to add.
- Chicken or Duck eggs
- A large bowl for mixing

1. Your dirts and powders should be added to the large bowl. You may also wish to add a bit of any complimentary waters, tinctures, perfumes, or washes to this mix as well, but don't overdo this or it will become waterier than will be of use.
2. Pick up the first egg you will use and hold it with both hands at heart level.[98]
3. Envision a bird of flame like a phoenix descending from the upperworld down and lending power to the egg and using your *vox magica*[99] state:

   "Supernal powers descend!"

4. Next, envision a black serpent of the watery depths, ascending from the underworld whilst using your *vox magica* to state:

   "Infernal powers arise!"

5. Envision these spirits of the upperworld and underworld meeting at your heart center and lending their power and life force to the egg you hold. Then envision the egg being imbued with power from all directions, allied to your work and state:

   "Reside in the heart terrestrial, the crossways betwixt all realms."

6. Then you will state:

---

98 For a similar example of this ritual blessing of eggs see *Crafting the Cauldron of Rebirth* in Chapter Ten.

99 The empowered magical voice employed in ritual and conjuration . See Chapter Ten for a deeper explanation of the *vox magica.*

"It is not my hands which perform this work, but the hands of that which breathed the first breath, uttered the first word, and crafted the first form."

7. You will then crack the egg into the dirt mixture and state:

   "Let this egg be that of both serpent and bird, from which all of creation is born."

8. You should thoroughly mix the egg into the dirt. You may then add more eggs or dirt to the mixture as needed to get a good consistency. You do not need to repeat the above with all additional eggs added.

This dirt mixture will not be so much like clay that you can sculpt with it. It is more like a cement mixture, which is why it is excellent for filling spirit vessels that can contain it. In fact, eggs were once used in this way to create cement and mortar in the past. Any vessel you are filling with the mix should be one that has decent air circulation. For instance, you wouldn't want to fill a spirit pot with this and then cover it with an airtight lid, as it will not allow the mix to dry and will likely lead to rot. Even with proper air circulation, this mix can occasionally smell a bit as it dries.

9. When you are adding this to a vessel like a horn, shell, or pot, you should add any larger solid objects, such as stones, bones, etc., before you add the dirt clay, or else work them in on top of it. Once this mixture dries, so long as you have the right ratio of dirt/egg it should harden fairly thoroughly.
10. An alternative to this, which makes a more workable clay, is to forgo the egg and simply mix your dirts, powders, waters, etc. directly into an air-drying clay as mentioned earlier in this chapter. This can be used for similar purposes or for creating sculptural forms as well.

On the Domain and Dirts of the Dead

Why might we work in the cemetery, and what types of magics might we engage with there? Firstly, it is a place where we can more easily call upon and meet with spirits of the dead. This could include ancestral dead, but also the spirits of influential, successful, learned, famous, or infamous folks whom we may wish to establish a relationship with so that they might assist us in our magics. We might also work in the cemetery to employ the spirits of death and decay. This could be worked to bring about an ending to a situation, such as an illness, to transform/transmute things, or for works of crossing and cursing.[100] We might also visit the cemetery to gather various *materia* as plants, stones, dirts, and other *materia* sourced from the cemetery will carry its virtues and may be employed in formulas and fetishes designed for working with the dead.

To this end, let us now explore proper etiquette for entering the cemetery when we wish to do magical work there, as well as some traditional methods for the collecting of various graveyard dirts that you might employ in your witchcraft.

Entering the Cemetery

It is best practice to enter the burial ground through the main gate when possible. When doing so, it is appropriate to knock three times upon the gate or stomp your foot upon the ground three times in order to announce your presence to the guardian of the gateway, as well as to speak aloud your intentions to do work within the cemetery. It is both customary and good manners to leave an offering at the gateway or entrance of some sort. Most commonly, this takes the form of tobacco, coins (often this is three pennies), and/or a bit of whisky poured upon the ground.

Next, you will also leave a similar offering for the guardian of the cemetery. Most accurately, this is the grave of the first person to be buried there. However, as this can often be difficult to identify, the first grave to the left of the main entrance acts as a stand-in for this grave, and its spirit is believed to ensure that the offerings go to the guardian proper. Both the offering at the gate and the grave show respect for the spirits who oversee the cemetery and curry their favor that we might be protected in our work.

---

100 Bear in mind that such malefic works are not generally undertaken lightly. And those who are not fairly adept in their practice are generally discouraged from engaging in these types of workings, or with such spirits, until they are skilled enough at cleansings, banishings, and exorcisms to ensure that these spirits do not become attached to us in parasitic ways.

Meeting the Dead

When exploring the cemetery, you may be searching for specific spirits to commune and connect with. Websites like Find a Grave and BillionGraves have searchable databases of cemetery records that may assist in determining any notable people who may be buried there. Conversely, you may simply wish to walk the cemetery and see if any particular gravesites stand out or seem to call to you. While traveling throughout the cemetery, it is always best practice to avoid whistling, mindlessly walking upon graves, and reading any of the names found on headstones aloud. That is, unless you wish to call the attention of the spirit whose name you are speaking.

When you find a grave you are looking for or one that seems to draw you, spend some time in silence there. Listen for any messages, note any bodily sensations you may have, or images that come to mind. If you feel an affinity with a particular grave, spend a bit of time communing with that spirit. This is a first meeting, we are not immediately beginning to work with this spirit, simply getting to know them. This type of work can be coupled with divination or mediumistic skills to begin a bit more of a conversation with the dead. You may also wish to follow up on this initial meeting by doing research into the person whose grave you have visited. Who were they in life? What were their accomplishments and struggles? Might they possibly make a good ally in your magical work?

Developing meaningful and trusting relationships with spirits often takes time. You might visit the grave on multiple occasions, perhaps leaving very simple offerings as feels appropriate. You might also check in with other spirits you work with, such as ancestral spirits, to ask if this spirit is one that you can trust. Many spirits of the dead tend to be almost forgotten, and there are a good number of them who are happy to have their name remembered and willing to assist us in our work in exchange for such remembrance and offerings.

Once you have established a decent relationship with one of these spirits, you may then consider asking for their assistance in your magical work. This is best confirmed by employing methods of divination, such as the simple methods mentioned earlier in this book, to confirm both their willingness to work with you as well as what type of payment they might like in return. When it comes to working with spirits of the dead, I recommend simple offerings such as tobacco, alcohol, coins, candy, fruit, flowers, and candles burned in their honor.

One of the most common ways of tying our magics to the aid and influence of the dead is the use of graveyard dirt. In cases where general graveyard dirt may be desired for necromantic, banishing, or crossing work, these will often be gathered from the gates of a burial ground or from a crossroad within the cemetery gates. However, when gathering *grave* dirt as opposed to *graveyard* dirt, it is about working with the spirit of the person to whom the grave belongs as the dirt from each grave carries a link to that specific spirit.

Grave dirts may be added to magical powders, oils, conjure bags, fetish objects, and used for dressing spell candles. When employing the dirt we call upon the spirit by name, remind them of their agreement to aid our work, remind them that the dirt has been previously paid for, and often, offer them an additional offering should our work be successful. I will often burn a candle in honor of the spirit or take flowers to their grave as a form of payment and sign of gratitude when they have aided me in a significant way.

Gathering Grave Dirts

When gathering grave dirts it is always best practice to be respectful and inconspicuous. Traditionally, once you have established a relationship with the spirit and they have agreed to work with you, you will take one scoop of dirt from the areas of the head, the heart, and the foot of the grave. You needn't take a massive shovel or garden trowel with you to do this. Often, a decent-sized spoon will work and can usually be quickly hidden in a pocket should prying eyes suddenly be upon you. In each hole, you should place a silver dime. As I was taught in traditions of Southern Conjure, and as reflected in my personal craft, these will usually be Mercury dimes. These are dimes that are no longer in circulation and are more appropriately known as "Liberty dimes," as the image they bear is meant to be a personification of Liberty. However, due to the winged helmet she wears, she has been more commonly seen as representative of Hermes/Mercury, the Greek/Roman psychopomp who transports the spirits of the dead.

Place a dime in each of the holes, cover with a bit of soil, and give thanks to the spirit. Be sure to bag or bottle the grave dirt you've collected and label it with the name of the person from whom it came, their birth/death dates, and the date collected. This dirt can then be brought home and worked with in the manner listed above. It is suggested that graveyard dirts be stored in places other than the bedroom, kitchen, or bathroom if possible. This is to avoid inviting too much of the presence of the dead into these places of sleep/sex, nourishment, and cleansing.

Types of Graves and Dirts

Though each spirit will have their unique areas of agency, experience, and expertise. There are some general suggestions for various types of spirits, and by extension grave dirt, that we may wish to work with for various purposes:

- **Soldier:** Soldiers are often believed to be good at following orders, carrying out magical missions, surveillance, and protection
- **Judge:** Judges can be worked with when we wish to enact judgment upon another or when we are seeking justice. Of course, the type of judge and their track record play heavily into this. In reflection of this, there are various traditional conjure workings which call for the dirt of a friendly judge, an upstanding judge, a corrupt judge, or a hanging judge (Meaning a judge who has sentenced people to death). Working with judges is understandably a common practice when involved in court cases and legal proceedings.
- **Spiritual Leaders:** Those who have served as spiritual or magical leaders and teachers may be incredibly helpful in our own spiritual, psychic, or magical development. Ideally, these will be individuals whose beliefs and practices align with our own. Surprisingly, though, you may find that spiritual teachers from other traditions may be more than willing to assist you in your work.
- **Performers:** This can include actors, singers, musicians, dancers, artists, authors, or athletes. These spirits can often assist us in excelling in these realms and acquiring fame, but also in gaining confidence if we struggle with public speaking and performing in front of others.
- **Child:** The spirits of children are particularly effective at bringing joy and laughter. They are also often worked with to help bring prosperity. However, you must always remember that you are generally dealing with a spirit that carries a childlike innocence and naivete, and that these spirits can sometimes be pranksters as well.
- **Doctor:** These spirits are connected to the realm of health and healing. Again, the life, expertise, and track record of the particular doctor will impact their areas of healing and their effectiveness.

Leaving the Cemetery

When leaving the cemetery, it is best practice to perform a quick cleansing before you leave. This is designed to ensure that any parasitic entities or hungry ghosts do not attach themselves to us or follow us home. One of the most common cleansings I perform upon leaving the cemetery is to take two silver-colored coins, the denomination does not matter, and pass/rub them all over your body. Be sure to get your head, back of neck, hands, and feet. Then, when leaving the cemetery, these should be dropped as you exit the cemetery gate without looking back. You should also endeavor to return home on a different route from which you arrived. This is intended to confuse any last spiritual entities that might desire to follow you home.

On returning home, you may wish to wash your hands, shoes, and head with consecrated water or use the *Hungry Ghost Spray* listed in the formulary section. An infusion of Pine needles and Angelica, or Florida Water, spritzed over oneself works well for this as well.

On the Heartstone and Other Stones

Stones and pebbles may be collected from various places and worked with in a very similar manner to dirts. We might also draw upon the historical, mythological, and folkloric attributions of gems, crystals, and minerals when employing their spirits in our work as well. There is also no shortage of resources for researching the chemical, geological, and magical properties of stones available to the witch. For some suggestions on more in-depth sources, see the end of this chapter.

Stones may serve as additions to the load of a spirit vessel, or in the case of the Heartstone, they may serve as its center. The Heartstone may be viewed as a form of *baetyl* or *baetylus.* In essence, a stone that functions as a sacred *locus* of spirit or deity. The term is translated as "house of god," and the *baetyl* is treated as the earthly body of a deity and an object of both power and devotion. A *baetyl* might be made from any stone so long as the devotee recognizes it as inhabited by the sacred. As they are literally stones fallen from the heavens, many historical examples of *baetyls* were made from meteorites. In other examples, such as at the Sanctuary of Aphrodite in Cyprus, an ancient stone venerated as the goddess is a naturally formed stone of black basalt.

In a mythic sense, centralized sacred stones might be seen as representative of the first mountain that bridges the upper, middle, and underworld, or as the primeval mound from which all of creation springs forth. Omphalos stones, like the one located at the Temple of Apollo at Delphi, are stone markers meant to represent the center of the world and have historically been treated with similar reverence. Such sacred stones are found throughout the ancient world, and comparable examples are found by different names cross-culturally.

In Yorubaland, the Orisha Eshu is often represented by *yangi* stone, a form of laterite stone which serves as his earthly body. Such stones range from fairly small to quite large in size, with larger examples often found in marketplaces, crossroads, and the entrance to homes. *Yangi* are ritually washed with sacred herbs and fed blood as a part of their birthing, and liquid offerings such as palm oil are poured directly upon the stone to feed Eshu.

In the Afro-Cuban religion of Lucumí, nearly all Orisha are built around stones that serve in many ways as representative of the material body of the Orisha. These stones are ritually prepared and usually housed within ceramic or wooden vessels along with additional tools and items specific to that Orisha. Additionally, during the ceremony of *kariocha,* when a person becomes a priest within the religion, the head (*Ori*) of the priest is regarded as a "stone" which is ritually cleansed and prepared for receiving and merging with the Orisha they are being made to.[101] Within certain instances of the Afro-Brazilian tradition of Quimbanda, a stone serves as the axis around which a spirit pot or *assentamento* is made. These vessels serve as the physical embodiment of an Exu or Pomba Gira, which, in addition to the stone, are further empowered by the addition of appropriate dirts, herbs, and other *materia,* as well as objects, and tools aligned to the specific Exu or Pomba Gira it is intended to house.

In the ancient world, cairns of stacked stones were created to serve as the dwelling place for deities such as Hermes or the Cailleach. Within Hindu practice, certain stones are treated as sacred representatives of the *lingam* of Shiva, and fossilized ammonites known as *shaligrams* are regarded as being inhabited by gods. Domestic gods and household spirits are often found residing within stones as well. An example of such is the

101 Jesse Hathaway-Diaz, in discussion with author, March 2024.

Kurinyi Bog spirits of Russian folklore, who live within hagstones and protect the hens of a property, with their name translating quite delightfully to "Chicken God."[102] Meanwhile, several traditions throughout Europe recognize the hearthstone or foundation stone of the home as the primary dwelling place for household spirits.

Within our work here, the heartstone serves as our *baetyl* and is the axis or nucleus around which the effigy or fetich is often built. As its name implies, it may be viewed as the heart of the body/vessel we are constructing for a spirit. It is the throne that the spirit we are embodying might rest upon. In many cases, should a fetich or effigy become damaged or broken, so long as the heartstone is preserved, we are able to reconstruct the spirit vessel from this central point with relative ease. The type of stone may be varied, but through the act of conjuration and ritually preparing the stone, we are able to tailor our heartstone to the work of the spirit vessel.

When selecting a stone to function as the heartstone for a spirit vessel, there are many approaches we might take. Firstly, we might consider the location the stone is collected from. In this case, it is less about what a stone looks like or what it is made from, but instead how it relates to the nature of a place and how that location has influenced it. For instance, similar to our considerations when sourcing dirts, if we are creating a spirit vessel meant to align with spirits of material wealth or to draw upon luck, we might search for a stone near a financial institution or a casino, respectively. For works related to knowledge and learning, we might look for a stone from near a library or an esteemed university. For movement or cleansing, perhaps we might choose a stone from a river. For travel, we might choose a stone from near a railroad track, highway, or airport. When in doubt, as it is the meeting place of spirits, a stone respectfully paid for and gathered from a crossroad will serve quite well.

We might also consider the size, shape, or color of the stone. Stones that are longer and more phallic in shape tend to be worked with when we wish to work with a more active, aggressive, or masculine power. Whereas more spherical stones, or those shaped reminiscent of a vulva, might be worked with to draw upon more receptive, generative, or feminine power. That said, though stones can be worked with through a gendered lens, this

---

102 Carol Rose. *Spirits, Fairies, Leprechauns and Goblins: An Encyclopedia.* (W. W. Norton & Company, 1996) 188.

is far from the only possible way we might take their shape into account. Stones with a sharp edge may serve well when the goal of a fetich is defense, to cut things away, or to cause division. Flatter stones might be selected for creating stability or a solid foundation. Whereas smoother stones might be chosen in cases where we wish to foster ease and amiability. In the case of color, we may search for stones that share color associations in alignment with the spirit we are working with, or that are reflective of our goal. White stones might be chosen for purity, cleansing, and alignment to the upper world and its spirits. Red stones might be chosen for works of action, passion, and attack, or to align with spirits and works of the middle world. And Black stones might be chosen for works of warding, protection, necromancy, or to align with spirits of the underworld.

Lastly, you might choose stones based upon their mineralogical makeup and the virtues commonly attributed to them within legend and lore. For those who have an affinity for working with the spirits of particular gemstones and minerals, this will be a natural fit. As previously mentioned, meteorites were often used as *baetyls,* and here they might serve well when crafting idols representative of sky gods and spirits with celestial or extraterrestrial origins. Spirits of lightning and storms might be served well by the use of fulgurite[103] for a heartstone. In cases where the goal is for an effigy or fetich to serve the role of attracting things we desire, I have found great success when employing lodestones.[104] An interesting example of the use of a lodestone in this manner can be found in the *Greek Magical Papyri* where a lodestone serves as the heart of a waxen effigy designed to draw positive attention and prosperity.[105]

Quartz has been celebrated in many cultures for serving as both a reservoir and transmitter for spirits. The use of quartz scrying spheres comes to mind here. I have known several accomplished witches who will turn to quartz as the material of choice when engaging in this type of work. Bear in mind that these needn't be beautifully polished, faceted, or cut specimens. When I have employed quartz in the past, I've had good results working with naturally occurring quartz pebbles, like those often found in riverbeds or on seashores.

---

103 A form of naturally occurring glass created by lightning strikes.

104 A naturally occurring form of magnetized iron.

105 *PGM IV.* 3125-71

PRAXIS: Preparing the Heartstone

Once we have chosen a stone to function as the heartstone of our fetich or effigy, there are several ways we might prepare it before it is added to our spirit vessel. Firstly, we may wish to cleanse it with consecrated water and suffumigate it with an incense such as the *Clearance Incense* listed in the Formulary section. This can be done to clear away any spirit attachments the stone may have that are not aligned to the new role it is being birthed into. During this process, you may wish to speak out loud and say something to the effect of:

> *"By the power of my word, and this hallowed smoke, may this stone be cleansed and made free of any and all previous attachments and associations that are not aligned to the work of ________. Let any spirit counter to the work of ______ be swiftly carried upon the winds to be granted new homes and new forms allied to their nature."*

Depending on what kind of vessel/fetish it is intended to be added to, I will then wash the stone in the *Aqua Vitae* formula provided later in this book. Instead, I might elect to prepare a wash for the stone with herbs, tinctures, perfumes, waters, alcohols, etc., that are aligned to the work at hand. If the heartstone is meant to serve in a vessel for a specific deity or spirit, I will choose elements aligned to that spirit for inclusion in the wash. Likewise, if it will be used in a fetich or poppet for a particular magical purpose, such as love drawing or magical protection, I will choose *materia* for the wash aligned to that task.

I will sometimes suffumigate the stone again after this wash with either tobacco smoke, or an incense such as the *Suffumigant of Spirit Calling* in the formulary section, or with another smoke that is allied to the purpose the stone will serve. For instance, if it is for a protective effigy, I may pass it through the smoke of myrrh. If it is for an attraction and seduction fetich, I might employ the *Breath of Eros* smoke mentioned in the formulary section. After the stone has dried, I will sometimes paint or draw appropriate sigils or symbols upon the heartstone that are aligned with the spirit and work. I will then apply a bit of an appropriate magical oil, such as the *Spirit Summoning* formula to the heartstone to even further align it to its work.

Throughout all of this work, I am usually speaking and praying aloud and telling the heartstone what its purpose will be in this work as the heart or center of this effigy, poppet, or fetich. I will partner with it and inform it of its new role and responsibility within the greater work of the spirit vessel that is crafted around it.

Lastly, I will bring fire to the heartstone by briefly passing it through the flame of a candle three times whilst saying:

> *"Fire within and without, heart without and within. Be now the seed of spirits, and the foundation upon which the kingdom of this fetich/vessel/effigy is built."*

The heartstone may then be placed within the spirit vessel as best suits its construction and your ritual workflow.

On Animal Materia

When working with animal *materia,* in addition to many of the questions posed earlier in this chapter regarding *materia,* there are often some additional considerations at play. It is best to ask ourselves the following questions:

- Am I drawing upon the spirit of this species as a whole, the spirit of this specific animal, or a combination of the two? For instance, are you calling upon the spirit of Coyote, or of this specific coyote?
- Was this animal *materia* provided in a way that I am ethically comfortable with? This will vary from one practitioner to the next. But it is always preferred to work with animal *materia* that has been gifted by nature, sustainably collected, and done so with minimal harm or distress to the animal. When working with naturally shed feathers, antlers, or snake skins, or found seashells this is of little concern.
- Is it legal to collect or possess *materia* from this animal. Is it a protected or threatened species?
- Does the spirit of this animal require any healing or offerings to work best as a partner in my work? If you are working with the spirit of an animal that died a violent death, such as being hit by a car, you may wish to partner with its spirit to soothe and calm it before working with it.

When searching for animal *materia*, you may wish to explore forests, fields, ocean shores, and other wild landscapes to find animal bones and such that have been offered up by nature. Again, it is always appropriate to give offerings before taking anything from these places. For those who are inclined, there is also the option of salvaging animals that have died as roadkill. For this, there are many resources available in print and online in the realm of "vulture culture" that discuss the best and safest ways for processing animal parts for use. Whenever harvesting any animal parts, it is always important to understand the potential health risks and legality of doing so. As this will vary quite a bit on a case-by-case and location-by-location basis, I am unable to cover all considerations here, but again, I have provided several resources at the end of this chapter for examining these things further.

As we work with animal parts, we should consider the nature of the animal and the parts we are using. For instance, depending upon the particular animal, I often associate teeth with sustenance, communication, and protection. The foot bones of an animal tend to relate to movement or travel. As such, the foot bones of a fox may be worked with for cunning movement and trickery, a rabbit's foot may be associated with swiftness and escape from misfortune, and the foot of a tortoise might be associated with slow and steady movement. Claws serve a number of purposes. The claws of a badger are often used for burrowing, so they may be worked with in cases where we wish to hide away or dig something up. Alternatively, a bobcat uses its claws not only for climbing and defense, but for snagging its prey. So, we might work with the spirit of Bobcat and its claws for capturing the things we desire or that sustain us.

Animal shells often speak to defense as well as domesticity. As such, they tend to make excellent charms for household protection. Additionally, as mentioned previously, animal horns and shells make excellent vessels which we might load with other magical *materia* for the crafting of fetiches. For this, it often works well to pack the vessels with the *dirt clay* mentioned earlier or to seal these vessels with resin or wax to keep everything within them secure.

Animal skulls may be employed in a number of powerfully magical ways, whether to call upon the spirit of a specific animal or to enlist the virtues of its entire species. They are particularly well-suited for housing land spirits and familiar spirits, or as central vessels in the crafting of a fetich. When a witch's Fetch presents itself in animal form, the skull of a corresponding creature may be chosen as a vessel for its temporary habitation. In this role, the skull serves as a locus through which the witch might better commune with and understand this aspect of the self, while also providing a means of training the witch to send the Fetch forth from the body with greater ease and clarity.

Skulls used in such workings can be washed, suffumigated, or dressed in oils, then loaded or adorned with sigils and magical *materia* to align them with their intended spirit. They may be incorporated into larger spirit vessels and shrines, or worked with on their own. Fresh botanicals can also be rubbed into the bone to color the skull and imbue it with verdant virtue, or it may be anointed with successive layers of tinctured myrrh to sanctify and empower it. As with other fetiches, the skull may then be further hallowed through rites and methods detailed later in this book, becoming not only a physical anchor for spirit but a consecrated tool of deep sorcerous potential.

As human beings also fall into the category of animalia, all of these same possibilities and considerations come into play whenever we are working with human remains. Though, understandably legal and ethical questions are often heightened in these cases. Once again, I do not advocate for desecrating or disrespecting the dead. That said, there are currently legal means for acquiring human bones and skulls in many places, and many witches will avail themselves of this option in the crafting of spirit vessels. When working with human remains we are by extension working with a human spirit that we must respectfully partner with. This may feel more natural for some of us as opposed to, say, interacting with the spirit of a tree, because we can more easily relate to the human dead given our shared human experiences. We must also determine if we are working with the spirit of the person to whom that actual bone/skull belonged in life, or if we are working with human remains as a means to call upon other spirits of the dead, as both are options in this work.

Much like working with grave dirt, this touches upon certain realms of necromantic work, which are best reserved for those who have developed a level of adeptness in spirit work. Not because the dead are inherently dangerous, but because working with the dead can occasionally draw the attention of parasitic entities or hungry ghosts. In approaching this work, we must first be able to trust our mediumship/divination and be able to banish any entities that prove to be troublesome. To aid in this you will find several options listed in the formulary which may be employed when cleansing and exorcism are required.

Recommended Additional Reading

Titles on Botanical Magic

The Green Mysteries: An Occult Herbarium by Daniel Schulke. Three Hands Press. 2023

Plant Lore, Legends, and Lyrics by Richard Folkard. Sampson Low, Marsten & Company. 1884.

Oxford Dictionary of Plant-Lore by Roy Vickery. Oxford University Press. 1995.

Titles on Mineralogical Magic

A Lapidary of Sacred Stones: Their Magical and Medicinal Powers Based on the Earliest Sources by Claude Lecouteux. Inner Traditions. 2012.

Gemstones of the World by Walter Schumann. Union Square. 2013.

The Witching Stones: The Lore and Craft of the Essential Crystals, Gemstones, and Minerals to Empower Your Magic by Nicholas Pearson. Weiser Books. 2025.

Crystal Basics: The Energetic, Healing, and Spiritual Power of 200 Gemstones by Nicholas Pearson. Destiny Books. 2020.

Conjuring Dirt by Taren S. Moon Books. 2023.

Divine Dirt: The Art of Using Dirt in Magic, Ritual & Spellcraft by Charity L. Bedell. Llewellyn Publications. 2024.

Titles on Animal and Necromantic Magics

Death's Head: Animal Skulls in Witchcraft & Spirit Work by Blake Malliway. Crossed Crow. 2022.

The Bones Fall in a Spiral: A Necromantic Primer by Mortellus. Crossed Crow. 2023.

Of Blood and Bones: Working with Shadow Magick & the Dark Moon by Kate Freuler. Llewellyn Publications. 2020.

Vulture Culture 101: A Book For People Who Like Dead Things by Lupa. Independently Published. 2019.

Skull Scrying: Animal Skulls in Divinatory Trance Work by Lupa. Independently Published. 2015.

Fang and Fur, Blood and Bone: A Primal Guide to Animal Magic by Lupa. Independently Published. 2020.

The cauldron of rebirth in ritual use.

A selection of fetiches made by the author.

An effigy within the Triangle of Arte.

The enshrined skill as a spirit vessel. From the author's collection.

Spirit vessels created by the author.

Smoking pipes and an herbal blend employed for ritual use.

A collection of the ritual implements from the author's collection. Pictured are a flute for spirit calling, various styluses, and two spiritus vitae tubes. One of coyote bone (left) and another of elderwood (right).

The author grants the breath of life to an effigy.

Fetiches crafted from a coyote skull and a seashell alongside a beeswax effigy.

Examples of effigies sculpted from air-drying clay.

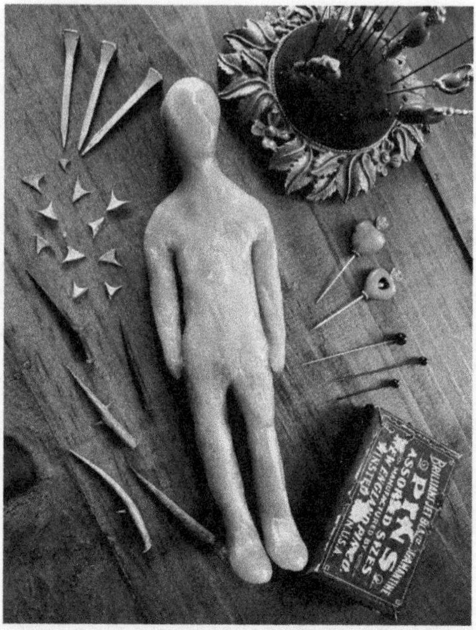

A beeswax effigy surrounded by pins and thorns.

Two cloth effigies with decorative elements created by the author.

A hand fetich for beckoning and blessing made by the author.

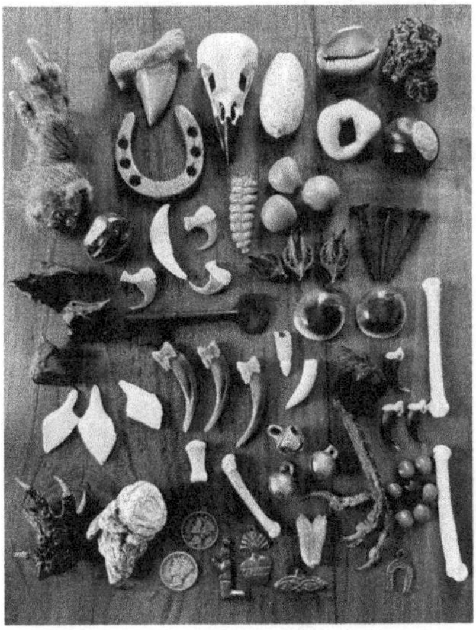

Various magical materia including botanical, animal, mineralogical, and human made items.

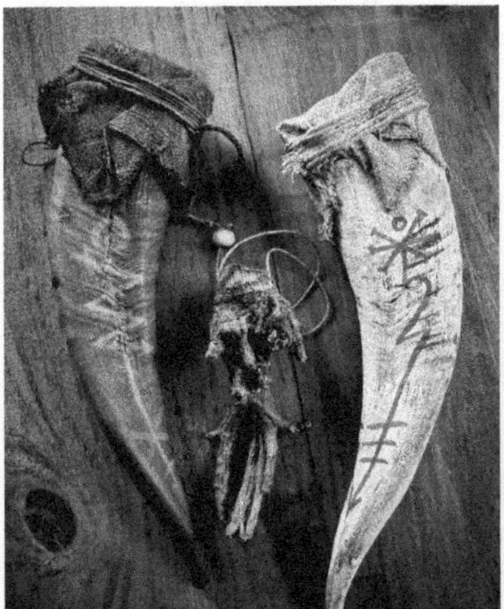

An angelica root fetich carved with a face and framed by twin goat horn fetiches as described in the Horns of the Witches' Devil working.

A healing poppet laid upon a bed of herbs for protection and blessing.

Ceramic effigies created by the author.

Part Three: Ensouling the Effigy

Chapter Ten

Spiritus Vitae: On the Arte and Act of Enspiriting Objects

Here we bring together many of the disparate threads we have gathered throughout this work and braid them into a cord, which will encircle the arte that is the namesake of this book. We will explore approaches towards ensouling the effigy, enlivening fetiches, and enspiriting *maumets.* The methods I put forth here are those that have proven effective and valuable to me and represent a more heavily ritualized approach. If you are new to this work, it is my hope that you will experiment with the methods as they are presented here. In time, however, with a proper level of experience and an understanding of the magical mechanisms at play, I encourage you to make your own alterations as necessary and develop a more personalized approach to this work.

The possible methods for enspiriting objects may range from simple conjurations to ritual processes which take several weeks or even months. This is all determined by both the witch's personal craft and the needs/ requests of the spirit in question.

My general approach towards the work of enspirited objects tends to follow this pattern:

1. A spirit is contacted and pacted, a desire is revealed for which a spirit might be sought, or we are simply inspired to create.

2. A vessel that will house the spirit is crafted or chosen.
3. The spirit vessel is given a ritual death, and/or an exorcism.
4. The vessel is then interred into a symbolic tomb/womb where it will gestate for a time.
5. The spirit vessel is then resurrected and reborn, and the *breath of life* is given.
6. The spirit of the vessel is named, and its role, function, and limitations are affirmed. This is often accompanied by recitation and signing of any formal pact you may have made with the spirit.
7. In the case of effigies and poppets, the body is aligned.
8. The vessel/spirit is then given any further fortification it may need. It is then enshrined, cared for, and worked with in the manner agreed upon with the spirit it serves.

In previous chapters, we have discussed the ways we might engage with and employ existing spirits, as well as concepts around creating *maumet* spirits (step 1). We have also explored the reasons and methods for creating effigies and fetiches (step 2). In this chapter, we will focus on the heart of this work (steps 3-8) and discuss methods for ritually ensouling or enspiriting the objects that will serve as spirit vessels. We will also examine some of the tools common to this process, as well as provide some examples of ways we might go about this work.

As previously stated, the enspiriting of objects tends to take three primary forms. Firstly, when creating an idol or fetich meant to assist in our work with an existing spirit or deity, we are ritually aligning the idol/fetich with that spirit, offering it a vessel, and inviting the spirit to dwell within the vessel. Secondly, when crafting a *maumet,* we are bringing forth and ritually birthing the spirit that will be aligned with the effigy or fetich. Lastly, in the case of a poppet meant to represent a living person, what we are doing is actively tethering the effigy to a part of their spirit. This will be explored more in the following chapter.

On the Breath of Life

One of the threads woven through the binding of this book is the idea that breath is the primary vehicle for spirit. As we have seen, the *spiritus,* the breath, is found both at the literal and mythological birth of humanity.

It is the whisper that inspires us to create new forms. It is the *vox magica* that speaks desire into form and chants, charms, and conjures the spirits. Air, breath, and voice are inseparable from our understanding of spirits and spirit work. And it is through the breath that we shall ensoul the effigy.

The work of enspiriting/ensouling ties together all of these concepts. The witch is the bearer of the inspired mind, the breath which grants new life and new forms, and the voice which calls, conjures, pacts with, and names spirits, and which makes requests, gives instruction, and offers prayer. Through the art of ensouling an effigy, we fully step into the role of the witch as a midwife of spirits. Further, we complete a cycle that begins with the initial inspiration to create and concludes with the act of enspiriting that which has been created. The *breathing out* of what has been *breathed into* us.

Before beginning this work, we may wish to prepare ourselves by cleansing and blessing the mouth with the wash mentioned in the *formulary* section of this book or simply by rinsing the mouth with a bit of rose water or a tincture or infusion of vervain (*Verbena officinalis*). Rose is a plant that exalts, purifies, and protects. Whilst Vervain, a plant also known as Enchanter's Herb, has long been associated with magical potency, empowerment, and, from my experience, is an effective aid in spirit conjuring. Such mouthwashes are intended to purify and fortify both the mouth and the breath.

There are various approaches towards bringing fire and life to the breath. I will give a method here which I have found incredibly effective in this arte as well as further suggestions for alterations which may be employed when granting the breath of life. I encourage you to experiment with these approaches and, once you have worked with them as presented here and feel good about them, make alterations as is necessary and appropriate to your own work.

PRAXIS: Stoking the Witchfire and Setting the Brow Alight

Witchfire is a term for the innate power possessed and cultivated by the witch. This may be stoked, strengthened, and directed through the use of breath. Further we may draw upon other points of power to augment and increase the witchfire. In this method, we are utilizing a form of rapid breathing to build up and concentrate witchfire in the belly and send it out through our breath.

1. To begin, you will start taking slow and intentional inhalations and exhalations. You should concentrate on taking breaths from the diaphragm. This is the muscle just below your rib cage and above your belly. When done properly, a diaphragmatic breath causes this area of the abdomen to rise and fall slightly with each breath while your chest and shoulders remain fairly stationary. If you find that your chest and shoulders are rising/falling with each breath, it is best to correct this, continue practicing, and return your focus to breathing from the diaphragm.
2. As you are doing this, envision that there is a fire within your belly or solar plexus area. This fire is representative of your power as a witch. Though this power often courses throughout our bodies, many witches envision this power as being housed within an internal cauldron or hearth. With our breath, we are awakening and building this fire. Imagine each breath as though it were a bellows feeding oxygen to the fire, and with each breath, the fire's strength, power, and brilliance grow.
3. During your inhalations, this fire should be further fortified and augmented by tapping into and drawing in ambient power from the universe around you. This often takes the form of drawing down celestial power from the upper world, drawing chthonic power up from the underworld, and drawing upon power from the land in the middle realm.[106]
4. As you are inhaling, draw power down from the upper world, the supernal realm of celestial powers. Envision it descending down through the crown of your head and adding power and life to the fire in your belly. This may appear as a luminous golden light.
5. Next, draw power up from the underworld, the infernal realm of ancestral wisdom. Envision it ascending up through your feet and legs and adding both power and life to the fire in your belly. This may appear as a luminous greyish/silver light.
6. Finally, draw power in from the middle world, the terrestrial realm of material structure and biological life. Envision it entering

106 Though the points we might draw power from are certainly not limited to these, and the more advanced practitioner might apply their ingenuity in any manner of ways here.

through your lungs and adding both power and life to the fire in your belly. This may appear as a red colored mist indicative of the blood of life and vitality.

7. Envision all of the power and vitality you have drawn upon coalescing within the witchfire in your belly.
8. Next, you will begin breathing more rapidly with shorter and shallower breaths. Begin slowly and build up to more rapid breaths.
9. As your breath grows more rapid, envision the purpose towards which your witchfire will be directed. This may involve envisioning the purpose that a *maumet* will fulfill, the image or sigil of a spirit or deity that an effigy or vessel will house, or the image of a person for which a poppet is being made. As you continue your breathing, envision this purpose/image as existing at the center of your brow, growing stronger and beginning to shine like a bright star upon your brow.
10. At this point, the fire in your belly will be the initial source of *power and life* that you are granting to the spirit vessel. Whereas the images and intentions conjured for the work that you are building up and cultivating at the brow will be tied to the *identity and instruction* of the spirit vessel.
11. Your breath should become more and more rapid as you envision both the fire in your belly and the star upon your brow growing in strength and radiance.
12. Once you have built your breath up and you feel that both belly and brow radiate with power, you will take a final deep inhalation and then exhale upon the effigy/fetich to grant it the breath of life. As you do so, you should envision that the power you have drawn in to fuel the witchfire as rising up in your throat, while the radiance that has formed at your brow is traveling down to your throat through the sinuses. You will then envision them both joining in your mouth, combining as your breath, and expelled from your body as you transfer them as the breath of life to the fetich/effigy that you are enspiriting.
13. Lastly, transposition can and, more often than not, should be employed as a part of granting the breath of life. This is the act of aligning the breath of life to a source outside of yourself. The way this is done is that, once you have taken in that final

inhalation, using the *vox magica* you will make a declaration of transposition, aligning the breath of life with its true source. You will state this aloud and immediately follow it with an exhalation of the breath of life.

Examples of this type of declaration might be:

- "It is not my breath which gives you life, but the breath of the creator of all things."
- "It is not my breath which gives you life, but the breath of [*insert spirit or deity*] themself."
- "It is not my breath which gives you life, but the breath of [*insert name of person whom a poppet is meant to represent*] themself."

This is helpful because, except for in rare cases where we might wish for an effigy or fetish to exist as a direct extension of ourselves, it is more appropriate that the living breath granted it be intentionally aligned to the most appropriate source and not heavily tethered to ourselves. In this work, the witch fulfills the role of one who harnesses, acts as a conduit for, and directs the breath of life. We are not its source. The act of drawing ambient power and vitality from other realms is intentional so that we might refine, sculpt, and transmit it to the spirit vessel.

Notes, Suggestions, and Alterations on the Breath of Life

- If you are new to this kind of breathwork, it is not uncommon to feel a bit lightheaded. Start breathing slowly and don't overexert yourself. You don't want to cause yourself to faint. You may wish to practice the exercise of building up rapid breath outside of ritual practices to become comfortable with it first.
- Though the above may sound complex upon first reading, I assure you that with practice, the act of stoking the witchfire, setting the brow alight, and passing the breath of life often happens in a matter of minutes. You will find that the more you become familiar with the methods involved, the more naturally you are able to engage with them.

- In addition to the work of this book, this method of empowering and enlivening objects is well suited to the hallowing of all manner of items from ritual tools and amulets, to incense and oil formulas. It may also be somewhat altered to infuse a place with the will of a witch by exhaling and envisioning your power and breath completely filling a space and influencing all it touches.
- The method provided here is sound and effective as-is for ensouling fetiches/effigies. However, further on in this chapter, we will explore additional ways to augment the work of the breath with ritual tools and sacred smokes.

On the Breath of the Gods

For those skilled in spirit flight or conjuration, in cases where you have developed a relationship of trust between yourself and the deities or spirits you are working with, you may wish to draw power/breath/life directly from the deity or spirit. I usually approach this by going forth in spirit flight and meeting with the spirit in the Otherworld. By this point, any negotiations, agreements, and pacts around the creation of this vessel should already be fairly well established.

I will then ask the spirit to temporarily gift me some of their power/breath so that I might carry it within me from the Otherworld to the embodied realm. With mutual consent, whilst still interacting with them via spirit flight, the spirit will usually exhale a small spark of their essence and power that I will inhale, adding it to the witchfire in my belly. In addition to this, I have also, on occasion, had spirits transmit some of their power to the star upon my brow and reveal sigils to me that they wish to see incorporated into the effigy or vessel in some way. Once my exchange with them has concluded in the Otherworld, I will then return from my spirit flight to the embodied realm and begin the work of ritually birthing the effigy/fetich and granting it the breath of life.

Though I share this technique here because I have personally found it effective, as always, exercise discernment in this kind of work and be warned that this type of exchange with spirits falls into more advanced realms.[107] You should not allow too much time to pass between taking on some of a spirit's power and transferring it to the designated vessel. Ideally, not more than an hour. You should also not attempt this with spirits you do not know well and trust, or with spirits whose general nature contributes to physical, spiritual, or mental illness and instability.

PRAXIS: The Serpent's Breath

The following is a breathing technique used for the *drawing in* of power. This may be used to draw upon ambient power from a space or to draw up power from the land. This is added to the witchfire in the belly to give it greater strength and to augment it as necessary.

1. Begin with your mouth resting in a relaxed position, only slightly open. Lips slightly pursed. Your tongue should be pushed forward with the tip just behind your top front teeth, but not touching them.
2. Focus upon the point you are drawing spiritual power from. This might be a point in the landscape, it may also be ambient power from a crowded room, or you may be drawing power from a spirit's vessel or shrine.
3. Next, breath is drawn in through the teeth, often making a soft hissing sound. It is then envisioned drawing this power into the witchfire of the belly, where it is purified and refined. You should be "tasting" the air while drawing in power from a chosen source to see what, if any, information accompanies it about its source and uses for the power. Build up a reservoir of the chosen power within the Solar Plexus.
4. Next, exhale through the nostrils, allowing any elements of the power you have drawn in that are not in service of your work to be released and returned.

---

107 In taking on a piece of a spirit's power, you will want to ensure that it is fully purged from your body when giving the breath of life. When in doubt, you can do a *Stoking of the Witchfire* exercise one to three times afterwards on its own and exhale into the earth to return any power which is not yours. You may also do a cleansing or banishing on yourself in place of or in addition to this.

This fairly simple technique can also be used for drawing in a bit of power/spirit from objects, places, or people in order to "taste" them and gain insights or visions about them. More advanced applications of this include drawing in a bit of a spirit's essence in order to transfer it to another form, drawing out illness in order to transform it, and stealing power from another. All of which have their own points of concern and possible dangers to weigh. As always, proper considerations around consent and ethics, as well as discernment about where you are sourcing power from, should be employed.

On the Vox Magica

The power of our breath within magic is further shaped by the intentional application of voice as a magical tool. This becomes what may be referred to as the development and use of the *vox magica*. This is a Latin term that essentially translates to "magical voice". Though this term is often applied to barbarous incantations and calls found in magical manuscripts such as the *Greek Magical Papyri*, here I apply it more broadly to the coupling of witchfire with speech.

Spoken word is one of the first ways the witch alters their reality and begins the work of manifesting their will and desire. An idea, an inspiration, remains within the crucible of the skull, nestled and hidden within our own bodies. It is a spark waiting to be unleashed upon the world and fanned to a flame, or else hidden away, deprived of oxygen, until its ember fades to ash. When we speak forth our desires and call forth the spirits, a monumental shift begins. That which was once contained within us begins to unfold upon the world around us. What once existed only as synapses and the tickling of nerve endings has now been set forth as breath and vibration that extends outward from us. It fills the space around us, it alters the air around us, it calls forth and calls out. Even if measured only by the production of soundwaves, our voice creates something new in the world.

With this in mind, it is unsurprising that so many creation myths begin with the universe being spoken into existence. In the *Popol Vuh* the Mayan deities speak the world into being. Within various Kemetic myths, the universe begins at the word of gods, or by the call of the Benu bird, whose crying out breaks the silence of nothingness and begins creation. Even within the Book of Genesis, we find the universe spoken into existence, things coming into being, and granted life simply by being spoken of and named. Much of magic relates to speech, and spoken charms, incantations, conjurations, and evocations are all made powerful by employing the *vox magica.*

Though many witches and magicians may not use the term *vox magica* to describe this practice, I'm quite certain that most effective magical practitioners employ the magical voice, consciously or otherwise. To understand that we possess power, that our breath possesses power, is to understand how powerful our words can be. Words can ensnare or shatter a heart. They have the power to build and destroy nations. More germane here, when passed through the curled lips of an effective witch, words are truly no idle thing.

Whether we acknowledge this or not, our words are always influencing the world around us. When employing the *vox magica* we seek to further differentiate our everyday commonplace speaking from a more magically powerful and intentional use of our voice in magic. For many experienced witches, this often done by a slight shift in mentality, an increased focus and intensity lent to our speech. Perhaps a subtle or pronounced shift in the timbre and cadence of our voice, or a variant focus on where we are drawing our breath.

For those who wish to further cultivate the empowered word, an exercise I have found helpful is similar in manner to the breath of life exercise above. You should envision the witchfire within you burning brightly, as well as envision the star upon your brow alight and shining with luminous light. If you feel you need to lend greater power to either belly or brow, you may perform the breathing exercises of stoking the witchfire from above and draw ambient energy within yourself.

Now, similarly to when we combined the light of the brow and the witchfire in the earlier exercise and exhaled the breath of life, you will envision this coupling happening whenever you are speaking magical words, conjurations, commands, charms, and the like. Here, the witchfire fortifies and augments our speech through an intentional infusion of power and purpose. The use of the *vox magica* may be expressed through whispered words, shouted commands, seductive song, extemporaneous glossolalia, and vibrating tones which reverberate throughout the cosmos. When we speak with the magical voice, we are drawing from our source and connection to magical power. With practice and with proper application, the witch may create and destroy by words alone.

On The Witch's Tools

Over the years, I have employed a variety of tools in the ritual work of crafting and conjuring effigies and fetiches. Though some of the primary tools, such as the Death Shroud, the Cauldron of Rebirth, and the Triangle of Arte, will be discussed in greater detail later on. Here is an overview of certain ritual implements that you may wish to procure and have available to you when engaging in this work.

The Blade of Arte

The witch's knife is employed in demarcating ritual space, such as casting a circle or laying a compass. Within my approach to this work, the knife is primarily worked with when ritual banishing and exorcisms need to take place. Though within certain traditions, ritual knives such as the Wiccan athame might never be used for the physical cutting of anything, in my use of the witch's knife, I do employ the knife for cutting items such as cords and cloth within a ritual context. In this manner, the knife is often employed when I am decommissioning a maumet or a spirit vessel. The knife may also function as a ritual tool for commanding, casting out, and casuing harm to spirits if ever required. Within my work, its use in cord cutting and dismantling spirit vessels has more often been done as a ritual action denoting the conclusion of a spirit contract or severance of a spirit partnership as opposed to an act intended to cause harm or distress to a spirit.

The knife can be single or double-edged, and I leave it to the reader to determine what best suits their needs and desires. I recommend that the knife have a blade made of metal that contains iron, such as carbon steel or stainless steel, as iron has long been used in many cultures for protection from hostile spirits and exerting spiritual authority. Traditionally, such ritual blades will have a black handle, though this, too, is left to the reader. Many reading this may already possess such a ritual knife. But for those who do not, I will include a ritual for hallowing the Blade of Arte in the appendices section.

The Spiritus Vitae

The term *Spiritus Vitae* is Latin for "breath of life". Though here we are not discussing the magical act of passing the breath, but instead a tool that may be employed by the witch for this specific act. The *Spiritus Vitae* is a small straw or tubelike device that the witch blows through when passing the breath of life.

Though this tool is not entirely necessary for passing the breath, I find that it helps refine and focus the breath and further empower and augment it within ritual. I encourage the reader to be led by their intuition and ingenuity in sourcing and crafting such a tool. In my craft, I employ two separate forms of *Spiritus Vitae* when doing this work. The first is a length of Coyote bone that has been hollowed out so that air can be blown through it. I primarily use this when working more heavily with spirits of the dead, animal spirits, and chthonic spirits. The other is a short stick of wood from an Elder tree (*Sambucus spp.*) that was ritually collected and hollowed out to make it usable. I employ this one when working with plant spirits and land spirits. I find that having these tools and working with them repeatedly in this manner lends an increased power to the act of ritually granting breath.

The materials I have chosen for these are reflective of my own spirit pacts and the revelations they provide. Though I'm sure the reader can see how and why a tool made of botanical material may be better suited for dealing with plant spirits, whilst a bone tool may be better for working with animal spirits and the dead. When choosing such a tool for yourself, you can use my own experience as inspiration and work with branch and bone. Or instead, seek out other straw-like tools to serve in your personal craft. You might wish to make a *Spiritus Vitae* of bamboo, or even go a very different direction and craft one from clay, or dedicate a hagstone to the art of passing breath. What matters most is that it is something both effective and sensible for you.

The Pipe and Ritual Smokes

At times, I will couple the power of breath and voice with botanical suffumigants. This is done by taking an herbal smoke into the mouth or lungs so that the breath/mouth may be empowered by the botanical spirits and power of the blend I am using. This smoke may be incorporated into the Breath of Life ritual, or it may be blown upon spirit vessels to cleanse, empower, invigorate, and "feed" them. This may be empowered with witchfire and also be coupled with the *vox magica* so that both words of power and tendrils of botanical smoke intertwine their magics.

For this, the witch may wish to dedicate and consecrate a pipe to their magical work, or perhaps even separate pipes for different types of workings or different herbal blends. I have a couple of pipes that are reserved exclusively for this kind of work and have served me well over the years. That said, the witch might simply smoke botanical blends in rolled cigarette form if they prefer.

All the usual caveats apply here when we speak of smoking anything. Pretty much all smoke is carcinogenic to a greater or lesser degree. So what can be done "safely" in this regard is a sliding scale. Tobacco is a sacred plant medicine that is readily available and often worked with to fortify and call spirits. Though I do not advocate its exploitation or abuse, it is a common choice among many witches I have known, and the scent of pipe tobacco can be quite alluring to humans and spirits alike. There are many other plants that humans have been smoking for millennia, and there are, of course, plants you should never smoke. For those who wish to preserve their lungs, you needn't fully inhale the smoke for this kind of work to be effective; in many cases, the smoke may be taken only into the mouth.

That all said, readers should be very well aware of any allergies they may have and be well-versed on the nature, precautions, and risks around any plants they may consider smoking or even burning as incense. When in doubt, do a lot of research and start small. If this practice doesn't feel comfortable or desirable to you, there is no need to explore it for your craft to be effective. For those interested in employing herbal smokes with the work of breath and voice, there are a couple of blends listed in the formulary section that may be a good starting point.

The Stylus

The stylus is essentially a small stick that has a tapered and pointed end. It might be viewed in some ways as a miniature wand, as a tool for engraving, or as an awl for puncturing items. In my work, it is most commonly used for pointing to areas on a poppet that the witch wishes to exert influence upon. If the stylus you are using has a sharp end, it may be used for engraving sigils, names, or other words into a waxen, wooden, or clay effigy. It may also be used to pierce a poppet in a similar manner as one might employ pins. Though it is a more temporary form of magic than the fixing of pins.

I have employed several forms of stylus in my work. Some have been crafted of iron or silver with sharpened ends for piercing. I have made them from repurposed wooden or bone hair sticks with more blunted ends and found these to work wonderfully. The stylus may be worked with for hexing or healing and in any other magical works where the witch wishes to pinpoint a burst of magical power to be sent to the target of the poppet. It may also be used for pointing at various body parts in rites of transposition and awakening effigies. I have found with students of mine who have an aversion towards the idea of using pins in benevolent magic that the use of a stylus for directing power without piercing the effigy serves well as a good alternative for them.

Pins/Needles/Thorns

In contrast to the stylus, pins, needles, and thorns are specifically used for piercing and securing magical power into the body of a poppet. Though most people immediately associate piercing dolls with pins with works of harmful magic, the use of pins and thorns is first and foremost about fixing things in place. Where the stylus may be worked with to temporarily direct magical power towards a target, pins and the like are worked with for locking power in place so that it may influence the target for an extended period of time. In a manner, this might be seen as magically grafting a particular influence and intention upon the spirit of the target for good or ill.

The Cord

Cords may be single-use, or you may wish to have cords that are worked with again and again. Their primary usage here is in the work of binding. This is not only relevant to workings where we wish to physically bind an effigy so that the associated person or spirit is disempowered and kept from doing harm. Instead, this might also be approached by using the cord as a temporary marker that binds a person or spirit to an effigy for a limited time. In such cases, the witch should state in their crafting of the effigy something to the effect of:

> *"So long as this cord stays wound round this effigy, it will serve as a body for and extension of [insert name of spirit or person here]. At the time that this cord is undone or cut by me, the spirit of NN will no longer be bound to this form, and my work with them will be concluded."*

I have worked with cords in this way when I am temporarily housing a spirit in an effigy or when I am temporarily tethering the spirit of a living person to a poppet for healing or binding. The severing of such a cord works as an excellent way in which to signal that the working upon that person, or the pact and work with a spirit, is concluded. In many cases, the cord will then be burned afterwards.

When crafting cords, I will often braid together three sections of embroidery thread. This allows me to employ the *vox magica* to utter charms into the braiding, to program the purpose of the cord and how it will function, and to create cords with colors I feel are relevant to the working or spirit they are intended for. Much like approaches discussed earlier in relation to thread, the witch might also elect to empower the cord with botanical tinctures and oils appropriate to the working. You may also wish to speak aloud empowered words of healing, binding, hexing, or other declarations and then pass the braided cord through the lips, wetting it with the spittle to further empower the work. In cases when we are creating a poppet for healing, we might employ this last method but instead pass the cord between the lips of the person we are doing healing work for, should they be available.

Flutes and Whistles

Another method for augmenting and empowering the breath in my work has been the use of various wind instruments such as flutes, ocarinas, and whistles. These are primarily worked with to call and conjure spirits and are also occasionally utilized as a form of giving, offering, and devotion through the use of breath. Certain types of flutes, such as those made from Elderwood (*Sambucus spp.*), are well known for their efficacy in drawing spirits near. I will often have certain instruments dedicated to my work with specific spirits. In such cases, it is understood by the spirits I am working with that to play upon a particular flute is a call and conjuration of their presence and attention. These flutes are usually kept near the particular spirit vessel or shrine of those spirits when they are not actively in use.

Divination Tools

Though we have covered the importance of divination elsewhere in this book, it bears repeating that it is often an incredibly important part of our work with spirits. It is important that the witch have at least one method of divination that they are proficient in and that can reliably be worked with for communicating with the spirits that guide them in this work. In many cases, it is even better to have specific divination tools dedicated to different spirits, such as each of your primary spirits having dice, coins, or a deck of cards which function as your direct line of communication with that spirit.

On the Death of Things

Death is a welcome partner in our work, as for anything to shift from one form to another, it requires a sort of death, a marked end to its previous existence. Spiritual initiations require the death of who we once were so that we may be born into who we are meant to be. As a result, we find symbolic aspects of death and rebirth heavily embedded in the initiatory rituals of many spiritual traditions and cultures throughout the world.

In my work with enspirited objects, I view the process of enlivening fetiches and effigies as a process of initiation and transformation, of death and resurrection. In this approach, we are conjuring and pacting with the spirits of the *materia* employed in crafting the body, as well as any spirits relevant to the work. Primarily, those meant to be housed within the effigy or fetich. Though this approach might be applied to creating any enspirited object, it is particularly relevant in the case of *maumets.*

In these cases, all of the disparate material parts and associated spirits that make up the fetich or effigy are ritually and symbolically given a death and are put to rest for a period of time. This is the first step in transforming those spirits from their previous roles and individual existences into their new form, which incorporates all of the varied parts now functioning as one whole. It is no longer, for instance, the spirit of a pair of scissors, alongside the spirit of an angelica root, alongside dirt gathered from seven churches, etc. Instead, it is all of these things born forth in alignment, as a new form and a new spirit. It is given new life, a name, and a specific role and charge.

There are several approaches we might take in the death process of this work. We might simply speak to the disparate spirits of the effigy with our *vox magica* and ask them to release any attachments that do not serve the work of their new collective spirit. Some may prefer more traditional forms of spiritual cleansing/exorcism and consecration, such as the one provided later in this chapter. In the past, I have approached this work by placing the effigy overnight onto a dish or in a bowl containing dirt, which had been paid for and gathered from the crossroads of seven cemeteries, or literally burying the item in the ground. However, the method I currently employ most frequently is the use of the *Death Shroud.*

On the Death Shroud

The Death Shroud is a piece of fabric that the effigy or fetich may be wrapped within for a period of time to allow for its ritual death. I was fortunate enough to be gifted a fabric sheet that served as the Death Shroud for a very sweet elderly woman who passed away. The shroud is a sheet from the bed she passed away on, and her body was wrapped in it as it was transported to the funeral home. After asking her spirit for permission and assistance in this work and giving her offerings of thanks, I cut a smaller piece of the sheet to use as a Death Shroud in my work.

Understandably, this type of material will not be easily available or desirable to all, so there are other, more accessible methods through which a Death Shroud might be made. In its simplest form, this may be a piece of fabric that is white, which has been dedicated to the role and purpose of the Death Shroud. You may wish to infuse your Death Shroud with tinctures, infusions, or oils made from botanicals appropriate to funerary workings, such as Cedar (*Cedrus spp.*) or Willow (*Salix spp.*) You may also wish to dye it with appropriate natural dyes allied to the dead, such as Black Beans (*Phaseolus vulgaris*), or to decorate and empower it with sigils and symbols you feel are aligned to this work. I have included a drawing of the sigils I employ around the edges of the Death Shroud as revealed to me by the spirits I work with. You may use them as you feel called to by painting or drawing them around the edges of your shroud, or you may wish to simply leave it plain. As with most things discussed in this work, I encourage you to incorporate the elements you feel best suit your practice.

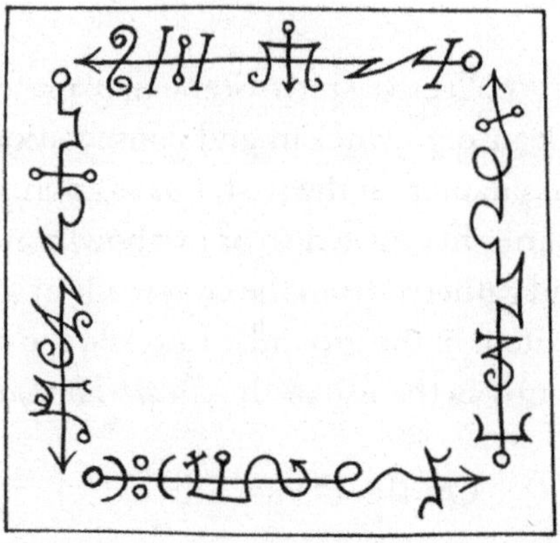

I suggest that you ensure the piece of fabric you choose is large enough to fully wrap whatever effigies, fetiches, and other spirit vessels you wish to create. In general, I have found that a square of fabric around eighteen to twenty-four square inches does well. It is also recommended that, in preparing the shroud for use, the fabric be taken to a cemetery and buried near the front gate for a full lunar month (full moon to full moon). In doing this, you should ask for the permission and assistance of the guardian of the cemetery gate and leave a small offering of three coins and some tobacco there for them. At the end of a lunar month, you will return to the cemetery, give thanks to the guardian of the gate, retrieve the shroud, and leave another offering of coins and tobacco.

PRAXIS: Working the Death Shroud

If you have a personal practice and preference for creating ritual space, such as casting a circle or laying a compass, you are encouraged to do so before this working as feels appropriate. To work the Death Shroud, the effigy or fetich is to be wrapped in the fabric, ideally so that it is not exposed to light. If possible, this is best done at sunset, as the setting sun is seen as the symbolic death of the day. When doing so, you will employ the *vox magica* and say something akin to the following:

> *"Death has come! Embraced you in her bony arms and wound you round in her shroud. Bidding you leave your old life behind. To shed as the serpent and cast off all things not in service of this effigy/fetich as a vessel for [insert name of spirit, or the living person in the case*

of a poppet] to serve in the work of [insert something here to describe how the objects will be worked with such as communication, healing, devotion, etc.]. Into the gates of Death you now pass, that you may rest and be reborn anew, no longer a creature of clay/stone/fabric, but as the body/home of [spirit/person name]."

The wrapped spirit vessel may be placed upon your altar, should you have one, or kept hidden away somewhere safe. As mentioned above, you may also wish to place it atop a dish of dirt gathered from seven cemetery crossroads to further aid the work. Wherever you place the spirit vessel, it should be left undisturbed for one full day at minimum, though ideally, I prefer to allow it to rest in this death state for three days.

On Cleansing and Exorcism

Before moving on to the process of gestation, I feel it is helpful to provide an overview of a simple exorcism that may be used in place of, or in addition to, the death and resurrection process. Exorcism, in this context, is an act of cleansing the object by casting out. It is a banishing of any attached spirit presence or influence that runs counter to the intended work of the effigy, fetich, or tool.

One primary advantage of the exorcism method is that it may be performed relatively quickly and does not require us to wait one to three days to move on to the next step. That said, I find this technique on its own tends to work best for preparing ritual tools or poppets rather than when ensouling more complex spirit vessels, particularly when creating *maumet* spirits.

If worked in conjunction with the Death Shroud method, I recommend doing this exorcism before wrapping the object in the shroud. Additionally, if you are inclined towards casting a circle, laying a compass, or simply spiritually aligning yourself, you are encouraged to do so before this working. If not, you may wish to at least call upon the aid of protective spirits to assist you and/or wear a protective amulet. This isn't particularly dangerous work; however, there is little harm in employing a bit of added protection whenever we are casting out undesirable spirits.

PRAXIS: A Simple Object Exorcism and Cleansing[108]

Items Needed:

- A small bowl of fresh water
- A small bowl of salt
- Charcoal and a censer for burning incense
- An incense for exorcism *(you may use a recipe listed in the formulary part of this book, or in a pinch, frankincense or pine resin work well).*

1. Once the items are laid out upon an altar or working surface, you will begin by pointing the index and middle fingers of your dominant hand, or pointing your Blade of Arte, at the bowl of salt and saying:

   "Blessings be upon you, O Creature of Salt, by the powers which created thee in such a form, may you be free from phantasm, falseness, and treachery. By the grace of Ghob and the intercession of the Gnomes,[109] may all spirits of impurity and uncleanness flee far away from thee. That they may cause neither hindrance nor harm to myself, nor behave in a manner contrary to the aims of my work. As the sun sets and rises, may it be so!"[110]

---

108 You will find similar ritual methods and wording at play in the *Consecration of Salt and Water* in the appendices section, as well as the *Hallowing the Blade of Arte* rite, which provides a good example of how cleansing/exorcism/consecration are often performed in tandem.

109 Ghob and the Gnomes are elemental spirits associated with Earth.

110 The blessings/exorcisms here are very loosely based upon those found in Roman Catholic liturgy, and which were subsequently employed in grimoires such as those attributed to Solomon and later adopted into Wiccan practices. I have always found the wording "creature of" to be an interestingly animist phrasing employed by the church. Here you will note that when speaking to the salt that instead of outright speaking of exorcism, we speak of blessings. This is because salt is generally viewed as a naturally incorruptible substance. Lastly, these exorcisms add an appeal to the elemental rulers and the elementals to aid in this work.

2. Next, point the index and middle fingers of your dominant hand, or your Blade of Arte, at the bowl of water and say:

 "I exorcise thee, O Creature of Water, by the powers which created thee in such a form, may you be free from phantasm, falseness, and treachery. By the grace of Nixa and the intercession of the Undines,[111] *may all spirits of impurity and uncleanness flee far away from thee. That they may cause neither hindrance nor harm to myself, nor behave in a manner contrary to the aims of my work. As the sun sets and rises, may it be so!"*

3. Take three pinches of the salt and add it to the water, saying:

 "The two made one, hallowed by Land and Sea. May this blessed water cast out all harmful specters, miasma, and malignity."[112]

4. Then the charcoal should be lit and placed in the censer. Once it is glowing red, point the index and middle fingers of your dominant hand, or your Blade of Arte, at the censer and say:

 "I exorcise thee, O Creature of Fire, by the powers which hath created thee in such a form, that you be freed from phantasm, falseness, and treachery. By the grace of Djinn and the intercession of the Salamanders,[113] *may all spirits of impurity and uncleanness flee far away from thee. That they may cause neither hindrance nor harm to myself, nor behave in a manner contrary to the aims of my work. As the sun sets and rises, may it be so!"*

5. Next, point the index and middle fingers of your dominant hand, or your Blade of Arte, at the incense and say:

 "I exorcise thee, O Creature of incense, by the powers which hath created thee in such a form, that you be freed from phantasm, false-

111 Nixa and the Undines are elemental spirits associated with Water.

112 For an alternate form of creating consecrated salt/water see the appendices.

113 Djinn and the Salamanders are elemental spirits associated with Fire.

ness, and treachery. By the grace of Paralda and the intercession of the Sylphs,[114] *may all spirits of impurity and uncleanness flee far away from thee. That they may cause neither hindrance nor harm to myself, nor behave in a manner contrary to the aims of my work. As the sun sets and rises, may it be so!"*

6. Add some of the incense to the charcoal while saying:

   "The two made one, hallowed by Fire and Air."

7. You will then dip your fingers into the water and sprinkle a bit over the fetich/effigy, then pass the object through the smoke at least three times while using the *vox magica* to declare:

   "I exorcise thee, by the powers which hath created thee in such a form that all spirits of impurity and uncleanness flee from thee, that you be freed from phantasm, falseness, and treachery, that all remnants of spirit which do not serve the appointed role and intended work of this effigy/fetich/vessel be cast away and scattered to the earth, that they may neither hinder nor harm myself nor behave contrary to the aims of my work. Let only that which is permitted by my desire remain, that this vessel may be suited to the work of [here you may wish to describe the purpose of the vessel and add any wording of your own or to call upon any spirits or deities which you have previously aligned with for their assistance]. As the sun sets and rises, may it be so!"

8. You should conclude this by using the index and middle fingers of your dominant hand, your witch's knife, or a wand, as is your preference, to trace an equal-armed cross three times over the effigy/fetich as a way of completing the exorcism and sealing the object from any further undesired outside influences. This type of exorcism may then be followed by the Death Shroud rite, if you like. It may also be followed by the work of tomb and womb detailed below, or you may wish to move directly to the rites of birthing, awakening, and dedication.

114 Paralda and the Sylphs are elemental spirits associated with Air.

On the Tomb, the Womb, and the Cauldron of Rebirth

The nature of the cauldron is deeply tied to the processes of death, transformation, and rebirth. By extension, tradition, and by the work of the witch, that which enters the cauldron does not emerge unchanged. Here we descend into the burial pit of the reddened earth. Traversing into the ochred caves of our early ancestors, where horned beasts were rendered by lamplight and first forms were crafted and carved. Here we return to the primordial blood-rich womb that sustains new life. It is here within the Cauldron of Rebirth, as a vessel which serves as both burial tomb and gestation vessel, that we will inter the effigy/fetich. Here it will remain as a seed planted in the earth, a child in the womb, for a period of incubation which allows it to gather greater strength and become further aligned to its new life and work. The use of the cauldron in this manner is something adopted into my effigy work in more recent years, which was heavily inspired by the work of Kamden Cornell in their book *On Needles and Pins.*[115] My approach includes some elements directly drawn from Kamden's use of the cauldron, with other adaptations and additions which reflect the spirits and symbolism present in my own practice. As they too share a deep understanding and passion regarding poppetry and enspirited objects, I highly encourage those interested to read Kamden's excellent book to examine their own use of the cauldron as well as benefit from their inspired approach toward the working of poppets and effigies.

The first method of creating the Cauldron of Rebirth is one that is fairly complex. With that in mind, I have provided alternative and potentially more accessible methods for creating a vessel of rebirth at the end of this section. Should you feel it appropriate to alter these workings to suit your practice and capabilities, I encourage you to do so. That said, as this is a primary method I have personally employed for ensouling effigies, I will first explain my own process for crafting the Cauldron of Rebirth.

You should begin by acquiring a cast iron cauldron, ideally one with a lid, that is large enough to fit any effigies/fetiches you plan to birth within. These types of cauldrons can often be found sold as Potjie pots. Bear in mind when looking for an appropriate cauldron that most cauldrons sold in occult shops and botanicas are coated in a black paint, which makes them

---

115 This book will be re-published as *On Pins and Needles* by Crossed Crow Books in early 2026.

unsuitable for this method of preparation. I will give an alternate method for preparing cauldrons that are already painted, and for other vessels to serve as the "cauldron" later. For this method to work, it is important that you use an uncoated, real cast-iron cauldron.

PRAXIS: Crafting the Cauldron of Rebirth

Items Needed:

- A good-sized, uncoated, cast-iron cauldron
- A bowl
- Rose water
- Tobacco, copal, dragon's blood, and juniper
- Tallow from a horned animal with cloven hooves
- Powdered red ochre (iron oxide)
- A naturally dropped bird feather (from a diurnal bird of prey, if possible)
- A snake shed
- A chicken egg
- Dirt gathered and paid for from seven crossroads
- Dirt gathered and paid for from a cemetery gate
- Dirt gathered and paid for from a hospital with an obstetrics unit or from a flourishing garden
- Additional dirts as desired
- A paint brush (silicone basting brushes work well for this)
- Oven glove or mitts, as needed
- A cloth rag or paper towel

1. Once you have chosen your cauldron, you will cleanse it by washing it with the rose water. If you wish to, you may use the *Vessel Cleansing Wash* in the formulary section or substitute consecrated water, a floral gin, or Florida Water cologne instead of rose water. To do this, simply dampen a cloth with the wash and wipe down the interior and exterior of the cauldron as well as the lid.
2. For this first part of the process, I encourage you to speak aloud extemporaneously and from the heart as you are inclined. It is

appropriate to employ the *vox magica* to speak conjurations to the spirits of the plants employed in the cleansing and preparation of the cauldron to ask for their aid in your work. Employ any words of exorcism and banishing that you are led towards to cleanse the cauldron and prepare it for use. You may also alter the earlier simple exorcism for this purpose, should you desire.

3. Next, you will blend together equal parts tobacco, copal, dragon's blood, and juniper into an incense, or create and work with the slightly more complex *Suffumigation for Spirit Vessels* found in the formulary section. This should be burned upon a charcoal, and the cauldron should be passed over it several times. Then it will be turned over and its interior allowed to fill with the smoke. Afterwards, it should be set down upright and allowed to rest until the smoke dissipates from within. The lid should be passed through the smoke as well. This process is equally about exorcising unsuitable qualities and lending new power to the cauldron.
4. You will then burn the bird feather to ash while envisioning the descent of heavenly and celestial powers of the upper world in the form of a bird made of sacred fire, while saying:

   "By the bird of flame, may supernal powers descend!"

5. Once it has fully burned, crush and powder the ash as necessary, then put the ash aside in a bowl for later use.
6. Next, you will burn the snake shed to ash while envisioning the rising of chthonic and ancestral power from the underworld in the form of a great black serpent, while saying:

   "By the serpent of the watery depths, may infernal powers ascend!"

7. Then put the ash from the snake shed into the bowl with the feather ash.
8. You will now add to the bowl just a pinch each of the dirts collected from seven crossroads, as well as the dirt collected from the cemetery gates and hospital/garden dirt. This dirt serves a paradoxical role as both the dirt of the burial mound and the fertile life-giving soil from which the spirit of the effigy might be grown, fortified, and

resurrected. In addition, you may wish to add dirts collected from other places of power as you feel appropriate. Just bear in mind that they will lend their influence to all that is born from the cauldron.

9. You should then heat a small amount of the tallow in a pot over a low heat until it melts.
10. Once it has melted, add the powdered red ochre to it until it is sufficiently colored. Add the combined ash from the feather and snake shed and the dirts to the melted tallow, ensuring to thoroughly mix them in.
11. This tallow mixture serves a multiplicity of roles in preparing the cauldron. Being sourced from a horned beast, it firstly calls upon the Witches' Devil, who is the horned lord of animals, granter of familiars, and magister of the eternal sabbath. Whereas the bird feather calls upon the upperworld, and the snake shed calls upon the underworld, the tallow speaks to the terrestrial animals of hoof and horn as creatures of the middle world. In creating my own cauldron, I chose to use buffalo tallow.[116] This was done to conjure forth the horned one in an early primeval aspect as the revered subject of paleolithic cave paintings, and the horned beast that gifts and sustains life. The tallow brings his presence forward and imbues the cauldron with his power. The red ochre is the blood of the earth womb and calls upon she who dwells deep in the caves, buried in the ground, she of the reddened hand, who brings forth life and new forms, the Clay Mother.
12. This mixture of tallow and ochre will be used to coat the interior of the cauldron, in an act calling back to the artistry of our ancient ancestors as the first crafters of image and form, and an acknowledgment of the cauldron itself as the primordial cave. Further, this serves to both protect the cauldron's interior and offer a crude form of "sustenance" to the spirits undergoing gestational transformation. The next step in this process involves heating the cauldron in order to polymerize the tallow and season the cauldron.[117]

---

116 Appropriate alternatives to buffalo tallow include deer, sheep, or goat tallow if you can source it.

117 A process by which fats are heated to a high temperature and become molecularly bonded to the surface of the iron.

13. The cauldron should be slightly warmed in an oven if possible, and then, wearing oven gloves and being careful not to burn yourself, the melted tallow, ochre, and ash should be painted or smeared in a thin layer with the brush onto the interior of the cauldron while it is still liquid. It is less important that this look perfect than that, as much as possible, the entire interior is coated. You may wish to use a cloth rag to apply the mixture to the cauldron if you find that works better.
14. Once it has been fully coated, you will heat your oven to 500°F (260°C) or as close to this as you can. Once it has reached max temperature, you will place your cauldron within the oven for ten to fifteen minutes. You should then turn off the oven and leave the cauldron within until it has completely cooled to the touch. Once the cauldron has cooled and has been removed from the oven, you should see that the interior is lined with a thin layer of red ochre and tallow, which has polymerized into a shiny coating.[118]
15. Once you have allowed the cauldron to completely cool, you will then take it to your ritual space, pick up the egg, and then hold it with both hands at heart level.
16. You will once again envision the descent of the bird of flame from the upperworld, whilst using your *vox magica* state:

    "Supernal powers descend!"

17. Next, envision the serpent of the watery depths, ascending from the underworld whilst using your *vox magica* to state:

    "Infernal powers arise!"

---

118 In some cases, some of the tallow may pool and harden at the bottom of the cauldron. This is okay if it happens. However, if this concerns you, instead of placing it upright in the oven you may wish to turn the cauldron upside down over a baking tray that can withstand high temperatures so that the excess tallow mixture runs out of the cauldron onto it.

18. Envision these spirits of the upperworld and underworld meeting at your heart center and lending their power and life force to the egg you hold. Then, envision the egg being imbued with life-giving power from all directions, state:

"Reside in the heart terrestrial, the crossways betwixt all realms"

19. Then you will state:

"It is not my hands which perform this work, but the hands of that which breathed the first breath, uttered the first word, and crafted the first form."

20. You will then crack the egg into the cauldron and say:

"Let this egg be that of both serpent and bird, from which all of creation is born."[119]

21. Next, you will add a further element of generative power to the working. This is done by adding three drops of your own blood to the cauldron. This can be accomplished by pricking the middle finger of your dominant hand. Alternatively, should you produce it, you may add your own semen in place of, or in addition to, the blood. When adding this, you should state:

"Let this blood/seed be as the life-giving force of all creation. No longer of mine, but of thine."[120]

22. This egg/blood/semen mixture should then be smeared all over the interior of the cauldron and left to dry. You will then conclude the preparation of the cauldron by saying:

119 Many creation mythologies speaks of the universe being born from an egg.

120 This line is an important one, and the power of your *vox magica* should be behind it in full force as it declares that the blood/semen is no longer tied to you as an individual. It is not a personal taglock drawing upon your own power, but instead behaves as a universal substance.

"From tomb to womb, and body to earth, a seed to soil.
Let what mustn't be perish.
Let what must be arise!
By the setting and rising of the sun, it is done!"

23. Then place the lid upon the cauldron and allow it to rest for at least a day before putting it to use.

On Alternative Vessels of Rebirth

Simpler methods for creating an appropriate gestation vessel may be employed by those for whom the above is either inaccessible or undesirable. You are encouraged to incorporate elements of the above as they suit your inclination.

If you find an appropriately sized cauldron but wish to forgo the use of the tallow and the process of polymerization, you might instead add the ochre to the egg mixture to create a crude form of tempera paint, which you may coat the cauldron with. To this, you can add the ashes, dirts, and blood/semen if you are called to. Alternatively, you could use a premade acrylic paint that is made from (or colored to look like) red ochre. Again, you may add the ashes/dirts/blood/semen to this paint as you are able and feel appropriate, with consideration of the purpose and roles of each substance.

If you have an aversion to a completely iron vessel, or you simply wish not to use a cauldron, I suggest considering an unglazed terracotta cooking pot with a lid. I have one of these that I've used on occasions where a heavily iron vessel was a contrary substance to the spirit I was seeking to work with. With this in mind, those who work with a diversity of spirits and wish to adopt the crafting of fetiches and effigies as a cornerstone of their practice might consider creating a second vessel using this method should they need it.

These kinds of terracotta pots are sometimes sold as curry pots, and one of the advantages here is that, though they don't have the same concentration of iron content. The clay they are made from is naturally colored by the inclusion of iron oxide, so the step of reddening the interior with ochre is generally unnecessary. Should you wish to include the other steps mentioned, I recommend dipping a rag in the melted tallow mixture and very lightly buffing it into the interior of the slightly warmed terracotta pot. The surfaces of these pots are often very porous, so they should accept the tallow and any other substances quite readily.

If you have found a vessel that you wish to serve in this role and the effigy you have created is too tall for its lid to be placed on top, an alternative is to place the effigy within the vessel and drape a piece of black fabric reserved for this purpose over it. This is primarily to allow the effigy to incubate and keep it from being exposed to direct light during the gestational period. Additionally, if a spirit has revealed particular symbols and sigils related to themselves, I will often inscribe those sigils with chalk on the outside of the cauldron and/or on its lid as a way of further empowering the effigy and allying it to the spirit it is meant to serve. This can be washed off the cauldron after each use.

Lastly, if you seek a much simpler form of rebirthing vessel to begin this work, an alternative is to cut out two pieces of red fabric in a rectangular shape and two pieces of black fabric in a rectangular shape of the same size. These are then sewn together on three sides to essentially make something that resembles a pocket or pillowcase. The interior lining should be the red fabric, while the black fabric serves as the exterior. Alternatively, you might simply place a premade red pillowcase within a black pillowcase, cleanse them with rose water, suffumigate them with the suggested blend above, and leave it at that. This serves the rudimentary requirements of providing a reddened interior which cradles, encompasses, and fortifies the effigy and a dark exterior designed to allow it darkness and rest.

What is important here is that the primary elements that invoke the sense of tomb, womb, gestation/incubation are present. Though the complexity of craft shouldn't provide an excuse to cut corners out of laziness, it also shouldn't be a barrier to our practice. I highly encourage those witches inclined towards this work to find inspiration where they may, alternatives where desired, and adaptations when necessary. We should never let the quest for the perfect be the enemy of the good.

It should also be noted here that between each use, the cauldron/vessel should be given a suffumigation with a mix of Copal (*Bursera sp.*) and Dragon's Blood (*Calamus draco*) resins or with the *Clearance Incense* listed in the formulary to which a tiny bit of Dragon's Blood has been added. This is intended to both cleanse and fortify it between uses.

On The Triangle of Arte

The *Triangle of Arte* is a concept found within various systems of grimoire and ceremonial magic and exists primarily as a space for the safe evocation of spirits. Symbolically, the upright equilateral triangle begins at a singular point representative of the one source of all being and ends in a straight line representing material form. In our work of ensouling the effigy, the triangle is viewed similarly when employed in the process of birthing spirits into material forms.

To create the Triangle of Arte, an equilateral triangle should be painted or drawn with a circle encompassing it. This should be made at least large enough so that the vessel of rebirth you are working with can sit comfortably within the triangle's center. The triangle may be created temporarily using chalk or created more permanently with paint or ink upon a cloth or wooden surface. You may wish to perform an exorcism and blessing upon whatever materials (chalk, paint, fabric, etc.) you use to create the triangle beforehand in order to align them to their intended purpose.

For my practice, I have created the triangle on a large circular piece of flat wood that can be placed on the floor, as well as a more portable version created on a piece of cloth that can be easily rolled up and stored away as needed. My triangle is framed by sigils designed to aid in the work of drawing spirits forth, these were revealed to me by familiar spirits through scrying. You are welcome to incorporate these sigils into your work as desired, replace them with symbols or names relevant to your practice, or simply utilize a simple triangle within a circle.

The triangle is most often placed upon the floor or the earth, though it may be placed upon an altar or table as is necessary. When in use, a candle is burned at each point. With a white candle placed at the lower right symbolizing generative forces, a black candle at the lower left symbolizing destructive forces, and a red candle placed at the uppermost point symbolizing lifeblood and rebirth.[121] These candles should ideally be dressed with a *Spirit Summoning Oil,* such as the one included in the formulary. In the absence of such an oil, you may offer prayer and conjuration over a portion of olive oil to charge it with drawing the desired spirits nearer. When lit, the candles are meant to activate and empower the triangle and to serve as a beacon that draws and contains the desired spirit to the triangle's center.

Though I will describe the triangle's use during the process of gestation and ensouling shortly, it is worth mentioning additional effective and valuable alternative uses for the triangle. In cases where one wishes to conjure forth a spirit, a censer of *Suffumigation of Spirit Calling* incense may be placed at its center, the candles lit, and the desired spirit called to be present and conjured into the circle. In this case, the smoke of the incense serves both as sustenance and substance for the spirit to present itself. During this process, attention should be paid to any images and forms that present themselves in the smoke.

In situations when I am calling upon an unknown spirit or one that is somewhat volatile, I will usually place the triangle outside of a ritually demarcated space, such as a magic circle/compass, which has been created for protection. In place of this, I might simply call upon the presence of protective spirits. You may also choose to wear protective amulets appropriate to your work. Should the witch desire an end to the session, the spirit should be given license to leave or be banished, the incense smothered, and the candles extinguished. Otherwise, if the interaction is an agreeable one, the session may continue until the incense and candles have ceased burning or the work has concluded. As necessary, additional banishing and exorcism may take place after the session to return your ritual space to a neutral state.

121 Here we are representing the necessity of the powers of both creation and destruction in a balanced craft, in the cycles of the world, and in the processes of life, death, and rebirth.

In order to engage in the work of scrying to communicate with spirits, a scrying stone, crystal sphere, or black mirror may be placed within the triangle. Once you are ready to begin the session, the candles are lit, and the spirit is conjured into the triangle. Similar methods to those above may be used for ending the session with banishing and exorcism done after the session has completed, as is felt necessary.

Lastly, I have also used the triangle for the empowering/enspiriting of magical formulas such as incense and oil blends, or talismans and amulets. This is done by placing the items within the triangle, lighting the candles, and calling forth a spirit to empower the formula or talisman. In these cases, the spirit called has been one with which I have had a previously well-established relationship that has been pacted with to do this work. The candles are left to burn down, and the spirit is given license to leave and offered gratitude before the items are retrieved from the triangle. Again, banishing and exorcism may take place after the session as necessary.

In a very simple approach towards ensouling an object, a witch might choose to forgo all previous steps mentioned (the Death Shroud and gestation) and simply place the effigy/fetich into the triangle and light the candles. You might then call to a trusted spirit you have an established a relationship with and ask for it to enspirit and empower the object. I find this is best reserved for objects that are meant to serve primarily as devotional icons. Still, in these cases it is recommended that you first ensure this approach is agreeable to the spirit in question and that you perform some form of exorcism/cleansing upon the effigy/fetich beforehand.

Ensouling the Effigy

Now that we have established the ideas of the breath of life, *the vox magica,* the tools, and given an example of creating a ritual death with the Death Shroud. I will illustrate the other steps involved in a rite of ensouling. Here I am going to be presenting this rite as it might look for the crafting of an effigy meant to represent a familiar spirit, because I believe it is one of the best illustrative examples for how this ritual process might look in its entirety. This same basic structure and approach may be applied to fetiches, *maumets,* statuary of deities, etc. The wording and such can be slightly altered as needed, so long as it follows the same general structure as laid out at the start of this chapter.

The Gestation Period

Once the effigy you have crafted has received a ritual death or exorcism, the cauldron or an alternate vessel of rebirth should be placed within the center of your Triangle of Arte. If you have used the Death Shroud to prepare the effigy, you will unwrap it as you place the effigy into your cauldron. Though this part of the ritual may be performed at any time, I find it particularly powerful to place the effigy into the cauldron at sunset, as this is a time of endings. While doing this, you should say:

> *"You are given to the earth. Committed to tomb and womb. That you may rest, that you may grow in power, and that you may be reborn into this world."*

Candles should already have been placed in candle holders at the points of the triangle. For this purpose, I suggest burning small chime candles, which usually burn for 2 hours or so. Once you have placed the effigy into the cauldron, you will then light the candles around the Triangle of Arte while saying the following:

> *"By the hand which creates,"*

Light the white candle.

> *"By the hand which destroys,"*

Light the black candle.

> *"By the star upon my brow and the light betwixt the horns,"*

Light the red candle.

You will call upon and conjure the spirit for whom the effigy is meant to serve. This should be something to the effect of:

> *"I conjure and call you forth NN! That you may find comfort and solace in the body here gifted to you. Let it be a vessel which pleases you, which fortifies you, and which strengthens our work in this world.*

Come forth and enter this cauldron. Enter this effigy that it may be a body, a foothold, and a locus for your power. Rest here now. Grow here now. Be strengthened here now."

Once you have felt the presence of the spirit and feel that at least a portion of its power has entered the cauldron, the lid should be placed upon it. Should you choose to, any sigils appropriate to the spirit may now be drawn with chalk onto the cauldron. The candles should then be allowed to burn out.

The period in which an effigy or fetich is left within a vessel of rebirth is often a good time to pay attention to any messages you may receive from the spirit you are working with. The duration of gestation may be anywhere from a single night to an entire lunar cycle. This will often vary depending upon the desires of the spirit being worked with, their requests, and the kind of spirit vessel. In most cases, if you are birthing a poppet, as we are linking the effigy to a living person already embodied in this realm, it shouldn't require more than a night within the cauldron. When creating *maumets* and fetiches, I have generally found that leaving them in the cauldron three to nine nights is best. With effigies meant to be receptacles for existing spirits, it has been anywhere between one night and a full lunar cycle. The time that each spirit may require to integrate into a material form to fulfill the role and tasks you have agreed upon can vary quite a bit. Again, when in doubt, divination is your friend.

During the period of gestation, it has been customary for me to burn new candles upon the triangle each night. This needn't be a grandiose ritual or display. In this case, you are essentially offering these candles to help fortify and protect the spirit during this phase of transition and alignment.

The Resurrection and Rebirth

Once you have reached the final day of the gestation period, candles should be lit at the corners of the Triangle of Arte once again whilst saying:

"By the hand which creates,"

Light the white candle.

"By the hand which destroys,"

Light the black candle.

"By the star upon my brow and the light betwixt the horns,"

Light the red candle.

The cauldron should be lifted and removed from the triangle. The side of it should be knocked upon three times to begin awakening the spirit within. The lid should then be removed and the effigy slowly lifted from the cauldron whilst saying:

"Resurrected and risen, you are! Brought forth in power and birthed in new form."

The effigy should then be placed within the triangle once more, whilst saying:

"Awaken now! Within this body. That you may be enspirited, enlivened, and empowered in the work of this world."

At this point, the breath of life exercise should be performed. During the transfer of breath, the effigy may be lifted towards your face as needed and desired. This is also the point at which you would incorporate the pipe/smoke and the *Spiritus Vitae* tool as a part of the transference of breath, as you are inclined and able. Additionally, you should not neglect to include a declaration of transposition before you pass the breath to the effigy. Once the breath of life has been given, you may place the effigy back into the triangle.

Naming and Affirming the Role of the Effigy

Now you will officially name the effigy. In cases where the effigy is created in service to a spirit or deity the name given will be the name of that spirit. If you are creating a *maumet,* you should have already created or divined a name for it. This can be anything which you feel best suits the *maumet,* from a conventional name you've chosen, to a name devised using acronyms or anagrams based on words and phrases of power, or perhaps a name which was revealed to you during the course of crafting the spirit or its gestation. If this is a poppet, you will name it on behalf of the person it is intended for. You may wish to couple the naming of the effigy with washing or sprinkling it with the *Aqua Vitae* and/or anointing it with the *Spirit Summoning Oil.* This may assist in further anchoring the spirit to the vessel. Alternatively, if there are washes or oils of your own devising relevant to the particular spirit, they may be used here. To formally grant the name, you should state:

> *"You are awakened to life, and I name you NN. That you may be known by and called by NN. And that you live now as an earthly vessel for the spirit of NN."*

This is then followed by a recitation of the role and responsibilities that the vessel and its associated spirit will fulfill. Here we are reaffirming the work the spirit is meant to do and how the spirit vessel will be worked with. Using an effigy for a familiar spirit in our example, this would take the form of saying something to the effect of:

> *"By the birth of this effigy, may you fulfill the role of teacher, ally, protector, and partner in our magic together. Bound by the agreements we have established. That you will come by the calling of your name. That we will work in allyship and peace. That this vessel may grant you stability and fortitude in your work in this world and serve as a locus for your influence and power in our work together. May this be as your body until such a time as our work will end and our bond be broken."*[122]

If you have created a formal written pact with the spirit that further outlines the agreed upon boundaries, roles, and responsibilities established between yourself and the spirit, it should be read aloud and signed by you. You should then state:

> *"It is not my hand which signs here now, but the hand of NN"*

122 See the final chapter for more information on breaking the bond. The use of the cord below is one example of this.

The contract is signed with the name of the spirit, and if it has revealed a specific sigil or seal to you, it should be included as well. Should you wish to employ the cord at this point it may be wrapped and tied around the effigy along with wording such as:

> *"Let the tying of this cord be a symbol of our bond, our agreements, and our work together. And by it, may you be bound to this effigy until such a time that our work and relationship may be severed by the intentional cutting of this cord. Upon such an occasion, you will no longer be bound to this form. This vessel will return in state to the materials from which it was crafted. And should it be desired by either party, both our work and relationship will be concluded."*

Bodily Alignment/Transposition
This is an element reserved for effigies. Here we are, in essence, further awakening and aligning the spirit to the body of the effigy by activating certain points on the body. For this part of the rite, you may wish to use a stylus to point to each part of the effigy being referenced as you state:

"May your mouth be as the mouth of NN.
That you may speak and bring forth messages as NN.
May your eyes be as the eyes of NN. That you may witness the world as NN.
May your ears be as the ears of NN. That you may hear my call,
my devotions, my petitions, my prayers, and my instruction.
May your nose be the nose of NN. That you may receive the blessing
of the sweet-smelling suffumigation gifted to thee.
May your feet be as the feet of NN. That you may
journey where needed with swiftness and ease.
May your hands be as the hands of NN. That you may
receive offerings given to thee and fulfill your work in this world.
May your heart be as the heart of NN. A center of stability and seat of life.
May your belly be as the belly of NN. A center of sustenance and power.
May your head be as the head of NN. A center for intellect and wisdom.
May your body be as the body of NN. An earthly vessel and locus of spirit.
Hail and blessings to you NN!"

Fortification and Enshrining

To conclude this work, I will usually feed and fortify the spirit by passing the effigy through the smoke of an incense appropriate to the spirit or the *Suffumigation of Ensouling* given in the formulary. It will then be enshrined wherever it is meant to live. This may be upon an altar, into a shrine specifically created for it, or another place you and the spirit have deemed appropriate. Lastly, I will often place further offerings in front of the effigy along with any tools and accouterments appropriate to the work of the spirit in order to welcome it. I will then let the effigy rest for at least a day before making any requests or beginning any serious work with the spirit.

Chapter Eleven

A Fragile Body of Stars: On Holy Idols and Poppetry for Balm and for Bane

The work of poppetry offers a wide spectrum of applications in our magical work. In this chapter, I hope to cover some aspects of this work in a bit more detail so that it may lead the reader towards inspiration in their own work. Additionally, we will explore possible approaches for preparing and sanctifying pre-existing statuary as sacred vessels aligned towards the spirits they are meant to serve. In this chapter I will be by providing two alternative rites of ensouling/hallowing for effigies that may be of particular use when working with poppets and statues. These may be slightly adapted and worked into the ritual structure provided in the previous chapter, if you like, or approached as standalone rites.

PRAXIS: Baptism and Hallowing Poppets

A very common manner by which poppets have been traditionally awakened and allied takes the form of a mock baptism. Though some witches may wish to employ a form of baptism which mimics the rite as it exists within Catholic or Protestant liturgy. If the individual that the poppet is meant to represent is of the Christian faith and has received baptism, a more Christianized form of this rite may prove more appropriate and effective. I encourage those who are inclined to research various rites of baptism as points of reference, should they wish to craft their own rite of baptism reflective of a Christian worldview. That said, I wish to provide here a form of enspiriting and hallowing for poppets that is fairly simple and somewhat more universal in its approach.

Prior to this rite, you may wish to perform the simple rite of exorcism and cleansing from the previous chapter on your newly created poppet.

For this rite, you will need:

- Your Triangle of Arte
- The *Aqua Vitae* blend from the formulary section, consecrated water, or a botanical infusion appropriate to the work of the poppet.
- The Suffumigation of Ensouling, frankincense resin, or copal resin
- Charcoal and a censer for burning incense
- *Spirit Summoning Oil* from the formulary section, a general Altar Oil or Anointing Oil, or olive oil that has been hallowed and made sacred for ritual use.
- Your stylus

Optional items:

- The *Spiritus Vitae* tool
- Ritual pipe and smoke
- A previously crafted cord

1. If you desire to, you may prepare your ritual space in the preferred manner, such as laying a compass, casting a circle, etc. Should you be working against an enemy or hostile person, you should consider employing additional measures of protection, such as wearing protective charms and partnering with protective spirits.
2. The poppet should be placed within the center of the Triangle of Arte, and the candles lit in the manner previously described. Your charcoal should be lit and a bit of the incense burnt upon it. You will then call to the spirit of the person for whom the poppet is meant to represent. In cases where the poppet is intended for baneful or coercive workings, it is usually most effective to summon their

spirit at a time when they are asleep, as most people's spirits are a bit more adrift from their bodies as they sleep, and they are more susceptible to influence.

3. The call may follow one of the formulas given below. These may also be altered and modified to be more specific to your work. The first call here is for calling upon the spirit of a person you are doing blessing work upon. The other is more aggressive, for people you are doing baneful workings, bindings, etc., on. You will begin by pointing the index and middle fingers of your dominant hand (or your Blade of Arte for hostile forces) at the poppet in the triangle. Employing the *vox magica,* say:

> *"I call you to come forth and be present here and now, spirit of NN, born into this world by [Mother's Name if known] and [Father's Name if known] on [Target's Birthdate]. Let my conjuration be as the voice of the creator, which gave you life and which unites all creatures. By my breath, by my call, and by the ancestors who preceded you may you be guided to this Triangle of Arte that a portion of your spirit be lent to this effigy that you may receive the blessings of [insert what type of working you are doing here]. Come forth by the figure, crafted in your image, that it may be as you are. As the sun sets and rises, may it be so! As it is spoken, so is it done."*

Alternatively:

> *"I call and command you to come forth and be present here and now, spirit of NN, born into this world by [Mother's Name if known] and [Father's Name if known] on [Target's Birthdate]. Let my conjuration be as the voice of the creator which gave you life and which unites all creatures, by my breath and by the breath within your lungs, obey my call as the commandment of the creator. By the avenging spirits of justice, of righteousness, and of retribution, may you be taken and brought forth to this Triangle of Arte that a portion of your spirit be lent to this effigy. Come forth by the figure, crafted in your image, that it may be as you are. As the sun sets and rises, may it be so! As it is spoken, so is it done."*

4. Once you feel the presence of the person's spirit, you will then dip your fingers into the *Aqua Vitae* and say:

   "It is not my hands which perform this work, but the hands of that which breathed the first breath, uttered the first word, and crafted the first form."

5. Then sprinkle the *Aqua Vitae* liberally upon the poppet whilst saying:

   "By water and earth and by these living waters may this effigy be awakened and allied to the life and spirit of NN, that this poppet shall be as they are and that whatsoever I shall bestow or enforce upon this effigy for blessing or bane may be granted to or visited upon NN in kind. As the sun sets and rises, may it be so!"

6. Next, pass the poppet through the incense smoke whilst saying:

   "By air and fire and by this hallowed smoke may this effigy be awakened and allied to the life and spirit of NN, that this poppet shall be as they are and that whatsoever I shall bestow or enforce upon this effigy for blessing or bane may be granted to or visited upon NN in kind. As the sun sets and rises, may it be so!"

7. At this point, the breath of life exercise should be performed. This is also the point at which you would incorporate the pipe/smoke and the *Spiritus Vitae* tool as a part of the transference of breath, as you are inclined and able to. Additionally, you should not neglect to include a declaration of transposition before you pass the breath to the effigy. For example:

   "It is not my breath which gives you life but the breath of [insert name of person whom a poppet is meant to represent] themself".

8. Once the breath of life has been given, you may place the effigy back into the triangle.
9. Use a bit of the *Spirit Summoning Oil* to anoint the forehead of the poppet and say:

"You are born and named as NN, child of [Mother's Name if known] and [Father's Name if known]."

10. Next, take up your stylus and touch it to the crown of the head of the poppet and say:

    "May your mind be as that of NN."

11. Touch the stylus to the mouth and say:

    "May your mouth be as that of NN."

12. Touch your stylus to each eye and say:

    "May your eyes be as those of NN."

13. Touch your stylus to each ear and say:

    "May your ears be as those of NN."

14. Touch your stylus to the nose and/or each nostril and say:

    "May your nose be as that of NN."

15. Touch your stylus to the chest and say:

    "May your heart be as that of NN."

16. Touch your stylus to the belly and say:

    "May your belly be as that of NN."

17. Touch your stylus to the head and say:

    "May your head be as that of NN."

18. Touch your stylus to each hand and say:

"May your hands be as those of NN."

19. Touch your stylus to each foot and say:

    "May your feet be as those of NN."

20. Next, use your index and middle finger to make the sign of an equal-armed cross over the poppet and declare:

    "You are no longer a poppet of [wax/cloth/clay], but the flesh, the sinew, muscle, bone, and blood of NN. Let your body be as the body of NN."

21. At this point, you may wish to tie a cord around the waist of the poppet as a ritual action, which seals the work. Again, this allows for this alignment to be undone and a quick way of releasing the poppet's ties to the spirit of the person it is intended for by simply untying or cutting the cord. To do this, the cord is wrapped around the poppet three times and tied at the navel of the effigy. When doing this, you should say:

    "By the wrapping of this cord may the spirit of NN be bound to this effigy that it shall be as they are. As it is worked for blessings or bane, so too will they receive the same. Until such a time that this cord is untied or cut by my hand, may they be so bound."

22. I will then usually conclude this by tying three knots in the cord and saying:

    "As the sun sets and rises, may it be so! As it is spoken, so is it done."

On Further Considerations for the Breath of Life

We will discuss cases where we may wish to create poppets as extensions of ourselves in a bit. However, I would like to clarify that a poppet designed to represent yourself will actively receive some of your own power/spirit via the breath. However, this is a very small link you are creating between yourself and the effigy. This process should not generally be viewed as though a portion of your spirit is being depleted from a finite pool. So long as the poppet doesn't fall into the hands of an enemy who is skilled at magic, you have very little to worry about regarding any form of soul loss or the like.

If you find that you are doing magic on behalf of a person who is accessible, aware of, and consenting to your work, it is ideal for them to be present to give the breath of life to the poppet themself. In such a case, you needn't go to all the trouble of conjuring the person's spirit into the triangle, as their presence as a part of the ritual is more than sufficient.

On Healing Poppets and the Body of Stars

In the process of creating and utilizing effigies for healing, we might stuff the poppet with healing herbs, dress it with healing oils, or pass it through suffumigation intended to bring health. As mentioned earlier in this book, a "bed of healing" can be crafted for the poppet from a box or basket lined in herbs such as Self-heal, Sage, and others appropriate to the person's condition. An effigy may have charms or songs of healing spoken over it with empowered breath. It may also have hands laid upon it for healing, and the witch may use a soft and repetitive stroking motion upon areas needing support.

Though this falls into the realm of more advanced work, when giving it the breath of life, the wording can be modified so that what is being passed to the poppet is only the spirit of the illness that the person is suffering. This is a form of transference where we seek to pass the illness to a new host and let it be taken away from the person afflicted. It is important, while doing this kind of healing work, that you have full awareness and consent from the person you are doing it for. It is also important that you are only passing the person's affliction to the poppet and nothing else of theirs.

Ideally, the person will be present and they can give the breath of life themself. It is also helpful if the poppet can be passed over their body. This generally takes the form of the witch holding the poppet and making three equal armed crosses each at the top of the person's head, the back of their neck, over their heart, the center of their back, over their belly, over their genitals, over their buttocks, over the palms of each hand, and the soles of each foot. If there is a particularly afflicted part of the body, this should also be given attention with at least nine crosses made over that area with the poppet. The poppet should then be taken to a cemetery, with proper protocols followed, and buried in order to allow the illness to "die" and return to the earth. This should ideally be done at sunset. Once the poppet has been buried, you should exit the cemetery without looking back.

For general healing work, I have created a poppet which is designed to be reused and re-enspirited. The poppet is gender neutral and fairly nondescript. It is created from cloth and has been given a heartstone and stuffed with healing herbs. It is intended for use when I need to offer some fast-healing support to a person and don't have time for more complex methods of poppet construction and ensouling. Along with it, I have crafted a cord that is allied to the poppet and made for reuse. The purpose here is for the cord to be wrapped around the poppet in the manner suggested in the earlier rite so that it will temporarily bind a person to the effigy in order for healing magic to be performed. Once I have completed the healing work, I will untie and unwrap the cord whilst declaring something to the effect of: *"Untethered and unbound, no longer is the spirit of NN tied to this effigy. May they go forth in good health and good cheer."* After this, I will pass the poppet and cord through the smoke of *Cleansing Incense* to ensure any ties to the person and the work are removed from the poppet and it is returned to a neutral state until it is required again for another person in need of quick healing.

When a specific limb or organ of the body is injured, it is usually fairly straightforward where we should work on a poppet. However, when working on an illness related to the endocrine system or the blood, it may be difficult to determine the areas of the effigy we should pin or otherwise direct our energy towards. One way we might address this is by applying ideas around astrological healing to our poppet.

Melothesia is an ancient form of medical astrology wherein different body parts and functions are associated with the planets and zodiacal signs. This attribution begins with Aries being associated with the head and the signs moving their way down to Pisces at the feet. Each of these associated parts of the body and signs is related to a variety of areas of healing. So you might choose to place a pin in that area of the poppet's body based upon the attributions below:

- **Aries:** Head, eyes, blood pressure, adrenals
- **Taurus:** Neck, shoulders, throat, ears

- **Gemini:** Lungs, arms, fingers, nerves
- **Cancer:** Chest, breasts, some body fluids
- **Leo:** Heart, spine, upper back, spleen
- **Virgo:** Abdomen, intestines, gallbladder, liver, pancreas
- **Libra:** Lower back, hips, kidneys, endocrines
- **Scorpio:** Reproductive organs, pelvis, urinary bladder, rectum
- **Sagittarius:** Thighs, hips, legs
- **Capricorn:** Knees, joints, bones, skin
- **Aquarius:** Shins, calves, ankles, circulatory system
- **Pisces:** Feet, lymphatic system

If you desire to create a reusable poppet of quick healing, you may wish to draw or paint the astrological signs upon appropriate parts of the effigy,[123] so that they may act as points of focus for your healing work. You may also wish to look further into these attributions and astrological healing to gain a greater perspective of its history and application.

It should be absolutely stressed here that magic alone is not a substitute for the great care and effectiveness that treating and addressing illness and injury which modern medicine can provide. This type of work is intended as something to be done in addition to addressing illness with the aid of your medical professionals. It is not a replacement for it.

On Hexing and Binding Poppets

I have already covered a discussion on ethics previously in this book, so I will not delve too deeply into the subject again, other than to say that it is my belief that each action has a reaction and a cost. In my experience, a witch who approaches hexing from a place of pursuing justice as opposed to indulging in pettiness or obsessive hatred is less likely to experience potentially undesirable consequences from this work. Additionally, as individuals who have, at least in theory, claimed their own personal power and sovereignty, I believe that it would be contradictory for a witch to allow themselves to be attacked without seeking to defend themself. Further, I believe that if you witness serious harm that you have the power to stop, and you do nothing, then you are complicit in that harm.

123 As is illustrated in the main image of this chapter and in the photographs section.

Should you wish to pursue works of binding and hexing, it is paramount that you are familiar with methods of personal magical protection and spiritual cleansing that you may employ in conjunction with this work. Often when dealing with hexing work, we are trafficking with spirits and working with *materia* that, by their nature, can behave as spiritual toxins. So it is always recommended that you perform proper cleansing and exorcisms after doing this sort of work.

On occasions where poppetry must be employed against someone who is a threat to the witch or the greater community, there are numerous approaches one may take. Of course, the poppet may be stuffed with various *materia* allied to and conjured with the purpose of causing misfortune to the target. In cases where the desire is to perform wasting magic designed to diminish the power, health, protections, or well-being of a target, the effigy may be made of wax and slowly melted away over a period of time. Similarly, a poppet of this sort may be made of unfired clay and buried in a cemetery, put into running water such as a stream, or put into a large jar filled with noxious materials such as storm water or vinegar and other aqueous substance so that as the effigy slowly breaks down in the water or earth the target wastes away. Another approach to this might be to craft an effigy from bread or even ground beef and place it upon an anthill so that it is slowly eaten away at. Poppets may, of course, be harmed by the use of pins and needles, the breaking of limbs, or by otherwise ritually dismantling them whilst still tethered to the target.

In cases where the desire is less to cause harm but instead stop a person from doing harm, similar to the execration figures discussed earlier in this work, a poppet may have its arms and legs bound. It may also be blindfolded or gagged. In some situations, binding magic may be done on a poppet to keep the person from doing harm to themself due to reckless or addictive behaviors. Again, when doing these types of binding, I recommend creating a braided cord that has been crafted and conjured for the specific behaviors you wish to bind.

In situations where a person has been spreading slander, a poppet may be crafted with an open mouth that can be stuffed with *materia* such as Slippery Elm *(Ulmus rubra)*, Cloves *(Syzygium aromaticum)*, or Alum, which are all allied to stopping gossip. The mouth of the poppet may then be sewn up or sealed with wax. In cases where the goal is to turn the work and words of an enemy against them, the poppet may be surrounded by mirrors or placed within a box lined with mirrors so that their own actions are reflected back upon them.

A much more benevolent approach to people who are behaving in potentially harmful ways is to speak suggestions which lead the person towards getting help or seeking peace over pins, dressing them with your spittle, and then inserting them into the head and heart of the poppet to transmit and fix these thoughts and desires onto them. I generally find that when a path towards peace and accountability is possible, it is usually a preferable and less taxing path to success than engaging in an all-out assault.

On Poppets as Personal Surrogates

Poppets may be prepared as an extension of the witch or to act as a form of stand-in. One possibility for this is to prepare a poppet that acts as a decoy and will take and absorb any malefic magical attacks or evil eye directed towards you. In preparing such an effigy, you should include some of your own taglocks (hair, fingernail clipping, etc.) within the poppet. It is ideal that when you are cutting your hair or trimming your nails to be added you speak in the *vox magica* and declare: *"Let this be taken by me that it may act in place of me. From me, but no longer of me."* This should be seen as an act of severance wherein the taglocks will draw attacks towards the poppet instead of you. In giving the breath of life, the same wording can be used. Let your purpose indicate that the poppet you are crafting will absorb any malefic magic or spiritual attacks. This sort of decoy poppet is best kept near your front door. Better yet, if it can be kept outside of the home but near the front. However, you will want to ensure it is not kept somewhere that it may be discovered by or tampered with by anyone who may wish you harm. If you ever find that the poppet has been damaged with no discernible cause, it should be buried somewhere far away from your home and retired. If it is kept inside the home, to keep it from acquiring too much malefic influence or evil eye, it is best to cleanse both it and yourself monthly with the *Cleansing Incense* in the formulary section, or more frequently if you feel you are under active magical attack.

In a similar fashion to the votary statues mentioned earlier in this work, you may wish to craft a surrogate poppet representative of yourself as a form of offering to any deities or spirits you wish to express an ongoing devotion to. Again, the wording of your hallowing and enspiriting should reflect its use as a token of your devotion and an extension of yourself so that you may be in communion with the deity whilst you are unable to be actively at their shrine so that you may receive their blessings and protection while you are away.

We may, of course, create poppets to draw our desires to us as well. For instance, in order to increase magical power you might craft a poppet which includes your own taglocks along with a lodestone for the heartstone and then load it with *materia* that reflects the botanical, mineral, and animal spirits you are allied to, or with appropriate *materia* that has been conjured to grant you psychic ability, wisdom, etc. So long as this type of poppet is well cared for, it may function in essence as a form of augmenting one's own spirit. For this kind of effigy, it is a good idea to include a cord that may be cut should you wish to sever the connection between yourself and the magical influence of the poppet. Such an approach may be utilized for all manner of purposes, from making oneself more confident, more prosperous, or more attractive. Of course, all the usual caveats apply that this should be an effigy that is kept in a safe space where it will not be touched or tampered with by others.

Lastly, similar in form to the work described for transference of illness, we may wish to create surrogate poppets which function as a repository for things we wish to rid ourselves of. In such a case, the poppet becomes a vessel into which we may pour parts of ourselves that we wish to be rid of and/or transmuted. This is particularly appropriate in cases where we wish to find clearance and healing from insecurities, self-sabotaging beliefs, addictions, past traumas, former spiritual and emotional attachments, or harmful patterns of behavior that are contrary to who we wish to be. Such a rite can be incredibly powerful, emotional, and cathartic.

When crafting and ensouling the poppet, you should be quite clear about the fact that the breath of life you are giving the poppet is representative of the behaviors you wish to be rid of and wish to heal. Keep in mind that this is often one step on a path towards personal transformation and healing. The practical work of seeking solutions, such as community support, therapy, and actively working on transforming yourself in other ways, is equally important. It is also very appropriate to call upon any protective deities and spirits you are allied to, as well as any known and unknown ancestors who support your greatest happiness, so they may assist in this kind of working.

It is usually best to create this kind of effigy from clay that is left unfired. When the effigy has been crafted and enspirited, it should be taken to a forest away from where you live and buried so that it may return to the earth and be transformed. You will notice this is similar in form to the wasting hex described earlier. However, the purpose in this case is to lay this particular part of yourself to rest. I have also witnessed people burning effigies crafted from paper and cloth for this kind of work. This is certainly an option, though I find that committing a poppet to the earth so that it may slowly be reintegrated and transformed is often more effective in cases where we hope for long-term results.

On The Enlivening of Statuary

As previously mentioned, there are various methods by which we might ritually prepare, empower, and align the devotional icons we wish to employ as representations of the deities, saints, and spirits we wish to work with. This helps transform a simple devotional image into a spirit *locus* and repository of their power.

Similar techniques are fairly common amongst various African Traditional Religions where statues intended to be representations of spirits are loaded with magical *materia* and ritually prepared before use. Within the cultus of Santa Muerte, devotees' statues are similarly prepared by loading the base of the statues with amulets, grains, seeds, and other magical *materia.* The statues are often bathed in a wash of various herbs and perfumes and suffumigated in botanical smokes to prepare them. In Buddhist tradition, the consecration of statues, especially those depicting deities, sometimes involves filling their hollow interiors with sacred objects such as mantra-inscribed scrolls and relics. This practice is believed to imbue the statue with a "soul," enhancing its spiritual presence. With this in mind, I wish to explore some ways we might apply similar techniques to our own craft.

Upon selecting a statue, unless it is already hollow or otherwise possesses a cavity in the bottom, we will want to consider ways we might make a space that may be loaded with magical *materia.* If the material the statue is made from allows for it, a hole may be drilled into the base of the statue so that it may be loaded. If this is not possible, other options include creating or buying a wooden plaque in which a cavity can be created that we can use as a base for our statue to stand upon.[124] Once the *materia* has been placed inside, the plaque may be affixed to the bottom of the statue, or the statue may simply be placed on top of it. If neither of these is an option, you may instead consider wrapping your chosen material in cloth to make a small packet or creating a pouch for the load, which may be tied or otherwise attached to the statue. We will discuss loading our statues in greater detail, but first, we should explore methods to cleanse and prepare the statue.

On Washing and Suffumigating the Statue

Before the statue is loaded, it is recommended that it be given a spiritual cleansing by washing or sprinkling it with consecrated water and passing it through the smoke of an appropriate incense such as the *Clearance Incense* or *Cleansing Incense* listed in the formulary section, or another appropriate cleansing incense. This should, of course, be coupled with spoken charms and prayers of cleansing over the statue. You might also employ the simple exorcism given in the previous chapter.

Once this is done, you may wish to thoroughly wash the statue in an infusion of herbs meant to draw the spirit which it will be dedicated to. You may choose to create an infusion from herbs sacred to the spirit or utilize the *Aqua Vitae* formula given later in this book. You may then follow the wash by passing the statue through the smoke of an incense allied to the spirit or utilizing the *Suffumigation of Ensouling* given in the formulary.

On Loading Statues

In choosing *materia* for loading your statue selecting appropriate botanical, mineral, or animal materials allied to the spirit/deity based upon their mythos, lore, and your relationship with the spirit in question is best. For example, imagine we were preparing a statue for the Greek god Apollo we might choose plants which appear in the myths surrounding him such as Bay Laurel, Hyacinth, Cypress, and as either are said to be the tree he was born under Olive or Palm leaves might be a worthy addition. Apollo is also allied to crows, wolves, and snakes, so provided we have access to items such as a crow feather, wolf's hair, and snake sheds, we might also incorporate them into the load.

124 For this, I find using a forstner or spade drill bit effective.

In some tales, Sapphire is said to be a stone sacred to Apollo, so perhaps we might include one. Given his solar associations, if we are unable to acquire a Sapphire or wish to include multiple stones, we might choose stones that also have associations with the sun, such as citrine or amber. You may wish to dedicate one of these stones as the heartstone for the statue as well, or choose one collected from a place that is allied to the influence of Apollo. The Arts, poetry, music, dance, archery, prophecy, and healing are all activities associated with Apollo, so perhaps you might seek out a stone from a music venue, an art school, an archery range, a hospital, or other appropriate place to serve as a heartstone for the statue. You may also wish to gather dirt from such places to include in the load as you feel are appropriate to the aspects of Apollo you desire to work with.

You may also wish to write out petitions, devotions, hymns, prayers, seals, symbols, or sigils for the spirit the statue is for, and either roll or fold them up very small so they will fit within the cavity, or ritually burn them and add the ashes to the load. If you have previously burned incense as a devotional offering to the spirit, these ashes may also make a good addition to the load you are creating.

In selecting materials for loading statues, go where your research and inspiration lead you. Now is a good time to call upon either the spirit you are dedicating the statue to, or a trusted familiar or deity, and do some divining upon the *materia* chosen for the effigy. This may allow you to refine your selection and determine if any items should be added or subtracted from the load you are creating for the statue. Once all *materia* for the load is confirmed, and you have conjured the spirits of the *materia* for their aid, you may wish to ask for the blessing of the spirit the load will be dedicated to by reading a traditional hymn, reciting a devotional prayer of your own design, or simply speaking from the heart as a part of this process.

Next, determine the logistics of how you will load the statue. If the opening in the statue you wish to load is quite small, you may wish to only include very small amounts of each of the items you have selected. Items may also be powdered and burned to ash as needed. When I am loading a statue, I will usually place any larger or solid objects into the cavity first and then mix together any powdered *materia* such as herbs, dirts, and ashes. These powdered objects will then be worked into an air-drying clay, or if I have enough dirt gathered from various places, I will use one of the methods described in the *Crafting of Dirt Clay* exercise located in Chapter Nine. Alternatively, you may wish to fill the cavity with melted wax or resin to seal it, or cover it by gluing a piece of cloth, paper, or leather over the opening.

On Awakening the Statue

At this point, you may wish to go through the death/gestation/rebirthing processes as laid out in the previous chapter. If you choose to go this route, it is always an excellent choice to time the birthing of the statue with any particularly relevant holiday, feast day, planetary day/hour, etc., that is traditionally significant to the deity or spirit. In lieu of this, allow yourself to be led by inspiration, divination, and necessity.

For the sake of expediency, you might wish to forego the more involved ritual processes of death/gestation/rebirth and instead move directly to ensouling and alignment. Below, I will give a suggested order of ritual operation for enspiriting and awakening the statue.

1. Prepare your ritual space as your practice/tradition dictates.
2. Place the statue within the Triangle of Arte and light the candles while saying.

   "By the hand which creates,"

   Light the white candle.

   "By the hand which destroys,"

   Light the black candle.

   "By the star upon my brow and the light betwixt the horns."

   Light the red candle.
3. Conjure forth the spirit/deity associated with the statue to be present in the Triangle of Arte.

4. Next, say to the spirit:

   "Awaken now! Within this body. That you may be enspirited, enlivened, and empowered in the work of this world."

5. The Breath of Life is given to the statue.
6. It is named for the spirit.
7. The Bodily Alignment/Transposition is performed.
8. Close your ritual space as you normally would.
9. The statue is then enshrined and worked with as a devotional *locus*.

Once complete, the statue becomes a much more effective *locus* of the deity/spirit you are working with. You should find with regular attention and devotion that in time this living statue will become a truly powerful repository for the presence and influence of the deity in your life.

CHAPTER TWELVE

Domestic Spirits: On Caring for and Cohabiting with Enspirited Objects

When engaging in this sort of work with regularity, you will eventually find yourself living in a house quite haunted by your own design. Each ritually enspirited object we are engaging with becomes another member of our spiritual ecosystem, which we bear some level of responsibility for as a reflection of the relationship we have established with the spirit that inhabits it. Depending upon your ability to manage relationships and responsibilities, this may be a lively, empowered, and enchanting ecosystem, or a chaotic and imbalanced, and draining one. With this in mind, this chapter is meant to provide some suggestions and best practices for living together with enspirited objects as well as approaches towards ending our relationship with spirits and retiring their material bodies should we ever need to.

On Cohabitation, Care, and Taboos

To work with enspirited vessels is to invite their spirits closer to us. As a result, this requires that we integrate them more thoroughly as partners in our daily lives. Though the expectations and responsibilities of this relationship will vary from spirit to spirit, some general points of consideration are worth highlighting here.

Firstly, *you* are the caretaker for the body of this spirit. As a part of the exchange provided by embodying spirits, the material form that you have crafted and ensouled for this spirit is now your responsibility to tend to and to protect. You should ensure that the effigy/vessel is kept safe from damage and harm and that it is periodically refreshed and cleaned when needed. Should the spirit's body ever become damaged or broken in any way, the witch should employ appropriate methods of divination/scrying/transvestion to determine why this happened.

A spirit vessel may simply break as a result of accident or age, so these possibilities should always be considered before immediately imagining worst-case scenarios. That said, it is important to determine if there are other potential forces at play when a spirit vessel is broken. In some cases, the vessel may have broken because the spirit has become stressed or overexerted in some way. This could happen because the spirit has taken the brunt of a magical attack sent your way, or because it has been working too heavily on your behalf without being properly fed and fortified. In other cases, a vessel may break because the spirit has simply "outgrown" the vessel and requires that you craft them a new vessel, which may include alterations more suited to the spirit's current needs.

It might also be that the spirit is displeased for some reason. In some cases, a spirit may react negatively to the addition or subtraction of people, pets, or other spirits to the home. They may also react to alterations of the home, such as construction or a move. To help avoid conflicts, it is always best practice to inform your spirits about the goings on of the home. Let them know if there will be any remodeling happening or a move. You should also inform spirits if someone (spirit, pet, or human) is moving in or out of the home, as well as if there have been any recent births/deaths.

A spirit's displeasure might also be related more directly to behaviors on your part. Perhaps you have neglected it, and the spirit is simply requesting more attention or offerings. The spirit may instead be upset with a recent choice you have made or other disrespect you have shown to it. Some spirit relationships come with certain taboos as a part of the relationship. These should be viewed in many ways as the boundaries that a spirit creates regarding what is/isn't acceptable, should you wish to have a relationship with it.

These taboos may be as simple as not being naked or engaging in sexual activity in front of the spirit's vessel, or not working with the spirit while unshowered or otherwise unclean. They may also include things like refraining from using foul language or engaging in malefic magic with or around the spirit. In other cases, the taboos may inform where the spirit vessel should be placed, such as being kept on the floor, in the kitchen, or higher than all other spirit vessels and representations in the home. Some spirits do not get along well with each other and may not wish to share an altar or room. For instance, in my work, there are spirits I work with of a more diabolical and/or chthonic nature that do not wish to be near any spirits, *materia,* or ritual practices of a more celestial or angelic nature. The opposite is true of some of the more celestial spirits I work with.

Spiritual taboos may also include greater restrictions on your own lifestyle choices such as avoiding certain kinds of foods, not touching or working with certain magical *materia,* wearing or not wearing certain clothing, or staying away from certain types of people, spirits, or activities. Occasionally, a broken spirit vessel may be a warning from a protective spirit about potentially harmful or risky behaviors or relationships we are engaging in, or a sign that they are upset about an established taboo we have broken.

In the case of spirits that you share a close bond with, it is important to ensure they are informed of major life changes, including milestones such as marriages and spiritual initiations. More often than not, these spirits may be consulted and approached for their counsel and blessings regarding the course of our lives. So the announcement of such changes usually comes as little surprise to those around us with whom we are close and trust, but it is a sign of respect nonetheless.

It is paramount that the witch always remembers that just like our relationships and the responsibilities we have to other people, spirit relationships may range from very simple and transactional exchanges to those that require a large amount of trust, devotion, and sincere commitment. Examples of more serious forms of relationships include dedicating yourself to the formal priesthood of a spirit or deity, or committing to a form of spirit marriage. Such commitments should never be approached lightly or simply from a desire for power and clout. I have personally witnessed the unfortunate results of more than one magical practitioner who fell victim to their own hunger and hubris in the pursuit of spirit companions and became spirit-sick and detached from reality as a result. It is up to each witch to exercise their own discernment in determining when and if the exchange requested by a spirit and the requirements of the relationship serve their greatest good and exist in a balanced or imbalanced form. When in doubt, seek the advice and counsel of trusted practitioners/friends to help keep you grounded and point out any of the things you may not be seeing.

On Offerings

The things that our spirits might require or request as offerings are as diverse as the spirits themselves. Most commonly, material offerings take the form of incense, perfumes, food, and libations of water, coffee, various alcohols, or other drinks. Offerings may also be given in the form of flowers or other botanical *materia* placed near or upon the spirit vessel. Similarly, a spirit may occasionally request an offering of stones, bones, or other *materia* sacred to it. We may also give offerings of coins and paper money, precious and semiprecious stones, and jewelry. Occasionally, a spirit may require an offering of a new tool to aid it in its work. Sometimes this will take the form of giving the spirit a small version of a tool, such as a miniature weapon or farming tool, a divination tool, or a small crown. Other times, it may entail dedicating a tool to the spirit that you will be using to work with it, such as a ritual tool or divination deck.

As for food offerings, some spirits will enjoy simple fruits, bread, butter, cream, various alcohols, coffee, water, meats, and more complex cooked offerings, or even a bit of the foods we prepare for ourselves. Candles and tobacco, either in raw form or the smoke, are also very common offerings depending upon the spirit.

I would be remiss here if I did not also mention the often-controversial topic of giving spirits blood offerings. Throughout history, many spirits have been fed and fortified with blood. This has been more common within societies that lived much closer in relation to the animals they raised, killed, and butchered for their own sustenance. In many cases, when blood was fed to a spirit, it was given with deep reverence and from an animal which would then be eaten by the person or community. Here, the blood becomes a literal lifeforce given to the spirit, which, in truth, would likely otherwise go to waste.

From a contemporary lens where we are so often removed from direct exposure to the cycle of life and the animals we eat, it is very easy to malign practices of animal sacrifice and treat them as taboo or barbaric. However, I must ask the meat-eating reader if they have ever thrown out meat that has rotted in their refrigerator and gone to waste or tossed out a half-eaten burger. In contrast to this, I believe it's worth considering what is more disrespectful and barbaric to an animal: raising it in a more open environment, treating it as sacred, and giving its lifeforce to the spirit world, or having animals raised in factory farms where they may never see the sun, processing them in industrial facilities, and selling them as fast food or letting them rot in a grocery store or fridge. How often do we treat the animals we eat as sacred?

Animal sacrifice has had a long tradition throughout most world religions, and this is almost universally approached as a sacred process. It is worth noting here that the literal root of the word *sacrifice* means to "make sacred".[125] In many traditions that engage in animal sacrifice, a part of the belief system is that by giving its life in this way, the animal's spirit will be uplifted and elevated in the cycle of reincarnation. Within those traditions that currently engage in animal sacrifice, there are usually training protocols and even ritual initiations that an individual must undergo to be granted license to perform this work.

This all said, though there are some exceptions to this, I do not believe that the average contemporary witchcraft practitioner is well-equipped enough to ethically, effectively, and humanely engage in this type of offering, as most will lack the proper resources, training, and cultural context for it. So it is not something I can advocate for in good conscience amongst modern witchcraft practitioners in general. However, to pretend it doesn't exist quite prominently within some corners of this arte would be incredibly disingenuous. With this all considered, you should be very clear with any spirits you work with what your limitations are in this regard. There are plenty of spirits that will not request or require this kind of offering and still provide quite effective results.

By extension, we should also discuss the possibility of giving small amounts of your own blood or other bodily fluids to spirits in offering. There are many historical examples of witches reportedly giving blood as an offering to their familiar spirits. Though I do have some personal experience here, this is not something I generally recommend to the

125 *Sacrifice | Etymonline,* https://www.etymonline.com/word/sacrifice

beginner or even intermediate practitioner. Even amongst more advanced witches, it is not something that should be done except with a spirit that you fully trust and are on equal or greater footing with as far as control and power dynamics are concerned. This type of act becomes a solemn communion between witch and spirit that deeply bonds you both and should generally be reserved as the rare exception rather than the rule.

If a spirit ever requests something of you that may cause you harm, or you are uncomfortable with, you need to take a serious step back and critically assess the relationship. Your safety and personal boundaries should be treated as sovereign. Ideally, you will have experienced elders, teachers, or friends to turn to who will also help guide you with their insights into what your best course of action should be. This also extends to cases where a spirit may request sexual or other bodily fluids as a form of offering. Tread carefully here, should these situations arise, and always err on the side of safety and caution. There are witches I have known who engage in this work with spirits they are intimate with, and it has indeed enriched their lives. I have also known witches who have been led down a road of obsession and sickness by their own lack of judgment and critical assessment when working with spirits. All of the above should be seen neither as an endorsement nor a condemnation of these kinds of offerings. I only wish to highlight that these types of exchanges deserve serious scrutiny and that, though they do exist and in some cases are very meaningful and reciprocal exchanges, they can also have truly unfortunate consequences for the witch who rushes into them without full consideration and developed discernment.

Our offerings may be given as a part of our regular work with spirits, when making a specific request, or as a form of payment given upon the completion of a request. Offerings of food, drink, and flowers are usually left overnight at minimum, or at maximum until they begin to spoil. An interesting phenomenon noted by many who engage with spirits is that our offerings will sometimes stay fresh for an extended period of time. I have personally seen this happen when giving fruits and flowers to my spirits, where they will sometimes last much longer than fruits or flowers from the same bunch that weren't given to spirits. Conversely, there may be times when an offering spoils very quickly. In either of these cases, it may be beneficial to do a bit of divination to determine the reason, if any, behind such anomalies.

When disposing of offerings, there are several options. In almost all cases, once a food offering has been given to a spirit, it should not be consumed by a human. After food, drink, and flower offerings have been given for a time, it is perfectly acceptable to discard them in one of two ways. Items can be left in nature or placed in the trash. I have seen some witches act as though placing items in the trash is somehow offensive or not "sacred". This is absolute hogwash and reflects our disconnected suburban fantasies around purity and cleanliness more than it does anything about the true nature of spirits. As I said earlier in this work, the spirits of rot and decay are important, and they are a part of the retinue of spirits who receive discarded offerings. Your discarded offerings will rot and be eaten, whether they are placed in your backyard or within the trash. Either is acceptable in most cases, so follow your own intuition and do what feels right and is most practical.

If over time a large amount of monetary offerings have accumulated in a spirit's shrine, it is appropriate to eventually spend it on something nice for the spirit such as decorations for its shrine or a new tool. Alternatively, monetary offerings may be given to a charity on behalf of the spirit or otherwise be given to the less fortunate.

Overall, one of the most important offerings we can give to our spirits is our time, attention, and devotion. As with any relationship, the more we put into developing our connection with a spirit, the more likely it is that the relationship will grow and become stronger. Speaking to our spirits, offering breath, song, prayer, and devotion, and expressing our gratitude are all important components in strengthening our relationship. Additionally, the more a spirit vessel is worked with, the more it will be strengthened as a *locus* for that spirit's power.

A spirit vessel shouldn't be crafted only to sit upon a shelf and collect dust, whilst hoping that the spirit will grant us blessings and aid. We must regularly feed, fortify, and work with our spirits and their material forms to reap the greatest rewards from our relationship with them. Though our spirits should provide for us in kind and we shouldn't feed our spirits simply to make them fat, we should take care not to starve them either. If we neglect a spirit's vessel or shrine, it is not uncommon for that spirit's presence to weaken and wane. Sometimes this leads to a spirit essentially becoming dormant until it is fed and given attention again. In other cases, the spirit may totally abandon the vessel and its relationship and loyalty to you if it has been neglected.

The spirit may act up to get your attention by appearing in dreams or other ways. It may also do things to annoy or distract you, such as causing your divination to be confused, causing accidents or items to break, or by acting out in other ways. This type of behavior can range in intensity from simply a nuisance to very upsetting. So it is important when this type of thing occurs that you do your best to address it, attend to the spirit, and salvage the relationship if possible. Just like the human people and pets in your life, spirits don't tend to do well when starved and neglected.

On Breaking the Bond

At times, our relationship and work with a spirit may reach a necessary conclusion. In many cases, particularly those involving *maumet* spirits, it may simply be that the work we have contracted the spirit to do has ended. In other cases, it may be that our relationship with the spirit is no longer compatible with our spiritual trajectory, or even that the spirit stops working for us and makes it known one way or another that they wish to end the partnership. In rarer cases, it may be that our relationship with a spirit has become unstable, undesired, or volatile.

As I have previously mentioned in this work it is highly recommended when we are birthing a spirit vessel or entering a spirit pact that we include verbiage that provides ritual or practical actions that allow for the ending of our relationship to the spirit. This agreement might be something as simple as the intentional cutting of a cord tied around the spirit vessel or the dismantling and destruction of the vessel itself. In other cases, it may be as elaborate as including an agreement such as:

> *"If ever it be decided that our relationship should end and you should vacate this vessel, I will carry this fetich three times backwards and counterclockwise around an oak tree to signal the end of our work. At which time we will go our separate ways in peace."*

Whenever the time comes to end a relationship with a spirit, you should verbally express your intention to end the relationship to cut ties and explain why. It is always proper to give the spirit thanks for any work it has successfully performed and assistance it has given. It is also common and usually appropriate to give the spirit a final offering of some kind as a sign of your gratitude. To assist in approaches towards ending our relationships with spirits and their effigies, fetiches, or vessels, I am including some suggested workings here as a template you might employ or adapt in your work should you ever need them.

PRAXIS: A Rite of Releasing

The following rite is designed for cases when you are ending your work with a spirit on good terms. Firstly, you should consider why you are ending your work together and determine if this decision is the best option. For instance, if you have created a maumet for acquiring employment, you may wish to ask the spirit if it is willing and able to assist you in maintaining and advancing in your employment should you continue working together. If so, you may wish to continue the relationship so long as you both agree to the new arrangement.

In other cases, it may be that the spirit is not providing consistent or quality results. In this instance, you may wish to determine if the spirit needs something to better do its work. Perhaps it simply requires clearer direction, more consistent or alternate offerings, or even that it needs to be given a tool of some kind to better do its work. It is up to you to determine if the requested needs are acceptable and if you choose to continue the relationship.

If you are ending the relationship simply because you are currently not in need of the type of assistance the spirit specializes in you may wish to speak with the spirit and determine if it's best to simply keep the spirit vessel safely stored away somewhere in case you wish to engage the spirits assistance and services again in the future. Here you are essentially putting the spirit vessel and your relationship with the spirit into a form of stasis. The point here is that it may not always be necessary to formally end your relationship and decommission/dismantle the spirit vessel.

If you determine the relationship should be ended, let the spirit know this and again, let them know why. Give the spirit a final offering and thank it for its service. Let it know that the following day you will be concluding your work together. To break the bond with a spirit, you will do the following:

1. Establish ritual space as is appropriate to your personal craft and tradition.

2. Call upon any assistant and protector spirits to aid you in this working.
3. Place the spirit vessel into the Triangle of Arte and light the candles as usual.
4. If the spirit vessel you have created includes any of your personal taglocks or has ever been fed with your own spittle, blood, or other bodily fluids, you should speak the following or some variation of it as is appropriate to your work:

   "By the aid of my ancestors and those spirits which watch over and protect me, I call back any and all essence of spirit belonging to me which is tied to this vessel. Let that which may still sustain and serve me be returned to me, and that which is no longer of use be forever severed from me and returned to the earth."

5. You should now take three deep breaths in whilst envisioning any remaining attachments within the vessel that belong to you and may still serve you being drawn from the vessel and into your body.
6. Call and conjure the spirit into the triangle and then speak the following or some variation of it as is appropriate to your work:

   "I offer you my gratitude, NN, for the assistance you have given and the work you have done. I ask you now to withdraw your attachment to this effigy/vessel/fetich and let it return to the materials from which it was made. This vessel will be dismantled, and by your withdrawal from it and its destruction, our work with and responsibilities to each other will be ended. May you go forth with blessings and in good cheer. May there ever be peace between us. Hail and farewell to you, NN!"

7. Let the candles fully burn down from the Triangle of Arte.
8. You should then take the spirit vessel and dismantle it as much as possible, ideally while in ritual space.
9. As you dismantle the spirit vessel, you should keep its pieces together in a box, bowl, or bag for later disposal. No part of this vessel should be reserved or reused.
10. Afterwards, any natural elements from the vessel should be returned to the earth in some way. They may be disposed of at a

crossroads, buried in the earth, or taken and disposed of at some other place, such as a cemetery or forest, as is most appropriately determined by your own divination or intuition.

11. Any parts of the spirit vessel that are not biodegradable are best discarded in a trash receptacle away from your home.
12. Close your ritual space as you normally would.
13. If you feel it is necessary, you may wish to conclude by suffumigating your ritual space, your home, and the place where the spirit was enshrined with the *Clearance* or *Cleansing Incense.*
14. You may also wish to do a cleansing on yourself by utilizing the *Cleansing Bath* provided in the formulary or by another preferred method.

PRAXIS: A Rite of Spirit Vessel Exorcism and Banishing

This is a working designed for the more forceful eviction of a spirit from a vessel and termination of all ties to the spirit and its influences. It should be reserved for the rare case where a spirit relationship has become unstable or unhealthy.

To perform this work, you will do the following:

1. Prepare yourself with any protective amulets, such as the *Protective Hexentache* discussed in the Selection of Workings part of this book, and anoint yourself with the *Oil of Protection* from the Formulary.
2. Establish a protective ritual space as is appropriate to your personal craft and tradition.
3. Call upon the aid of any deities and spirits which stand as your protectors.
4. You will then place the spirit vessel into the Triangle of Arte and light the candles as usual.
5. If the spirit vessel you have created includes any of your own personal taglocks or has ever been fed with your own spittle, blood, or other bodily fluids, you should now speak the following or some variation of it as is appropriate to your work:

"By the aid of my ancestors and those spirits which watch over

and protect me, I call back any and all essence of spirit belonging to me which is tied to this vessel. Let that which may still sustain and serve me be returned to me, and that which is no longer of use be forever severed from me and returned to the earth."

6. You should now take three deep breaths in whilst envisioning any remaining attachments within the vessel that belong to you and may still serve you, being drawn from the vessel and into your body.
7. Call, conjure, and if necessary, command the spirit into the triangle. Pointing your ritual blade at the vessel in the triangle, you should then speak the following or some variation of it as is appropriate to your work:

"By the intercession, aid, and authority of those spirits who stand as my protectors [name them here], I formally terminate my relationship with you NN. I command you now to withdraw your attachment to this effigy/vessel/fetich and let it return to the materials from which it was made. This vessel will be dismantled, and by its destruction, our work with and responsibilities to each other will end. By the burning of these candles and the destruction of this vessel, any and all ties between us are severed. Our work is concluded, our agreements are null and void. You will retire to some place far away from this place and no longer engage with any part of my life. Begone and forever exorcised from this vessel and this place. By the power and authority of [name your protective spirits again], so shall it be done."

8. Conclude by tracing three equal-armed crosses in the air over the vessel with your ritual knife.[126]
9. Let the candles fully burn down from the Triangle of Arte.
10. You should then take the spirit vessel from the triangle and dismantle it as much as possible while within ritual space. It may be appropriate here to state something to the effect of:

"It is not my hands that destroy this vessel, but the hands of [insert name of protector spirit]."

126 Those who are inclined may make a banishing pentagram over the vessel or trace sigils of exorcism and protection over it instead.

11. As you dismantle the spirit vessel, you should keep its pieces together in a box, bowl, or bag for later disposal. No part of this vessel should be reserved or reused.
12. You should give thanks to your protector spirits and perform any additional banishing rituals on your ritual space and home.
13. You may wish to suffumigate the remaining pieces of the vessel, your ritual space, your home, and the place the spirit was enshrined with the *Exorcism Incense.*
14. The bag/bowl/box you have put the pieces into should then be covered with the Death Shroud and left for a day.
15. Afterwards, any natural elements from the vessel should be disposed of at a crossroads or a cemetery.
16. Any parts of the spirit vessel that are not biodegradable are best discarded in a trash receptacle far away from your home.
17. Close your ritual space as you normally would.
18. After disposing of the pieces it is best to conclude by further suffumigating your ritual space, your home, and the place where the spirit was enshrined with the *Clearance* or *Cleansing Incense.*
19. You may also wish to do a cleansing on yourself by utilizing the *Cleansing Bath* provided in the formulary or by another preferred method.

PRAXIS: A General Rite of Exorcism and Banishing

The following is a rite designed for the exorcism and cleansing of a space from unwanted spirit influences. It may be adapted to suit a ritual space or your entire home as needed.

Items Needed:

- Bowl of consecrated water
- *Clearance* or *Exorcism* incense from the Formulary or an appropriate substitute
- The Blade of Arte

The Ritual:

1. If desired you should ritually prepare yourself and the space as feels most appropriate such as by laying a compass, casting a circle, and wearing a protective oil such as the *Oil of Protection* or any protective fetiches or amulets.
2. Do the basic alignment from chapter three then state:

   "I call now to those spirits who serve as both protectors and allies. I call to my ancestors and to the spirits who walk with and watch over me, both known and unknown, named and unnamed."

   (Now call upon the aid and authority of any specific protective and guiding spirits to assist you in this work.)
3. If exorcising your home stand at the threshold of your front door. If cleansing a ritual space stand at the threshold of the room's door, or in the center of the room as is appropriate. Take three slow breaths and say forcefully aloud in your *vox magica:*

   "What has no rightful claim here, hear me.
   Procul, O Procul Este, Profani!"

4. Sprinkle consecrated water upon the threshold or floor. Light the incense and carry it with you.
5. Take up your Blade of Arte and beginning at the northernmost point of the space walk widdershins (counter-clockwise) around the full boundary. As you walk, speak with clarity and force:

   "I walk these bounds as kin of the land,
   as a child of the crooked path.
   You who linger with ill intent,
   you who feed where you have not been fed,
   you who fester, curse, or cling
   I see you.
   I name you as unwelcome.
   I name you the banished!"

6. Stop at each quarter if in ritual space, or at each corner, window, and door if doing a whole room or house. Enforce your will and sovereignty into the space by using the Blade of Arte to make an X in the air (tracing top right to bottom left and top left to bottom right) and say:

    "Let no foulness find a foothold here.
    Let no tongue whisper poison here.
    Let no eye that means harm find welcome.
    Here I lay the mark and cast you out.
    Never to pass this way again
    This is warded. This is mine."

7. Sprinkle some consecrated water. Suffumigate with the incense and carry on until the whole space is done.
8. Return to the center or heart of the space or to the threshold. Raise your Blade of Arte pointed to the sky, and declare:

    "By water and salt, by smoke and by fire,
    by the authority of those spirits who stand with me and by my right as Witch,
    I cast out all spirits of malice and malcontent, of misery, and misfortune.
    I cast out all that creeps unseen, unknown, unwelcomed, and unwanted.
    Flee to your holes!
    Fly into the dark that waits beyond the hedge.
    Withdraw into silence.
    Depart this place.
    Be gone!"

9. Breathe out sharply three times then say:

    "To those who dwell here in peace,
    Who are faithful, who guard, and who watch
    I give you my gratitude.
    This space is now clean.

This house is kept.
Let only those who are invited come in truth and goodwill pass through.
By the setting and rising of the sun, it is done.
As it is spoken, it is so."

10. Take down any ritual space you have erected and perform the basic alignment as needed.

Part Four:
A Book of Secrets

Formulary

Presented here is a collection of recipes for incense, oils, and other formulas that might serve as an aid in the workings throughout this book. You will likely note that many of the botanicals mentioned here recur throughout these formulas. Oftentimes, in manners intended both for the calling in and casting out of spirits. This serves to illustrate the dual nature of many botanicals that aid in both calling in helpful spirits aligned to our work whilst exorcising those which are unwelcome.

These formulas reflect botanical allies that have proven effective in my own work in this realm. That said, in keeping with the approaches mentioned in this book, it is highly recommended that the witch ally with and conjure the spirits of the botanical *materia* they are working with to awaken their virtues and bring them into alignment with each formula. The witch should employ their own inclinations and ingenuity as well as use the *vox magica* to speak words of blessing and hallow each formula once completed.

Clearance Incense

For clearing and cleansing a space, an object, or yourself of unwanted spirit influences prior to, or after ritual workings. The incense is to be burned upon charcoal.

- 1 pt Pine resin *(Pinus sp.)*
- 1 pt Copal *(Bursera sp.)*

- 1 pt Cedarwood chips *(Juniperus virginiana)*[127]
- ½ pt Juniper tips *(Juniperus sp.)*

This incense should be coarsely ground and stored in a glass vessel.

Prior to burning the incense for the first time, the following sigil should be drawn on white paper in dragon's blood ink or another red ink.

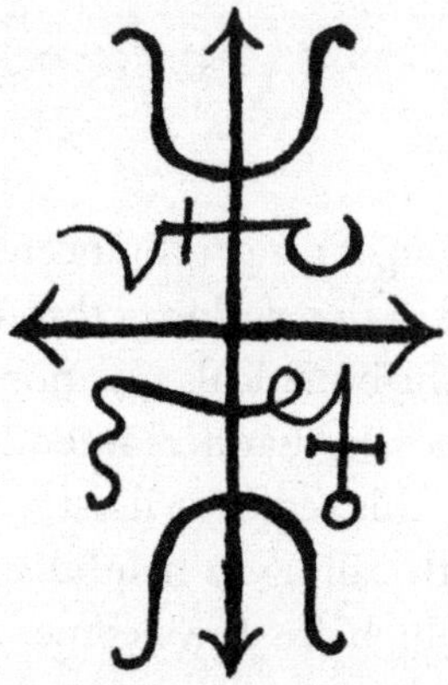

The sigil should be burned to ash and the resultant ashes blended into the incense to further empower the blend.

Cleansing Incense

Another for cleansing a space, an object, or yourself of unwanted spirit influences prior to, or after ritual workings. The incense is to be burned upon charcoal.

- 1 pt Frankincense *(Boswellia sp.)*
- 1 pt Myrrh *(Commiphora myrrha)*
- 1 pt Cedarwood chips *(Juniperus virginiana)*
- ½ pt Fumitory *(Fumaria officinalis)*
- ½ pt Rosemary *(Salvia rosmarinus)*

127 Many of the trees considered cedars will do well in these blends. Though it is technically a Juniper, I prefer the Eastern Red Cedar as it is native to my locale and has a long history of use in sacred suffumigations for calling and casting out spirits.

This incense should be coarsely ground and stored in a glass vessel.

Prior to burning the incense for the first time the following sigil should be drawn on white paper in dragon's blood ink or another red ink.

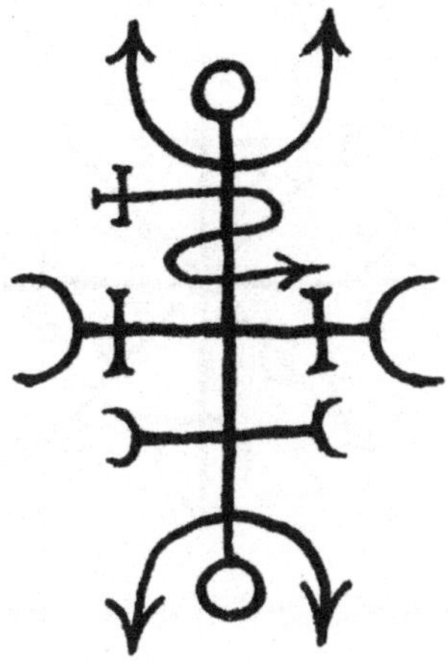

The sigil should be burned to ash and the resultant ashes blended into the incense to further empower the blend.

Exorcism Incense

For the forceful casting out of unwanted spirit influences from a place. The incense is to be burned upon charcoal.

- 1 pt Red Cedarwood chips *(Juniperus virginiana)*
- 1 pt Dragon's Blood *(Calamus draco)*
- ½ pt Myrrh *(Commiphora myrrha)*
- ½ pt Rue *(Ruta graveolens)*
- ½ pt Mugwort *(Artemisia vulgaris)*
- ¼ pt Dried Onion skins *(Allium cepa)*
- ¼ pt Garlic powder *(Allium sativum)*
- ⅛-¼ pt Asafoetida resin *(Ferula sp.)*

This incense should be coarsely ground and stored in a glass vessel. Due to the inclusion of Onion skins, Garlic, and Asafoetida, this formula is quite powerful, and its scent can be intense. You should avoid inhaling it directly, and windows should be opened in the rooms you are suffumigating with it.

Prior to burning the incense for the first time, the following sigil should be drawn on white paper in Dragon's Blood ink or another red ink.

The sigil should be burned to ash and the resultant ashes blended into the incense to further empower the blend.

A Spray Against Hungry Ghosts

This is a spray for casting off malignant and parasitic spirits and hungry ghosts. It may be used to spritz the ritual space and/or yourself after doing necromantic works and working in burial grounds or after engaging with unsavory spirits. It may also be used to spray around doorways and windows to protect and clear the home when necessary.

Soak equal parts Juniper (*Juniperus spp.*) needles and Pine Needles (*Pinus spp.*) in gin to make a tincture.[128] Let this sit for a full lunar month from one full moon to the next. It may then be strained and transferred to a glass spray bottle for ease of use.

Alternatively, if for some reason you don't have easy access to fresh Juniper and Pine needles, you may add 7 ml each of the essential oils to a 4 oz glass spray bottle and fill the rest with gin.

---

128 Ideally, choose a juniper-heavy gin for this.

Evocation Incense

For the conjuration of spirits, particularly where the desire is to provide a smoke medium by which they might appear. This is a blend best burned in a censer within the Triangle of Arte to aid in the manifestation of spirits. The incense is to be burned upon charcoal.

- 2 pt Mastic *(Pistacia lentiscus)*
- 1 pt Dittany of Crete *(Origanum dictamnus)*
- ½ pt Aloes/Agarwood powder

This incense should be ground to a powder and stored in a glass vessel.

Prior to burning the incense for the first time, the following sigil should be drawn on white paper in dragon's blood ink or another red ink.

The sigil should be burned to ash and the resultant ashes blended into the incense to further empower the blend. This same sigil may be used in the same way for the following two recipes.

This is a relatively costly blend to create, as all of the botanicals included are fairly rare. Additionally, it can be difficult to procure sustainably harvested aloeswood, so please research your sources. The two recipes for *Suffumigations of Spirit Calling* that follow are somewhat more accessible options.[129]

A Suffumigation of Spirit Calling

For the conjuration of spirits, particularly where the desire is to provide a smoke medium by which they might appear. This is a blend best burned on a charcoal in a censer within the Triangle of Arte to aid in the manifestation of spirits.

- 1 pt Dragon's Blood *(Calamus rotang, et al.)*
- ½ pt Frankincense *(Boswellia spp.)*
- ½ pt Cassia *(Cinnamomum cassia)*
- ½ pt Calamus root *(Acorus calamus)*

This incense should be ground to a powder and stored in a glass vessel.

Again, there are some sustainability concerns around both Frankincense and Dragon's Blood resins, and the reader is encouraged to do their research on sourcing.

Another Suffumigation of Spirit Calling

For the conjuration of spirits, particularly where the desire is to provide a smoke medium by which they might appear. This is a blend best burned on a charcoal in a censer within the Triangle of Arte to aid in the manifestation of spirits.

- 1 pt Red Cedarwood chips *(Juniperus virginiana)*
- 1 pt Juniper berry *(Juniperus communis, et al.)*
- 1 pt Copal Blanco *(Bursera jorullense, et al.)*
- 1 pt Tobacco *(Nicotiana spp.)*

This incense should be ground to a powder and stored in a glass vessel.

---

129 Always bear in mind that, though certain botanicals may aid spirit work in general, it's always worth considering if a spirit is allied to a particular materia when crafting your formulas. For instance, Myrrh has traditionally been associated with Mars, Saturn, and the Moon. So it may be more appropriate to use when crafting formulas for calling spirits of a martial, saturnian, or lunar nature.

The materials for this blend are generally more accessible and sustainable than the previous two. For the tobacco, it is best to use naturally cured tobacco with no additives. If you prefer not to include the tobacco, it can be omitted from the recipe.

Suffumigant for Awakening Bones

An incense for the feeding and empowering of osseous remains in spirit work. This is a most appropriate choice for preparing skulls to serve as spirit vessels. It is to be burned upon charcoal.

Combine equal parts:

- Dragon's blood *(Calamus rotang, et al.)*
- Myrrh *(Commiphora myrrha)*
- Rabbit Tobacco leaves *(Gnaphalium obtusifolium)*
- Bay Laurel *(Laurus nobilis)*

This incense should be ground to a powder and stored in a glass vessel.

Suffumigant for Spirit Vessels

An incense for preparing and empowering any bottles, jars, urns, shells, horns, cauldrons, or any other containers intended to house spirits. It is to be burned upon charcoal. The vessel should be held upside down over the burning incense allowing it to fill with the smoke and coat the interior of the vessel.

Combine equal parts:

- Benzoin Siam resin *(Styrax tonkinensis)*
- Fennel seed *(Foeniculum vulgare)*
- Tobacco *(Nicotiana spp.)*
- Dragon's Blood resin *(Calamus rotang, et al.)*
- Rabbit Tobacco leaf *(Gnaphalium obtusifolium)*
- Juniper berry *(Juniperus communis, et al.)*
- Vervain *(Verbena officinalis)*
- Rosemary *(Salvia rosmarinus)*

This incense should be ground to a coarse powder and stored in a glass vessel.

Suffumigation of Ensouling

For use during the process of enspiriting effigies and fetiches. It is often employed both prior to the gestation process and/or after the birthing/naming/transposition rites as a way of concluding the work and further fortifying the spirit within.

Combine equal parts:

- Cedarwood chips *(Juniperus virginiana)*
- Frankincense resin *(Boswellia spp.)*
- Dragon's Blood resin *(Calamus rotang, et al.)*
- Vervain *(Verbena officinalis)*
- Life Everlasting *(Helichrysum spp.)*

This incense should be ground to a powder and stored in a glass vessel.

Prior to burning the incense for the first time the following sigil should be drawn on white paper in dragon's blood ink or another red ink.

The sigil should be burned to ash and the resultant ashes blended into the incense to further empower the blend.

An Oil of Protection

An oil for protection from potentially antagonistic or harmful spirits and against malefic magic.

To a 12 oz glass jar, add:

- 1 pt Dried Angelica root *(Angelica archangelica)*
- 1 pt Dried Nettle *(Urtica dioica)*
- 1 pt Dried Rue *(Ruta graveolens)*
- 1 pt Dried Celandine *(Chelidonium majus)*
- 1 pt Dried St. John's wort *(Hypericum perforatum)*

Cover this with a carrier oil such as olive oil, sweet almond, or jojoba oil, and then seal it tight. Let this sit for a full lunar month from one full moon to the next, being sure to shake up the contents each day whilst speaking prayers of blessing over the oil. After the lunar cycle has ended, the oil may be strained and transferred to a glass bottle. The following seal should be drawn upon white paper in black ink and added to the bottle.

This oil may be used to anoint the brow, wrists, back of the neck, navel, and soles of the feet to offer protection. It may also be used for dressing candles, amulets, tools, and spirit vessels designed for spiritual protection, and may be used for tracing equal-armed crosses over doorways and windows to protect home and temple alike.

Transvection Oil

To aid in spirit flight.

To a 12 oz glass jar, add:

- 1 pt Dried Mugwort *(Artemisia vulgaris)*
- 1 pt Dried Calamus root *(Acorus calamus)*
- 1 pt Dried Chamomile *(Matricaria chamomilla, et al.)*
- 1 pt Dried Cinquefoil *(Potentilla spp.)*
- 1 pt Dried Rose petals *(Rosa spp.)*
- 15 drops Clary Sage *(Salvia sclarea)* essential oil
- Small pinch of Henbane seed *(Hyoscyamus niger)*
- Small pinch of Datura leaf *(Datura spp.)*[130]

Cover this with a carrier oil such as olive oil, sweet almond, or jojoba oil, and then seal it tight. Let this sit for a full lunar month from one full moon to the next, being sure to shake up the contents each day whilst speaking prayers of blessing over the oil. After the lunar cycle has ended, the oil may be strained and transferred to a glass bottle. The following seal should be drawn upon white paper in black ink and added to the bottle.

This oil may be used to anoint the wrists, temples, brow, inner elbows, backs of knees, and the soles of the feet prior to attempting spirit flight.

130 Both Henbane and Datura are poisonous plants so please exercise caution in their use or omit them should you wish to.

You may also wish to use it to dress candles that might be burned whilst engaging in transvection.

An Oil of the Sight

For aiding in spirit sight, communication, and divination. It may be used to anoint the brow/third eye, behind the ears, and wrists for this. It may also be used for the dressing of candles, talismans, and divination tools.

To ½ oz of a carrier oil, such as sweet almond or jojoba, add:

- 13 drops Clary Sage *(Salvia sclarea)* essential oil
- 11 drops Frankincense *(Boswellia sp.)* essential oil
- 6 drops Bay Laurel *(Laurus nobilis)* essential oil
- 6 drops Anise (*Pimpinella anisum)* essential oil

Add a pinch each of the following dried herbs to the bottle:

- Mugwort *(Artemisia vulgaris)*
- Eyebright *(Euphrasia officinalis)*
- Yarrow *(Achillea millefolium)*

The following sigil should be drawn upon white paper in black ink and added to the bottle.

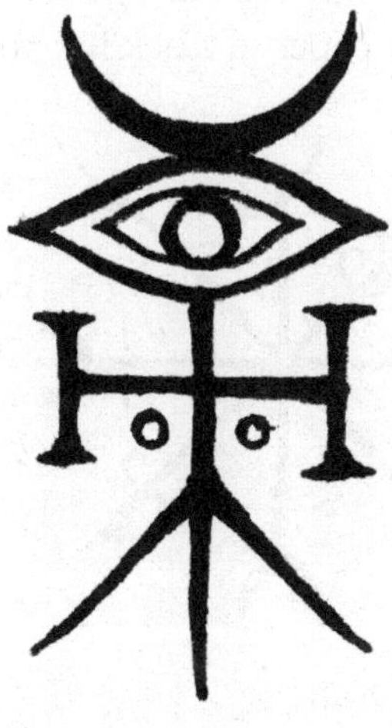

Spirit Summoning Oil

An oil which may be used to dress candles for the Triangle of Arte or for altars and shrines. It may be used to dress amulets, talismans. effigies, fetiches, and ritual tools where the desire is to entice a spirit to dwell therein. And it may be applied to scrying tools for drawing spirits near as well.

Into a glass jar place the following:

- 1 tbsp Dried Rose petals *(Rosa spp.)*
- 1 tbsp Dried Rosemary *(Salvia rosmarinus)*
- 1 tbsp Dittany of Crete *(Origanum dictamnus)*
- 1 tbsp Dried Life everlasting *(Helichrysum spp.)*
- 1 tbsp Ground Copal resin *(Bursera spp.)*
- 1 tbsp Ground Myrrh resin *(Commiphora myrrha)*
- 1 tbsp Ground Opopanax/Erythraea Myrrh resin *(Commiphora erythraea)*
- 1 tbsp Ground Frankincense resin *(Boswellia spp.)*

Cover this with a carrier oil such as olive oil, sweet almond, or jojoba oil, and then seal it tight. Let this sit for a full lunar month from one full moon to the next, being sure to shake up the contents each day whilst speaking prayers of blessing over the oil. After the lunar cycle has ended, the oil may be strained and transferred to a glass bottle. The following sigil should be drawn upon white paper in black ink and added to the bottle.

To further empower and fortify this, you may wish to add:

- 13 drops Myrrh *(Commiphora myrrha)* essential oil
- 13 drops Opoponax *(Commiphora erythraea)* essential oil
- 13 drops Frankincense *(Boswellia spp.)* essential oil
- 13 drops Rosemary *(Salvia rosmarinus)* essential oil

Aqua Vitae - A Wash for the Birthing of Spirits

This is a formula that may be employed during the preparation of spirit vessels, which aids in housing a spirit within. It may be used to wash the heartstone intended for a fetich or effigy, as well as for washing the interior of jars, bottles, boxes, shells, and horns intended to serve as spirit vessels. It also may be used to wash, or added to a spray bottle and spritzed upon, a completed effigy or fetich after the death process and prior to the act of ensouling.

Into a 24 oz glass jar, add equal parts:

- Fennel *(Foeniculum vulgare)*. The chopped up fresh bulb and fronds are ideal, but dried fennel seed will do as well.
- Dried Life Everlasting *(Helichrysum spp.)*
- Dried or fresh Vervain *(Verbena officinalis)*
- Dried or fresh Calamus root *(Acorus calamus)*

Fill the jar completely with high-proof Vodka. Allow the jar to sit for a full lunar cycle from one full moon to the next.

Three days prior to the end of the lunar cycle, you will need to place a Resurrection Plant *(Selaginella lepidophylla)* in a bowl or deep dish of water and allow the plant to unfurl its leaves and become green and vibrant with life. At the end of the lunar cycle, the plant should be removed from the water and allowed to dry and close itself up again.

Once it has been worked for this purpose, this plant should only be worked with for creating more *Aqua Vitae* and not for any other magical purposes. Take 8 oz of the water that remains in the bowl, strain it if you like, and put it aside. Any remaining water can be poured in front of your front door to bring blessings of renewed vitality, health, and prosperity to the home.

Strain the vodka from the 24 oz jar and add it to a clean and new 32 oz glass jar. Add the water from the Resurrection Plant to this blend to complete it and store the *Aqua Vitae* in a cool place away from direct sunlight when not in use.

Vessel Cleansing Wash

For washing the interior of bottles, jars, urns, shells, horns, cauldrons, or any other containers intended to either house or birth spirits in order to give them clearance and prepare them for use.

To a 24 oz glass jar add:

- 1 pt Dried Rosemary *(Salvia rosmarinus)*
- 1 pt Dried Rose petals *(Rosa spp.)*
- 1 pt Dried Chamomile *(Matricaria chamomilla, et al.)*
- 1 pt Dried Juniper berry *(Juniperus communis, et al.)*
- 1 pt Dried Hyssop *(Hyssopus officinalis)*

Fill the jar with gin and allow it to sit for a full lunar cycle, beginning and ending on the dark moon. Then strain the herbs out, add the menstruum to a 32 oz glass jar, and top off with 8 oz of consecrated water.[131] Store in a cool, dark place when not in use.

A Cleansing Wash/Bath for Body and Home

A wash that may be used as a bath for spiritual cleansing and to remove unhealthy spirit attachments. It serves well as a wash after doing heavy work with unstable spirits or crossing/hexing work. It may also be added to mop water, or used to wash around doorways and windows for cleansing the home or temple.

To a large basin or bowl add:

- 1 gallon of consecrated water
- 1 handful of Fresh Sage *(Salvia officinalis)*
- 1 handful of Fresh Rosemary *(Salvia rosmarinus)*

131 See appendices.

- 1 handful of Fresh Mint *(Mentha × piperita, et al.)*
- 1 handful of Fresh Basil *(Ocimum basilicum)*
- 1 handful of Fresh white Rose petals *(Rosa spp.)*
- 1 handful of Fresh Hyssop *(Hyssopus officinalis)* or 15 drops essential oil
- 1 handful of Fresh Lavender flowers *(Lavandula spp.)* or 15 drops essential oil

Macerate and knead the fresh herbs in the water whilst using the *vox magica* to pray for spiritual cleansing and clearance until they are thoroughly worked and their juices and essential oils have integrated into the water. Once complete, strain out the herbal *materia.*

To use as a bath, you should first take a normal bath or shower as usual. Then the wash should be poured over the head and allowed to run down and completely cover the body. Alternatively, you may wish to use a washcloth soaked in the bath and wash your body in it from the head down. As the wash flows down the drain, pray for it to remove any spirit attachments or malefic energy as it goes.

A Wash of Casting Out

This serves as another wash designed for exorcising spirit presences for places and objects.

- Vodka
- 1 pt Dried Tansy *(Tanacetum vulgare)*
- 1 pt Dried Rue *(Ruta graveolens)*
- 1 pt Dried St. John's Wort *(Hypericum perforatum)*
- 1pt Dried Hyssop *(Hyssopus officinalis)*
- 1 pt Dried Angelica root *(Angelica archangelica)*

Add all of the herbs to a glass mason jar and cover with the vodka. Seal the vessel and allow it to steep for a lunar cycle, periodically agitating the jar. After this time, strain the tincture you have made and store it in a sealed glass vessel. A bit of this wash may be added to water in order to dilute it a bit. This water can then be used for washing items, sprinkling around the home or ritual area, or added to mop water and baths for casting out unwanted spirits.

A Wash for the Mouth When Calling Spirits

This wash is designed to cleanse the mouth, fortify the voice, and offer protection during spirit conjuration.

To a glass jar add:

- 4 oz of gin
- 1 tbsp of Dried Rosemary *(Salvia rosmarinus)*
- 1 tbsp Dried Vervain *(Verbena officinalis)*

Seal the jar and keep it in a dark place for a lunar cycle from one full moon to the next. At the end of the month, strain out the herbs and add 2 oz of food-grade Rosewater. Store the blend in a glass dropper or spray bottle.

Administer several drops or 1-2 sprays to coat the mouth prior to calling spirits.

To Add Fire to the Voice When Calling Spirits

Take seven grains of Cardamom *(Elettaria cardamomum)* for alluring, or Guinea Pepper *(Aframomum melegueta)* for commanding, or a mix of both and chew them allowing their heat to pass to the tongue, coat the mouth, and empower the voice for the calling of spirits.

The Breath of Eros

A smoking blend for amorous and lustful works.

Combine together:

- 1 pt Dried Raspberry leaf *(Rubus idaeus)*
- 1 pt Dried Rose petals *(Rosa spp.)*
- 1 pt Dried Damiana *(Turnera diffusa)*
- ½ pt Dried Catnip *(Nepeta cataria)*
- ½ pt Dried Passion Flower *(Passiflora incarnata)*

Store in a glass vessel. This may be added to the ritual pipe and used for blowing upon poppets and fetiches in love drawing and sensual workings or for seasoning the breath when engaging in charms and incantations of the same.

A Smoke of Spirit Transference

A smoking blend for use in granting the Breath of Life to effigies, fetiches, and the like.

Combine together:

- 2 pt Pipe Tobacco *(Nicotiana spp.)*
- 1 pt Vervain *(Verbena officinalis)*
- 1 pt White Willow bark *(Salix alba)*
- 1 pt Mugwort *(Artemisia vulgaris)*
- ½ pt Mullein *(Verbascum thapsus)*
- ½ pt Rabbit Tobacco leaves *(Gnaphalium obtusifolium)*

Store in a glass vessel. This should be smoked in the ritual pipe and used when passing the breath of life to spirit vessels to strengthen and empower the work.

Smoke of the Hallowed Tongue

A pre-ritual smoking blend which blesses and fortifies the breath and *vox magica* for incantations and the calling of spirits.

Combine together:

- 1½ pt Mullein *(Verbascum thapsus)*
- 1½ pt Mugwort *(Artemisia vulgaris)*
- 1 pt Lavender *(Lavandula spp.)*
- 1 pt Rose petals *(Rosa spp.)*
- 1 pt St. John's Wort *(Hypericum perforatum)*
- 1 pt Vervain *(Verbena officinalis)*

Store in a glass vessel.

A Sachet of Dreaming

For those who wish to engage in dream magic as a form of engaging with spirits. The following botanicals may aid in creating more vivid dream experiences.

- 3 pt Dried Mugwort *(Artemisia vulgaris)*
- 2 pt Dried Lavender *(Lavandula spp.)*
- 1 pt Dried Agrimony *(Agrimonia eupatoria)*

These should ideally be added to a muslin bag which has the following sigil drawn or painted upon it.

This is best prepared on the full of the moon, and all herbs should be conjured towards the purpose of spirit dreaming. The sachet should be placed within your pillowcase or beneath it when you wish to engage in oneiric spirit work.

Salt Dough

This dough may be used for making small effigies and is very well suited to crafting figures for protection. For this purpose, it is best to use consecrated salt and water in this mix.[132]

132 See appendices.

To a large bowl, add:

- 1 cup flour
- ½ cup consecrated salt
- ½ cup consecrated water
- Additional ground herbs, ashes, and dirts (optional)

Add the dry ingredients to the bowl first and slowly add the water while stirring it into the mix. This may then be kneaded to make it into the consistency of dough. You may then mix a bit of any herbs, dirts, and ashes which are appropriate to the purpose your effigy will serve.

Shape the effigy into the desired form and allow it to air dry until fully hardened. These may be painted with acrylic paints afterwards or left as is.

Cinnamon Dough

This dough may be used for making small effigies and is very well suited to crafting figures for prosperity and wealth magic or those designed for love and lust works.

- 1 ½ cup powdered Cinnamon
- 1 cup applesauce (unsweetened)
- 1 to 2 tablespoons of craft glue (optional)
- Additional ground herbs, ashes, and dirts (optional)

Add the applesauce and glue to the bowl first and slowly add the cinnamon powder while stirring it into the mix. This may then be kneaded to make it into the consistency of dough. You may then mix a bit of any herbs, dirts, and ashes which are appropriate to the purpose your effigy will serve. Shape the effigy into the desired form and allow it to air dry until fully hardened.

Herbal Doughs

Herbal doughs are made by combining powdered botanicals, ashes, and dirts, and then adding a binder of some sort. They can be tailored to the work at hand by altering the chosen *materia*. As the formula is changeable, this is not an exact science and may require some experimentation on your part.

When making doughs of this sort, I have usually used about 4 cups of the dried and powdered material and added it to a bowl. Next, I will dissolve 1 part Gum Arabic into 2 parts of very hot or boiling water. This gum arabic/water blend should be added bit by bit into the powdered *materia* and stirred in until it is at a dough-like consistency. You may need to moisten the powders first and allow the mix to sit for a while in order to bind into a workable consistency. Once it has become workable, form it into the desired shape and allow it to air dry.

A Selection of Workings

The following operations bring together many of the approaches explored throughout this work. They are presented so that the reader might perform them as written, or make judicious alterations as best suits their own craft. It is my hope in sharing them here that they may give a good illustration of the manner in which such workings as are implied throughout the course of this book may be crafted and formatted to suit your own work.

A Protective Hexentasche

This *hexentasche* or witch's bag may serve the witch well in offering protection against antagonistic, parasitic, or malevolent spirits whilst engaging in spirit work and when traveling the Otherworld. As all of the *materia* mentioned here offers multilayered protection, depending upon how you conjure the *materia* during its creation, the hexentasche may also be created to serve in providing protection against evil eye, malefica, and misfortune for yourself, in the home, or while traveling.

This approach towards the crafting of *hexentaschen* may be viewed as a general template for crafting such bags. By altering the *materia,* sigilization, and wording, this template may be reworked for crafting any number of *hexentaschen* to align with whatever purpose the witch desires.

Items Needed:

- 4x4 in square of white cloth or a premade cloth pouch
- Red string
- Angelica root *(Angelica sp.)*

- Agrimony *(Agrimonia eupatoria)*
- Rue *(Ruta graveolens)*
- Vervain *(Verbena officinalis)*
- Mugwort *(Artemisia vulgaris)*
- St. John's wort *(Hypericum perforatum)*
- Dill *(Anethum graveolens)*
- Consecrated salt[133]
- One small iron nail
- A small heartstone taken from the center of a crossroad

1. In the center of the cloth, draw or paint the following seal in red. This is a simple form of a sigil I have worked with many times for protection.

2. Once the ink/paint from the sigil is dry, flip the cloth over and add a pinch each of the herbs to the center to make a little mound. Place the iron nail in the center.
3. Hold the heartstone in your dominant hand, rap it three times on the table and say:

> *"By the spirits who stand behind me,*
> *who walk beside be,*
> *and who laid the path before me.*
> *I call you to attention as heartstone and aid.*
> *By the supernal,*

133 See appendices.

(Touch stone to your brow.)

By the infernal,

(Touch stone to your feet.)

And by the path betwixt."

(Touch the center of your chest.)

4. Put a bit of your spittle on your thumb and rub it into the stone while saying:

   "Sentry, soldier, sword and shield,
   Seen and unseen,
   In this world and the other."

5. Place the stone in the center of the cloth on top of the other *materia.*
6. Pull up the four corners of the cloth towards each other to make the cloth into a bundle while saying:

   "By the four corners of the earth.
   Drawn to crossroads center.
   From which I will go forth with ease.
   Protected from all harm, misfortune, and spirits of calamity."

7. Pull the excess cloth tight, making a little bag of the cloth. Then wrap the string three times around the "neck" of this to close the bag.
8. While doing this, say:

   "Thricely wound throughout and about."

9. Tie three knots in the string to seal the bag, as you do so, add a bit of spittle from your mouth onto the knot and say:

   "You are awakened."

(Tie knot.)

"You are empowered."

(Tie knot.)

"You are alive."

(Tie knot.)

10. Impart the *Breath of Life* to the bag.
11. Give the spirit of the bag a name and speak aloud any specific requests or directions you may have for the spirit of the bag. The hexentasche may then be held, worn, or placed on an altar when doing ritual. It may also be hung over a door or placed in a vehicle for protection.
12. On occasion, you may wish to feed and fortify the bag by passing it through the smoke of Dragon's Blood, Tobacco, or Myrrh incense.

Nest of the Genius Loci

The Latin term *Genius Loci* references the spirit of a place. More specifically, in this working we are creating a spirit vessel as a locus for honoring the spirit of the land we live upon. We might approach this *Genius Loci* and ask for its aid in offering protection and good fortune to the home and its inhabitants in exchange for attention and regular offerings. Through this, we are granted a greater gateway for engaging in a reciprocal relationship with the land we live upon.

Though the *Genius Loci* may take many forms, depending upon location, cultural transmission, and firsthand experience, one of the more common forms of such land and household spirits is that of a serpent. That in mind, for the purposes of this working we will be employing that same serpentine imagery while conjuring forth the *Genius Loci.* If your own experience of the spirit of the land you are upon varies, please feel free to alter this working as best suits the spirit in question.

Items Needed:

- A small opaque lidded vessel such as a small urn, pot, or jar
- A tool for digging
- A small mixing bowl
- Coins or tobacco
- Small twigs, leaves, grasses, and brush respectfully gathered from around your home
- A complete snakeshed (optional)

Begin by washing out the vessel you have chosen with consecrated water or the *Vessel Cleansing Wash* from the formulary. If you live near a body of water, you may wish to add some of the water from your land to this. You may then wish to further prepare the vessel by censing the inside with the *Suffumigant for Spirit Vessels* or with Tobacco or dragon's blood smoke.

13. You will then take a trowel or spoon for digging as well as the small mixing bowl outside of your home. Go to your front door and look for a small stone about the size of a walnut to serve as the heartstone for the vessel. Give thanks to the land and leave a small offering. If you can't easily find a stone near the entrance to your home, search in and around the land for a stone that feels suitable.
14. Next, take a scoop of dirt from near the door and add it to the bowl. You should then place a coin, a bit of tobacco, or other appropriate offering into the hole. You will then go to each of the four corners of your home or of your property, doing the same until you have five scoops of dirt from the land in total.[134] Bring the bowl inside and mix the earth together thoroughly. You may wish to clear out any rocks or botanical matter from the dirt.
15. If you are inclined, you may wish to further wash the vessel with *Aqua Vitae* at this point. You should then take enough of the commingled dirts to fill the vessel 1/3rd of the way. Next, you will

134 In the case that you live in an apartment or multi-unit home, you should treat the front door and corners of the building as the places where you will gather the stone and dirts from.

use the small twigs, leaves, grasses, and brush you have gathered from around the property to make a bit of a "nest" atop the dirt in the vessel.

16. You will now prepare the heartstone in the manner mentioned earlier in this work. You may also wish to wash it in *Spiritus Vitae* and dress it with the *Spirit Summoning Oil.* Wrap the heartstone with the snake shed and then place it within the nest you have created in the vessel.
17. Next, you should take the vessel and place it with its lid off within the Triangle of Arte, either near your front door or by the hearth of your home if you have one. Ideally, you should place this on the floor if possible. If the vessel will fit within the Cauldron of Rebirth it may be employed in this work as well. Create ritual space as is appropriate to your practice. Light the candles of the Triangle of Arte and burn a bit of the *Suffumigant of Spirit Calling* if you are inclined. Then, employing the *vox magica,* summon forth the *Genius Loci* by stating:

"I call to you Genius Loci.
Sacred serpent, spirit of this land,
You who lie coiled beneath root and stone,
Who moves through veins of ochre, iron, earth,
I conjure you with open hands and steadied breath.

Be welcomed to this home and hearth,
And find solace and respite in this hallowed vessel,
That there may be peace between us,
That you may be honored and fortified,
And in turn that we who dwell here may be protected and prosperous.

Watcher of the Thresholds,
Keeper of the Land,
Stir from your slumber,
Come forth and be welcomed here."

During this conjuration, you should pay attention to any images that come to mind or messages received. With the imaginal eye, it is not uncommon to witness the *genius loci* appear in the form of a serpent, enter into the vessel, and coil around the stone within. The candles should be allowed to burn down. Once they have, you may place the lid on the vessel if it is not within the cauldron. Ideally, the vessel should be left in place overnight, if possible, before it is enshrined in a more permanent place in the home. This vessel is most appropriately enshrined in a central location of the home. It would be well placed near a hearth, in the kitchen near the stove, or near the front door. With time and regular devotion and offerings, it will become a powerful locus for engaging with the spirit of your land.

Offerings should be given to the *Genius Loci* frequently, particularly at the turn of seasons, during holidays, and if there are any major changes made to the home or land. This could include people joining or leaving the home and new construction to the home or property. It is appropriate to tell the *Genius Loci* of the household goings-on and needs regarding stability, prosperity, protection, and good fortune. Common offerings tend to include candles, incense, milk or cream, beer, wine, water, butter, bread, and flowers and fruits from the land. These offerings may be placed before the vessel for a night and then given directly to the land.

Of course, it is up to the witch to develop their own unique relationship with their own unique land spirits, so that in mind, all of what has been shared here should be taken as general suggestions. When moving to a new home it is customary to inform the *Genius Loci,* communicate your gratitude for its blessings, and gift it a final offering. You should then bury the vessel somewhere on the property. Ideally, near the front door.

The Sentry Maumet

This is a rite for crafting a *maumet* to act as a protector for yourself and your home. The spirit created serves as a defense against intrusion, theft, maleficium, and a guardian against harmful spirits. The working as written here utilizes clay; however, this can be adapted to making a figure from wax or cloth, or employing a readily made statue and loading it with materia.

Items Needed:

- A durable air-drying clay
- Seven herbs of protection. These should ideally be a mix of both

Martial and Solar herbs, such as nettle, chili, angelica, Saint John's wort, rue, basil, and rosemary.

- A heartstone collected from a place you associate with protection, such as an old military fort, police station, or from near a security gate. Alternatively, you may choose a gemstone with martial virtues such as carnelian, red jasper, or garnet. The heartstone should be prepared as usual. You may also wish to dress it in *Oil of Protection.*
- Dirt from the four corners of your home/property.
- Dirt from any places you associate with protection. Those who are skilled at necromancy might consider including dirt from the grave of an honorable soldier, which has been respectfully gathered and paid for.
- A thorn from a protective tree such as hawthorn, honey locust, or blackthorn. Or a miniature sword or iron nail.
- Any other *materia* or decorative elements that you associate with protection. For instance, you may wish to include animal materia such as claws and teeth or the quills of porcupines for defense, and include bones or fur from a rabbit for alertness.

1. Powder the botanical *materia* as finely as possible and mix it together with any dirts you have collected. Ensuring you are conjuring the *materia* towards its purpose as you go. This should then be kneaded into the clay, which will become the body of your sentry.
2. You should craft the effigy in a way that it is standing at attention. You may wish to sculpt its face so that it appears fearsome and intimidating. You should ideally create the *maumet* so that one of the arms is extended or raised, as this will hold the thorn or sword you have chosen. The heartstone should be inserted into the heart area of the *maumet* whilst sculpting it. If you so desire, you may also write out instructions for the kind of protection the *maumet* will provide, which may be rolled or folded up very small, or burned to ash and placed within the head of the *maumet.*
3. You are encouraged to be led by your own ingenuity, creativity, and intuition in this process to include aesthetic elements that you feel add to the strength and power of the *maumet.* You may wish to make its eyes from *nazar* (evil eye) beads. Give the *maumet* a small shield in addition to the sword, or dress or paint it with

protective colors. This particular *maumet* will be allied primarily to Mars, so adorning it or painting it in red is appropriate. You may also wish to sculpt or paint sigils of protection and alertness upon the *maumet.* Once the *maumet* has been crafted, allowed to fully dry, and adorned as you like, you should secure the thorn/sword into its hand if it is not already.

4. You may now go through the process laid out earlier for giving the *maumet* a death, rebirth, and ensouling it. Being clear to give the *maumet* specific instructions on the types of protection you wish it to provide. One important element in the birth of this *maumet,* however, is that the rites of resurrection and rebirth, naming and affirming its role, and bodily alignment should ideally be timed so that they happen during the day (Tuesday) and hour of Mars.[135] Essentially, you are birthing this *maumet* to be under the patronage of Mars as a soldier and guardian.
5. Once the *maumet* has been completed, it should ideally be enshrined somewhere near and facing the front door of the home. Speak to the *maumet* and give it offerings at least monthly. It is appropriate to give it offerings of martial incenses such as myrrh or dragon's blood, and red candles. It may also be given items such as chili peppers and coffee as offerings, which are both martial in nature but also serve to fire up the *maumet* and keep it alert in times when you feel additional protections are required.

To Conjure a Prosperous Spirit

The following is a work to craft a *maumet* spirit vessel for both drawing and maintaining financial stability, as well as creating opportunities for building prosperity.

Items Needed:

- A suitably-sized vessel for the spirit to reside within. For this, I prefer a brass vessel or a gold colored pot, cauldron, or urn, but anything that you feel is suited to this working will do. In fact, this

135 See appendices.

sort of working could be beautifully adapted to using a small safe, cashbox, or piggy bank as the vessel.

- A good-sized lodestone, which will serve as the heartstone of the *maumet.*
- Lodestone food (iron filings)
- Something gold, this can be very small, such as a piece of gold-plated jewelry.
- Something silver, this can be a very small such as a piece of silver jewelry.
- Seven of each of the following coins:[136]
    - Pennies
    - Nickels
    - Dimes
    - Quarters
    - Fifty-cent pieces
    - Dollar coins
    - Coins from different countries
- Dirt gathered from seven different banks, ideally, one of these should be your own.
- Dirt from the four corners of your home and also the four corners of your place of work, if applicable.
- Seven pieces of pyrite (fool's gold)
- A mixture of seven money-drawing herbs, such as calendula, chamomile, cinquefoil, cinnamon, basil, patchouli, and alfalfa, which should be made into an infusion to be used as a wash.
- Any other *materia,* such as precious stones, which you personally associate with wealth and prosperity.

1. Prepare the vessel by utilizing consecrated water or any of the washes and suffumigations from the formulary you feel are best suited to the work, such as the *Vessel Cleansing Wash* and the *Suffumigant for Spirit Vessels.* The lodestone should be prepared as the heartstone as has been previously described, being sure to conjure

136 If you do not live in the United States or cannot source these various coins, please adapt the coins and denominations as necessary. Ultimately, the point here is to have 7x7 coins for a total of 49.

the lodestone to attract wealth, prosperity, and opportunity while doing so. Both the lodestone and the vessel you are using should be washed/spritzed with *Aqua Vitae.* In lieu of this, you may wash them in the infusion of money-drawing herbs.

2. The coins, the pyrite, the gold, and silver pieces should all be washed in the infusion of seven money-drawing herbs and set aside. The dirts should be commingled and made into a dirt clay by the methods mentioned previously in this work. Ideally, during this process, you should add a bit of the herbal infusion and *Aqua Vitae* to the dirts. The bottom of the vessel should be lined with a layer of the dirt clay. In the center of the vessel the gold and silver pieces should be buried in the dirt.
3. Next, the lodestone should be placed in the center atop the dirt, and the coins should then be added surrounding the lodestone. The seven pieces of pyrite should be placed surrounding the lodestone as well, and any of the other *materia* you have selected should be incorporated into the vessel as well now.
4. You may wish to engage in scrying or transvection to connect with the spirit taking form in the vessel and determine more about its nature, including the name you will give to the spirit.
5. You will now go through the process laid out earlier for giving the *maumet* a death, rebirth, and ensouling it. If the vessel is too large, you may wish to simply drape the Death Shroud over it during the death process. And similarly, as a vessel of this kind is unlikely to fit inside of your Cauldron of Rebirth, you may instead place it in the center of your Triangle of Arte and cover it with a red cloth and then a black cloth for the gestation period.
6. After the vessel has been given the breath of life and named, you should then sprinkle some of the lodestone food upon the heartstone to feed it. This is the primary manner by which you will feed and fortify the *maumet* spirit. The vessel should be given a good-sized pinch of lodestone food at least monthly, but ideally weekly, as you speak to the spirit and request continued prosperity, opportunity, and financial stability.
7. You may also offer additional coins and paper money to the vessel periodically when making requests of the *maumet* or giving thanks for good fortune by placing the money within the vessel. Green

candles and incense can also be burned near the vessel to occasionally feed and fortify it. In time, the vessel may accumulate large amounts of coins and money which you have given as offerings. If the vessel becomes too full of these, you should clear some of the monetary offerings out from the vessel, and the money should then be donated to a charity or given to someone less fortunate than yourself. The vessel should be kept somewhere safe where it may be seen and interacted with somewhat frequently.

A Vessel of the Greenwood

The following is an outline for crafting a spirit vessel for establishing a relationship with a patron spirit of the Greenwood. This spirit is intended to serve as a teacher and ally in building your knowledge and understanding of the kingdom of flora. It may serve as an aid to those witches who wish to deepen their work and wisdom in areas of magical and medicinal herbalism and all work with the plant kingdom. This patron spirit may assist the witch in empowering herbal formulas, charms, and medicines. As well as offering inspiration and revelation regarding the nature of the botanical spirits we wish to know better and serves as a locus for your personal patron of the forest, field, and garden.

Items Needed:

- A suitably sized vessel for the spirit to reside within. For this, let intuition and inspiration be your guide. I have found that an earthenware vessel with a lid, such as one made from terracotta, is best, as a somewhat porous clay lends itself well to the work of the vessel. Of course, a handcrafted vessel made from native wild clay would be ideal for this; however, do not allow the perfect to be the enemy of the good in this regard.
- A tool for digging
- A small mixing bowl
- Paper and a pen with green ink
- Green paint and a small brush

- A small green or natural beeswax candle[137]
- A stone respectfully gathered and paid for from the center of a woodland crossroad to serve as the heartstone.
- A small amount of dirt respectfully gathered and paid for from seven woodland crossroads. These should ideally be gathered from the center of crossroads found in wild and verdant places such as woodlands, meadows, and marshes. This could be hiking trails or those game trails made by the travel patterns of animals.
- A small amount of dirt respectfully gathered and paid for from seven different "forest" edges. This could be gathered from places that stand as liminal points between the greenwood and the realm of humans. Appropriate places might include the edge of a forest, meadow, marshlands, desert, or hedgerow depending upon your locale.
- A small amount of dirt respectfully gathered and paid for from a garden or orchard. This should be a cultivated place where plants are grown. If you have your own garden, a bit of dirt from there is an excellent choice.
- While you are gathering the above dirts you are encouraged to pay attention to the botanical life around you. If you encounter any plants with whom you have an established allyship, affection, or appreciation for you are encouraged to respectfully gather a bit of it, such as a leaf, flower, or seed, for inclusion in the vessel. These should then be dried before use.
- Additionally, if you have any botanical *materia* from other patron plants that you work with, you should have a small amount of dried *materia* from these available as well.

1. Once you have gathered all of the items, you should mix all of the dirts together into the bowl. All of the botanical *materia* should be powdered as finely as possible and added to the dirts as well. Next, prepare the vessel by washing it and suffumigating it with

137 For this sort of work, I recommend using the thin beeswax candles often found in Orthodox churches. These are excellent as they tend to burn for between twenty to thirty minutes and are well timed for the duration of this rite. I would avoid choosing candles with an excessively long burn time, as you will need to wait for the candle to completely burn before concluding the rite.

appropriate options from the formulary section, or at minimum, wash it with consecrated water and suffumigate it with an incense such as copal, frankincense, or tobacco smoke. Prepare the heart-stone in the usual manner as is appropriate to this vessel.

2. You will then prepare your ritual space in your preferred method by laying a compass, casting a circle, etc. If it is at all possible, you should perform this part of the working outdoors. The bowl of dirt/herbs should be present and placed upon the ground or your altar. You should also place the vessel and heartstone near the bowl. You should have a paper and pen nearby as well.
3. The candle should be placed standing within the center of the bowl of dirt. If you are inclined, it is most appropriate to dress the candle with a bit of *Spirit Summoning Oil.* You may also wish to burn a bit of a *Suffumigation of Spirit Calling*. The purpose here is to call forth and connect to the Spirit of the Greenwood[138] and ask that it come forth to provide a sigil and name for itself that you may utilize for work with this vessel.
4. Once all items are ready and your ritual space is prepared, you will light the candle in the center of your dirt/herb blend in the bowl. Then you will employ the *vox magica* and conjure forth the spirit of the Greenwood by this wording or by that of your own devising:

"Spirit of lush gardens and green growing wilds,
Who transforms light into the verdant blood of all flora,
Who breathes through and sustains all life,
By that very breath I call to you!

You who are the seed, the root, the stalk, the trunk, the branch, the leaf, the bud, the blossom, and fruit I call to you.

Keeper of poisons and medicines,
Witness to bounty and blight,
Patron of meadows and marshlands, forests and fields, gardens and groves,

138 The Spirit of the Greenwood should be understood as that which oversees all plant people. For some, this spirit is personified as the greenman/woman.

And all places the plant people dwell,
Grant me audience and aid,
Reveal to me both name and sign that I may better know thee by.

I call you forth, Spirit of the Greenwood,
As a seeker of your wisdom and revelation,
That I may be aided in magic and medicine,
That I may be both student and steward of your mysteries.

Hail to thee, Spirit of the Greenwood!
Hail to thee, Spirit of the Greenwood!
Hail to thee, Spirit of the Greenwood!"

5. Once you feel the conjuration has been sufficient and the presence of the Spirit of the Greenwood near you should seek to discover both a sigil and a name by which you will know the Spirit of the Greenwood. This may be done by employing scrying and mediumistic abilities for revelation. Or by engaging in transvection to step into the Otherworld, meet with the spirit, and request that it grant you a sigil and name that you may call it by.
6. Once both a name and sigil have been revealed to you, be sure to write them down so they are not forgotten. Allow the candle to fully burn down and eventually extinguish itself in the dirt.
7. You may continue on to this next part of the working immediately if you desire or on the following day.
8. You should paint the sigil that was revealed to you with green paint on the interior or exterior of the vessel, or both, as you are inclined, and it should be allowed to thoroughly dry.
9. You may then add the dirt/herb mixture to the vessel as is, or make it into a dirt clay to line the bottom of the vessel with. This should only fill the vessel about ⅓ of the way up. The heartstone should then be placed in the center of the vessel.
10. You will then go through the death, rebirth, and ensouling ritual processes for the vessel. If the vessel is too large you may wish to simply drape the Death Shroud over it during the death process. You may also place it in the center of your Triangle of Arte and cover it with a red cloth and then a black cloth for the gestation

period, in lieu of employing the cauldron. When naming the vessel, you will use the name revealed to you by the Spirit of the Greenwood for calling upon it.

11. Once this vessel is completed, it may be enshrined upon an altar or kept near any place where you study or practice botanical artes. This may become a spirit locus for engaging with the Spirit of the Greenwood through acts of mediumship, transvection, and scrying. And a place where you may offer devotion and make requests. The Spirit of the Greenwood may grant aid in works of blessing and bane, and of both growth and withering in equal measure.
12. When you seek to better know a particular plant and strengthen your allyship with it, it is appropriate to add a pinch of powdered *materia* from that plant to the vessel. Alternatively, should the vessel be made of an appropriately porous clay, it may have the fresh leaves and blossoms of botanical allies rubbed upon its surface so that they may color and impregnate the vessel with their virtues. Similarly, botanical tinctures and oils may be applied to the interior or exterior of the vessel. You may also wish to arrange seasonally appropriate botanicals gathered from your locale around the vessel as an act of devotion. Candles may be burned before the vessel, and fragrant smoke may be offered to it as well.

A Fetich of the Hallowed Hand

Here, the hand becomes an emblem of the Crafter aspect of the witch's tripartite soul and representative of our work in this world. It is essentially a *maumet* spirit; however, it is also linked to your own work, artistry, agency, and magic.

This fetich serves as an aid to the work of the hands and ensures we are skillful in that which we create or draw with them. This is somewhat open to interpretation for the witch. It may aptly apply to anyone who is an artisan or crafter by trade or truly anyone whose hands are an integral part of their work, so in truth this fetich is an assist to nearly anyone who might recognize the hand as a symbol of agency and power.

The reader is encouraged to meditate a bit upon the nature of their hands. How do you use them? How do they serve you? How are they reflective of your work in the world? What do you wish to create, draw near, and hold tight with them?

Additionally, this fetich also serves in the work of beckoning forth the things we desire as well as in procuring, securing, or stealing of luck. This in mind, this sort of fetich might also be employed for success in gambling and the procuring of wealth.

The vessel for this fetich should be in the shape of a hand. For our purposes here, though, I will be using a repurposed porcelain doll hand/arm as an example. These types of doll hands are usually hollow and make a perfect vessel for loading with your chosen *materia*. They are also often small enough to be easily carried on the person. However, this fetich could take many forms and may be altered should you instead wish to sculpt a hand from clay or wax, to make one from cloth, or even repurpose an old glove you have previously worn for it. Or you might instead choose to work with one of the wooden hands used as artist's models by hollowing out the base so that it may be loaded with *materia*. It is suggested that you choose or create a hand which is reflective of your dominant hand, meaning if you are right-handed, the fetich you are making should be of a right hand as well.

Items Needed:

- A hollow doll's hand made from porcelain or other durable material.
- A small stone to serve as a heartstone. This may be a small stone from a crossroads if you like. Though lodestone may be well suited to the work of beckoning and drawing skill, opportunity, and luck to you. However, you may choose any stone which you feel is best suited to the nature of this fetich.
- Fingernail clippings from both of your hands.
- A Lucky hand root *(Orchis spp.)*
- Cinquefoil herb *(Potentilla spp.)*
- Calamus root *(Acorus calamus)*
- Laurel leaf *(Laurus nobilis)*
- Chamomile *(Matricaria chamomilla, et al.)*
- An alligator paw
- Animal claws. These should ideally come from an animal that uses their claws to catch their prey. If you have a pet cat, you may even use the claw caps that they naturally shed.

- Feather or claw of a crow[139]
- A human finger bone
- Dirt respectfully gathered and paid for from the graves of skilled artisans, craftspeople, writers, or magicians.
- Dirt gathered from the four corners of a busy crossroad
- Dirt gathered from any places appropriate to this work. This may include places such as art schools and galleries, places where artists markets take place, casinos, etc.
- Any other botanical, mineralogical, or animal *materia* which you feel is well suited to this work. This is a fetich meant to enhance your own skill and work in the world, so allow yourself to be guided by what this means to you.

1. Prepare the heartstone and vessel in the usual manner. The botanical *materia* and any items which may not easily be loaded into the cavity of the doll's hand should be ground down into a powder. Though it is not entirely necessary, leave the animal claws, bones, and lucky hand root whole if possible.
2. The heartstone should be placed inside the doll hand along with any of the other whole *materia*. The powdered *materia* should be mixed with the dirt and a dirt clay, then made from them. This should then be used to completely fill the cavity of the doll hand and secure all *materia* inside. This should be allowed to dry before moving on.
3. Once dried, it is recommended that you engage in a bit of scrying or transvection to connect with the spirit you most associate with the work and nature of this fetich. This may be a spirit you work within the realm of artistry, creativity, or luck. Or this may take the form of connecting specifically with the Crafter part of yourself to better understand its role in your work in this life. During this process, you should open yourself to receiving any sigils or symbolic elements which might be incorporated into the fetich, as well as a name that you might give to the maumet upon its birth.
4. You may then embellish the hand in whatever manner you are led to. You may wish to paint it with sigils or colors that have

139 Crows are incredibly cunning creatures who also make and utilize tools. Possession of crow *materia* is not legal in all places, so please do your research.

been revealed or are representative of skill, artistry, and luck to you. You may wish to make a small bracelet of beads or thread for the hand. You may wish to cover the open end of it with beads or cloth. Or even make the arm into a pendant so that it may be easily worn. This is a fetich which should absolutely reflect some of your own personal creativity and artistry.

5. Once complete, the fetich should go through the death, rebirth, and ensouling ritual processes. When naming the *maumet*, you will use the name revealed to you, or give it one of your own devising. This fetich may be carried upon your person or enshrined somewhere near where you do your artistic, vocational, or magical work. It may be periodically suffumigated with incense smoke or dressed with oils to strengthen, feed, and fortify it. In times when you desire assistance in building your skills and artistry, or in bringing good fortune to you, the *maumet* should be petitioned for its aid.

An Oracular Maumet

The purpose of this *maumet* is to assist the witch in receiving clear messages during divination, scrying, dreaming, and mediumistic work. The example here will center on crafting a fetich from a large seashell. However, this working may be altered for making an effigy or spirit pot for the same purpose should you desire it.

Items Needed:

- Paper and a pen with black ink
- A large seashell. For this type of fetich a nice 3-5 inch turbo shell is an excellent option.
- A small stone from a crossroads or seashore to serve as the heartstone.
- A pinch each of thirteen different plants of divination. For this, I suggest choosing a mixture of botanicals under the patronage of the Moon (intuition), the Sun (prophecy and revelation), and Mercury (communication and magic). Some suggested options are:
    - Mugwort *(Artemisia vulgaris)*
    - Aniseed *(Pimpinella anisum)*
    - Water lily *(Nymphaea alba)*

    - Poppy *(Papaver spp.)*
    - Clary sage *(Salvia sclarea)*
    - Orris root *(Iris germanica)*
    - Yarrow *(Achillea millefolium)*
    - Bay laurel *(Laurus nobilis)*
    - Eyebright *(Euphrasia officinalis)*
    - Calendula *(Calendula officinalis)*
    - Cinquefoil *(Potentilla spp.)*
    - Vervain *(Verbena officinalis)*
    - Dill *(Anethum graveolens)*
- Those who wish for assistance in cartomancy should procure a duplicate of the primary deck you use and burn it to ash.[140] Ensure the deck is reduced to as little ash as possible.
- Seven pearls
- A small piece of silver or a silver mercury dime
- Seven small stones with a natural iridescence to them. This could be small chips or beads of moonstone, labradorite, or opal.
- Dirt from seven crossroads gathered in the day and hour of Mercury[141]
- Sand from the seashore gathered during the day and hour of the moon or on the full moon[142]
- Any other *materia* which you associate with divination and psychic ability, and are inspired to include.

1. The heartstone should be prepared in the usual manner, and the shell should be washed and suffumigated as usual.

---

140 This should not be approached as a form of destroying the deck so much as condensing its power into a powdered form that may be worked into the fetich. It is excellent to use the same sort of deck that you use, if possible. However, if this is not possible, you may opt to simply use a generic or miniature tarot or playing card deck, or even print the images of all the cards on a piece of paper and burn that instead.

141 See appendices.

142 If you do not live near the sea and are unable to procure this sand, you may instead substitute dirt gathered from a lakeshore or riverbank. It must be from a place where water touches land.

2. On the piece of paper, you should draw the following seal:

3. On the other side of the paper, you may write out instructions for how the *maumet* will assist in your work. This should then be burned to ash.
4. This ash, along with that of the divination deck you have burned (if applicable), should be added to a bowl. The herbs should be ground into a powder and mixed together with the ashes, the dirts, and sand you have gathered should be added as well. This mixture should then be made into a dirt clay using the methods previously mentioned in this work.
5. You will add the heartstone to the shell as well as the silver piece/dime and any other materia you have chosen. Next, completely fill the shell with your dirt clay mixture. Lastly, you may insert the pearls and stones into the clay at the shell's opening by pushing them into the clay in a way that both keeps them secure and is visually pleasing to you.
6. Once complete, the fetich should go through the death, rebirth, and ensouling ritual processes. While the *maumet* is gestating, you are encouraged to engage in scrying or transvection to connect with the spirit taking form in the vessel and determine more about its nature, including the name you will give to the spirit as a part of its birthing process. Ideally, the spirit should be birthed and given the breath of life either during the full moon or during the day and hour of the moon.

Once complete, the fetich may be held whilst engaging in oracular, mediumistic, and psychic operations. It may be kept nearby when engaging in any form of divination as proximity to the fetich will aid in both receptivity as well as clarity. For those who engage in oneiric prophecy, you may wish to keep the shell near the bedside or under the pillow.

The relationship the witch may form with the *maumet* allied to this fetich will be quite individualistic and may, in time, take the form of actively working with this spirit as a form of familiar. Conversely, for some, this may simply function as a proximal relationship wherein the spirit is primarily worked with and called upon for aid when engaging in divinatory work and the like.

As with most fetiches, the shell may be passed through incense smoke and dressed with oils in order to feed and fortify its indwelling spirit.

Horns of the Witches' Devil

The working here is offered for consideration of the reader who has taken the entirety of this book to heart and explored it with thoroughness.

When crafting these fetiches the witch should already have an established understanding of and relationship with our Devil. This isn't an introduction; it is a greater conjuration, an amplification, and indeed a form of pact. Combined, these fetiches stand as representatives of our devil and may serve as a locus by which we might honor and call upon him.

These twin fetishes are mirrored siblings. One of light and one of shadow. Each set should be crafted from a matched pair of goat horns, which are meant to align with the Witches' Devil and assist in works both supernal and infernal. One horn tipped towards the earth to plow a chthonic furrow where baneful seeds may be sown. The other tipped towards the sky to rend the heavens that starlight might rain upon us and brighten our eyes. Each horn represents a path. One sinistral, the other dextral.

The horn of Malediction is allied to works of the nightside. Of necromancy, spirit flight, and spirit conjuration. Additionally, it aids in rites of obsession, binding, blasting, and blighting.

The horn of Benediction is allied to works of the daytide. Of healing, divining, and the conjuring of fortune and favor. Additionally, it aids in rites of blessing, protection, and consecration.

Alterations may be made to the selected materia depending upon your inclinations and limitations. I absolutely understand that many of these items may be quite difficult for the average person to acquire; they are, however, the ones I have used in crafting these same horns for myself and others, so I list them here as an example of the complexity that this manner of work might develop. It should be understood that all items listed have been conjured to purpose and, where appropriate, paid for in offering. That all in mind, there is no set recipe for our Devil, and you should endeavor to craft these items in a way reflective of your own desires and your relationship with him. What must be understood here is the nature of each of these fetiches and what aspect of our Devil and by extension our magic they are meant to represent.

General Items Needed:

- A pair of cleaned goat horns sourced from the same goat
- Dirt collected and paid for from seven crossroads and split into two portions
- Red paint and smaller brushes
- Two bowls
- Eggs
- The Triangle of Arte

For the Horn of Benediction you will need:
Items that can be powdered.

- Dried and cut/powdered Angelica root.
- Dried Sage (*Salvia officinalis*).
- Dried Saint John's Wort (*Hypericum perforatum*).
- Dried Rowan berries (*Sorbus spp.).*
- Dried Hawthorn (*Crataegus spp.*).
- Dried Rose petals (*Rosa spp.*).
- Dried Calendula (*Calendula spp.).*
- Dried Bay (*Laurus nobilis*).
- Dried Rosemary (*Rosmarinus officinalis*).
- Dried Rue (*Ruta graveolens*).

- Dried Avens root (*Geum urbanum*).
- Dried Cinquefoil (*Potentilla spp.*).
- Dried Devil's Shoestring (*Viburnum alnifolium or other spp.*).

Items that should be kept whole.

- Quartz pebble or crystal to serve as a heartstone
- A human finger bone from the right hand
- An antique skeleton key
- Goat field dirt (dirt from a place goats have trodden)
- Dirt gathered and paid for from seven churches

For the Horn of Malediction you will need:
Items that can be powdered

- Sulfur
- Dried Chili Pepper (*Capsicum spp.*)
- Grains of Paradise (*Aframomum melegueta*)
- Dried Valerian Root (*Valeriana officinalis*)
- Dried Datura leaf and flower (*Datura spp.*)
- Dried Belladonna leaf and berry (*Atropa belladonna*)
- Dried Mandragora root (*M. officinarum or M. autumnalis*)
- Dried Mullein (*Verbascum thapsus*)
- Dried Mugwort (*Artemisia vulgaris*)
- Dried Wormwood (*Artemisia absinthium*)
- Blackthorn (*Prunus spinosa*)
- Wasp nest
- Snake bones
- Cremains that you have pacted with
- Lightning-struck wood

Items that should be kept whole

- A small piece of onyx or obsidian to serve as a heartstone.
- A human finger bone from the left hand
- An iron nail

- Goat field dirt (dirt from a place goats have trodden)
- Dirt gathered and paid for from seven cemetery gates

For the initial preparation, you will want to have sifted any dirts and powder the botanical *materia* (and any other *materia* possible) to as fine a powder as you are able. Take care to wear protective respiratory equipment and gloves when powdering, as some of these herbs are poisonous. The materials for the Horn of Benediction should be kept in a separate bowl from those of the Horn of Malediction. To each bowl, one half of the dirt gathered from seven crossroads should be added.

The fetiches may be crafted within ritual space as desired, though it is not entirely necessary so long as the materia has been conjured and the witch is focused upon their task and the purpose of the fetich they are crafting.

To Craft the Horns

Each should be made separately. If you like, you may include ritual timing in the crafting, such as making the Horn of Malediction during the dark or waning moon and making the Horn of Benediction during the full or waxing moon.

To make the horns, you will begin by using the methods listed in the *Crafting Dirt Clay* praxis listed in chapter nine to blend together all of the dirts and powdered materia for each horn. Next, you will add just a bit of your dirt clay mixture to the inside of the hollow goat horn. For the Horn of Malediction, you should be using the horn from the left side of the goat, whereas you should be using the right horn for the Horn of Benediction.

Once you have added a small amount of the dirt clay, next add the solid items. Keeping in mind that items such as the key, the nail, and the finger bones should be positioned inside the horn so that they are pointing towards the tip. Once all of your solid items are placed within, continue to fill the horn the rest of the way until it is fully packed. Do this for each horn and allow them to dry.

Once dry, you may wish to cover the end of the horns with cloth as is shown in the photos section of this book. You should then decorate the horns with paint as you like. Though this is optional, I roughly painted the Horn of Benediction in white whilst painting the Horn of Malediction in black. You should, however, paint the sigil of each horn upon it in the red paint:

Horn of Malediction

Horn of Benediction

The Ritual

Prior to beginning, you should have given the horns a ritual death using the Death Shroud, or by doing the cleansing/consecration as laid out in Chapter Ten.

The Gestation Period

Once the horns have received a ritual death or exorcism, the cauldron or an alternate vessel of rebirth should be placed within the center of your Triangle of Arte. If you have used the Death Shroud to prepare the horns, you will unwrap them as you place them together into your cauldron/vessel.

1. You should create ritual space by laying a compass, casting a circle, or employing another form of creating ritual space specific to your practice.
2. Though this part of the ritual may be performed at any time, I find it particularly powerful to place the horns into the cauldron at sunset, as this is a time of endings. While doing this, you should say:

"You are given to the earth. Committed to tomb and womb. That you may rest, that you may grow in power, and that you may be reborn into this world as the twin crowning powers of our Devil."

3. Candles should already have been placed in candle holders at the points of the triangle. For this purpose, I suggest burning small chime candles, which usually burn for two hours or so. Once you have placed the fetiches into the cauldron, you will then light the candles around the Triangle of Arte while saying the following:

"By the hand which creates,"

Light the white candle.

"By the hand which destroys,"

Light the black candle.

"By the star upon my brow and the light betwixt the horns,"

Light the red candle.

4. You will call upon and conjure the Witches' Devil now with these or other words of your choosing:

"I conjure and call you forth, Witch Father,
Crooked One, bearer of many masks,
That your wisdom, challenge, and cunning may take root in the vessels crafted in your name.
A horn of starlight and cunning,
another of shadow and bone,
One of the sunwise road and one of the widdershin shadow.
A body complete, shaped by arte and by oath.
Come forth and enter!
Enter these horns that they may be your throne, your altar, a cloven hoofprint stamped upon the world.
Let them be for you a seat of power, a crossroads between the worlds.

Rest here now, be strengthened here now,
Coil about and within here now,
Let your fire grow within the cauldron as the light betwixt the horns,
A fire which empowers these fetiches and sets light upon the brow."

5. Once you have felt his presence and feel that at least a portion of his power has entered the cauldron, the lid should be placed upon it. Should you choose to, any sigils appropriate to him as have been revealed may now be drawn with chalk onto the cauldron. You may also draw the sigils of the horns given above. The ritual space can be closed, and the candles should be allowed to burn out.
6. Allow the horns to gestate here for seven nights. During the period of gestation, burn new candles upon the triangle each night.
7. During this time, should it be appropriate for the witch and their relationship with our Devil, you may draft a more formal pact, keeping in mind all that has been put forth in this book to this point. This isn't an act to be approached with frivolity and abandon, and the author assumes no responsibility for those who advance too eagerly out of hubris or unfettered desire.
8. After this time (ideally at midnight on the final night), ritual space should be created, candles should be lit at the corners of the Triangle of Arte once again whilst saying:

"By the hand which creates,"

Light the white candle.

"By the hand which destroys,"

Light the black candle.

"By the star upon my brow and the light betwixt the horns,"

Light the red candle.

9. The cauldron should be lifted and removed from the triangle. The side of it should be knocked upon three times to begin awakening the fetiches. The lid should then be removed and the horns slowly lifted from the cauldron whilst saying:

   "Resurrected and risen, you are! Brought forth in power, and birthed in new form."

10. The horns should then be placed within the triangle once more, whilst saying:

    "Awaken now! Within this body.
    Come now, Crooked One, Witch Father, Mask-Bearer,
    You whose name is etched upon ancient ruins and the heart of the faithful.
    By hoof and horn, by breath and by blood,
    By plow of the field and iron upon the anvil,
    I summon thee as no stranger,
    But as one who has been alit by your flame,
    And awaits at the twilight crossroads."

11. At this point, the breath of life exercise should be performed. During the transfer of breath, the horns may be lifted towards your face. Benediction should be in your right hand, and Malediction should be in your left hand, close but not touching, and the breath of life blown between them. This is also the point at which you would incorporate the pipe/smoke and the *Spiritus Vitae* tool as a part of the transference of breath, as you are inclined and able. If using the *Spiritus Vitae,* the horns may be left lying in the triangle as needed while giving the breath if lifting them is not possible. Additionally, you should not neglect to include a declaration of transposition before you pass the breath to the horns. Once the breath of life has been given, you may place the horns back into the triangle and say:

"I name thee The Horns of The Devil.
By the first flame of the first forger,
Breaker of chains, stealer of fire,
Bearer of the witch's mark and teacher its ways.
The serpent coiled round the root which ascended, crowned by the heavens.
The star that falls again and strikes the brow alight.
You who plow the furrow and rend the skies,
Come forth and stand now before me,
Neither above nor below, but together at the crossroads center.
As ally, as challenger, and as co-conspirator."

12. Pick up the horns again and state:

"These horns I raise in your image.
One for the supernal,
One for the infernal.
One for benediction, bright and shining,
One for malediction, cold and severe."

13. Briefly touch the tip of the Horn of Benediction to the flame of the white candle on the Triangle of Arte and say:

"Hallowed be the Horn of Benediction."

14. Briefly touch the tip of the Horn of Malediction to the flame of the black candle on the Triangle of Arte and say:

"Hallowed be the Horn of Malediction."

15. Now, at the same time, briefly touch the tips of both horns to the flame of the red candle on the Triangle of Arte and say:

"Dextral and Sinistral,
Starlight and Shadow,

Breath and Blood,
Joined as one by witching fire."

16. Place the horns back in the triangle. If you have created a formal written pact that further outlines the agreed-upon boundaries, roles, and responsibilities established between yourself and the spirit, it should be read aloud and signed by you.[143]
17. Conclude by saying:

"May your cunning lie coiled within them,
Your flame alight betwixt them,
Your breath and my voice awaken them.
Let them be as your crown within this world.
Let them speak, and call, and strike when I command.
Let them be the Devil's horns.
Let them stand as a bridge to your power and gnosis,
And a boon upon the land your witches walk.
Come Horned One, and be honored.
Come Witch Father, and be enthroned.
Come Devil, and dwell."

18. You may close your ritual space in the usual manner.

These horns may then be worked with as such:
The Horn of Benediction is allied to all works of the dextral path, of blessing, and the Supernal Realm. Particularly, works of cunning, luck, and fortune, benevolent protection, healing, and consecration.

The Horn of Malediction is allied to all works of the sinestral path, of blasting, and the Infernal realm. Particularly in works of nocturnal spirit flight and spirit conjuration, of necromancy, and in rites of obsession, attack and defense, binding, and blighting.

Each may be carried or held as a fetich to grant the benefits allied to it and to call this aspect of our Devil nearer. They may also be worked with

143 For further information and an example of this, please see P*RAXIS: Creating a Formal Pact* in Chapter Five

similarly as one may with a wand or the Blade of Arte. When enshrined together or laid upon the altar or elsewhere, a red candle may be placed between them and devotional hymns or conjurations spoken to call upon the ear and aid of him.

Through this, they may serve as a gateway of revelation to the witches' arte entire.

Afterword

In bringing the body of this work to a close, I want to thank you, the reader, for joining me on this somewhat long and crooked road exploring approaches towards a magical arte which is very dear to me. One which is a cornerstone of my own practice, and that I believe deserves to be as central within discussions and practices of contemporary witchcraft as any other form of magic. The works of spirits, of hands, of craft, of breath, and of creation are ours as witches.

It is my hope that the spirit of this book has perhaps "breathed into" you in some small or significant way and that my efforts here will have enriched both your art and arte going forward. If this tome has served in extending a witching hand across to the Otherworld and opened some eyes a bit wider around our ideas concerning spirits, personhood, and bodies, I will be quite pleased. If it has inspired you to more consciously and actively enspirit, and in turn be enspirited by, the world around you, and to perhaps take up this arte more actively, then it will have done its work, and I will be grateful to have aided in its creation.

Go forth.
Do good things.
And make good magic.

Appendix One: Planetary Magic and Attributions

Below is a collection of information on planetary associations, plants, and squares that may serve the reader in choosing magical materia and working with planetary spirits.

Saturn

- **Areas of Rulership:** Boundaries, limitation, discipline, justice, death, the occult, binding, teaching, time, history, wisdom, patience, punishment, imprisonment, malefic magics.
- **Colors:** Black and Grey
- **Common Symbols:** The scythe, hourglass, veil, shadows, scales
- **Element:** Earth
- **Metal:** Lead
- **Astrological Rulership:** Capricorn, Aquarius
- **Day of Week:** Saturday
- **Places:** Cemeteries, morgues, museums, ruins, libraries, borders and hedgerows, prisons, places of stinking and rot like bogs and junkyards, slums, caves and mines, basements, retirement and hospice homes
- **Numbers:** 3, 9, 15, 29, 333
- **Geometry:** Triangle
- **Animals:** Cow, Crocodile, Ass, Crow, Goat, Raven, Mole
- **Plants:** Aconite, Belladonna Yew, Cypress, Hemlock, Datura, Hellebore, Asafetida, Myrrh, Costus

- **Archangel:** Tzaphkiel/Cassiel
- **Olympic Spirit:** Aratron

Jupiter

- **Areas of rulership:** Politics, influence, law, organized religion, sovereignty, rulership, wealth, expansion, growth
- **Colors:** Royal Blue/Purple
- **Common Symbols:** Scepter, Crown, Crook
- **Elements:** Air/Water
- **Metal:** Tin
- **Astrological Rulership:** Sagittarius, Pisces
- **Day of Week:** Thursday
- **Places:** Political capitals and places of legislative assembly, courthouses, religious institutions, universities, banks, granaries
- **Numbers:** 4, 16, 34, 64, 444
- **Geometry:** Square
- **Animals:** Eagle, Bull, Ram, Stag, Wren, Sturgeon, Goose, Centaur, Gryphon
- **Plants:** Agrimony, Alfalfa, Cinquefoil, Bayberry, Sage, Hyssop, Cedar, Fir, Fumitory
- **Archangel:** Tzadkiel
- **Olympic Spirit:** Bethor

Mars

- **Areas of rulership:** Warfare, passion, athleticism, courage, anger, strength, energy, vitality, protection, vengeance, violence.
- **Color:** Red
- **Common Symbols:** Weaponry, blood, hammer, anvil, whip
- **Element:** Fire
- **Metal:** Iron
- **Astrological Rulership:** Ares, Scorpio
- **Day of Week:** Tuesday
- **Places:** Battlefields, gymnasiums, sports arenas, police stations, army barracks
- **Numbers:** 5, 25, 65, 125, 555

- **Geometry:** Pentagon, pentagram
- **Animals:** Boar, Horse, Wolf, Ram, Bear, Basilisk, Scorpion
- **Plants:** Black pepper, Cayenne, Rue, Mustard, Nettle, Thistle, Dragon's blood, Ginger
- **Archangel:** Khamael/Samael
- **Olympic Spirit:** Phaleg

The Sun

- **Areas of rulership:** Joy, fame, success, spiritual and intellectual illumination, healing, ego, fortune
- **Colors:** Yellow/gold/orange
- **Common Symbols:** Halo, lance, cymbals, gold coins
- **Element:** Fire
- **Metals:** Gold and brass
- **Astrological Rulership:** Leo
- **Day of Week:** Sunday
- **Places:** Mountain tops, temples, palaces, performance halls.
- **Numbers:** 6, 36, 111, 216, 666
- **Geometry:** Hexagon, hexagram
- **Animals:** Lion, Falcon, Bee, Tiger, Puma, Phoenix
- **Plants:** Cinnamon, Bay, Angelica, Chamomile, Frankincense, Heliotrope, Sunflower, Calendula
- **Archangel:** Michael
- **Olympic Spirit:** Och

Venus

- **Areas of rulership:** Beauty, pleasure, sensuality, prosperity, sexuality, love, fertility, art, culture, attraction, allure.
- **Color:** Green/Pink
- **Common Symbols:** Mirror, necklace, heart, girdle, harp
- **Element:** Earth
- **Metal:** Copper
- **Astrological Rulership:** Taurus, Libra
- **Day of Week:** Friday
- **Places:** Beauty salons and spas, bathhouses and brothels, art galleries

- **Numbers:** 7, 49, 175, 343, 777
- **Geometry:** Heptagon, heptagram
- **Animals:** Dove, Lynx, Peacock, Sow, Frog, Pidgeon
- **Plants:** Benzoin, Geranium, Rose, Violet, Bergamot, Clover
- **Archangel:** Anael
- **Olympic Spirit:** Hagith

Mercury

- **Areas of Rulership:** Travel, commerce, communication, education, trickery, healing,magic, music, gambling, luck
- **Color:** Orange/light blue/mixed colors
- **Common Symbols:** Caduceus, winged helmet or shoes, dice
- **Element:** Air
- **Metals:** Mercury/Aluminium
- **Astrological Rulership:** Gemini, Virgo
- **Day of Week:** Wednesday
- **Places:** Crossroads, casinos, marketplaces, airports, railways
- **Numbers:** 8, 64, 88, 260, 888
- **Geometry:** Octagon, octagram
- **Animals:** Baboon, Ape, Cock, Coyote, Dog, Magpie, Jackal
- **Plants:** Dill, Caraway, Lavender, Mastic, Storax, Lime, Licorice, Marjoram
- **Archangel:** Raphael
- **Olympic Spirit:** Ophiel

The Moon

- **Areas of Rulership:** Emotions, dreams, intuition, divination, illusions, hospitality, community and populace, increase/decrease
- **Color:** White/Silver
- **Common Symbols:** Crescent, bow and arrow, perfumes
- **Element:** Water
- **Metal:** Silver
- **Astrological Rulership:** Cancer
- **Day of Week:** Monday

- **Places:** Oceans and lakes, commons and parks, gardens, nurseries, hotels, restaurants
- **Numbers:** 9, 13, 81, 369, 999
- **Geometry:** Nonagon, Nonagram
- **Animals:** Crab And Shellfish, Deer, Hare/Rabbit, Badger, Dog, Owl, Unicorn
- **Plants:** Camphor, Eucalyptus, Jasmine, Anise, Ylang Ylang, Willow
- **Archangel:** Gabriel
- **Olympic Spirit:** Phul

On Planetary Identifiers for Plants

What follows is a catalog of traditional markers used to discern the planetary sympathies of plants. The identifiers here are drawn primarily from Richard Folkard's *Plantlore, Legends, & Lyrics* and Heinrich Cornelius Agrippa's *Three Books of Occult Philosophy*. These traits, subtle and overt, may serve the practitioner in identifying which celestial current, or currents, a given botanical is most readily allied to.

Saturn
Plants that grow in wastelands, borders, ruins, and cemeteries. Those that bear black fruits and berries, or bear no fruits at all. As well as those which are sour, that taste of rot and death, are poisonous, and that stupefy. Lastly, slow-growing plants, funerary plants, and those that live a very long time.

- **Leaves:** Coarse or hard, hairy, dry or withered, often ill-favored in form or hue.
- **Flowers:** Dull, pallid, greenish or dirty white, sometimes pale red; often prickled, hairy, or otherwise displeasing to the eye.
- **Roots:** Tend to sprawl outward in a meandering or discursive fashion.
- **Scent:** Putrid, fetid, like damp soil.

Jupiter
Plants that grow very tall, spread or increase rapidly, or stand as royalty of the Greenwood. Those that nourish the body, those that taste pleasant and sweet, as well as those which are somewhat astringent and sharp.

- **Leaves:** Smooth, gently pointed, with subdued veining and a bluish-green cast.
- **Flowers:** Generous and well-formed, bright, transparent, often tinted rose, blue, yellow, or flesh-toned, succulent and luminous.
- **Roots:** Small, fine, with shorter hairs, spread throughout the soil.
- **Scent:** Subtle and pleasing, uplifting to the mind.

Mars

Those that are bitter and tart, or that cause burning or tears. Those plants with thorns and needles. Those that bear red flowers and berries, or with bloodlike sap. Those that grow in deserts, on battlefields, or near sports arenas and gymnasiums.

- **Leaves:** Rigid, pendulous, sharply pointed, those that are thorny or cause irritation, those that bring heat, sometimes bitter or biting on the tongue.
- **Flowers:** Vivid, volatile in hue; red, or a mix of colors including crimson, green, blue, or purple, prone to quick change, and sometimes abundant in seeds.
- **Roots:** Dense with fibrous strands that snake aggressively through the earth.
- **Scent:** Sharp, acrid, heady, sometimes overwhelming.

The Sun

Those plants that follow or turn towards the Sun. Those that are sun-loving and thrive in the summer. Those bearing bright and pleasing fruits, such as various citrus species.

- **Leaves:** Succulent, often deeply veined with thick stalks; hues range from golden-green to tawny, sometimes with red stems.
- **Flowers:** Brilliant yellows and radiant golds, sometimes violet; striking and full of solar vitality.
- **Roots:** Strong and vertically anchored, not spreading far but holding deep.
- **Scent:** Bright and agreeable, bold, medicinal, clarifying, strengthening to the senses, particularly vision and thought.

Venus

Those that are sweet tasting, oil-bearing, and delectable. Those that are heavily perfumed, aromatic, and pleasing. Those that excite arousal. Those plants that bear sweet and delicious fruits and produce intoxicating flowers. Those that grow in lush gardens, near beauty salons, bathhouses, and brothels.

- **Leaves:** Large and lush, soft, vibrant in tone, emerald or blushed, often broad and abundant.
- **Flowers:** Delicate, lovely, commonly blue, white, or rose; visually alluring and generously borne.
- **Roots:** Quick to appear, but shallow, springing freely and with ease.
- **Scent:** Sweet, subtle, alluring and pleasing to both senses and spirit; gently invigorating.

Mercury

Those of a mixed or complex flavor. Those with mixed colors of flowers. Those that grow quickly. Those with shorter leaves. Plants quicken the mind and speech. Those that grow near crossroads, airports/railroads, and marketplaces.

- **Leaves:** Varied in shape, but typically neat and pleasant to behold.
- **Flowers:** Many-colored and manifold in form; bright and cheerful.
- **Roots:** Those that sink deep into the earth and fan wide.
- **Scent:** Penetrating, elusive, and quickening, refreshing to both heart and mind.

The Moon

Those that are camphorous, cooling, and watery. Those with white flowers, night-blooming, or become more fragrant at night. Those with silvery leaves. Those that grow in or near the water, in parks, or in public squares.

- **Leaves:** Pale, succulent and fleshy, with pronounced pith and thick veins; dark bottle-green or silver-washed.
- **Flowers:** Muted, white, pale yellow or soft green, watery, mellifluous and sweet, night-blooming.
- **Roots:** Thrive in water or wet soil, but often shallow, prone to rot, and short-lived.

- **Scent:** Mild to the point of absence; cool, damp, like rainfall, or with a soft savour of honey.

On Planetary Hours

The division of time according to planetary rulership is an ancient practice found in the magical traditions of the Hellenistic world, later absorbed into medieval and Renaissance occultism. Its roots lie in Chaldean astronomy, where the seven classical planets: Saturn, Jupiter, Mars, the Sun, Venus, Mercury, and the Moon were arranged according to their apparent speed through the heavens. This order, known as the *Chaldean Order*, is the foundation of planetary hour calculation.

Each day is ruled by one of the seven planets and is further divided into twenty-four planetary hours, beginning at sunrise and proceeding cyclically through the Chaldean sequence. This system not only maps planetary influence onto the flow of the day but also allows for choosing ritual timing, which supports our magical operations by aligning them with sympathetic planetary forces.

This method, while simple in essence, has a long tradition and is a practical means of employing celestial powers within terrestrial rites. As such, you can time your magical workings to occur on the planetary days and planetary hours most advantageous to their purpose. For instance, if you were doing work regarding legal matters, you might choose to time your workings to the planetary day and hour of Jupiter (Thursday). If you were crafting a *maumet* to aid in dreaming and spirit communication, you might craft it on a Monday (Moon) during the hour of Mercury.

Below are instructions for determining which planet rules each day and for calculating planetary hours. It should be noted that there are now many computer programs and apps that can quickly and easily do this for you as well.

Calculating Planetary Hours

The Chaldean Order

To begin, one must commit to memory the planetary sequence:

Saturn - Jupiter - Mars - Sun - Venus - Mercury - Moon

This is the order in which planetary hours proceed, and it always repeats.

Determining the Planetary Day
Each day of the week is ruled by a planet, corresponding to the *first hour after sunrise:*

- Sunday – Sun
- Monday – Moon
- Tuesday – Mars
- Wednesday – Mercury
- Thursday – Jupiter
- Friday – Venus
- Saturday – Saturn

Whichever planet rules the first hour after sunrise also rules the entire day.

From there, you cycle forward in the Chaldean order for each subsequent hour.

How to Calculate the Hours
Planetary hours are not equal segments of sixty minutes (except when near the equinox). Instead, the span from sunrise to sunset is divided into 12 equal daytime hours, and sunset to the next sunrise is divided into 12 nighttime hours. These will vary in length depending on the season and your location.

Step-by-Step Guide:

1. Find local sunrise and sunset times for your exact location and date. These can be found in weather apps or astronomical calendars.
2. Calculate the length of daylight
   - Subtract sunrise from sunset.
   - Example: Sunrise at 6:00 AM, Sunset at 8:00 PM = 14 hours of daylight.
3. Divide the daylight span by 12 to get the length of each planetary hour (daytime).
   - Example: 14 hrs x 60 min = 840 min ÷ 12 = 1 hour and 10 minutes per planetary hour.

4. Apply this same process to the night:
    - From sunset to next day's sunrise.
    - Example: Sunset at 8:00 PM, Sunrise at 6:00 AM = 10 hours of night.
    - 10 hrs x 60 minutes = 600 min ÷ 12 = 50 minutes per nighttime planetary hour.
5. Assign the planetary rulers:
    - Start at sunrise with the ruler of the day.
    - Move forward in the Chaldean Order, hour by hour.
6. Repeat as needed through the night.

A Working Example

Let's say it's Tuesday (ruled by Mars). Sunrise is at 5:45 AM, and sunset is at 8:15 PM (14.5 hours of daylight).

- 14.5 hrs x 60 min = 870 min ÷ 12 = 72.5 minutes per planetary hour.
- The first planetary hour (from 5:45–6:57 AM) is ruled by Mars.
- The second hour (6:57–8:10 AM) is ruled by the next in Chaldean Order: Sun.
- Then Venus, Mercury, Moon, Saturn, and so on…

This continues until sunset, where you calculate the night hours in the same fashion. Below is a table which helps illustrate the order of the planetary hours based on each day.

Daytime Hours Chart

Hour	Sunday	Monday	Tuesday	Wednesday	Thursday	Friday	Saturday
1	Sun	Moon	Mars	Mercury	Jupiter	Venus	Saturn
2	Venus	Saturn	Sun	Moon	Mars	Mercury	Jupiter
3	Mercury	Jupiter	Venus	Saturn	Sun	Moon	Mars
4	Moon	Mars	Mercury	Jupiter	Venus	Saturn	Sun
5	Saturn	Sun	Moon	Mars	Mercury	Jupiter	Venus
6	Jupiter	Venus	Saturn	Sun	Moon	Mars	Mercury
7	Mars	Mercury	Jupiter	Venus	Saturn	Sun	Moon
8	Sun	Moon	Mars	Mercury	Jupiter	Venus	Saturn

Hour	Sunday	Monday	Tuesday	Wednesday	Thursday	Friday	Saturday
9	Venus	Saturn	Sun	Moon	Mars	Mercury	Jupiter
10	Mercury	Jupiter	Venus	Saturn	Sun	Moon	Mars
11	Moon	Mars	Mercury	Jupiter	Venus	Saturn	Sun
12	Saturn	Sun	Moon	Mars	Mercury	Jupiter	Venus

Nighttime Hours Chart

Hour	Sunday	Monday	Tuesday	Wednesday	Thursday	Friday	Saturday
1	Jupiter	Venus	Saturn	Sun	Moon	Mars	Mercury
2	Mars	Mercury	Jupiter	Venus	Saturn	Sun	Moon
3	Sun	Moon	Mars	Mercury	Jupiter	Venus	Saturn
4	Venus	Saturn	Sun	Moon	Mars	Mercury	Jupiter
5	Mercury	Jupiter	Venus	Saturn	Sun	Moon	Mars
6	Moon	Mars	Mercury	Jupiter	Venus	Saturn	Sun
7	Saturn	Sun	Moon	Mars	Mercury	Jupiter	Venus
8	Jupiter	Venus	Saturn	Sun	Moon	Mars	Mercury
9	Mars	Mercury	Jupiter	Venus	Saturn	Sun	Moon
10	Sun	Moon	Mars	Mercury	Jupiter	Venus	Saturn
11	Venus	Saturn	Sun	Moon	Mars	Mercury	Jupiter
12	Mercury	Jupiter	Venus	Saturn	Sun	Moon	Mars

Planetary Squares (Kameas)

A planetary square, sometimes called a *kamea*, is a magical construct formed through the arrangement of numbers within a square grid in such a way that each row, column, and diagonal yields the same total, known as the *planetary number*. These squares are each associated with one of the seven classical planets and are used within various systems of occult practice, particularly in talismanic magic and spirit conjuration.

Each planet's square is based upon a specific number of rows and columns, determined by its numerical scale in the traditional Chaldean order. In this approach, the numbering of planets follows a classical understanding of heavenly bodies, where one represents what is farthest from Earth and most enduring/slowest moving, whereas nine is seen as the closest to Earth.

1. The Eternal Ineffable Divine
2. The Vault of the Stars
3. Saturn
4. Jupiter
5. Mars
6. Sun
7. Venus
8. Mercury
9. Moon

The squares reflect this numbering. For instance, the square of Saturn is 3×3, that of Jupiter is 4×4, and so on, culminating in the square of the Moon, which is 9×9. These configurations are not arbitrary. They are rooted in a worldview that sees numbers not merely as quantity, but as quality, resonance, and presence.

These squares are talismanic engines, encoded with the harmonic signatures of a planetary power. When inscribed, activated, or embedded into ritual objects, they serve to draw down and anchor the spirit and influence of the corresponding planetary sphere and its associated spirits.

In practical terms, these kameas may be mindfully drawn or otherwise created in a form where fetiches, effigies, and formulas may be placed atop them and imbued with the virtues of the corresponding planet. The planetary square may also be approached as a field upon which sigils may be constructed by connecting the sequence of numbers that correspond to the letters of the name. The resulting figure is not merely symbolic; it is a vessel through which that planetary force is entreated, conjured, and occasionally contained.

When working with these squares, it is wise to consider them not just as tools of operation, but as spirits in themselves. As patterned intelligences formed of order, resonance, and will. They are both a key and a lock, offering structured means through which the planetary virtues may be called into the world of matter.

Saturn = 15

4	9	2
3	5	7
8	1	6

Jupiter = 34

4	14	15	1
9	7	6	12
5	11	10	8
16	2	3	13

Mars = 65

11	24	7	20	3
4	12	25	8	16
17	5	13	21	9
10	18	1	14	22
23	6	19	2	15

Sol = 111

6	32	3	34	35	1
7	11	27	28	8	30
19	14	16	15	23	24
18	20	22	21	17	13
25	29	10	9	26	12
36	5	33	4	2	31

Venus = 175

22	47	16	41	10	35	4
5	23	48	17	42	11	29
30	6	24	49	18	36	12
13	31	7	25	43	19	37
38	14	32	1	26	44	20
21	39	8	33	2	27	45
46	15	40	9	34	3	28

Mercury = 260

8	58	59	5	4	62	63	1
49	15	14	52	53	11	10	56
41	23	22	44	45	19	18	48
32	34	35	29	28	38	39	25
40	26	27	37	36	30	31	33
17	47	46	20	21	43	42	24
9	55	54	12	13	51	50	16
64	2	3	61	60	6	7	57

Luna = 369

37	78	29	70	21	62	13	54	5
6	38	79	30	71	22	63	14	46
47	7	39	80	31	72	23	55	15
16	48	8	40	81	32	64	24	56
57	17	49	9	41	73	33	65	25
26	58	18	50	1	42	74	34	66
67	27	59	10	51	2	43	75	35
36	68	19	60	11	52	3	44	76
77	28	69	20	61	12	53	4	45

On the Generation of Sigils from Planetary Squares

To draw forth a sigil from a planetary square is to translate the name of a spirit, intention, or desire into a form that the planetary spirits may recognize and respond to. This is best done during the planetary day and hour of the planet you are seeking to ally with. Creation of this sort of sigil is accomplished through a process of numerical transmutation, wherein letters are converted into numbers, and those numbers are then used to trace a path across the kamea associated with the corresponding planetary force. To create sigils from the squares you will follow the steps below:

1. **Select the Proper Square:** choose the square that corresponds to the planetary spirit or influence you are working with.
2. **Convert the Name into Numbers:**
    - Using a system of letter-to-number correspondence—typically based on Hebrew *gematria,* Greek *isopsephy,* or a custom magical alphabet—convert the name or phrase into a sequence of numbers. For our example we will be using the simple Latin order: A=1, B=2, ..., Z=26.

    - For instance, the name *ANAEL* (a spirit of Venus) using the Latin system would yield:
    - A = 1, N = 14, A = 1, E = 5, L = 12
    - So the sequence becomes: 1 – 14 – 1 – 5 – 12
- Once converted, adjust any numbers that fall outside the square's range by reducing them. For Venus's 7×7 square (numbers 1–49), this step may not be necessary. For smaller squares like Saturn's 3×3 (1–9), reduction is essential, usually via numerological reduction (e.g., 24 becomes 2+4 = 6).

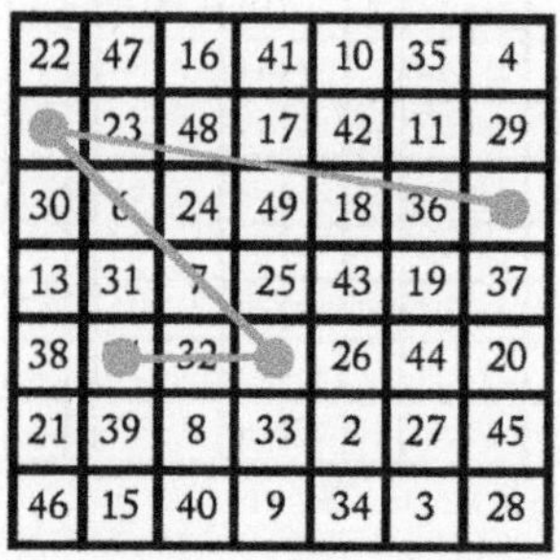

3. **Plot the Points:**
    - Each number corresponds to a cell within the planetary square. Beginning with the first number, mark a point. From there, draw a line to the second number, and so on, creating a path that travels across the grid. This path becomes a sigil charged with both the geometry of number and the force of the planet it resides within.
    - Usually small circles will be used to mark the beginning of the line and a small line (almost like crossing a letter T) to mark the end.
    - If a letter repeats (e.g., 1 → 1), a loop or crossed line may be used.
4. **Enliven the Sigil:**
    - Once inscribed, the sigil is not yet active; it holds potential, but not presence. To quicken it, within ritual context: during the proper planetary day and hour, suffumigate it with an incense aligned to the planet and/or anoint it with an appropriate oil while speaking the spirit's name and conjuring the spirit. These sigils may be drawn on parchment, etched in metal, or burned into wood as suits your needs and capabilities. The sigil may then be set within a talisman, placed upon an altar, or hidden within a vessel as is appropriate to your working.

Appendix Two: Common Color Associations

As mentioned earlier in this book, I believe that it is incredibly beneficial for the witch to consider their own associations as experiences when attributing the meaning to symbols such as color. That said, I felt it may be helpful to provide some common color associations used in contemporary magic and witchcraft as a point of reference for the witch to consider when designing their spirit vessels and choosing colors for paints, cloth, thread, etc.

Black

- **Planetary Association:** Saturn
- **Symbolism:** Protection, banishment, endings, death, mystery, concealment, absorption, introspection, transformation
- **Magical Workings:** Banishing, binding, and heavy protection. Necromancy death rites. Obfuscation and concealment. Defensive and warding magic. Cursing and counter-magic.

White

- **Planetary Association:** Moon
- **Symbolism:** Purity, spiritual light, clarity, truth, peace, elevation, sacredness
- **Magical Workings:** Purification, cleansing, and creating peace. Blessing, consecration, and healing. Ancestor work and the elevated dead. White is often treated as an "all-purpose" color.

Red

- **Planetary Association:** Mars
- **Symbolism:** Passion, lust, strength, blood, vitality, desire, anger, courage, action, movement, defensive protection
- **Magical Workings:** Protection, strength, and defense. Creating lust, passion, motivation, and action. Athleticism and vitality.

Orange

- **Planetary Association:** Mercury
- **Symbolism:** Creativity, attraction, confidence, stimulation, joy, ambition, exchange
- **Magical Workings:** Safe travel and road opening. Inspiration, creativity, communication, and commerce. Attraction, opportunity, and overcoming obstacles. Learning and memory.

Yellow

- **Planetary Association:** Sun
- **Symbolism:** Intellect, clarity, logic, learning, eloquence, attention, joy, success
- **Magical Workings:** Joy and contentment. Study, logic, and revelation. Personal radiance, magnetism, confidence, and charisma. Bringing truth to light and spiritual illumination.

Green

- **Planetary Association:** Venus / Earth
- **Symbolism:** Fertility, prosperity, bounty, health, abundance, nature, grounding, growth
- **Magical Workings:** Money drawing, employment, and financial stability. Plant and land-based magic. Growth, health, and bodily renewal.

Blue

- **Planetary Association:** Jupiter
- **Symbolism:** Peace, healing, justice, emotional truth, loyalty, influence
- **Magical Workings:** Protection from the evil eye and peace. Legal matters and justice. Financial growth. Works to ensure success and that you are seen favorably by others.

Purple

- **Planetary Association:** Jupiter/Moon
- **Symbolism:** Power, mysticism, sovereignty, psychic insight, spiritual authority
- **Magical Workings:** Divination and spirit sight. Magical empowerment and elevation. Spirit communion/mediumship. Wisdom, command, and magical power.

Brown

- **Planetary Association:** Earth
- **Symbolism:** Stability, practicality, grounding/earthing, animals, the home
- **Magical Workings:** Hearth and home magic and protection. Animal magic, including healing animals and working with animal spirits. Land magic and working with spirits of place and the home. Stability, patience, and legal matters.

Grey

- **Planetary Association:** Mercury/Moon
- **Symbolism:** Ambiguity, neutrality, invisibility, illusion, liminality, subtlety
- **Magical Workings:** Glamour, masking magic, invisibility, and obfuscation. Walking between worlds, spirit flight, or spirit negotiation.

Silver

- **Planetary Association:** Moon
- **Symbolism:** Lunar power and spirits, intuition, reflection
- **Magical Workings:** Lunar and dream magic. Mirror magic, reflecting harm, reversals and scrying

Gold

- **Planetary Association:** Sun
- **Symbolism:** Solar power, glory, divinity, wealth, success, enlightenment
- **Magical Workings:** Success and prosperity workings. Solar worship and devotion. Favor, glory, charisma, recognition. Personal illumination and radiance.

Appendix Three: Creating Consecrated Salt and Water

While an example of this was given earlier in this book I wanted to provide it its own section here as a quick reference for any readers who may not be familiar with creating these items for ritual use. Here I also give a variant phrasing for this work that I have previously used with students of mine. You are encouraged to revisit the example from the *Simple Exorcism and Cleansing* to compare the two and craft your own phrasing as you like.

Though it is likely older, this form of salt/water exorcism and consecration finds its roots in Catholic liturgy where it is employed in the making of holy water. In these rites the wording "creature of salt" has always struck me with its implied animism. From there it became incorporated into traditions of grimoire magic before finding its way into ceremonial magic and contemporary witchcraft. These two simple elements: salt and water when magically awakened and set to purpose may be employed as powerful allies in works of both exorcism and of hallowing.

Items Needed:

- A small bowl of salt
- A small bowl of water

The Rite

1. Create a ritual space however best suits your own craft and practice. Have the bowls of salt and water on a table or altar.

2. Place your hand over the bowl of Water and using the *vox magica* say:

   "I exorcise thee, O creature of Water, that every kind of phantasm may retire from thee, and be unable to harm or deceive in any way. I cast out all impurities, uncleanliness, and malignity of spirit that you be most properly hallowed and sanctified in the eyes of the old ones onto the work of the Arte. May it be so."

3. Place your Hand over the Salt and using the *vox magica* say:

   "Give blessings to thee, O creature of Salt, that every kind of phantasm may retire from thee, and be unable to harm or deceive in any way. I cast out all impurities, uncleanliness, and malignity of spirit that you be most properly hallowed and sanctified in the eyes of the old ones onto the work of the Arte. May it be so."

4. Next add three pinches of the salt to the water and state:

   The two made one, hallowed by Land and Sea. May this blessed water cast out all harmful specters, miasma, and malignity.

5. Close your ritual space as usual.

This consecrated water may then be used for spiritual cleansings, exorcisms, and consecrations, where it may be sprinkled about a place and upon items or added to baths and washes. The salt may be used in similar ways as well, and for making more consecrated water in the future. Both the salt and water may be saved for later use, though if the water ever goes stagnant, it may be discarded.

Appendix Four: Creating Ritual Space

In cases where the witch desires to create a place of power and/or containment for ritual purposes, particularly when protection is added, desired, or when ensouling spirit vessels in a more formal way, Laying a Compass or Casting a Circle may be an ideal approach. Below, I am providing a simple example of both. Laying a Compass is an approach towards creating ritual space which is more common to streams of contemporary traditional witchcraft, whereas Casting a Circle is a more common approach utilized by contemporary witches more broadly, particularly those who have taken influence from Wicca. There are similarities in both of these approaches as presented here, and there are *many* variations on how these rites may be performed depending upon tradition and inclination. These are only singular examples, and the reader who is newer to this is highly encouraged to delve deeper and experiment with a variety of practices in determining the best way to establish a ritual space for themself.

Laying a Compass

1. Choose a suitable place of working where you won't be disturbed. Preferably outdoors when possible. Traditionally, a compass may be 9 ft. However, work within whatever space limitations you may have.
2. Make sure to clear the area of any clutter where possible.

3. If working outdoors, you should ensure you have gained permission of the spirits present to work there, and you should provide offerings to the spirits of the land.
4. Perform an alignment exercise as you feel is necessary.
5. Standing at what will be the center of the Compass, begin by stomping your foot thrice upon the ground and saying:

"I give honor to the spirits of this place, to the Genius Loci, and I ask for your blessing and for safe passage from this realm into the Otherworld."

6. Then place your arms across your chest with one hand upon each shoulder and say:

"I call upon the Ancestors and the Mighty Dead to come forth, bear witness, and aid in this work of the Craft."

7. Beginning in the East, walk in a circle three times around the boundary of the Compass. You may wish to point your hand at the ground or use a ritual tool such as the *Blade of Arte* to symbolically or physically circumscribe the boundary of the compass. As you are walking the perimeter, say:

"Thout, tout a tout, tout,
Throughout and about,
Once around for the world above,
Once for the world below,
And once around for the world between!
For the Plot, for the Field, and Furrow!"

8. Then return to compass center.
9. From center, face the East, hold your hand in a hailing sign,[144] and state:

144 A hailing sign would be raising your arms, or at least your dominant arm, with elbows bent and hands upwards. Palms and fingers should be flat and facing outwards.

"Spirits of the East awaken, arise, and stand with me as protectors and witnesses!
May the way be opened and may the compass be hallowed."

10. From center, face the South, hold your hand in a hailing sign, and state:

"Spirits of the South awaken, arise, and stand with me as protectors and witnesses!
May the way be opened and may the compass be hallowed."

11. From center, face the West, hold your hand in a hailing sign, and state:

"Spirits of the West awaken, arise, and stand with me as protectors and witnesses!
May the way be opened and may the compass be hallowed."

12. From center, face the North, hold your hand in a hailing sign, and state:

"Spirits of the North awaken, arise, and stand with me as protectors and witnesses!
May the way be opened and may the compass be hallowed."

13. Then stand at center with your right hand pointing to the heavens and your left to the earth and state the following:

"Spirits of the Upperworld Descend."

14. Bring your right hand down and place it upon your left shoulder.

"Spirits of the Underworld Ascend."

15. Bring your left hand up and place it upon your right shoulder.

"I stand at Compass center."

16. Allow your Left arm to fall to your side.

    "With the Witch Mother to the left of me."[145]

17. Allow your right arm to fall to your side.

    "And the Witch Father to my right
    I stand at Compass center
    As it is spoken it is so!"

18. Here any ritual and magical work will now be done.
19. Once complete you will stand at the Compass center and say:

    "By the Witch Mother and Witch Father.
    By the Spirits Above, Below, and Center.
    Let my works and words go forth and let the Compass be raised."

20. From center, face the North, hold your hand in a hailing sign, and state:

    "Spirits of the North go forth in good faith, with both blessings and gratitude."

21. From center, face the West, hold your hand in a hailing sign, and state:

    "Spirits of the West go forth in good faith, with both blessings and gratitude."

22. From center, face the South, hold your hand in a hailing sign, and state:

    "Spirits of the South go forth in good faith, with both blessings and gratitude."

---

145 You may wish to replace Witch Mother/Witch Father here with the names of any deities or spirits which stand as your patrons, protectors, or guides.

23. From center, face the East, hold your hand in a hailing sign, and state:

    "Spirits of the East go forth in good faith, with both blessings and gratitude."

24. Beginning in the East, walk in a circle three times around the boundary of the Compass in the opposite direction from that which you laid the compass. You may wish to point your hand at the ground or use a ritual tool to symbolically or physically erase the boundary of the compass. As you are walking the perimeter, say:

    "Rentum Tormentum!
    Rentum Tormentum!
    Rentum Tormentum!"

Casting a Circle

Items Needed:

- Consecrated water in a small bowl (or the consecration of salt/water can take place at the start).
- Incense and a burner of some sort

The Ritual

1. Choose a suitable place of working where you won't be disturbed. Traditionally, a circle is said to be 9 ft. However, work within whatever space limitations you may have.
2. Make sure to clear the area of any clutter where possible.
3. Have your incense/burner and your consecrated water on an altar or nearby surface.
4. Perform the alignment exercise as you feel is necessary.
5. Pick up the consecrated water and, beginning and ending in the East, walk around the perimeter of the circle whilst sprinkling it and saying:

"By Earth and by Water let this circle be sanctified and consecrated unto the work of the Arte. Let it stand as a barrier of protection, a space betwixt and between, and a vessel of containment for the magic crafted within. By my hand and in the name of Witch Mother and Witch Father,[146] *may it be so."*

6. Place your hand over the incense and say:

    "I exorcise thee, O creature of Perfume, that every kind of phantasm may retire from thee, and be unable to harm or deceive in any way. I cast out all impurities, uncleanliness, and malignity of spirit that you be most properly hallowed and sanctified onto the work of the Arte. In the names of the Witch Father and Witch Mother, may it be so."

7. Then light the incense and, beginning and ending in the East, walk around the perimeter with it whilst saying:

    "By Fire and by Air let this circle be sanctified and consecrated unto the work of the Arte. Let it stand as a barrier of protection, a space betwixt and between, and a vessel of containment for the magic crafted within. By my hand and in the name of Witch Mother and Witch Father, may it be so."

8. Next, beginning and ending in the East, walk the perimeter of the circle *three times* using the index and middle fingers of your dominant hand or your Blade of Arte to point at the ground, directing your will and energetically creating the circle. This is commonly done by envisioning/visualizing/feeling your power/energy streaming forth from your fingertips and creating the boundary between your ritual space and anything outside of it. This will appear/feel different to different people, and the way it is envisioned from one practitioner to another may vary greatly. For some practitioners, they envision this as a boundary of protective fire, for others as a mist or glowing energy. Some may have difficulty seeing this in the mind's eye and may only feel the

146 Again, replace these names as you are inclined.

energy streaming down their arm and out of their fingers. Some may feel nothing at all; that is okay, particularly for the beginner.

It should also be noted that, though you are tracing a circumference for the circle, once it is cast, it is most commonly envisioned as a dome encompassing the area of working, or as a sphere with half above ground, and half below.

9. As you are walking the circle and directing your energy, speak the following:

   "I conjure and cast you, O Circle of Arte in the name of the Witch Mother and Witch Father that you may stand as a place between this world and the Otherworld. Let all malignity, falsity, and calamity be cast out. Let this circle stand as a barrier of protection and Vessel of Transmutation. Dually consecrated and thricely traced. By my hand, and by my will, the circle is cast!"

10. Next, face the East and state:

    "I summon, stir, and call thee up, mighty spirits of the East. May you be welcomed and stand as both wardens and watchers of this Circle of Arte and grant your aid to the rites performed herein."

11. Next, face the South and state:

    "I summon, stir, and call thee up, thou mighty spirits of the South. May you be welcomed and stand as both wardens and watchers of this Circle of Arte and grant your aid to the rites performed herein."

12. Next, face the West and state:

    "I summon, stir, and call thee up, thou mighty spirits of the West. May you be welcomed and stand as both wardens and watchers of this Circle of Arte and grant your aid to the rites performed herein."

13. Next, face the North and state:

"I summon, stir, and call thee up, thou mighty spirits of the North. May you be welcomed and stand as both wardens and watchers of this Circle of Arte and grant your aid to the rites performed herein."

14. Return to the center of the circle, and state:

"I call upon and welcome the Witch Mother and Witch Father to be present and stand witness within this Circle of Arte. And I ask that you lend your blessing and aid to the rites performed herein."

15. It is now that any ritual/magical work would traditionally take place. In the case of doing this to simply practice circle casting, I suggest you sit within this space and try to sense any changes from the way the room or space felt prior to casting. You may also wish to use this space and opportunity to meditate or offer devotion to any particular spirits you are aligned with.
16. Once ready to close the circle, you would begin in the center and say:

"I give thanks to the Witch Mother and Witch Father for standing as witness and aid to the rites performed within this Circle of Arte. May you ever be welcomed and may there ever be peace between us."

17. Facing the North, say:

"I give thanks to the Spirits of the North for standing as wardens and watchers and for your aid in the rites performed within this Circle of Arte. May you ever be welcomed and may there ever be peace between us."

18. Facing the West, say:

"I give thanks to the Spirits of the West for standing as wardens and watchers and for your aid in the rites performed within this Circle of Arte. May you ever be welcomed and may there ever be peace between us."

19. Facing the South, say:

    "I give thanks to the Spirits of the South for standing as wardens and watchers and for your aid in the rites performed within this Circle of Arte. May you ever be welcomed and may there ever be peace between us."

20. Facing the East, say:

    "I give thanks to the Spirits of the East for standing as wardens and watchers and for your aid in the rites performed within this Circle of Arte. May you ever be welcomed, and may there ever be peace between us."

21. Next, walk the circle three times, counterclockwise, beginning and ending in the East. As you do so, use your pointed hand/fingers or *Blade of Arte* as before, but this time envisioning/feeling the boundary of the circle dissipating/being cut and any excess energy/power from it returning to the earth. When done, state:

    "May the Circle of Arte be open. By my hand, by my will, and by the Witch Mother and Witch Father, it is done."

22. Lastly, you may wish to perform the alignment exercise again as you feel is necessary.

Appendix Five: Hallowing the Blade of Arte

The following ritual is designed to assist the witch in ritually preparing their Blade of Arte. This blade serves in creating ritual space as well as in works of hallowing and exorcism. Further, for those witches who are inclined, it may be used as a tool in the crafting or dismantling of enspirited objects.

Items Needed:

- A knife to serve as your *Blade of Arte*
- The Triangle of Arte
- Small bowl of oil (olive oil or the *Spirit Summoning Oil* are best)
- Consecrated water (see appendix one)
- Incense of some sort. The *Suffumigation of Ensouling* may be a good choice here.
- Two small bowls to hold the oil and consecrated water

The Ritual

1. Choose a suitable knife to act as your Blade of Arte.
2. Place oil and consecrated water each in a separate bowl.
3. Create your ritual space as your personal practice dictates.
4. Light the candles for the Triangle of Arte as usual.
5. Place the blade into the Triangle of Arte.
6. Sprinkle the knife with the consecrated water whilst saying:

"By the hallowed waters of life let this blade be sanctified and consecrated unto the work of the Arte. By my hand and in the name of the Witching Gods,[147] *may it be so."*

7. Place your hand over the incense, and say:

   "I exorcise thee, O creature of Perfume, that every kind of phantasm may retire from thee, and be unable to harm or deceive in any way. I cast out all impurities, uncleanliness, and malignity of spirit that you be most properly hallowed and sanctified in the eyes of the old ones onto the work of the Arte. May it be so."

8. Then light the incense and take the knife from the triangle to suffumigate it with smoke whilst saying:

   "By this perfume of plenty let this blade be sanctified and consecrated unto the work of the Arte. By my hand and in the name of Witch Mother and Witch Father, may it be so."

9. Place your hand over the bowl of oil, and say:

   "I exorcise thee, O creature of Oil, that every kind of phantasm may retire from thee, and be unable to harm or deceive in any way. I cast out all impurities, uncleanliness, and malignity of spirit that you be most properly hallowed and sanctified in the eyes of the old ones onto the work of the Arte. May it be so."

10. Dip your fingers into the oil and lightly anoint the blade of the knife while saying:

    "By this blessed oil do I hallow the Blade of Arte. That it may increase in power by each waxing of the moon. That it may never turn upon the hand who wields it now. That it may act as faithful servant, companion, and protector until the end of my days."

---

147 Please feel free to put in any spirit or deity name you like here such as "the creator", "Hekate", etc…

11. Breathe the breath of life on the blade.

    "Once for the road of the starry heaven,"

12. Breathe the breath of life on the blade.

    "Once for the road which leads below,"

13. Breathe the breath of life on the blade.

    "And once for the crossed roads betwixt all realms."

14. (Though this is not required, here you may wish to prick your finger and rub a bit of your blood upon the blade of the knife.) If you do so you should recite the following:

    "I give forth my life blood and seal the pact of the blade. That by my blood given, you shall thirst for no more, and by our covenant you shall be born as Blade of Arte."

15. Then state:

    "By my breath, and by my blood, you are born forth anew to serve in the work of the Arte.
    In the eyes of the old ones, it is done."

16. You may wish to formally give the blade a name now that will only be known by you.
17. The blade should be placed in the Triangle of Arte. The candles should be allowed to burn down, and the blade left overnight. The next day, you may wipe any excess oil/blood from the blade and store it as is most appropriate.
18. Close your ritual space as usual.

As always, though I strongly encourage you to work this rite as written, please feel free to alter this rite as feels most appropriate and organic to your practice and comfort level.

Appendix Six: Example of a Formal Written Pact

The example given here is to provide the reader with an example of what a written pact *might* look like. The scenario this was crafted around represents a witch entering into a more formal relationship with a spirit and essentially making it their familiar. This format and wording can be changed as best suits the spirit you are working with and the nature of the pact.

Being a solemn accord between the Witch and
the Spirit known as the Thorn-Bound One

Beneath the waxing crescent moon, on the seventh night of the seventh month, in the year two-thousand and twenty-four, let it be known that I, NN witch and walker of crooked paths, do enter into a sacred accord with the spirit known to me as the Thorn-Bound One, called also He Who Waits in the Bramble, to establish a bond of mutual trust, exchange, and obligation.

This pact is made in full consciousness, without coercion, and in alignment with the laws that govern the hidden paths and the spirits who walk them. This pact has been crafted under the watchful eyes of those spirits who serve as my protectors and allies; my ancestors and the spirits who walk with and watch over me, both known and unknown, named and unnamed. It shall be enforced by the judgment and necessity of *[insert protector spirit name]*.[148]

Of the Spirit's Duties

The Thorn-Bound One, who has appeared to me in spirit flight, in dreams, and the arte of scrying, shall henceforth take up the role of familiar, ally, and ward. Under the terms of this accord, the spirit shall:

- Provide instruction to me in the hidden artes of the craft, particularly those aligned with baneful herbcraft, dream-working, and the ways of concealment and obfuscation.
- Guard me in times of vulnerability during spirit flight, rites of necromancy, conjuration, or workings wherein the soul is laid bare.
- Provide warning through omen, dream, or subtle sign should harm, hex, or spiritual peril draw near.
- Walk beside me in spirit when I cross into the deeper realms, and steady my return with cunning and care.

Of the Witch's Offerings

In return for these acts of service and companionship, I, NN, do pledge the following:

- On each dark moon, a single drop of my blood shall be given to the fetich, which will serve as a shared vessel of our accord.[149]
- Once each week, a libation of black coffee or red wine shall be poured at the threshold in your name.

---

148 This last line can simply read "my protector spirits". However, it is much more preferred that you have established spirits who protect you and can specifically be named here. In cases where the spirit you are working with exists in a hierarchical structure, you may instead put the name of a spirit it answers to or one more powerful than it. It should be understood that this enforcing spirit will hold both parties responsible for keeping up their end of the pact.

149 Please see my points about blood use in Chapter Twelve. This is included for illustrative purpose as opposed to being representative of something which belongs in all pacts.

- Within three nights of this signing, I shall craft a fetich from serpent skin, yew wood, and other materia allied to and agreed upon by the Thorn-Bound One. This shall serve as a house of your spirit and mark our bond, and a copy of this contract will be burned to ash and placed inside of it.
- At some point during the waxing moon of each month, I shall burn dragon's blood incense and speak your name in devotion or spell, that your presence might be ever called into the world through word.

These offerings shall be made with sincerity and regularity, as befitting the dignity of a true familiar spirit. Should any be missed through illness, necessity, or imbalance, I shall make reparation at the soonest possible hour.

Of Term and Boundaries

This pact is entered into without a fixed end, and shall remain in effect for as long as it serves both parties in good faith.

Should the spirit withdraw from the duties herein, or should the witch neglect the agreed offerings for one full cycle of the moon without cause, apology, or reparation offered, the pact may be reassessed or dissolved.

In such an event that this partnership should need to be dissolved I will speak words of unbinding, make a parting offering of red wine and bitter herbs, and ritually extinguish the bond by means of the destruction of the fetich.

A period of thirteen moons shall pass before a new pact between the same parties may be forged, unless otherwise agreed in spirit by both.

Of Signature and Seal

This pact has been confirmed by means of black mirror scrying and the fall of divinatory dice, through which the Thorn-Bound One gave sign of assent.

> *Let this document serve as a testament to our accord, witnessed by the eyes that do not sleep and under the enforcement of [insert protector spirit name]. By the setting and rising of the sun, it is done.*

Signed and sealed:

(Insert personal sigil here if you have one, and then sign both your birth name and any magical name you may have.)

(Using transposition to let your hand act on behalf of the spirit, insert spirit sigil here if you have one, and then sign any names or titles you know the spirit by.)

Witnessed and enforced by the spirit:
(Again, using transposition to let your hand act on behalf of the enforcing spirit, insert spirit sigil here if you have one, and then sign any names or titles you know the spirit by.)

Dated this:
Seventh Night of the Seventh Month, Under the Waning Crescent in the Year MMXXIV

Glossary

Here are collected terms that appear throughout this book, along with their working definitions. Please note that you may find divergent definitions for some of these terms elsewhere. As with many things in the realm of magic, there are often variant understandings of similar terms from one practitioner to another. This is provided as a resource to assist readers in understanding such terms and the ways they are utilized and meant to be understood within the context of this work.

Animism: The belief that things have spirits. This often extends to animals, plants, and natural phenomena, and may also include human-created objects, structures, concepts, and art.

Anthropomorphism: Attributing a human likeness or qualities upon nonhuman beings.

Conjuration: Gaining the attention of a spirit and bringing it forth as a being we can communicate and engage with.

Contagion Magic: A form of sympathetic magic that operates by the principle that things once in contact continue to influence each other even after separation. In other words, if two objects, beings, or materials were once physically connected, they remain spiritually linked across space and time. Through the bond of that former contact, one can influence the other. See also Taglock/Personal Concern

Crafter: In a tripartite understanding of the witch's spirit, this aspect of ourselves is aligned with the middle world and mediates between the guidance of the Grand Genius and the instincts of the Fetch. The Crafter is concerned with the actual doing of things in the material realm. It is equally concerned with ensuring that we are physically safe and provided for, and also that we are being led by a sense of greater purpose. The Crafter enacts the manifestation of our highest potentialities as met and balanced by our practical needs and desires. While we are in this incarnation, the Crafter is the most identifiably "self" part of ourselves and is often equated with the ego.

Effigy: Any sculptural representation of a human or humanoid form intended for magical purposes. This includes statues, dolls, puppets and mannequins.

Embodied/Physical World: The material world as we experience and understand it through the conscious interpretation of sensory input, symbols, and memories.

Ensouling/Enlivening/Enspiriting: These words are used interchangeably in this work and refer to the act of ritually housing a spirit within a material object or body. In some cases this may crossover with the concept of conjuration and refer to awakening and allying with the indwelling spirit already present in an object.

Enspirited: Any material form which possesses an indwelling spirit.

Fetich: (fetiches plural) A fetich is a portable material object meant to serve as a spirit vessel and an object of magical power. Though it is often an assemblage of various materials, in some cases it may be a single object, such as a root, stone, or animal paw that serves as a spirit locus. The fetich is not defined by its form here so much as by its function. An element worth highlighting is that a fetish is not simply a magically powerful object; it is an object that houses a spirit. The spelling here employs an archaic form of the word fetich in an effort to more clearly differentiate the magical object from conflation with other associated ideas found within psychology and philosophy.

Fetch: In a tripartite understanding of the witch's spirit, the Fetch is the part of self that is primarily associated with our survival instincts and the more primal drives within us. It is often associated with the chthonic realms, and in some traditions it may be referred to as the "lower self" or "shadow". The fetch is the spirit which is sent forth during transvection. It may appear in human form as a kind of "doppelganger", and/or take on the form of an animal.

Familiar Spirit: Also sometimes referred to as a puckril, imp, or magistellus. A familiar is a spirit of any kind that the witch allies with, learns from, and/or is protected by. Historically familiars have most commonly been said to be fairies, demons, or spirits of the dead who worked on behalf of the witch, granted her power, and/or taught her witchery. Many witches will have a primary familiar they work with whilst also working/pacting with additional spirits on a long-term or temporary basis.

Grand Genius: In a tripartite understanding of the witch's spirit, this is the aspect of self aligned to the supernal realm/upper world. It is this spirit that acts as a guide upon the path of our life's work. It functions in the realm of ideas and ideals and is the primary conduit for the transmission of inspiration, revelation, and spiritual gnosis. The Grand Genius, as I have come to understand and approach it, is somewhat comparable to concepts such as the personal daimon of Greek antiquity, and the Holy Guardian Angel as understood by many occultists. The Grand Genius is generally viewed as representing the highest expression of and potentiality for ourselves. It is this aspect that reincarnates, and it is believed to be the most enduring part of ourselves.

Hallowing: The ritual act of making something sacred and recognizing it as magically empowered. Hallowing is essentially synonymous with consecration.

Imitative/Image Magic: Imitative magic is a form of sympathetic magic based on the principle that "like produces like". Implying that by mimicking or representing something, you can influence it magically. In other words, the act of creating an image, a representation, or performance of an action can cause the corresponding action to happen in reality.

Infusion: An herbal extraction created with water.

Load/Charge/Bundle: A collection of magical materia enclosed within the body of an effigy or other spirit vessel designed to help empower it.

Materia: Throughout this work, the term *materia* primarily refers to the magically powerful items we employ when crafting spirit vessels. This can also be extended to include all of the botanical, mineral, animal, and other elements that we recognize as being magically active and spiritually potent allies within our rituals and spellwork. This can also at times include formulas, oils, powders, candles, etc., that we employ in our craft.

Maumet: A term used within this work to refer both to a 'created' spirit and the object which serves as its body. In earlier historical usage, this term was diversely employed to refer to; an idol, a 'false' or 'pagan' god, an image/statue of a household spirit, a poppet/effigy, or to reference a

person who acts on behalf of or does the bidding of another. A maumet might be housed within an effigy, fetich, or any other kind of spirit vessel.
Otherworld: The realm of spirits, which is largely invisible to human beings without employing spirit flight or psychic faculties.
Pacting: Establishing an explicit or implicitly negotiated agreement with a spirit. This could include but is not limited to agreements regarding the type of role the spirit will play, the type of work that will be done together, what type of offerings/compensation will be received in return, any taboos placed upon the witch's behaviors, the way a spirit might be called/contacted, the creation of boundaries for the relationship, and agreements upon how and when the relationship may be ended.
Panpsychism: The belief that all things possess some form of consciousness, and by extension, that the universe is conscious.
Poppet: A doll intended to serve as a stand-in or substitute for a person or animal for the purposes of magic.
Shrine: A permanent or temporary location treated as the home of a spirit and engaged with for magical or devotional purposes.
Spirit: Spirits are patterns of consciousness of varying complexity that we are able to communicate and engage with by practical or magical means. A spirit may have a material body/form it is associated with or be disembodied. In the course of this writing, spirit is usually used in reference to disembodied patterns of consciousness. Terms such as "Others" and "other-than-human persons" are also employed in this work in reference to spirits.
Spirit Vessel: Though this is often applied quite appropriately to bottles, jars, boxes, and other forms of containers, a spirit vessel is any object that is meant to serve as a body or house for a spirit.
Sympathetic Magic: Sympathetic magic is the broad magical principle that things which are connected or similar can influence one another at a distance, even when separated. Sympathetic magic is magic based on correspondence, connection, and symbolic association and holds to the belief that if two things are linked, either by resemblance, by past contact, or by similarity in representation, they can affect each other magically. Though the concept is an ancient one, the phrase "sympathetic magic" was popularized by the Scottish anthropologist Sir James George Frazer in his work The Golden Bough. Frazer divided magical thinking into two types: Sympathy through Similarity (Imitative Magic) and Sympathy through Contact (Contagious Magic).

Taglock/Personal Concern: An item that is spiritually tied to the target of a spell. The concept being that those items once in contact with a person, or which are a part of their body (contain dna), also carry some essence of their spirit so that what is enacted upon the taglock will affect the person from whom it came. Examples of this include hair and fingernail clippings, bodily fluids, articles of clothing worn by the target, and items such as jewelry from the target. This may also extend to items such as photographs of the individual and samples of their handwriting.

Tincture: An herbal extraction most commonly created with alcohol but may also be made with vinegar or glycerine.

Transvection: Also known as spirit flight, hedge crossing. The act of sending forth the spirit, more specifically the fetch, from the body to traverse the material realm, or more commonly, travel into the Otherworld. Similar practices are sometimes referred to outside of a traditional craft context as 'astral travel' or "shamanic journey"

Vox Magica: The magical voice as empowered by the witchfire and intentionally directed towards creating magical effect or conjuring spirits.

Wash: Any liquid solution employed in the process of creating spirit vessels. A wash may be made with infused or tinctured herbs, perfumes, alcohols, consecrated water or otherwise empowered waters such as those gathered from natural places. Washes are often worked with as a method for cleansing and hallowing

Witchfire: The inherent and cultivated magical power of the witch, which is envisioned as stored, stoked, and refined in the belly.

Bibliography

Abram, David. *The Spell of the Sensuous: Perception and Language in a More-Than-Human World.* Pantheon Books, 1996.

Agrippa von Nettesheim, Heinrich Cornelius. *Three Books of Occult Philosophy.* Edited by Donald Tyson. Translated by James Freake. Woodbury, MN: Llewellyn Publications, 2018.

Ankarloo, Bengt, and Clarck Stuart, eds. *Witchcraft and Magic in Europe: The Middle Ages.* University of Pennsylvania Press, 2002.

Ankarloo, Bengt, and Stuart Clark, eds. *Witchcraft and Magic in Europe. The Period of the Witch Trials.* University of Pennsylvania Press, 2002.

Auryn, Mat. *Psychic Witch: A Metaphysical Guide to Meditation, Magick & Manifestation.* Llewellyn Publications, 2020.

Betz, Hans Dieter, ed. *The Greek Magical Papyri.* Chicago Univ. Press, 1986.

Booth, Abigail. *The Wild Dyer: A maker's guide to natural dyes with projects to create and stitch.* Princeton Architectural Press, 2019.

Coleman, Martin. *Communing with the Spirits: The Magical Practice of Necromancy.* Xlibris, 2005.

Cornell, Kamden. *On Needles & Pins: A Witch's Book of Poppetry and Figure Magic.* Acorn, 2021.

Cunningham, David Michael, Taylor Ellwood, and Amanda R. Wagener. *Creating Magickal Entities: A complete guide to entity creation.* Egregore Publ, 2003.

Davies, Owen. *Popular Magic: Cunning Folk in English History.* Bloomsbury Publishing PLC, 2007.

Dickie, Matthew W. *"What Is a Kolossos and How Were Kolossoi Made in the Hellenistic Period?" Greek Roman and Byzantine Studies,* February 11, 2011, 237–57.

Domínguez, Ivo. *Spirit Speak: Knowing and Understanding Spirit Guides, Ancestors, Ghosts, Angels, and the Divine*. New Page Books, 2008.

Duffy, Martin. *Effigy: Of Graven Image & Holy Idol.* Three Hands Press, 2015.

Ellwood, Taylor. *Walking with Magical Entities*. Independently Published, 2020.

Ellwood, Taylor. *Walking with Spirits*. Independently Published, 2020.

Folkard, Richard. *Plant Lore, Legends, and Lyrics.* Sampson Low, Marsten & Company. 1884.

Froome, Joyce. *Wicked Enchantments: A History of the Pendle Witches and Their Magic*. Palatine Books, 2010.

Ginzburg, Carlo. *Ecstasies: Deciphering the Witches' Sabbath*. Translated by Raymond Rosenthal. S.l.: University of Chicago Press, 1991.

Gary, Gemma. *Traditional Witchcraft: A Cornish Book of Ways*. Troy books, 2008.

Hall, Nathan M. *Path of the Moonlit Hedge: Discovering the Magick of Animistic Witchcraft*. Llewellyn Publications, 2023.

Harvey, Graham. *Animism: Respecting the Living World.* Hurst & Company, 2017.

Harvey, Graham, ed. *The Handbook of Contemporary Animism*. Routledge, 2015.

Horne, Roger J. *A Broom at Midnight*. Moon Over The Mountain Press, 2021.

Howard, Michael. *By Moonlight and Spirit Flight: The Praxis of the Otherworldly Journey to the Witches' Sabbath*. Three Hands Press, 2019.

Hunter, Devin. *The Witch's Book of Spirits*. Llewellyn Publications, 2017.

Kelden. *The Witches' Sabbath: An Exploration of History, Folklore & Modern Practice*. Llewellyn Publications, 2022.

Lancre, Pierre de. *On the Inconstancy of Witches: Pierre de Lancre's tableau de l'inconstance des mauvais anges et demons (1612)*. Edited by Gerhild Scholz Williams. Arizona Center for Medieval and Renaissance Studies, 2006.

Lewis-Williams, J. David. *The Mind in the Cave: Consciousness and the Origins of Art*. Thames & Hudson, 2016.

Levack, Brian P., ed. *The Oxford Handbook of Witchcraft in Early Modern Europe and Colonial America*. Oxford University Press, 2015.

Miller, Jason. *Consorting With Spirits: Your guide to working with invisible allies*. Weiser Books, 2022.

Normand, Lawrence, and Gareth Roberts. *Witchcraft in Early Modern Scotland: James VI's Demonology and the North Berwick Witches*. Liverpool University Press, 2022.

Pearson, Nigel G. *Treading the Mill: Workings in Traditional Witchcraft*. Troy Books, 2017.

Sandars, N. K., trans. *The Epic of Gilgamesh*. Penguin, 1977.

Shadow, Sirian. *Spirit Work: A Guide to Communicating & Forming Relationships with Spirits*. Sirian Shadow, 2022.

Schulke, Daniel A. *The Green Mysteries: Arcana Viridia - An Occult Herbarium*. Three Hands Press, 2023.

Schulke, Daniel A. *Idolatry Restor'd: Witchcraft and the Imaging of Power*. Three Hands Press, 2023.

Schulke, Daniel A. *Viridarium Umbris: The Pleasure Garden of Shadows*. Xoanon Limited, 2005.

Sophistes, Apollonius. *Construction and use of Ancient Greek poppets*, 1996. http://opsopaus.com/OM/BA/GP.html.

Swain, BJ. *Familiar Unto Me: Witches Sorcerers and Their Spirit Companions*. Independently published, 2023.

Swain, BJ. *Living Spirits: A Guide to Magic in a World of Spirits*. Independently published, 2018.

Valiente, Doreen, and Evan J. Jones. *Witchcraft a tradition renewed Evan John Jones with Doreen Valiente*. Hale, 1990.

Wilby, Emma. *Cunning-folk and Familiar Spirits: Shamanistic Visionary Traditions in Early Modern British Witchcraft and Magic*. Sussex Academic Press, 2013.

Wilby, Emma. *The Visions of Isobel Gowdie: Magic, Witchcraft and Dark Shamanism in Seventeenth-Century Scotland*. Sussex Academic Press, 2013.

Index

I-L

M-N

O

P

S